THE CINEMA
DREAMS ITS
RIVALS

THE CINEMA DREAMS ITS RIVALS

*Media Fantasy Films
from Radio to the
Internet*

Paul Young

University of Minnesota Press
Minneapolis
London

Chapter 5 first appeared in slightly different and shorter form as "The Negative Reinvention of Cinema: Late Hollywood in the Early Digital Age," *Convergence: The Journal of Research into New Media Technologies* 5, no. 2 (1999): 24–50, guest edited by Ross Harley. Reprinted with permission.

Published by the University of Minnesota Press
111 Third Avenue South, Suite 290
Minneapolis, MN 55401-2520
http://www.upress.umn.edu

Library of Congress Cataloging-in-Publication Data

Young, Paul, 1968–
    The cinema dreams its rivals : media fantasy films from radio to the
    Internet / Paul Young.
        p.   cm.
    Includes bibliographical references and index.
    ISBN 13: 978-0-8166-3598-6 (hc) — ISBN 13: 978-0-8166-3599-3 (pb)
    ISBN 10: 0-8166-3598-6 (hc : alk. paper) — ISBN 10: 0-8166-3599-4
    (pb : alk. paper)
    1. Mass media in motion pictures.   2. Fantasy films—History and
    criticism.   I. Title.
    PN1995.9.M39Y68 2006
    791.43'6552—dc22

                                                            2005035510

Printed in the United States of America on acid-free paper

The University of Minnesota is an equal-opportunity educator and employer.

15 14 13 12 11 10 09 08 07 06   10 9 8 7 6 5 4 3 2 1

To my grandparents' generation
and
for Kate

Contents

Introduction: The Perpetual Reinvention of Film

> In spite of our confident labeling of media, genres, styles, and the like, every phenomenon is subject to new perceptions regarding its very identity.... With each technological or social shift, cinema [has] found itself subject to redefinition—as photography, as illustrated music, as vaudeville, as opera, as cartoon, as radio, as phonography, as telephony, and so forth. One reason why linear history is an illusion is that even the most basic objects and categories on which that history would be based have no permanent identity.
>
> —Rick Altman, "Deep-Focus Sound: Citizen Kane and the Radio Aesthetic"

In 1992, New Line Cinema released Brett Leonard's *The Lawnmower Man,* a spectacular fantasy about the digital universe of cyberspace that is also a warning against realizing that fantasy. After rehearsing options that range from computer-generated puzzles and first-person shooter video games to CD-ROM interactive education, Leonard's film presents virtual reality (VR) as the ultimate payoff of digital media progress: a 3-D game one climbs inside, represented on the movie screen by computer-generated animation that puts 1982's trapped-in-the-mainframe fantasy *Tron* to shame. Despite its fascination with VR, however, *The Lawnmower Man* shows the medium perverting the sweet nature of the mentally handicapped Jobe (Jeff Fahey), with disastrous results. After Dr. Angelo (Pierce Brosnan), a behavioral scientist who experiments with VR on chimpanzees for a military contractor, augments Jobe's intelligence with a cocktail of psychotropic drugs, hypermediated education, and VR, Angelo's bosses take over the project and transform Jobe into a military superman. But their plan backfires when Jobe, now somehow able to wreak telekinetic and telepathic havoc, decides that only a digital fist can heal the world's political wounds. At the climax, Jobe enters cyberspace as pure consciousness and nearly commandeers the global telecommunications network before Angelo destroys his "creation." The poster for *The Lawnmower Man* stresses that Jobe's transformation has upset the orders of both nature and culture: "God made him simple—Science made him a God." By the end of the film, little doubt remains that the reach that digital technologies grant their human inventors exceeds humanity's ethical grasp. Angelo, the postmodern Prometheus, should have left the "natural" hierarchy of smart above slow, and powerful above powerless, just as it was.

The Lawnmower Man received some attention from feminist scholars for its mangling of Donna Haraway's hypothetical postindustrial subject, the cyborg. Haraway imagines the cyborg as a hybrid subjectivity, unbound by such ideological dichotomies as male/female and technology/nature. She makes playful use of her construct to challenge the anachronistic persistence of these categories, and the hierarchies they maintain, in a global economy where technology has become the new nature.[1] Jobe becomes cyborg-like to the extent that digital interactive technology reconstructs his subjectivity, overriding the power relations thrust upon him by his physiological limitations. But in the end, the film confirms the very dichotomies that Haraway's work seeks to undermine. When Jobe invites his girlfriend Marnie to make love in cyberspace, their bodies melt into one another like multicolored taffy, but then, without warning, he rapes her brain with beams of digital energy that penetrate her virtual body with the force of an explosion (Figure 1). The horrible image of Marnie being pummeled by energy bolts from Jobe's "primal mind" spectacularizes the film's rejection of technological identity politics and insists that the female is always already other to the male. Throughout the film, men are scientists, capitalists, and self-made virtual powerhouses fed on aggressive video games, while women remain mothers, housewives, consumers, demanding harpies, sexually available decorations, and victims of male (techno-) aggression.[2]

The central role of technology in cinematic representations of gender trouble comes as no surprise. But another kind of cultural struggle is on display in this film, one that deserves to be more fully documented, for it resonates with a theme central to Hollywood films about technology. The technological primal scene of Marnie's rape is part of a history of media

Figure 1. Jobe's virtual reality avatar turns grotesque. Frame enlargement from
The Lawnmower Man (1992).

fantasies that dates back to the emergence of the American cinema. If we
consider films about other media at all, we probably think first of *mediaphobic* films like *The Lawnmower Man*: horror stories that speculate about
the hidden dangers of fascinating electrical media. Like films about television from the 1950s and '60s such as *The Glass Web, All That Heaven
Allows, It's Always Fair Weather, A Face in the Crowd, The Seven Year Itch,*
and *The Apartment, The Lawnmower Man* rakes a new and untested mass
communications medium over the coals for failing to disclose its social
consequences. In the films I've just listed, new media's sins range from
heightening one's sense of isolation to allowing a killer to frame another
for his crime. While Leonard's film similarly (if more pyrotechnically)
excoriates VR, it also straddles a mediaphobic fence: the spectacular images and enveloping sounds of its long computer graphics (CG) sequences,
the most sophisticated film graphics of their kind in 1992, anticipate and
even solicit the spectator's fascination with VR, even while they portray
a shared digital world as nothing more or less than a battlefield for the
future of the human race.

By having VR both ways—as utopia and as horror show—*The Lawnmower Man* accurately reflects the fact that mediaphobia was only half the
story that American culture told itself about digital media at the time. In
1992, Leonard's ambivalent vision of VR was recognizable as a reaction to
an equally novel but more developed and domesticated technology: the
World Wide Web, known to most Americans through news stories about

hackers and computer crime or by way of semi-utopian hacker fantasies like Hollywood's own *WarGames* (John Badham, 1983). Untested by all but research scientists, college students, the military, and the few thousand PC and modem owners linked through CompuServe and other pre-Internet network service providers, the computer network circa 1992 was an ambiguous "space" where communication was free, open, largely unregulated, and apparently unregulatable thanks to the Web's piecemeal network structure. Where early on-line communities like the Well and independently published magazines like *Mondo 2000* imagined the Web as a paradise that was theirs for the shaping, *The Lawnmower Man* takes a more jaundiced view, implying that precisely the freedom and openness of the network make Jobe's crimes possible, even inevitable. If a childlike man can learn to use global telecom to invade the homes and brains of others, and no coherent regulations or surveillance yet exist, what's to stop a disgruntled programmer, a hacker, or a Net-addicted juvenile delinquent from making similar trouble in the digital world outside the movie theater?

Described this way, the mediaphobia expressed by *The Lawnmower Man* and its antitelevision siblings of the previous generation may seem like a case of sour grapes on Hollywood's part, and, indeed, this is how the relationship between mediaphobic films and the industry that produces them is commonly understood. On this view, behind public floggings of TV or cyberspace lies the film industry's paranoia that new media will "kill" film. But early in my research about the film industry's relationships with competing media, and especially with entertainment technologies marketed for home use, I found that what William Uricchio has called the "struggle for media identity" takes place on too many fronts and in too many different registers—economic, technological, formal, discursive— for a single theory to encompass them all.[3] These complexities also undermine the various attempts to formulate a unified theory of media "evolution" adequate to all mass media. Even if we subcategorize mass media by their technological capabilities (such as live and/or recorded, sound and/or image, print and/or pictorial-representational), social functions (person-to-person communication, news delivery, entertainment, art), or encoding procedures (digital and/or.analogue), we risk losing a sense of the effects of institutional history on not only what kinds of information a medium carries and how it is carried but on how industry and consumers *think* about the medium, and in turn, how those ideas about its nature affect both production and reception.

Thus I have limited the scope of my own intermedia interests to ask a deceptively simple question: How has the American cinema represented the consumption of newer media, and specifically media that differ from film in terms of their liveness—the simultaneity of the transmitted event or text with its reception—and their situatedness in the private sphere? How do *media fantasy films,* especially those released when the future of the cinema's rival was still an object of vigorous speculation, confront the fantasies that circulated about those media? And what do these films have to tell us about the history of Hollywood's conception of its audiences, as new media introduce more pointedly interactive models of media consumption than the cinema has historically offered? *Immersion*

I take this tack partly to counterbalance the overemphasis on technological specificity and difference that characterizes much intermedia analysis at present. My intent is to apply the brakes to a tendency that follows from that overemphasis, namely, the interest in producing a poetics for one medium, or even multiple media, as an entrée into figuring out how each makes meaning on its own terms. I have nothing against attempts to formulate new media poetics. Without periodic examinations of film and video aesthetics, for example, film and media studies as a field would have trouble keeping up with new developments in technology and technique. Some such texts, like John Ellis's *Visible Fictions,* skillfully avoid treating a medium's "qualities" as ahistorical or inherent.[4] Too often, however, we treat media poetics as an end in itself. That is, we forget to treat a poetics for what it really is: not a definitive analysis of the limits of a medium's capabilities but rather a description of what is *done* with a medium at a specific time and within a specific culture.

Now, I am not going to pretend that I have found a way out of the cave of my own historical and cultural experience of media uses and conventions and now stand blinking in the sunlight of empirical reason. But by focusing on cinema's discourses about new media rivals, I hope to provide a reminder that media discourses operate at many levels—including the claims about the medium's intrinsic qualities made by inventors and engineers, marketers, thinkers, mass-media critics, and consumers—to shape media identity as surely as does technology. I wish to support this reminder by producing a record of some of the pressures that a few new-media paradigms of textuality and address have exerted on an industrial institution that is approaching its century mark: Hollywood cinema. The film industry as a whole would very much like to shape the collective understanding of "its" medium, "film," so that the public's view is identical to *its* understanding of what film is, as if the one equals (or must equal) the other and can never change. If I succeed at nothing else in the pages that follow, I hope to demonstrate that, when Hollywood cinema puts new media and their discourses on display, it inadvertently recognizes just how incorrect this equation is—that is, how much Hollywood's textual conventions and modes of address shift from period to period, rival to rival, and even film to film, in part because new rival media have proposed a different set of possibilities for media communication and textuality.

Although recent histories of Hollywood's relations with other media industries have become increasingly sensitive to discursive issues, three problems in particular continue to trouble this subfield of film and media studies. In the interest of inviting the reader to judge how well or how poorly this book avoids these snags, I will address them briefly in turn. To oversimplify rather drastically, I'll pose these problems in the form of typical answers to the general research question "What does the history of the cinema have to do with the histories of other media?"[5]

1. *The Ontological-Evolutionary Answer: Film history and the histories of other media have little to do with each other, because the cinema evolves according to intrinsic laws.*

André Bazin, one of the most sweeping and inventive "grand theorists" of film, has been accused of portraying film history this way, as an evolutionary progression toward a cinema that would offer an experience indistinguishable from experiential reality.[6] From mummies and Quattrocento perspective drawing to photography to films with sound and color, the cinema of Bazin's famous essays "The Ontology of the Photographic Image," "The Evolution of the Language of Cinema," and "The Myth of Total Cinema" anthropomorphically seeks a perfect simulation of reality, incorporating other media technologies (such as sound recording and amplification) along the historical path to help it complete its illusion.[7]

In media studies more generally, the extreme version of this answer belongs to Jean Baudrillard and Friedrich Kittler. Although they seem to agree with Marshall McLuhan that media affect and shape each other by mutual ingestion (a point to which I will return), for these critics, the technological base of each medium determines in the last instance the rules that govern that medium's textuality and the experience of its users. "A medium is a medium is a medium," Kittler avers in *Discourse Networks 1800/1900*. "Therefore it cannot be translated."[8] Kittler reveals his contempt for "media history" as opposed to his own field, "media science," most overtly when he writes in a 1994 essay that media theorists who lack knowledge of "higher mathematics" merely hinder the progress of media studies.[9] Similarly, Baudrillard acknowledges his McLuhanist roots when he proclaims that mass media are "'not *coefficients* but *effectors* of ideology.' . . . In short, [for Baudrillard] media do not mediate; they are anti-mediatory and intransitive."[10] Raymond Williams makes perhaps the most elegant case against such blatantly determinist claims in *Television* (1974) when he argues that descriptions of "intrinsic" media qualities are better understood as "explicit ratification[s] of particular uses," "factors and norms [that] are themselves effects" rather than ineffable causes of "new" human behaviors or social formations: "For if the medium—whether print or television—is the cause, [then] all other causes, all that men ordinarily see as history, are at once reduced to effects":

> Technological determinism is an untenable notion because it substitutes for real social, political and economic intention, either the random autonomy of invention or an abstract human essence. . . . On the contrary, the reality of determination is the setting of limits and the exertion of pressures, within which variable social practices are profoundly affected but never necessarily controlled.[11]

Thus Williams criticizes the determinists' argument while refusing to turn it upside down and suggest that intention and use have *full* control over a medium's conventional applications; a radio cannot be used to mix cement just because we fantasize that it *could*.

Williams's certainty that this balanced view, in which a culture exerts intention—and struggles within itself for the right to exert that intention—always within the bounds of "limits and pressures" brought to bear by both technological possibility (at the invention stage, where specific intentions lead to specific capabilities) and technological restrictions (at the implementation, textual production, and distribution stages), led him to suggest, too optimistically, that "the particular rhetoric of McLuhan's theory of communications is unlikely to last long" (Williams, 122). But, as Williams knew, "struggle and argument" over the conventional uses and institutional identities of media do not end when the institutions settle into a pattern (129). And as in media practice, so in media theory: the continuing debate between determinist and antideterminist theories signifies that the struggle to define not merely one communications medium or another but "mass media" as a category of technological cultural production in the twentieth and twenty-first centuries is by no means finished. In fact, the debate itself is regenerated by perpetual adjustments and transformations in such media practices as textual forms (think of how dramatically the pacing and framing of commercial films has changed across genres since *Jaws*) and means of distribution (recall that studios' desire to lease films to television interests forced cinematographers to compose wide-screen frames with the "TV-safe area" taped onto their viewfinders).

That said, the Ontological-Evolutionary Answer has obvious attractions, including its rhetorical elegance and its certainty that media have absolute identities that need only be discovered and described. But historians who teleologize a medium in this way pay a heavy price in terms of the descriptive value of their theories. McLuhan's *Understanding Media* (1964), for example, avers that technologically based media from print to film and television struggle through misguided, conservative uses and textual forms until they at last "progress" to the point where they assume the forms most appropriate to them (see my discussion of answer 3, below). I would submit, however, that these "appropriate" media forms are merely the forms that McLuhan lived with and studied, the forms that had (thus far) won the struggle to dominate the collective imagination of television, film, and the other media he describes. In film theory, versions of this teleological tendency date back to Vachel Lindsay's *The Art of the Moving Picture* (1915) and Hugo Münsterberg's *The Photoplay* (1916) and depend (as Lindsay does in particular) on the art-history paradigm in which a medium undergoes a life cycle, passing from experimental to classical to baroque phases at a staunchly Kantian distance from social and political realities. But this theory snags even more obviously when applied to film than when it is used to explicate the plastic arts, for reasons that I believe an intermedia account is better equipped to explain than a single-medium poetics.[12] Film may be an aesthetic medium and a communications medium, but it is also the medium by which the capitalist industries that shape and define it communicate specific messages in specific ways at different times, under internal and external conditions and pressures that may be altogether unrelated to a medium's technological base.

For example, as early as 1902 the cottage industry of American film made a quarter-turn from tableaux, gag films, and *realités* toward more complex, multishot narratives (partly under the influence of trends in French and British film) in order to attract continued patronage at a time when the novelty of the projected moving picture had begun to falter. Even more complex narratives were produced by 1908 in reaction to condemnations of film's representational crudeness when compared to fiction and legitimate theater. When Progressives and politicians attacked film theaters as threats to public morality, film producers had to consider new textual forms that might answer the critics and lure respectable patrons to the nickelodeons, or risk letting the entire industry crumble under public pressure. Even technological "improvements" to the cinema were catalyzed by extratechnological, institutional events. Sound film was introduced only when two upstart film studios, Warner Bros. and Fox, tried to turn themselves into giants, and other studios capitulated, each for different immediate reasons.[13] And in the 1950s, as box-office revenue plummeted to all-time lows, Twentieth Century Fox and other studios used widescreen, 3-D, and blockbuster epics with heretofore unimaginable special effects to compete with television and the increasing privatization of American leisure it symbolized.[14] At every stage in its history, the identity of film mutated not because of an intrinsic logic of "progress" but because of crises forced by social and economic exigencies.

2. *The Box-Office Answer: The cinema fears losing business to new media that compete with it for the American entertainment dollar, and so it lashes out at them through negative representations in films, boycotts of performers who work in rival media, and other forms of negative publicity.*

This answer might be nicknamed the "sour grapes" argument. By its very nature, it can never expand very far beyond factual observations or descriptions of films. Although few recent critics have adhered strictly to this answer, I believe it has become so commonsensical that we practically hear it echoing in our heads when watching a film like *Will Success Spoil Rock Hunter?* (Frank Tashlin, 1957), with its hilarious commentary on the bigness of CinemaScope compared to the minuscule TV screens of the mid-fifties. As Janet Wasko demonstrates, however, "the myth of Hollywood's technophobia," the belief that, during times such as the inception of broadcast TV, the film industry feared media competitors would destroy the cinema, stems from the misguided assumption that the main business of Hollywood studios was and is the production of films, when exhibition, distribution (which for nearly three decades now has included the lucrative market of VHS and DVD sales and rentals), and cross-marketing (of tie-in toys and the like) have historically represented Hollywood's bottom line.[15]

Wasko, Michele Hilmes, and Christopher Anderson have already begun to debunk the myths of Hollywood's radiophobia in the 1920s and 1930s, and its videophobia in the 1950s and onward, by examining the tricky behind-the-scenes relationships among Hollywood business interests, new entertainment technologies, and the broadcast industry. The "Radio Ban" of 1932 has often been cited as proof of the film industry's fear of radio stealing its audiences, but this event turned out to have been insisted on by theater operators, not production studios, and was quite toothless and short-lived—more a publicity event than an expression of intermedia malice.[16] At the beginning of the sound era, Warner Bros. and Paramount bought radio stations for publicity purposes, and Paramount plotted to buy the CBS radio network (see Hilmes, chapter 3). To make more trouble for the Box-Office Answer, early sound films generally portray radio in a positive light, glorifying (and borrowing) its stars and reveling in the narrative possibilities of backstage intrigues at radio stations (as I will discuss in chapter 3). And while it's tempting to view such films as *The Glass Web* (1953), *Network* (1976), *Poltergeist* (1982), and *The Truman Show* (1998) as expressions of contempt for TV, in fact the major studios have been producing shows for network broadcast since the 1950s and, then as now, would lose a sizeable chunk of their domestic gross if they lacked broadcast, cable, satellite, VHS, and DVD as means to package, repackage, sell, and rent theatrical films and made-for-TV programs ad infinitum. If Hollywood films exude suspicion about TV—and they do so constantly—whatever relationship these films have to the industry's self-definition must be more complex than economic fear and loathing.

3. *The Cannibalism Answer: Film's relationship to another medium is defined by each medium's ingestion of the other's qualities and capabilities.*

Although McLuhan makes intransigent pronouncements about the natures of media from electric light to TV, *Understanding Media* also allows that newer media "cannibalize" forms, formal strategies, and styles from elder media, as early film did with theater (an old saw, but useful as a starting point), and as television eventually did with film. I agree with this answer in principle, except that, in McLuhan's view, the media seem to cannibalize each other under their own steam; producers, technicians, executives, and other busybodies just obstruct proper digestion. McLuhan, one of the godfathers of contemporary media studies and one-time masthead "Patron Saint" of *Wired* magazine, is exceptionally good at identifying subtle differences among media practices but insists that the differences are intrinsic. To him, media technologies develop teleologically, finally becoming "themselves" like biological species reaching adulthood. Even when he acknowledges the institutional contrast between home TV and public film viewing, for example, he presents the contrast as the inevitable outcome of technological difference. When he sees the "cool," participatory medium of TV being filled with content that doesn't fit his definition of TV, he dismisses historical fact as untelevisual: "When hotted up by dramatization and stingers, [TV] performs less well because there is less opportunity for participation."[17]

But if the content of a medium works against the medium's own properties, as McLuhan claims is the case even in his own example, then clearly the medium does not entirely determine the nature of what it transmits, nor can it mandate how that transmission will be received. While on the one hand he argues that television the medium shapes its programming in a way that makes viewers feel they are part of a "global village" composed of people both on the screen and watching other TV sets, on the other he claims that some programming misunderstands the "cool" nature of television and therefore puts off viewers rather than absorbing them into the village. To apologize for McLuhan by characterizing these two notions as compatible would be to underestimate the absoluteness of McLuhan's technological determinism. Indeed, the contradiction damages McLuhan's version of the Cannibalism Answer, for if television truly makes everything that passes through it "televisual," then TV producers and networks would never have thought to borrow conventions from film and theater to develop televisual forms.

Yet the Cannibalism Answer has consistently produced the most nuanced and historically provocative reports on film's intermedia identity. Lev Manovich's *The Language of New Media,* for example, hails film—and specifically *The Man with the Movie Camera* (1929), Dziga Vertov's celebration of the new Soviet Union and of the manipulations of the visual world made possible by this "kino-eye"—as a crucial point of comparison for understanding such specifically digital elements as the database, and the aesthetic and stylistic conventions that have been derived from these capabilities. Even (and especially) in the age of digital telecom, he argues, "cinema is now becoming *the* cultural interface, a toolbox for all cultural communication, overtaking the printed word."[18] His goal is to describe the technological parameters of digital art, and he meets that goal admirably by outlining a poetics of new media; to describe mutual influence between digital media and film is not his intent. But while Manovich provides an extremely useful account of how digital media have transformed some filmic conventions and circumvented others, his approach to media history exudes a noncausal and agentless tone I can only describe, awkwardly, in a sentence like the following: "Then X happened, and new possibilities were born." Manovich's evidently cavalier approach to the development of a medium's conventions of representation, textuality, and usage undercuts the force of his claims about which properties "belong" specifically to new media and which do not. A reader who wants to interrogate intermedia *history*—that is, one who seeks sustained discussions of how social forces, cultural conventions, or economic interests affect a medium's development—may simply be the wrong reader for *The Language of New Media*. In any event, the facts of media invention that Manovich reports do not perform historical analysis by themselves.

Jay Bolter and Richard Grusin's *Remediation: Understanding New Media* homes in on intermedia history, much more specifically than Manovich's book, on its way to theorizing the forms and aesthetics of digital media. Bolter and Grusin construct a metatheory of media development that rivals McLuhan's in its suppleness and its reach backward for precedents and origins of so-called new media. "Remediation" means that "new" media borrow conventions of the "old" in the process of constructing their own brands of realist representation, while at the same time old media incorporate aspects of the new in an attempt to reanimate their appeal to consumers:

> A medium is that which remediates. It is that which appropriates the techniques, forms, and social significance of other media and attempts to rival or refashion them in the name of the real. A medium in our culture can never operate in isolation, because it must enter into relationships of respect and rivalry with other media. There may be or may have been cultures in which a single form of representation (perhaps painting or song) exists with little or no reference to other media. Such isolation does not seem possible for us today, when we cannot even recognize the representational power of a medium except with reference to other media.[19]

Bolter and Grusin deal with the ontological-evolutionary implications of their version of the Cannibalism Answer by placing themselves at one remove from the history they trace. They don't believe that media tend toward erasing the signs of their mediation; rather, they argue, the media themselves are caught up in this ideology of inevitability and a desire for the real:

> In most cases, the goal [of digital effects in film] is to make these electronic interventions transparent. The stunt or special effect should look as "natural" as possible. . . . Hollywood has incorporated computer graphics at least in part in an attempt to hold off the threat that digital media might pose for the traditional, linear film. This attempt shows that remediation operates in both directions: users of older media such as film and television can seek to appropriate and refashion digital graphics, just as digital graphics artists can refashion film and television. (48)

Here the authors attribute a medium's dominant identity to the triumph of corporate desire, which manifests itself in what James Lastra has called "standards and practices," conventions that an industry like Hollywood legitimates as quality standards.[20] At one level, I could not agree more with Bolter and Grusin's version of the Cannibalism Answer: an institution's collective *belief* that its medium has a unique identity has been crucial to critical arguments about the persistence of the production conventions that anchor the classical Hollywood cinema. Indeed, I will argue that one function of Hollywood's standards and practices is to protect classical conventions from the encroachment of new media's forms while allowing classicality to pick and choose bits of those forms in order to rejuvenate Hollywood film for audiences who might consider classical cinema outdated. However, *Remediation* focuses so intently on describing how the ideology of standards and practices works that the fact that the gravitational pull of realism *is* an ideology—not simply a description of how media are, or how media must be—fades quickly from the book's purview, as do the economic relations and political forces that overdetermine how a medium is used and perceived.

What is unsatisfying about all three of these answers is that, particularly if taken up one at a time, none adequately addresses how malleable media identities are in discursive and material practice, even if their dominant definitions seem little changed.[21] To put it another way, they open up only slender opportunities for recognizing that media identities have discursive layers that lie beneath—or, rather, have been buried beneath—their technological bases. The similarity or dissimilarity between, say, a two-way medium such as the telephone and a one-way medium such as broadcast radio or television may be for its users less a matter of ontological or mechanical difference (such as one-way versus two-way communication) than a matter of discursive overlap that might actually make the two media seem quite similar. Such overlap stems from multiple rhetorical and ideological factors at once: sales pitches and press reviews; suspension of disbelief on the part of users; a conventionalized confusion between hearing or seeing an event "live" and literally participating in what takes place during that event; or an ideology that depends upon lumping media effects together as representative of a larger trend, as when producers, pundits, or consumers compress many technologies into a category like "digital media" and use that category to signify progress, democratic ideals, greater realism, the destruction of the nation's moral fabric, and so on. Uricchio takes this kind of discursive intermedia overlap seriously when he discusses how turn-of-the-century expectations of live image transmission affected the reception of early cinema.[22] Even describing radio, television, and the Internet as "new" media that differ intrinsically from film misrepresents the history of intermedia relations, since (I would suggest) each representational, electrical medium that was developed after projected film hit the market between 1894 and 1896 overlaps with film in such conventions as narrative structure, visual framing, sonic spatial cues, or spectatorial address.

So why *does* a media fantasy film like *The Lawnmower Man* exhibit such paranoia about new media—particularly media such as video games and the Web, from which Hollywood might extract profits, cultural cachet, and novel technological and representational strategies otherwise unavailable to it? I contend that media fantasy films do indeed express anxiety about new media's competition with the cinema, but that they do so in ways that speak less to economic competition than to the qualities of "film" as a medium as compared to its newer rivals. The comparison of media's qualities that such fantasies undertake, however, is a blind for what is more fundamentally at stake for Hollywood in addressing new media: the maintenance of the Hollywood cinema as an *institution* that is and will remain distinct from competing media institutions.

The "new" media institutions I will discuss in what follows provide products from the same general category that Hollywood promises— entertainment—but they compete with the Hollywood cinema in an institutional way that has repercussions far beyond simple economic competition, for they promise communication *among* users as well as communication of image and sound *to* users. The media I have chosen to focus on—radio, television, and the Internet—were relatively easy for me to choose (from among such others as the telephone, citizens' band (CB) radio, cellular networks, and so forth) because these three media, like film during its first two decades, offered as one of their attractions the *possibility* of expanded social exchange, or what I will call *interactivity* out of deference to the "new" paradigm that dominates discussions of "new" digital media (a paradigm that, as I hope to show, actually has a rich mass-media history that predates the home computer modem by at least seventy years). Partly due to Hollywood's success at institutionalizing film as an entertainment medium, the broadcasting and digital telecom industries moved quickly to develop prefabricated and repeatable textual forms. However, radio, TV, and digital media texts have depended on models of address and reception that differ in at least three profound ways from the classical cinematic model: (1) the possibility of media-enabled social exchange; (2) "live" transmission; and (3) private consumption in the home. I will discuss these differences at greater length below. For now, I will simply say that Hollywood's on-screen fantasies about these media during their incipient phases return obsessively to these distinctions between film and home-media reception with equal parts denial of their pleasures and envy at the cinema's technological incapacity to replicate them.

In focusing on Hollywood's media speculations from periods "when old technologies were new," I am following the example of Carolyn Marvin, who coined the term *media fantasy* to describe how Western nations negotiated the meanings and futures of new and ambiguous electrical media in the nineteenth century. Media fantasy, Marvin writes, has revealed "what thoughts were possible" about new media during their emergence "and what thoughts could not be entertained yet. . . . Such dreams are never pure fantasy, since their point of departure is a perceived reality. They reflect conditions people know and live in, and real social stakes."[23] Because they broke the barriers of time and space in bewildering new ways that were impossible before electricity, media like the telegraph, the telephone, and the electric light seemed to guarantee massive political changes as well. These changes were expected to stem from the new forms of social contact and the new opportunities for intercultural engagement and confrontation that electrical media seemed to initiate. But these possibilities did not have the same connotations in everyone's imaginations a century ago any more than such possibilities do today in the digital age; and those connotations, then as now, generated a myriad of narratives about "proper" hierarchies of knowledge and power, the changing social meanings of space and time, the problems of cultural, ethnic, and sexual difference, and the ever-shifting line between public sphere and private sphere. Media fantasies are not merely chimeras but determining factors in the future uses of the media in question:

> Fantasies help us determine what "consciousness" was in a particular age, what thoughts were possible, and what thoughts could not be entertained

yet or anymore. . . . [They] develop their own traditions in the conversation society has with itself about what it is and ought to be. Such dreams
are never pure fantasy. . . . They reflect conditions people know and live
in, and real social stakes. (Marvin, 7–8)

Thus *fantasy* for Marvin aligns closely with what Arjun Appadurai
prefers to call the *imagination*—flights of fancy, inspired by media consumption, that lead the dreamer to speculate on the practical applications
of her dreams:

> The idea of fantasy carries with it the inescapable connotation of thought
> divorced from projects and actions, and it also has a private, even individu-
> alistic sound about it. The imagination, on the other hand, has a projective
> sense . . . of being a prelude to some sort of expression, whether aesthetic
> or otherwise. Fantasy can dissipate (because its logic is so often autotelic),
> but the imagination, especially when collective, can become the fuel for
> action.[24]

Though I take Appadurai's point that "fantasy" can too easily be taken as a
synonym for escapism, in fact I would prefer to retain fantasy as an analyti-
cal category precisely because fantasy *seems* so self-contained, so detached
from real conditions, and so devoid of political affect, even to itself. In
fact, however, the strongest pejorative connotations of the term—delusion,
impossibility—make fantasy texts all the more useful for reconstructing
the forgotten futures of film and its rivals. Fantasy may be the only node of
cultural practice from which we can excavate the most fervent wishes and
strongly held beliefs, both destructive and socially progressive, that saturated the emergent identities of media before becoming obscured by institutional conventions and sheer, mundane familiarity. No adult American
today would even flinch while watching a filmed train rush the camera,
but in 1896 such films ignited countless fantasies in the minds of viewers.
Although it is probably not the case that those viewers dove under their
seats to avoid being run down, they were fascinated by the visceral force
exerted by these enormous, ghostly images, and speculated voluminously
about the futures of communication and knowledge that this shocking yet
technologically familiar new medium might bring.

Media fantasies both express and act as crucible for the public imagination regarding a medium's purposes and effects. At the same time, they
remind us that the dominant economic and political structures that accrue
to media are not inevitable. Rather, they develop as the result of competition among various definitions and possibilities that circulate in multiple

mass-cultural forms. Through diligent historical research that takes short stories, cartoons, science fiction, and letters to the editor into account, alongside "expert" opinion in professional journals, Marvin demonstrates that media are pliant entities with "no natural edges." As such, the modes of usage that eventually come to define media depend on social discourses concerned to make sense of or to exploit media, not solely on the intrinsic properties of a technology. In the process of collating specific kinds of fantasies, Marvin troubles the second-nature quality of technology and thus challenges modernity's monumental fantasy of technological progress, its certainty that universally positive social change must follow technological change.[25]

Media fantasy films represent one of the American film industry's most ideologically potent interventions in debates about media futures. They also reveal a network of utopias and anxieties that orbit around the Hollywood cinema's own status as a predominantly classical, predominantly narrative medium. In their monumental study *The Classical Hollywood Cinema,* David Bordwell, Janet Staiger, and Kristin Thompson argue that Hollywood cinema as we know it, and as audiences have known it since the mid-1910s, is a technological, formal, and organizational paradigm engineered to fulfill specific purposes, such as serial production, predictable profitability, the possibility of novelty within a durable narrative framework, and resonance with cultural forms and values familiar to its target audiences (such as melodrama, the novel, the short story, and the well-made play). Hollywood, like most industries, prefers predictability to change because change necessitates costs: it requires that new forms be engineered, new technologies employed, new technicians brought in and old ones trained for new tasks, and new practices standardized. At the same time, the practical impact of change must be dampened as much as possible at every level, from production and distribution to exhibition practice and the expectations of film viewers.[26]

I do not dispute that there was, and is, such a thing as the classical Hollywood cinema, nor that classicality remains the zero degree of Hollywood filmmaking, perhaps more so in the past three decades than in the two decades that preceded *Jaws* (1975), after which the popularity of thrillers and adventure films convinced studios that industry growth depended on the pursuit of the neoclassical blockbuster.[27] But media fantasy films offer a much-needed opportunity to discuss classicality as one discourse about film's identity among many discourses, against our tendency to consider it *the* definition of film qua medium that permanently overshadows all the others. Although the historical argument of *The Classical Hollywood Cinema* is eminently materialist and historicist compared to the Ontological-Evolutionary Answer, it also has a catch that makes film's intermedia history harder to frame: it envisions classical form as invulnerable to historical circumstances that do not directly or literally affect the film industry, as if the industry's collective desire for stability can (and does) stave off any but the most minor shifts in standards of form, style, or address based on extraindustrial—or indeed intermedia—factors.

Hollywood's practical interests continue to determine the dominant discourse about the nature of film—that point I cannot dispute. But it is also true that the discourse itself has changed dramatically since classical film became the norm. From somewhat different critical perspectives, Rick Altman, Miriam Hansen, and Bill Nichols have each taken issue with the argument fronted by Bordwell, Staiger, and Thompson that classical Hollywood narrative cinema is durable enough to absorb everything from new technologies to stylistic trends in new-media competitors without experiencing more than a minor ripple on its surface.[28] For these critics, and others attempting to revise cinematic reception theory from microhistorical perspectives, the concept of a *dominant* modality overstates the importance of certain structuring elements, such as plots (and shooting or editing patterns) that center primarily on characters and their goals, to Hollywood film's consistency over time.[29] Perhaps it would be more productive, instead, to think of a "dominant" definition of a medium as an ideological construct in the most materialist sense. Classical cinema, in other words, is not an ephemeral identity for film arising from false consciousness but a discursive definition imposed and maintained by material forces such as economic strategies of production and profit-making, standards and practices enforced at every level of production from direction to light-hanging to training editors to know the "right" way to edit dialogue scenes, and—of course—the existence of thousands and thousands of films that adhere closely to the tenets of classicality. And, like any discursive definition, classicality can never entirely suppress the fact that it is only one possible definition of film among many, many others.

However exhaustively researched and argued its claim, *The Classical Hollywood Cinema* and its various sequels account unevenly for elements of Hollywood films that affect spectatorship as profoundly as do their structural elements. Special effects, stars, the spectacular and emotional swings of melodrama, comic gags, dance numbers, and stylistic and storytelling excesses of all sorts (such as the dank shadows and impossible plots of film noir)—all of these elements trouble classical coherence in their own way, by introducing extrafilmic discourses into reception (such as the star's life outside the studio), jerking a narrative to an unlikely conclusion, or stopping a plot altogether for the sake of an isolated image or event that offers pleasure on its own terms. But the paradigm of classicality is so supple for Bordwell and his collaborators that, in the final analysis, no resistance to it can even be said to exist; in their view, the most radical stylistic innovation or spectacularly unmotivated event can be redeemed as classical by applying such concepts as the familiarity of genre conventions, functional equivalents (as when a long tracking shot picks out story elements rather than ceding the task to editing, the latter being the more conventional choice), and, of course, the unified ending, under the thumb of which no stray element, apparently, can ever escape or even be recalled by viewers as anything but integral to the story once the film is over. If classicality is a code of Hollywood law, *The Classical Hollywood Cinema* seems to function as much as a police force to defend and protect the integrity of that code as it does as a chronicle of its development.

If Bordwell et al. perform such a policing function as critics, then media fantasy films could be called their equivalent in Hollywood itself. Specifically, I will argue, media fantasy films function within Hollywood output as rhetorical defenses of classicality against those newer media rivals that offer very different, more deliberately *social* forms of reception to their users. James Lastra has used Pierre Bourdieu's conceptualization of the "universalizing mediation which causes an individual agent's practices, without explicit reason or signifying intent, to be nonetheless 'sensible' and 'reasonable'" to describe how "the norms of classical continuity construction" have shaped the Hollywood labor force's "predispositions toward practice" in a more-or-less mystified way, as when the definition of "correct" sound recording during the transition to synchronized sound changed from an "absolute fidelity" model to a model that subordinated acoustic spatial cues to dialogue intelligibility and storytelling cues.[30] I take from Lastra's example a mode of thinking about classicality that casts it as an unconscious or preconscious preserve of rules driving technical practices, rules that, however pliant, always have boundaries. These rules imposed upon the uses of celluloid (or, by 2006, digital video) make Hollywood movies more than simply instantiations of a value-free medium, *film,* but rather the utterances of an institution called *Hollywood cinema.* The distinction is not mere hair splitting, however conventional it has become to use "film" and "cinema" interchangeably. Hollywood's production practices work in tandem with exhibition practices, reception practices, and discourses about film as a medium to solder the idea of film tightly to what is merely (if *merely* is the right word) a *possible* (not necessary) definition, "the Hollywood film," and to keep the two concepts equivalent in the collective imagination. In my experience, at least, common parlance recognizes two essential categories of film: "the movies" (classical Hollywood narrative features) and everything else (documentaries, experimental films, "art" or avant-garde films, short subjects, animated films, and so on). Moreover, I will argue, Hollywood production practices contain within them an ossified, preconscious ideology of what film must be like in order for it to remain distinct from other media, and thus indispensable—and an equally preconscious, equally ossified ideology of what "film" must *not* be like.

If we want to continue to use the idea of mediaphobia to describe one position taken by the American cinema toward media rivals, one surely expressed by *The Lawnmower Man,* we might redeem such an interpretation from the trap of finding nothing but Hollywood's economic frustration in such a film if we recast the concept of *phobia* as a more specific kind of response that Hollywood makes to its media rivals. Freud's concept of phobia posits that every phobia shares the same unconscious purpose: to safeguard the subject from the revival of a repressed perception associated with the feared object or situation.[31] Although using psychoanalysis to interpret the intermedia "dreams" of the film industry in the form of films threatens to anthropomorphize Hollywood, Freud's definition of phobia illuminates what the institution of Hollywood stands to lose, and what its publics might stand to gain, from the success of new media and their unique paradigms of reception as a social activity, against Hollywood's "private-in-public" mode of reception, in which silence, undivided attention or absorption, and identification with characters are rewarded over and against engagement with other spectators.

Media fantasy films are expressions, in different periods and under different conditions—conditions determined by differences in new rival media and the fantasies they sponsor—of an ongoing institutional defense of classical form, address, and spectatorship. They recognize and appropriate some of the attractions of the other medium in question. At the same time, they deny that the Hollywood cinema itself could ever be renovated, its form and content revised, its modes of reception and interpretation put back up for grabs. I would go so far as to suggest that every film—*every* film, whether it deals openly with film or another medium or not, whether science fiction or romantic comedy—is both a discrete cultural text and a claim about the nature, qualities, and potentials of the medium that carries it. In media fantasy films, however, the film industry articulates most plainly its definitions of film at these critical moments of intermedia rivalry. Media fantasy films also perform another function, one as accidental as it is threatening to the stability of classical Hollywood form and address: they renegotiate the definition of film by recognizing the spectators' inevitable interest in media newer, stranger, more amorphous, and (in the case of radio, television, and the Internet) more technologically interactive than classical film.

As both Hollywood history and the Freudian model of phobia suggest, to describe these films as merely grouchy attacks on interactive media would grossly overstate the conscious agenda shaping the texts. Like mass-cultural texts in general as discussed by Fredric Jameson, media fantasy films offer their audiences at once an apologia for social hierarchies in general and a glimmer of resistance to those hierarchies, dialectically folded into the same narrative spectacle. Flashes of real resistance to structures of power are the necessary evils that mass culture must supply its consumers in order to make the inevitable textual reaffirmation of those structures easier to swallow.[32] I consider media fantasy films as the film industry's tactical responses to reception paradigms that differ from Hollywood's own. In Michel de Certeau's lexicon, *tactics* articulate on-the-fly resistance to the strategies by which institutions map individuals into an instrumental blueprint for reproducing existing power relations.[33] I appropriate the term here not to characterize Hollywood as a dispossessed underdog but to suggest the sketchy, half-composed quality of media fantasy films' "messages" about these new media, and the repressed possibilities for cinematic publicness—that is, text-grounded but relatively open social interaction at the point of public exhibition, including debate about the meanings of the film being shown—that this ambivalence regarding new media reveals.

When I argue that any of the media discussed here, film included, are more or less *interactive,* I realize that I am entering contested lexical territory and cannot afford to allow the term to remain as inclusive as I have thus far without further explanation. "Interactivity" in media history may be understood in much the way Philip Auslander understands "liveness," that is, as a historically variable discourse defined by way of intermedia comparisons. For Auslander, the nature of liveness depends on the opposition of certain kinds of performances to the concept of "the recorded" in different historical moments; indeed, broadcasting of events as they happen has become so synonymous with liveness in contemporary mass culture that simulcast video screens have become a de facto sign of "the live" even in arena rock concerts that feature the performers in the flesh.[34]

The definition of "interactive" I identify in Hollywood's representations of other media similarly depends on a network of oppositions that are constructed by emergent media institutions to identify the new technology in question. Lest my deployment of the term be misunderstood as blindly anachronistic, I should point out that fantasies and speculations about radio and television during their emergent periods never used the term "interactive." Indeed, it would seem strange for the term to have arisen in relation to these technologies even if it *had* been current in the 1920s or the 1940s, since neither broadcast radio nor broadcast television allows the audience to respond to or change media texts directly. However, the emergent-era fantasies of radio and TV portrayed these electrical wonders in ways that resonate with the current, digital definition of interactivity. *Interactivity,* then, refers here less to what Jens Jensen calls the *informatic* definition of the term, which includes the individual's manual-textual engagement with a media technology such as a video game or a Website, than to a *sociological* definition of interaction as engagement among subjects, whether that engagement takes place *through* a medium—using it as a communication channel between one subject and another—or directly *because* of it, as when viewers whisper to each other during a film or talk about statistics and plays during a televised football game.[35]

As Jensen has suggested, the categories of informatic and sociological interactivity blurred into each other in the early 1990s—the moment at which the term "interactivity" came into being—as digital technologies and their hands-on reception paradigms began to dominate media discourse and practice.[36] In fact, however, the intermingling of and confusion between these concepts of media-supported interaction is as old as the capitalist-nationalist exploitation of the printing press, which encouraged readers of mass-produced religious tracts, political pamphlets, newspapers, and novels to imagine themselves as united by their disparate but roughly simultaneous acts of reading and engaging with matters of widespread interest, even if they never spoke to another person who had read the same texts.[37] For Hollywood, the confusion of informatic interactivity with sociological interactivity has actually been quite useful and, in fact, as I will show, classical Hollywood has exploited this confusion to market its own media experiences as sociologically interactive, despite the industry's vested interest in suppressing social exchange in the theater and focusing spectatorial attention on the film alone (which I will discuss in chapter 1).

As the example of Jobe and Marnie's violent encounter in *The Lawn-mower Man* implies, although media films exploit new media for the purpose of reengaging spectators with cinematic worlds in new ways and strengthening the attractions of informatic interactivity, they also fix a bright narrative spotlight on mediated social interaction, an experience that Hollywood film appears unequipped to offer. But media fantasy films repeatedly superimpose the informatic and the sociological in their bid to position the cinema among its "live" and intersubjective rivals. As radio, TV, and the World Wide Web have shaped media consumption practices according to loose and amorphous paradigms of media consumption as social interaction, media fantasy films have been energetic participants in debates about the parameters of those paradigms. These films express the ways in which sociological interactivity both opposes and overlaps with cinema's construction of its own spectators as relatively silent, passive spectators who nevertheless watch movies in full public view—what we can call the public-in-private paradox of classical cinematic spectatorship.

In order to keep classical film viewing analytically distinct from person-to-person communication, I will refer to the sense of interaction that the absorbed classical film spectator experiences as *informatic intimacy*—an engagement with the screen and the characters it portrays that *involves* the spectator imaginatively but positions her or him as a voyeur, always apart from those characters. Media fantasy films have historically attempted in many different ways to make informatic intimacy simulate sociological interactivity—for example, direct-address singing in early talkies, the advent of CinemaScope, and first-person shots of virtual-reality landscapes are all products of such attempts—while simultaneously circumscribing actual social interactivity within the theater. But by focusing their attention on new media as *technologies*—mechanisms employed in very specific ways to shape messages and to organize their reception—these films call attention to the fact that classical cinema engages in manipulations of its own. In particular, the cinema directs the theatrical spectator to ignore the fact that the potential for sociological interaction among a diverse and heterogeneous group of people, the same utopian promise that broadcasting and home-computer networks make over and over again, exists on every side of the spectator's seat.

I have chosen to address films from the emergent period of each of my chosen new media, that is, the period between the first wave of heavy speculation about it and its reification into a stable, institutionalized set of forms. During these periods, the nature of each medium's challenges to Hollywood spectatorship was still uncertain. Trotting out a famous example of cinematic mediaphobia might help characterize some important historical differences between emergent-era media fantasy films and media fantasy films in general. Director Sidney Lumet and former television playwright Paddy Chayefsky's *Network* (1976), one of the most celebrated antitelevision films, appeared almost three decades after television cracked the mass market, while *The Lawnmower Man* was released amid a torrent of fantastical questions similar to those that greeted TV in the late 1940s: would this new medium bring atomized individuals and communities into closer contact with each other? Promote better understanding across regions and cultures? Provide more objective information than other, more jaded and corporatized mass media? Or would it disseminate half-truths, allow sex, violence, and advertising to invade the home, or homogenize experience to the detriment of democratic ideals, as network news is mobilized to do in *Network*?

Certainly these two films resemble one another in their concern not merely to *address* but to *dream* their media rivals. They construct their respective enemies out of a mixture of facts, criticism, and speculation drawn from contemporary discourses of television and digital media. What finally distinguishes *The Lawnmower Man* from *Network,* however, is that the rival medium fantasized by the former film is no more or less "real" or accessible to the majority of Americans than VR itself was by 1992, at least as far as most American media consumers were concerned. Immersive digital environments had been a staple of science fiction and fantasy across media even before William Gibson's groundbreaking cyberspace novel *Neuromancer* (1984), but at that time virtual reality existed as a usable medium for only a small number of researchers and engineers who had experimented with digitally simulated space since the 1960s.[38] By 1992, however, technological advances had made VR more feasible than ever, and the Web, though it too could only be accessed secondhand by most Americans (via news reports and other speculations), was already a magnet for speculations about unregulated, unrestricted communication and expression. Placed back into the historical-discursive context of its production and reception, *The Lawnmower Man* is not simply part of a smear campaign against digitality, but a speculation on equal terms with other speculations in a cultural struggle to define VR and the Internet—a debate about which technological capabilities and social functions would best serve the interests of users, and indeed what those interests were in the first place.

The first chapter brings Frankfurt School thought regarding the importance of utopian fantasies and lost possibilities to bear on the notion of media fantasy and explores early media fantasy films about film itself and its earliest audiences in order to suggest that, in terms of spectatorship and address, early cinema presented film itself as Other, a continual nuisance to the industry's intentions for it. By examining early film's fantasies about various kinds of spectatorship and collectivity in the context of this contested moment, I locate a powerful ambivalence about the future of the industry and the institution of cinema if private individuals were to control film the way they controlled such media machines as Kodak still cameras, telephones, and toy magic lanterns. Chapter 2 reads media fantasy films from 1908 to the dawn of sound against the backdrop of interactive fantasies dating back to Marconi's development of wireless telegraphy, later known as radio, into a two-way medium. Chapter 3 studies films of the early broadcast radio era (1919–1933), which overlapped with the emergent era of synchronized sound film. Radio fantasy films still bear the traces of the waning wireless-era debate over who was and was not allowed to make noise in the ether—a debate over the nature of media publicness that these films bring to bear on the discourse of cinematic identity.

The fourth chapter, on media fantasy films during the development of television, represents something of a break with the previous two, because at this point, for the first time since the early film industry competed with its own audiences to define film's institutional identity, the American cinema had to deal with a rival that transmitted moving images. TV threatened to impose its own paradigms for reception and interpretation onto the dominant discourse of audiovisual media textuality, paradigms that seemed poised to transform the reception of the elder medium's own moving pictures. Here I argue that television acted as a structuring absence for the cinema's identity as early as the mid-1940s. I recast a few key film noirs of that decade as media fantasy films that predict the terms for intermedia competition set later by 3-D, widescreen, and the blatantly videophobic films of the 1950s.

The fifth and final chapter examines late Hollywood production during the now-receding emergent moment of the World Wide Web, during which virtual reality and the Internet haunted the cinema with a form of reception that seemed even more remote from the cinema's than had the domestic consumption of TV. The potential political energy embedded in the mediaphilic myths of the moment, which Scott Bukatman has termed "cyberdrool," is made visible, in part, by the equal force exerted by digital-media films to negate that energy and flout computer-age optimism.[39] I deconstruct the digital mediaphobia of the 1990s into its major constituent parts by sifting through a cycle of Hollywood media fantasy that culminated in 1995, including *The Lawnmower Man*, *Hackers* (1995), *The Net* (1995), and *Strange Days* (1995). These films exploit two myths that circulated endlessly in computer discourses through the early nineties— the hacker myth and the myth of total media—and that became central to digital media films' equation of media-fostered sociological interaction with social disaster. At the heart of Hollywood's mobilization of these myths, however, lies a deeper concern with the fate of narrative cinema as the baseline definition of entertainment technologies shifts from narrative consumption to expectations of instantaneous intercommunication.

One reader of an early chapter draft joked that this book is less a study than a proposal for a field that might be called intermedial film studies. I repeat that joke here not to aggrandize the project but to recognize its limitations. The broad scope of the book's theoretical argument has prevented me from closely examining the aesthetics and representational strategies of film's competing media in favor of focusing on the cinematic constructions of those aesthetics and strategies, which media fantasy films reinvent in the process of reinventing the identity of film to suit the industry's purposes in each era I discuss.

What follows, then, is both a study of media fantasy films as a recurrent phenomenon in the American commercial cinema and a plea for sensitivity to irrational and fantastic presentations of new media beyond the bounds of science fiction. (Although this will no doubt seem an unfortunate decision to many, I have purposely *not* singled out science fiction for special scrutiny here, because I believe that cathecting too tightly to *literal* images of media in film can cause us to look past the media fantasies that hide, as it were, in plain sight.) I ask the kinds of questions I feel must be asked if we are to approach intermedia studies with the proper sensitivity to the pressures placed upon media reception—specifically, on each medium's (changing) construction of its ideal, "proper" spectator-auditor—by differences in textual practices and structures of reception, by historical and cultural variation among uses of media, and by discourses of hope and anxiety that we cannot dismiss as simply utopian delusion or dystopian hysteria. I reread these films as encoded missives from film history that speak the many opportunities that even the apparently hermetic structure of classical Hollywood has made available for its publics to reshape and rethink media in acts of legitimately collective negotiation—horizons of historically available interpretations that we can reconstitute, but only if we confront the films with two pieces missing from most accounts: the media fantasies that circulated outside the theaters at each moment and the crises of cinematic representation, narration, and address that the film industry perceived itself to be in when its competing media were new. In doing so, I take my cue from the energies for equitable communication—the chance of the spectator's commandeering the media to talk back to it or to make it speak for her—whispered in conspiratorial tones by the films themselves.

Rubes, Camera Fiends, Filmmakers, and Other Amateurs: The Intermedia Imagination of Early Films

L et me begin my examination of the cinema when old media were new with a blunt claim: Classical cinema is not a stage or a phase in the historical life of film. Nor is it a technological or even a technical trait intrinsic to, or "waiting" to be extracted from, the medium of film. Rather, it is a definition of the medium imposed upon it by an institutional process.[1] The major influences within this process include filmmaking practices (screenwriting formats, framing and editing strategies, acting styles, characterizations, modes of mass production), publicity and distribution practices (what advertising and planted "news" stories promise will be both recognizable and unique about each film, discourse about stars, strategies for manipulating desire for and profits of films by creating artificial scarcity of prints early in the run), and exhibition practices (the live prologue–short subjects–feature–trailers format, the positioning of patrons as theatrical spectators facing a proscenium screen, the ban on talking and other disruptive behavior). As each of these practices is relatively arbitrary rather than intrinsic to film, each must be invented, cultivated, and maintained, decade by decade, year by year, and even week by week and film by film.

The definition process of film as *classical cinema*, to borrow one of Stephen Neale's claims about film genres, is best described not as a system but as an ongoing "process of systematization,"[2] in which a series of related but discrete "systems" of film form and spectatorial address share the implicit goal of creating a specific kind of theatrical experience for the spectator that keeps her attention focused on the screen, deaf and blind to the spectators around her. Psychoanalytic film theory from the 1960s to the 1980s described this subject position clearly, if dogmatically, as that of a spectator who identifies both with a central character's goal and desires and with the camera that invisibly narrates the film from an omniscient position. She knows she is not really dreaming the film before her but forgets herself all the same, thanks to the darkness of the theater, the cause-and-effect pressure of the plot, the deftly causal arrangement of shot next to shot, the seamless relationship of musical score to onscreen events, and the effectively "public-in-private" sense one gets in the movie theater thanks to the agglomeration of darkness, rules of decorum (i.e. keeping mum so as not to break other patrons' concentration), and the spectacle of light, movement, eroticism, pyrotechnics, and bodies that unfolds on the bright rectangle that beckons to the viewer in the dark. As public as theatrical spectatorship is, the ideal spectator loses himself in the classical film as if engrossed in a novel.

But, as I will attempt to show throughout the book, there is no single, self-identical system of "classical cinema"—"cinema" here referring to any institution that enforces a relatively stable set of conventions for the production, distribution, and exhibition of films. The American commercial cinema is perpetually engaged in setting up institutional systems of production and reception appropriate to specific historical eras in terms of cultural antecedents, intertextual expectations about aesthetics, style, and entertainment, technological innovations in film and other media, and so on. As one more or less supple system comes together, as it did between 1907 and 1917 when D. W. Griffith, Alice Guy Blaché, Smith and Blackton, Carl Laemmle, Cecil B. DeMille, Thomas Ince, and myriad other industry leaders collectively produced the precedents for a reproducible, classical institution of filmmaking and film viewing, it nevertheless crumbles as quickly as it is built, and parts of it must be replaced or retrofitted before it has ever become a fully dominant system. For example, Griffith's Victorian moralizing and elaborate races to the rescue, which were practically cornerstones of classical storytelling, seemed outdated or rote almost immediately after taking audiences' breath away. In their place (though never displacing them entirely), DeMille and screenwriter Jeanie Macpherson borrowed some of Griffith's means of constructing an attentive spectator to erect a more contemporary and (sometimes) less bombastic form of melodrama that centered on the secular joys of eroticism and consumerism.[3]

Consider the following example: "Late" silent films released by the Hollywood studios in 1926–28, just as Warner Bros. released its first Vitaphone "talking" prologues, can still be called "classical" in their basic construction and especially in their appeal to that public-in-private spectator, but even a cursory glance at King Vidor's *The Crowd* (1928) reveals that, aside from the positioning of the spectator and the parameters of the classical institution that I have just outlined, much has changed in the fifteen-odd years between *The Crowd* and *The Cheat* (DeMille, 1915). By 1928, close-ups rather than three-quarter shots prevail, the acting has become more intimate and understated (thus taking advantage of the nearer framings), and what counts as a character goal and the achievement of that goal seems to have become much more flexible. In *The Cheat*, Edith Hardy (Fannie Ward) is blackmailed and forcibly branded by an evil "Oriental" aristocrat and part-time usurer (Sessue Hayakawa) and must come clean about their relationship in court in order to save her and her husband's good names; the goals and psychological-emotional stakes of the plot are as obvious as its melodramatic punch. *The Crowd*, by contrast, ends with destitute "everyman" Johnny receiving his first day's paltry pay for his job as a street juggler, and yet he enjoys an ostensibly happy ending in which he uses his wages to invite his estranged wife and son to see a vaudeville show that leaves them, and the humongous crowd that a series of dissolves exposes as enveloping them, enraptured by amusement and by how amusement unifies them. Although Johnny's position in capitalist society and in his own family now seems murky and even his goal—to be a better father and husband—is incompletely realized compared to the goals of characters in *The Cheat*, each film makes use of classical narrational properties to construct—ideally—an attentive, absorbed spectator who empathizes with the rises and falls of the protagonists.

But I cannot help but wonder how stable we can afford to call classicality as a system when that system changes so much from decade to decade that these films seem to hail spectators with entirely different expectations about goals, ethics, and even the physical actions of characters, not to mention expectations of visual style and montage. One answer to this conundrum is, of course, that film style and technology as well as social mores and cultural preconceptions of narrative, acting, and character change slowly and imperceptibly, so it is to be expected that changes to classical form that look radical when seen from a distance of years seemed like no changes at all to viewers. This logical assumption, however, does not change the fact that elements like cinematographic and editing conventions do change drastically from decade to decade, as even a quick skim of Barry Salt's invaluable *Film Style and Technology* will show.[4] The means by which the American cinema maintains classicality might thus be productively recast as a series of fragmentary systems rather than the retention of a single, monumental system. Classicality only *seems* to persist along a continuous line because emergent practices within each system overlap with dominant practices from another and residual practices left over from still another.[5] The fact that differences over time don't irreparably damage the ideal spectatorship experience I have described above is a testament to the success of a process that in fact takes *spectatorship* as its primary product rather than any specific classical film or even a specific style or format for Hollywood films. Specifically, films must render their discursive practices—that is, their technological base, revealed by any screening-time proof that the film was made rather than simply exists—invisible.

But we must not allow ourselves to take on faith that spectatorship practices, or even the positioning of spectators with respect to the screen and its unfolding events, remain utterly consistent over the years. A new student of film history might well compare DeMille's late silent film *King of Kings* (1927) with *It Happened One Night* (Frank Capra, 1934), find few variations between their styles of visual storytelling, and assume smooth continuity between silent and sound eras, never dreaming that the brief period of transition to sound (approximately 1926 to 1933) generated many Hollywood films that looked and sounded stilted, stagy, and crude compared to the films that preceded and followed. Every film produced by any Hollywood studio must be founded on recognizable classical practices, and it must exhibit adjustments of those practices to the vagaries of subject matter, technological changes in filmmaking and/or exhibition, and broader audience expectations that patch into the social and cultural terrains within which the films must be consumed—this last including everything from trendy subject matter to the future transformation of a theatrical release into a broadcast or cable television event and a VHS or DVD package that will be viewed under decidedly unclassical circumstances.[6]

I dust off the concept of the classical spectator position—the subject of Hollywood cinema who is at the same time its object, the agent of the "gaze" who is reified into a passive, film-hungry consumer by accepting the highly encoded and circumscribed version of agency that is joined at the hip to spectatorship—not to return to the psychoanalytic model of the duped spectator who experiences and interprets each film exactly as every other spectator does. On the contary, any viewer is a subject of ideologies but need not be (nor is she ever) wholly *subjected* to them by the film or by any other means.[7] Rather, my point is to characterize the classical subject position as a historical idea, or rather an ideal, that has remained since last century's first decade a driving force in Hollywood's development of institutional practices. Among institutions for the viewing and interpretation of moving picture texts, the institutional parameters to which we refer whenever we say "Hollywood cinema" are responsible for some of the most resilient practices in the medium's history. Hollywood cinema has also exerted more energy, more effectively, than any other cinematic institution to stabilize a specific aspect of its mode of reception, that is, to replicate the public-in-private character of watching movies in theaters no matter how circumstances, filmic and extrafilmic, might threaten it. Unsurprisingly, the success of classical narrative cinema has allowed it to hijack the collective imagination of film on a global scale; to any number of undergraduate film students and longtime cinephiles alike, there is simply "film" or "the movies" (character- and goal-driven products with more-or-less invisible narration and high production values) and then there are a crowd of minor, quirky subgenres: documentary (although *Capturing the Friedmans* and *Fahrenheit 9/11* have helped rehabilitate this form's public reputation), "art" films, avant-garde/experimental, "foreign," and the like.

It's little wonder, then, that as early as the twenties, with the publication of Terry Ramsaye's *A Thousand and One Nights,* and as late as Janet Murray's *Hamlet on the Holodeck* (1997), the popular definition of *film* qua medium has become synonymous with the institution of classical cinema. Not only do both Ramsaye and Murray conflate the two, they treat as fact the analogy of early cinema to an inarticulate infant waiting to reach its inevitable adulthood as an emotionally affecting narrative medium. Imagining a prehistory even more ancient than Bazin's "mummy complex," Ramsaye writes that "all art is pervaded" by the "single purpose" that American film circa 1926 so well fulfilled, that is, to provide "a living motion story of thrill and glory and pleasure."[8] In fact, however, the commonsensical, evolutionary aura of these claims betrays the ahistorical teleology that underwrites them, a sense of evolution as a continuous process that, as Rick Altman points out about some theories of genre evolution, flouts Darwin by forgetting that diachronic change in organisms is forced by discontinuous external conditions.[9] Classical Hollywood storytelling began to stabilize in the mid-teens partly in answer to debates that had built up steam since 1900—debates about how films should be made, what their primary content should be like and how it should be regulated and presented, and how audiences should behave when viewing them. These debates were often cast in the form of a discussion of the "nature" of the medium—as a "universal language" of pictures, which could be used for good as effectively as for ill—when in fact the discussion's goal was to negotiate a mutually desirable definition that could be imposed upon the medium.

These debates began in the Progressive press and church pulpits. But producers participated in the debates as well, not only through the motion picture trade press but also through their films. In attempting to fit reformist expectations without alienating or simply boring their core audience of middle- and working-class patrons, the members of the Motion Picture Patents Company (MPPC) and their rivals began to work harder than ever to legitimate the viewing experience. They did so by reaching for new textual benchmarks, the first of which were content centered: adaptations of literary and theatrical texts, historical events, Biblical subjects, paintings, and the like. They also followed the cue of Griffith's successful Biograph one- and two-reelers, which adapted the "high art" of Dickens, Longfellow, and Millet but also used specifically cinematic means to do it, insisting on shot-to-shot causality in one scene and symbolic parallelism in another. In other words, Griffith transmuted the conventions of literary narration ("Meanwhile, she thinks of her lost love . . .") into filmic "language" (for example, a shot of the man might be followed by a shot of the woman in an obviously different-looking space, staring blankly into an empty portion of the frame until a matted image of the man's face appears).[10] The difficulty for the producers, and for the exhibitors on which they depended, was to avoid being labeled peddlers of lurid spectacles without alienating their immigrant and working-class audience's desire for spectacle.

Looked at through the lens that I am attempting to grind here (without, I hope, grinding too many axes in the process), every film that American producers have released since the industry first came under reformist pressure may be interpreted as a film about the classical cinema and the struggle to maintain and reproduce it. Specifically, any classical film bears indentations left by the industry's collective attempt to mediate among four key elements, each of which exerts its own peculiar pull against the continuity of classical institutional practices: the medium of film and its specific (and changing) opportunities and limits; the engagement of multiple artists and engineers with film's possibilities; the social and production relations under which those engagements take place; and the audience that producers anticipate when they produce the film. Whether and how a version of classicality is maintained by the American commercial cinema depends in large part on how the actual, historical audience receives it—in the case of classical cinema, this means determining whether the discursive aspects of narration get in the way of what the industry has for decades considered the primary navigator of the spectator's attention and pleasure: storytelling.

Before story films began to dominate production by 1905–6, however, it seemed that every film laid out another forking path for film's future. The medium that early films fantasized about most energetically was film itself. Before I address those fantasies, though, I must reiterate the stakes of the act of generating media fantasy. For Carolyn Marvin, media fantasy demonstrates that the question of what a medium will be and do is much more than a question of what a machine can do or what its aesthetic or commercial future will be; it is a question about the relationship of public to private experience, who speaks and who is heard, who owns the media—both old and new—and who regulates them, and whether these structures of power and influence can or should persist.[11] The struggle over media identity is fought in magazines and newspapers, congressional hearings, advertising, in the texts of the emerging medium, and in the texts of the media with which it competes for the public "mindshare." This last is Donald Crafton's term (borrowed from the current advertising industry) for consumers' attention to and feelings about a product even when not directly in its presence, a hotly contested commodity among media industries. "What was at stake for the corporations that controlled the technology" of synchronized sound film, for example, was "to convince consumers that sound belonged to a particular manufacturing group and that the group enjoyed a 'natural' claim to exploit sound."[12]

Media industries continually traffic in comparisons of their product with other media products—precedents, rivals, and sibling technologies—in an effort to instruct the public in the corporate visions of their media's futures. Once the connotations of one medium have been installed in the public imagination of another, however, those connotations become difficult to control. Nothing guarantees that negative expectations of a medium will not infiltrate that mindshare or that users will make imaginative links between one medium and another, thereby fantasizing new uses that the producers never intended.

What Is This Thing Called the Cinématographe, the Biograph, the Kinetograph, the Eidoloscope . . . ?

Few periods offer richer and more wide-reaching precedents for tracking the negotiation of media identity than the emergence of the American cinema. The history of early cinema is, among other things, the history of a medium looking for an institution. Its developers had a major stake in defining it, to say the least: they needed stable markets, respectability, and a reproducible structure of film production that would encompass everything from the division of labor to conventions of screenwriting and directing.[13] But the drive for stability was challenged by public fantasies about the nature of film—fantasies that rushed to meet the industry's products and economic imperatives with the force of an onrushing train. What could film do? How did it do it? What other technologies did it resemble, and how did it differ from them or even best them at their own game? And if it did resemble other media that industry, government, and technological experts had used to demonstrate the progressive future of the nation, what new opportunities for engagement with the social world did it offer? This chapter is not intended as an exhaustive list of turn-of-the-century answers to these questions, but I do hope to hint at the variety of definitions of "film" lobbed by early films and lobbed back by their audiences. In particular, I hope to coax out of hiding a hardy strain of fantasies that imagined film as the newest example of that most remarkable of nineteenth-century accomplishments: machines that sent and received messages via the apparently occult power of electricity.

Although early films made an indelible impression on viewers, the identity of film as a medium was teasingly indistinct to producers and viewers alike. "Film" by whatever name, moving pictures, scenes, Kinetograph shows, and so on, was a contested idea that shifted from film to film, screening to screening, venue to venue, and spectator to spectator. During the first couple of years of projected cinema, up to 1897 or so, the film industry seemed too busy giving its audiences more films like the ones they praised the most to care about addressing a singular or even a general definition of the medium. The first films featured "actuality" subjects like exotic lands, earthquakes, animals and humans performing feats of prowess and pageantry, and gigantic machinery at work, as well as more overtly encoded matter such as raucous slapstick gags based on vaudeville acts and comic strips, patriotic subjects, and "blue" movies that exposed garters, shoulders, and ankles for all to see. The attraction of such fare depended mainly on the novelty of transforming anything that moved into a ghostly yet monumental and vivid representation, but as exhibitors called for still more novelty, producers experimented with more and more subjects, like the mythical Edison trying everything from piano wire to human hair in his search for the proper filament for the light bulb.

For their part, film exhibitors tested diverse presentation arrangements as well, depending on their economic means (which determined their access to the newest films and projecting equipment as well as the nature of their musical or spoken accompaniment), the spaces they had at hand, and the neighborhoods and venues in which they operated. Films were screened in vaudeville houses, at fairgrounds and amusement parks like Coney Island, in uptown New York auditoria, in makeshift storefront theaters, in churches and town halls visited by itinerant lecturers bearing mechanical novelties, before hundreds or only a handful of people. Each of these spaces carried its own rules and mores for audience behavior, and each also hailed audiences as belonging to a class or an intermingling of classes whose interests in the moving picture spectacle varied from the intellectual fascination provided by this scientific oddity to the astonishment and metaphysical thrills of witnessing this peculiarly magical magic lantern. Spectators ranged from upper-class aficionados of modernity's wonders, to middle-class thrill seekers, to working-class tenement dwellers who visited film venues to see friends or avoid going home as often as to wonder at the kinetic photographs of onrushing trains, pixilated furniture, and Russian cityscapes that moving pictures displayed.

Viewers had a wide spectrum of categories by which to judge exactly what the moving images they saw signified about the medium's novel powers over space and time, and also over the relationship between one human consciousness and another, as person after anonymous person appeared in a beach scene or a street parade, bigger than life but insensible to the viewer's presence. The judgments any given viewer might have made depended on the intersection of particular films with the viewer's knowledge of other technologies and their powers, social functions, and fantasized futures. As diverse as films were, the ambiguous experiences of these spectators were edged in the direction of speculation and fantasy by previous encounters with technological displays such as mechanical dioramas, magic shows, and phonography demonstrations, and by expectations about the technological future generated by other media and by the utopian and nationalist rhetoric that framed such demonstrations.

Although for the most part we can do no more than reconstruct possible extracinematic responses, contemporary writings about the first projected moving pictures suggest that, to its first viewers, film resembled technologies as diverse as the steam engine, the telegraph, the telephone, the phonograph, and the X-ray in that it wreaked havoc on the natural order of space and time.[14] Without projecting the centrality of the classical film text back onto a period in which the film itself was far from central, I think it crucial to consider the impact of specific subjects and specific films upon viewers' perceptions of intermedia similarity, because the machines and media that early films envisioned no doubt narrowed the technological contexts available to viewers at a given moment, or at least sharpened their awareness of which contexts might best explain the film experience. Consider the familiar example of the railroad engine, most infamously the one that rushes at the audience in three-quarter view in the Lumière Brothers' *L'arrivée d'un train à la Ciotat* (1896). As the railroad journey had already produced "rapid changes of scenery and point of view" that represented "the annihilation of space and time" as they had previously been experienced, and as the telegraph had split off communication from physical transportation for the first time in history, so film decoupled the continuous movement of reality itself from the time and place of its recording and transformed the visible properties of time and space into reproducible objects.[15]

Idealized visions of community had long saturated electrical communications fantasies by the time of the first projected films: world peace, an end to cultural misunderstanding, total empathy, indeed, a proto-McLuhanesque global village seemed the inevitable outcome of instantaneous communication. As Marvin describes them, nineteenth-century fantasies about new electrical media continually stressed an "instant mutual sympathy" expected to follow the media's virtual annihilation of space and time (Marvin, 198). The authors of an 1858 history of the telegraph, for example, claimed that the new machine intrinsically "binds together by a vital cord all the nations of the earth. It is impossible that old prejudices and hostilities should longer exist, while such an instrument has been created for an exchange of thought between all nations of the earth" (Czitrom, 10). Marvin quotes an 1885 *Electrical Review* speculation about the "universal intelligibility" of a vaguely imagined medium (whether it transmits information visually, aurally, or through code seems too mundane an issue to bother with) that the author nevertheless expected to appear any day—a "poetical telegraph" that would transmit historical events to such far-flung places as Cairo, Calcutta, and Rio, and by which "all corners of the earth are joined, kindled, fused" in interest and empathy.[16]

Like the electrical annihilation of space and time, this ideal of technologically induced democracy has its roots in popular discourse concerning the railroad engine. Long before the introduction of moving pictures, the train's uncanny transformation of space had attracted utopian wishes that technology contained the seeds of social transformation, as evidenced by a democratic vision conjured up by the French writer Constantin Pecqueur in 1839:

> By causing all classes of society to travel together and thus juxtaposing them into a kind of living mosaic of all the fortunes, positions, characters, manners, customs, and modes of dress that each and every nation has to offer, the railroads quite prodigiously advance the reign of truly fraternal social relations and do more for the sentiments of equality than the most exalted sermons of the tribunes of democracy. To thus foreshorten for everyone the distances that separate localities from each other, is to equally diminish the distances that separate men from one another.[17]

Pecqueur here makes a metaphorical equation between the effacement of literal distance between one place and another and the elimination of figurative "distances" between individuals, that is, cultural, racial, and class differences.

It is not exactly the train's power of rapid transit that effects this democratization; Pecqueur's diverse national and cultural subjects meet in the railroad car, squeezed together by chance, where their only ostensible similarity is their desire to reach the same destination. But the train's ability to abridge the distance between one point on the map and another seems to guarantee the effacement of passengers' differences. What Wolfgang Schivelbusch calls the "technological equality" experienced by passengers riding on the same train provides, in Pecqueur's rhetoric, "a continuous lesson in equality and fraternity." In other words, the passengers are equal in their desire to move, to be taken to a particular destination as rapidly as possible, but also in the fact that they are all moving, reduced to an essential state of bodies moving parallel to each other through space. No matter what social class or nationality they inhabit, these passengers co-commute using the most advanced, and most fetishized, technology that progress had to offer (in 1839, at least). In this sense, if no other, certain recognized distances between them have "shrunk" just as the space between them and their destination appears to the senses to have dramatically decreased.

Of course, these "transformations" are phantasmatic, for the literal distance between cities has not changed, nor have farmers or workers met bankers and managers in the middle in terms of class or status. But the rhetoric used by dreamers like Pecqueur invites us to confuse the fantasy of near-future changes with the actual situation the train creates, suggesting that the unreal quality of the train ride for its first passengers—the thrill and terror of immense speed, the proximity of dissimilar people, and the panoramic perception of the landscape itself whizzing past the windows that Schivelbusch stresses was a completely new, alienating phenomenon—irreversibly shook up all of reality, social as well as physical, making democratic utopias seem as inevitable as technological ones.[18] Fantasies about media like the telephone were continually swallowed up by the same ideology of social transformation. According to a prediction published in *Scientific American* in 1880, the telephone augured "nothing less than a new organization of society—a state of things in which every individual, however secluded, will have at call every other individual in the community."[19] Although the telephone was in actuality "not a democratic medium" at the time (Marvin, 153), the very fact of the technology and its communicative potential, like the fact of the railroad engine, underwrote fantasies of universal accessibility and intelligibility.

Early filmmaking constantly alludes to this problem of machine-driven publicness and contingency in more or less overt terms, positioning the cinematic publics as a more powerful, volatile force than the media receivers imagined by Marvin's electricians. Train films in particular alluded to the cinema's political energies by rehearsing the railway journey's own mythical claims to social transformation. First-person railway-journey films such as Edison's *Panoramic View of the White Pass Railroad* (1901), nicknamed "cowcatcher" films because the camera was sometimes positioned at the front of the engine, invited viewers to intermingle railway idealism with their ideas about film. In a fascinating precursor to the subjective boundaries that classical film imposes, viewers were in each case positioned as train passengers, particularly when cowcatcher films were shown in the mocked-up railway cars that served as screening rooms for the railway-cinema attraction known as Hale's Tours.[20] By casting the screen as an observation window, cowcatcher and panorama films echo the democratizing possibilities of the train in that they imitate one railway reality—rapid travel—and physically recreate another—the grouping of different "travelers," joined in virtual motion as they share the same landscape views—under the sign of a new and uncanny technology. As the Hale's Tours car was artificially jostled and the front window screen unfurled views of mountain slopes or canyons, viewers became film's passengers in more ways than one: they traveled virtually along with the long-take films, and they playfully took part in Pecqueur's fantasy of the passenger car as nation-in-miniature, updated and further democratized by cinema.

Such passenger-viewers would not have had to reach very far for such fantasies. Like the railroad, and the telegraph lines that tailed it around the country, film was touted by the pundits of the day as an intrinsically democratic technology that would foster instant understanding among the peoples it made visible to each other. The newness of the cinema and the strangeness of its powers attracted fantasies that closely resembled those built up around the world-shrinking powers of electrical networks and train travel.

Miriam Hansen has identified a broad discourse on film as a "universal language" operating during the cinema's first two decades. Imagined by editorial writers, film producers, and social reformers in terms of the communications revolution ushered in by the printing press, film seemed to materialize the long-imagined end to post-Babel confusion through the "allegedly zero prerequisite of linguistic skills" required to make sense of photographs. The "direct" photographic appeal of film was supposed to lead to its use as a medium for hieroglyphics or a "graphic Esperanto," through which the cultural ideals of technologically advanced societies could be transmitted via particular icons, a concept embraced with special verve by Vachel Lindsay and D. W. Griffith in the mid-teens.[21] This fantasy depended in large part on film's photographic basis, for the "unmediated" realism of daguerreotypes and photographs, which Samuel Morse called not "copies of nature, but portions of nature herself" in 1840, attracted copious speculations about photography's universal, instant intelligibility;[22] but again, the very existence of the new technology of cinema and its novel method of reproducing reality intensified the fantasy and practically ensured its introduction into the expanding family of democratizing media.

Despite their democratic rhetoric, however, the motive force behind these high-profile fantasies of electrical media and film was more likely cultural imperialism or the legitimation of capitalism than an interest in making the social or political public spheres more inclusive. The democratizing force attributed to electrical media generally assumed that everyone in the world was alike—or was yearning to be more Western, that is, more "civilized"—to begin with. In Marvin's words, "Instantaneous electric communication augured a universal language, usually thought to be English, and global harmony. . . . Always, new media were thought to hail the dawning of complete cross-cultural understanding, since contact with other cultures would reveal people like those at home" (193, 194). Magazines like *Electrical Review* and *Scientific American* erected one-way media scenarios obsessively when speculating about the social implications of a media-shrunken world but limited the use of point-to-point communication to Anglo-European cultures as a privilege of their most technologically (read: socially, politically, culturally) "advanced" citizens. Marvin notes that the point of origin and the subject matter of the imaginary "poetical telegraph" are strictly European; only the audience is nonwhite, pre-industrial, and unequivocally other. "While all corners of the earth were flatteringly 'breathless' in attending this apparent center of human drama, that center was oblivious to the possibility of uncertainty, misunderstanding, or hostility in encounters between cultures with different logics of experience, or indeed to the possibility that interest might ever lie elsewhere" (Marvin, 199).

The crucial point of discursive intersection between electrical media fantasies like the poetical telegraph and cinematic universal language is that the media public in each case is more virtual than actual. The writer of the poetical telegraph fantasy casts the messages worthy of transmission— reports of war, assassinations, and other national disasters—as "drama," "theater," something to be consumed passively and at a distance, without any expectation of or opportunity for deliberation between spectator-auditors and the events presented. This unidirectional vision of media communication differed little from the reality of contemporary electrical communication, over against the inclusiveness implied by the media fantasies. As Ithiel de Sola Pool writes regarding the idea of "two-way interaction in real time" in early telephone discourse, "This point, though understood, was discussed surprisingly little. . . . There was instead a tendency at first to anticipate that the phone would be an instrument for hierarchic interactions; giving instructions rather than negotiating and discussing." Sola Pool attributes this tendency to the fact that the telephone's first subscribers were business owners who mainly used it to interlink branch offices, as well as to the poor fidelity of early telephone technology.[23]

Like the poetical telegraph and other such fantasies, the myth of film as universal language was explicitly hegemonic. Between "recreated" historical scenes, literary and dramatic adaptations, and (after 1907) Griffith's innovations in narrational editing and psychological complexity, film was expected to "uplift" the masses to the cultural level of its more distinguished patrons (and to attract more of the latter class of patrons in the process).[24] The universal language of the moving picture was to be a language that told audiences something and made them feel something, not one through which spectators could talk back.[25]

The Spanish-American War films of 1898 demonstrate the ability of the new medium to abstract its ostensibly unified audience in this way. War-related films, from actualities to fiction films to outright fakes, organized spectatorial response around nationalist icons. Whether the views were actual or faked did not matter so much as their mediating effect between spectators at the theater or fairgrounds and other spectators watching the same views elsewhere, and the fact that they addressed viewers as homogeneous, patriotic masses whether or not they actually fit these descriptions. (Musser reports that such films often brought cheering crowds to their feet, though the intensity of the response varied from region to region, especially when films of McKinley, the "reluctant" commander-in-chief, were shown as part of war-film programs.)[26] Like even the most apparently communitarian fantasies of other electrical media, these films presumed a self-identical public, nationally (if not internationally) joined in its reverence for a superior culture and a noble cause.

As the telegraph, in the words of an 1858 history, would surely make it "impossible that old prejudices and hostilities should longer exist" according to the fantasies, the mere fact of seeing others as they were in life would automatically set people on equal terms as *masses,* demonstrate "the social world of 'Americans'" in an idealized sense, and assimilate immigrants into the larger whole.[27] As late as the release of Griffith's *The Birth of a Nation* (1915) and after, social reformers hailed the potential of film as a "universal language" by which the people of the world could be educated as well as finally communicate with one another sans translation for the first time since the mythical fall of Babel—a utopian dream that Griffith hoped to realize with his follow-up film, *Intolerance* (1916). Walter Benjamin might have cheered and cursed this fantasy at the same time, for by constructing an inevitable, egalitarian "dream world," the universal language fantasy recognizes that a new medium *could* provide a platform for the transformation of social relations. Its faith that the technology will effect change by itself, however, ignores the reality that the same capitalist system of privilege and profit that limits the public's access to existing technologies would also regulate the new. The hieroglyphic language of film was expected to wash the unwashed heathen by spreading Western values supposedly waiting to spring up in every culture (with the exception of the hordes of barbaric "darker races") and particularly in the United States, where urban immigrants held too tightly to their languages and customs. Rarely if ever was film explicitly imagined as a language through which the heathen could respond. *The Birth of a Nation*, the experts' favorite example of cinematic Esperanto, delivered an intolerant message to a "nation" of political subjects that Griffith and novelist-playwright-minister Thomas Dixon could not have more clearly envisioned as exclusively white.

Yet in spite of hegemonic media fantasies and equally hegemonic films, the exhibition conditions of early cinema strained against the restrictions imposed by electrical media fantasy. Projected film aggravated the dialectic between electrical media expectations and the reality of media experience in that film's only implemented form was as an amusement for a mass audience assembled in the public space of a theater. The railroad imagination of early film invited sociological interactions among viewers that the haphazard practices of exhibition could do little to define or control. The same was true for the electrical media discourses that films and their exhibition invited into the viewers' heads. Film's place in electrical media fantasy is a little difficult to grasp today, because film does not communicate instantaneously, nor does it allow patrons to interact with the screen as if it were a sort of videophone. But fantasies about television-like communication devices circulated as early as the invention of the telephone in 1875.[28] An 1889 fantasy concerning the "telectroscope," a proto-televisual device Edison was expected to invent in the very near future, presumed that the development of telegraphy and telephony would soon make "actual scenes . . . visible to people hundreds of miles away from the spot." In 1894, a writer interviewing Alexander Graham Bell topped off Bell's fantasies of shrinking the world via telephony by reporting that

> Professor Bell is convinced that in the near future it will be possible to see by telegraph, so that a couple conversing by telephone can at the same time see each other's faces. Extending the idea, photographs may yet be transmitted by electricity, and if photographs, why not landscape views? Then the stay-at-home can have the whole world brought before his eyes in a panorama without moving from his chair.[29]

If film could not match the literal simultaneity of this ideal, it did the next best thing by producing the moving "landscape views" and "panoramas" expected of the telegraph of the future. In 1895, Charles Henry Cochrane said of Edison's experimental "kineto-phonograph"—the closest thing to a "telectroscope" most Americans would hear about until the first experiments with mechanical television in the late 1920s—that its "possibilities . . . are almost endless. It may bring to our door sights and scenes which heretofore have been obtainable only by traveling in distant lands."[30]

As I have argued elsewhere, early cinema also invited many explicit and implicit comparisons with the telegraph.[31] In contrast to the telephone, the prohibitive cost of which restricted its private use to the economic elite, the telegraph was a public medium, called upon to perform civic functions that ranged from signaling firemen to delivering baseball scores or war news to eager crowds. Early "reality" films were promoted as more or less immediate experiences of distant places, political candidates, and news events (even staged ones) in ways that resonated with telegraphy practices, in that both involved *display*: telegraphic news "as it happened" often involved such displays of information as banners at newspaper or telegraph offices, magic lantern slides at vaudeville theaters, or fireworks signaling the outcome of political elections or other major events. News films, briefly popular at the turn of the century, took up the baton from that display culture and drew upon telegraphy's connotations of immediacy in the process, which was more easily done at the time, when the public's access to the telegraph was limited to displays and newspapers produced and consumed at a temporal remove (however slight) from the events they reported. The "living newspapers" of early cinema, such as Edwin S. Porter and George S. Fleming's *Kansas Saloon Smashers* (Edison, 1901) and *Execution of Czolgosz with Panorama of Auburn Prison* (Edison, 1901, a staged reenactment of the death of McKinley's assassin) did not display events live to their viewers, but they could be produced in a few hours and distributed mere days after the event in question, making filmic delivery nearly as rapid as the publication of wire-service stories to the public.[32]

Hansen provides another clue to the discursive relationships between film and live media by describing how early spectatorship fulfilled the conditions for what Oskar Negt and Alexander Kluge call an alternative public sphere. Hansen's definition of the *public* follows that of Jürgen Habermas, who characterized the classical public sphere (that is, the public sphere in its early Enlightenment manifestation as a physical space of unofficial but politically charged exchange among male landowners) as a historical category of bourgeois society "distinct from the Hegelian trinity of family, state, and civil society." The classical public sphere was founded on its critical and official distance from the state on an "equality" and "mutual respect" that ideally (though rarely in practice) offered universal access and "an autonomy grounded in the private realm" but that nevertheless excluded the private sphere from discussion.[33] Negt and Kluge argue that media production in late capitalism enables a kind of public sphere that excludes neither members of the "wrong" gender or race, nor the day-to-day conditions of the private sphere. Instead, it addresses those disenfranchised consumers who, although politically disempowered, constitute the majority of consumers of both mass-media texts and the products associated with them through advertising. Thus the mass media, and television in particular, create the "conditions for an explosion" of political energy by offering a shared "horizon of experience" in the form of programming that simultaneously indexes private life as a general idea and exposes to the politically disempowered the exclusion of their lived experience from the "official" public sphere. This horizon accidentally offers common ground for discussions of implicit affinities within and between social groups, shared realities like labor woes, childcare, class division and sexism across ethnic categories, racism across class lines, and so on.[34]

One space to which this promise could lead, if the structural possibilities afforded by media texts could be developed and organized by groups of viewers, is an alternative, nonbourgeois public sphere in which partial publics would take up the unkept promises of "meaning and totality" that capitalism and its media circulate, and take action to realize them beyond the "commodity nexus."[35] Hansen characterizes early cinema as a venue that "provided the *formal* conditions for an alternative public sphere," because it offered not only shared texts but also a public space where the texts were both consumed and discussed, and an "interactive" experience of attending films: "The neighborhood character of many nickelodeons—the egalitarian seating, continuous admission, and variety format, non-filmic activities like illustrated songs, live acts, and occasional amateur nights—fostered a casual, sociable if not boisterous, atmosphere."[36]

In this environment, commentary was not merely the preserve of film lecturers or on-site musicians. Early films, as Gunning has famously argued, were ambiguous, fragmentary texts, "attractions" that did not restrict the parameters of their own interpretation as classical story films have done for the past ninety-odd years. The "syncretic, presentational, and non-linear" representational mode of early films invited distracted viewing rather than absorption, and exhibition practices varied depending on the interests of exhibitors and of their (ethnic, regional, upscale, and so on) clientele; audiences themselves were thus encouraged to recognize cinema viewing as a unique and public event.[37] Thus projected film was more socially inclusive and contingent than the earlier, truly live, truly networked electrical media around which such democratic ideals were formulated in the first place. Public exhibition offered patrons literally immediate opportunities for interaction, expression, and organization, all for the price of a nickel or dime a head. The brevity of the films (the first Lumière and Edison films ran under a minute each), their exhibitionist and confrontational aesthetic, the infrequency of edits or changes in camera distance, and the presentation and organization of moving picture shows invited a range of audience responses much different from character identification or narrative absorption.

Indeed, the earliest films rarely drew attention for their individual merits. Rather, like the myriad technologies publicly demonstrated before it, the whole apparatus of film and the ways it remediated reality were the point of any given film show. In the tradition of technological displays throughout the industrial age, the cinematic apparatus was the main attraction that exhibitors sold to the public, while perhaps the most common meaning attributed to the shows was "technological progress" itself, coupled with the way that, symbolically at least, such a demonstration made progress inclusive and democratic.[38] Viewers collected together before the Vitagraph or Biograph, as they had in previous decades to see demonstrations of the telegraph and the telephone, united by their awe and a sense of collective ownership of the medium to which the shows gave them collective access. At the same time, going to a film show in 1896 was a technological shock—a cross between riding a roller coaster and working on an assembly line. The screen flung visual equivalents of urban shocks and distractions—speed, rapid changes in times and places, inexplicable transformations, even onrushing railroad engines and automobiles—at its audiences and invited the same whoops, laughter, squeals, and questions about the technology encouraged by attractions at Coney Island. Nickelodeon owners did not allow spectators access to kinetograph cameras or projectors (which set these shows at a vast operational remove from the hand-cranked, single-serve Kinetoscope peepshows that displayed the first moving pictures), nor did the screen offer opportunity to exchange ideas with the people it displayed, but the confrontational images and the distracting, carnivalesque atmosphere of early screenings fostered communication within the theater in ways that the institution of a "respectable" performative art like ballet or legitimate theater did not.

Exhibitors and producers, however, found this sociable definition of film a liability. One problem was that early cinema's stress on novelty, rapid change from "view" to "view" (an early term for a single short film), and images that many critics found socially inappropriate (such as aggression toward authority figures or images of underdressed dancers) presented film as a curiosity first and foremost, but curiosity alone could not sustain viewers' attention for long. By 1904, a scene of elephants shooting the water chutes at Coney Island was no longer a selling point simply because it was caught on film; most New Yorkers could easily take the train to see the same show in the pachydermic flesh.[39] Under these uncertain conditions, and before the rise of market research, the search for paradigms and functions that would meet audience interests resembled a desperate cycle of trial and error. Musser argues that the Spanish-American War of 1898 boosted the film industry by offering it a new identity as war correspondent, at least for as long as there was war news to report.[40] While performing a function previously reserved for the telegraph, war films also posited film as a technological mirror of America's colonial mastery. This novel role cast a dual shadow of imperialism and consumerism upon the electrical media fantasy of universal understanding, as if the neighborhood theater were the armchair colonialist's answer to the Fotomat: "In the operation of this wonderful piece of mechanism," wrote the *Austin Statesman* in 1900, "photography and electricity join hands and grim visaged war is portrayed while you wait."[41]

Without spectacular news stories to report, however, the "living newspaper" function could not sustain the film industry any more predictably than had the cinema of attractions. Producers professionalized the business of producing films early on by establishing patent trusts, instigating serial production, rewarding technical proficiency, and pushing toward vertical integration. But by 1908, the site-specific and interactive practices of viewing these increasingly sophisticated films suggest that, in an emphatic sense connected to market predictability and the text's (and thus its producer's) authority over its primary meanings, film was still an *amateur's* medium, a hit-or-miss affair that had yet to be defined by replicable textual formulae or by a stable set of social functions. As Charlie Keil shows, the demands for "good" stories and "good" photography that hit the film trade press around 1907 were plotted on an uneven foundation of conflicting criteria. As a group, neither the critics nor the producers whose products they reviewed knew exactly what standards they were looking for, but they were convinced that comparing film to legitimate theater and still photography held the key to discovering them.[42] As long as producers experimented with clarifying and standardizing film form, and as long as exhibition interspersed films with other entertainments that reflected neighborhood interests, the production companies remained bricoleurs. They could not yet claim to have mastered the medium as a maker of meaning. Edison, Biograph, and their smaller competitors shared a level playing field with every exhibitor who had a constituency to serve, and every distracted pleasure seeker who wandered into a nickelodeon.

I am not suggesting that film developed teleologically from this point forward until it at last resembled some form that producers and critics had long imagined; indeed, both groups knew better which contemporary practices they disfavored than which practices they could tentatively approve. But I must stress, as Gunning, Hansen, and others have suggested before, that the urge to stabilize film reception saddled the industry with an imperative to develop a resilient, commercial film form. One way or the other, if the industry was to survive its social critics and the rowdiness, confusion, and happily sociable distractedness of viewers, it would have to "program" its audience to watch attentively by textual means and, if possible, by limiting and shaping the extratextual influences of exhibition spaces.

A second problem facing the attempt to shape a profitable identity for film was its unnerving power over space and time, and the restlessness that this power incited in its audiences. If the original "mobilized gaze" of modernity belonged to the Baudelairean *flâneur,* who pinned people and commodities alike under his "window-shopping" gaze as he strolled the industrial city, early films commodified the gaze itself. Like the panorama and diorama before it, they sold the very act of looking to audiences eager to *see* technology, and to see *with* it into another place. But early films also outdid the panorama by mass-producing that gaze, distributing it across the nation and around the world, and selling access to its pleasures for a pittance.[43] Benjamin and Kracauer, the major figures (along with sociologist Georg Simmel) behind the "modernity thesis" relating industrial culture to the emergence of film, characterized this form of looking as a simulation of the experience of urban alienation. The fragmented kineticism of film returns the blasted urban subject's alienation in the face of transportation machines, crowds, and factories to her in the form of distracting amusement, with mixed results: going to the motion picture show compounded urban alienation and provided a homeopathic remedy for it at the same time, while offering city dwellers an opportunity to grasp their own alienation as an object they could name, ponder, and perhaps connect for the first time back to the social conditions that determined their lives.[44]

Without disputing this redemptive interpretation, I suggest that recent theorization of early film viewing as a mediated form of modern shock has overlooked the suggestive relationship between "shock" and the discourse of electricity at the end of the nineteenth century. Benjamin drew from Baudelaire an explicitly electrical invocation of urban innervation: "Moving through traffic involves the individual in a series of shocks and collisions. At dangerous intersections, nervous impulses flow through him in rapid succession, like the energy from a battery. Baudelaire speaks of a man who plunges into the crowd as into a reservoir of electrical energy."[45] Even before the first living newspapers wired the identity of film in a parallel circuit with the "lightning lines" of telegraphy, the anonymous *New York Times* review of the first Edison program at Koster and Bial's in 1896 saw sparks flying from a very similar source: the crowd of spectators.

> When the hall was darkened last night a buzzing and roaring were heard in the turret, and an unusually bright light fell upon the screen. Then came into view two precious blonde young persons of the variety stage, doing the umbrella dance with commendable celerity. Their motions were clearly defined. When they vanished, a view of an angry surf breaking on a sandy beach near a stone pier amazed the spectators. The waves tumbled in furiously, and the foam of the breakers flew high in the air. A burlesque boxing match between a tall, thin comedian and a short, fat one, a comic allegory called *The Monroe Doctrine,* an instant of motion in Hoyt's farce, *A Milk White Flag,* repeated over and over again, and a skirt dance by a tall blonde completed the views, which were all wonderfully real and singularly exhilarating. For the spectator's imagination filled the atmosphere with electricity, as sparks crackled around the swiftly moving, lifelike figures.[46]

If read against the backdrop of instantaneous communications media like the telegraph and the telephone, which predated projected cinema by some fifty and twenty years respectively, the reviewer's electrical metaphor articulates the meaning of this "exhilarating" experience not as shock alone, but *immediacy* and *communication.* The crackling sparks please rather than endanger, and they unify the crowd rather than atomize it. As links in a circuit of human electrons whose "imagination" (note the collectivizing singular noun) "fill[s] the atmosphere with electricity," they registered in the reviewer's own imagination as meeting the screen images halfway, in a singularly modern and self-consciously communal fashion. He recognizes that the medium acts as a lightning rod that draws out this collective imagination, but he also acknowledges that crowds supply the speculative energy that makes the spectatorial *event* as exciting as the medium of film itself.

Yet the exact nature of the sparks incited by this moving picture show is left indistinct. What precisely does "imagination" mean to the reviewer? Does it imply that the audience and the reviewer fancied that they witnessed a live transmission from afar? Or does it convey a sense of danger that attended this communal excitement, in an era of frequent labor and race riots, not to mention frequent auditorium fires (particularly when some film projectors were equipped with improperly shielded electric motors)? The ambiguity of the *Times*'s terminology reflects a contemporary wariness about electricity that provides a clue to the review's implications. Electricity, as David Nye shows, symbolized by turns both progress and destructiveness throughout the nineteenth century. Harnessing this natural phenomenon made it no less unruly. It could light streets and homes one second, and execute criminals or errant circus animals the next, as frequent moviegoers well knew from watching films like *Execution of Czolgosz* and *Electrocuting an Elephant* (Edison, 1903; an actual electrocution of an errant circus animal—perhaps the first snuff film). In 1909, the prolific W. Stephen Bush injected some of this ambivalence into his own electrical description of film viewing when he wrote in the film business journal *Moving Picture World* that film patrons "gifted with a little imagination and the power of speech will begin to . . . try to explain [the screen story] and tell their friends and neighbors. This current of mental electricity will run up and down, wild, irregular, uncontrollable."[47]

By honing his own electrical metaphor to describe the *conversation* rising from an "excitedly" chatting crowd, Bush's review completes a circuit of its own. After thirteen exuberant but frustrating years, the industry Bush addressed had come to see the excitement its films produced as a problem, because vocal opinions and interpretations gave nickelodeon shows the unwanted flavor of cheap amusement. Bush's commentary plugs the cinema into paranoid electrical fantasies about inexpert users of media—Native Americans, society ladies, African Americans, island "savages," and other types—and the fear that accompanied those fantasies: when it appeared that new media might become so accessible as to accidentally amplify the voices of politically excluded groups, Marvin shows, electrical experts spun out nightmarish narratives in which these amateurs exploited the media to overturn the same social and cultural hierarchies that regulated media reception.[48] In an age of overt and violent struggles among economic classes and ethnicities over the definition of a properly "American" identity and the rights of citizenship, neither government nor private enterprise could afford to give the masses such access to *filmic* meaning, and to the ears of other members of their cinematic publics, without installing some kind of editorial control.[49]

Indeed, envisioning the audience as electrified and electrifying in terms of face-to-face social interaction envisions film as an honorary electrical medium if not an actual one. I must make clear here that film became an object of this dire strain of media fantasy by dint of the resemblance between the *institutional* future toward which early film exhibition pointed—a cinema characterized by the sociological interactivity that had characterized "legitimate" theatrical and operatic performances in the United States through most of the nineteenth century—and the similarly uncertain futures of telephony and other duo-directional media during their emergent phases.[50] Lacking obvious mechanical or institutional means to control film viewers' access to each other the way that, for example, Bell Telephone and Western Union managed their networks, film shows engendered distracted and vocal audiences. For film producers, whose products were screened in whatever order exhibitors wished and with whatever sound accompaniment they chose, the challenge was to determine the relationship of film to its audiences and the effects—real, perceived, imagined—of films and of the conditions of their reception on social relations, via the films themselves as much as this was possible.

A forgotten future of the cinema is made visible here by the very act of negating it: a form of spectatorship that defines the experience of film as a self-conscious relationship among exhibitor, screen, viewer, and other viewers. In this future, the institutional form imposed on collective film viewing would support idiosyncratic group dynamics, and might in turn encourage site-specific modes of interpreting films. That future was, in a predigested and unself-conscious way, the present of early cinematic spectatorship. For his part, Bush presents the *lecturer* as a solution to that clear and present danger. To play out the electrical metaphor that Bush initiates, the lecturer acts as a master electrician who "repairs" filmic communication by shorting out the viewers' figurative transmitters—or to put it better, their independent faculties of interpretation, which would include their ability to negotiate filmic meaning with other viewers—and enticing them to bask in the cool light of his reason and experience instead: "The gifted lecturer will gather up and harness this current of expressed thought. . . . [The] errant sparks will fly toward him; the buzz and idle comment will cease." If it was indeed possible to experience early cinema as telegraphic not only in its "lightning" delivery of news but in its overtly public character, then going to the moving picture show seems to have literalized that character, at least for Bush, in terms of the kind of unsupervised person-to-person exchange that had been successfully eliminated from telegraphic practice half a century before.

A third problem blocking the stabilization of the industry was that interaction in the darkened theaters was becoming unmanageable. As Bush's advice suggests, rhetorical gestures extrinsic to the films such as lectures, live music, and the arrangement of "views" into semicohesive programs reduced the ambiguity of screened images and bracketed the theater's functions as an alternative public sphere. But the effectiveness of these strategies evaporated in the contingent atmosphere of neighborhood nickelodeons, where audience and exhibitor had equal freedom to transform the meanings of the theatrical event according to local interests and shared knowledge. Illicit activities, both actual and feared, ranged from the criminal to the sexual. Nickelodeon shows were among the few public events that an unchaperoned woman could attend without automatically being accused of indecency, but this did not prevent Progressives and other social critics from criticizing movie houses for harboring indecent activities. A patriotic song played by a fiddler would shunt the meaning of a film displaying a national flag in a narrowly patriotic direction, but satirical music offered other possibilities for interpretation, whereas no change in the music from that played over the previous image screened would leave its significance primarily up to the viewer.

On Christmas Eve 1908, as has been reported many times, the mayor of New York declared the city's film venues a threat to public morality and temporarily shut them down. By that time, the production industry had been trying to climb out of the cultural gutter of "cheap amusements" for nearly a decade. Most producers filmed more culturally acceptable content than train collisions, antiauthoritarian gags, or blue movies by 1908, but "quality" pictures based on poems, classical drama, operas, and historical events could not improve film's reputation by themselves. Respectable content won skirmishes with reformers but only inched toward an end to the war to transform spectatorship, for the audience's familiarity with such material—much of which was considered less highbrow then than it is today—meant that producers of quality films could fall back on the episodic structure of the earliest narratives and rely on the audience's intertextual "electricity" to fill in the missing plot and character information.[51] By relying on the audience to supply extracinematic knowledge, and the exhibitor to supply the necessary editorial context, producers surrendered their authority over filmic meaning, and the meaning of film itself, to factors over which they had little control.

But 1908 was also a landmark year for the institutionalization of American film for another reason. Filmmakers had begun to borrow features of the bourgeois realist novel—character psychology, causal narration, narration of simultaneous actions, and the like. By doing this, and by avoiding distractions like presentationality and self-reflexivity, the film industry asserted more control over both film spectatorship and the identity of film. The importation of these literary and dramatic tools represented a step toward addressing spectators the way that novels addressed their readers: as functionally identical subjects who all enjoyed and desired a specific form of storytelling. This universal subject position or, better put, mass-produced experience of a film could effectively be detached from that film and "given" to the spectator in the form of a predisposition to another film constructed according to the same principles of narration.[52]

This *classical* discourse of universality represents a major shift from the universality projected by electrical media discourses and reflected by Bush and the *Times* reviewer. In that discourse, universality refers to the medium's inclusion of all discussants in the construction of meaning, a public constructed by the fact (rather than just the content) of the medium. McLuhan's "global village" of TV provides a surprisingly useful example of this model of universality, at least in theory: the village is composed of those who share, or have the potential to share, the experience of the same broadcasts. In other words, the medium does not connect them literally through the screen; rather, common experience connects them imaginatively to each other. While U.S. culture casts TV primarily as a home medium (although, as Anna McCarthy shows, to label TV "primarily" domestic ignores the millions of televisions viewed in public places), this imaginative publicness is a key element linking the discourse about TV to the ideals of the classical public sphere.[53] In the eighteenth-century café culture described by Habermas and Benedict Anderson, the propertied men who considered themselves informed political subjects were *readers,* linked not only by their regular congregation in a public place and their lack of official public office but by the fact that they read the same newspapers and books. With that common "horizon of experience" to ground them, they eventually pushed their discourse beyond literature and the news of the day to debate and affirm political goals (see Habermas, 33).

But in the American film industry after 1908–1909, the increasingly eloquent narrator function that told stories via the formulaic application of framing and editing was employed as a tool to *reduce* the interactive character of theatrical film exhibition. As I've mentioned, critics who hailed film as a universal language during the proto-classical era also praised it for excluding the masses from the process of making meaning. Instead of defining the meanings of films for themselves and each other, spectators were increasingly imagined as subjects defined from without, by ethically and patriotically didactic stories told in gripping ways. Viewers willing to attend to details of plot and characterization were rewarded with greater readerly comprehension.

If the mid-teens myth of film as a natural language drew on Western culture's faith in photography and electricity to convey reality objectively, it conveniently (perhaps even purposely) forgot how ambiguous the "pure" images of early cinema had been just a few years earlier. It banished the shocks and distractions of early cinema—the rapid changes in places and times shown on the screen, the long-shot framings that distanced viewers from characters, and other elements that kept viewers' imaginations grounded in the situation of exhibition along with their bodies—to the historical ghetto of unrealized media fantasies, where forgotten futures are doomed to be misremembered as wrong turns that did not fulfill a medium's inevitable calling. In other words, the rush to laud film as finally reaching its potential as a universal language may not be the sign of the producers' and reformers' success after all. Rather, it seems a willfully premature attempt to put an end to the proto-classical era's debate about film's institutionalization, a debate that conveniently mistook itself for a debate about the nature of the medium.

Looking at Looking: Keyholes, Kodaks, Screens

Before the installation of classical production and exhibition practices, screen fantasies about film and spectatorship were perhaps the primary method through which producers commented on the medium and its audiences. I will go even a bit further and suggest that, before the success of the French *films d'art* and the "quality films" of Shakespeare plays and biblical and historical subjects, self-portraits of film in early cinema were an important means by which film producers negotiated spectatorship practices directly with viewers. The literal and figurative terms of the negotiation are still visible in Hollywood films today, in sublimated ways, but it will be easier to identify classical-era media fantasies as fantasies about film if we use early cinema's self-portraits to begin examining those terms.

The discussion that follows builds upon Miriam Hansen's discussion of Edison's *Uncle Josh at the Moving Picture Show* (Edwin S. Porter, 1902), a film that takes an overtly didactic approach to taming audience interactions. Perched in a low balcony to the left of a screen proclaiming the "Edison Projecting Kinetoscope," the rube Josh throws himself into the task of spectatorship, dancing "with" a "Parisian" dancing girl, going hysterical at the sight of the Black Diamond Express, and attempting to pick a fight with an amorous farmer over a country girl. Hansen argues that the point of *Uncle Josh* for its intended viewers is that Josh mistakes filmic images for reality. By doing so, it makes both Josh and the garrulous audiences of attractions films look ridiculous, and implicitly congratulates the spectator for knowing better than the rube on the screen. *Uncle Josh* thus marks itself as a transitional film, an attempt to mediate the historical tension between attractions and story films. As it draws together the heterogeneous pleasures of presentational genres under the rubric of a simple story, "the narrative clearly articulates a pressure for these pleasures to become integrated, subordinated to a more mature mode of reception."[54]

Many early films scrutinize that same pressure, but not always or not only from the perspective of exhibition. The first few years of the cinema are rife with films about photographers and cinematographers whose own activities, not the actions of their consumers, produce the unpredictable results. In *Photographer's Mishap* (Edison, 1901), an amateur shutterbug gets hit by a train while attempting to photograph it, and nearly gets hit again by a second train that enters the frame from behind the camera. *The Camera Fiend* (AMB, 1903) has a more moralizing tone. In a long-shot tableau of a lakeshore, a man with a Kodak—the Fiend—takes pictures while a young boy falls into the water and struggles to swim to shore. When a woman appears and seems to ask what the matter is, the Fiend gestures to indicate he is taking the boy's picture, upon which the woman reacts violently to the mishap and runs out of the frame. She returns a moment later with another man, who jumps in to save the boy, and as the hero pulls him from the water, the Fiend grudgingly assists but only uses the arm that isn't operating the camera. In *The Story the Biograph Told* (also called *Caught by Moving Pictures,* shot by A. E. Weed; Biograph, 1904), a technician shows an office boy how to run the real thing, a Biograph moving picture camera, and the boy immediately uses his new skill to film the boss inviting his secretary over for a lap-sit. And one of the most elaborate films, *Bobby's Kodak* (shot by Billy Bitzer; Biograph, 1908), begins with young Bobby's distinguished-looking father giving him a small Kodak, which the boy (portrayed by the "juvenile" star of many Griffith films, Bobby Harron) puts to less-than-distinguished tasks. He secretly photographs the family cook sitting on a policeman's knee in the kitchen, Mother rifling though Father's pants pockets for money, his sister petting in the parlor with her beau, and finally Father stealing a kiss from his secretary. The climax stages an explicitly cinematic show, in which Bobby projects stereopticon slides of his photos on a very large screen in the parlor for the assembled household.[55]

All four of these fantasies about film display the anti-authoritarian spirit of many early story films. Neither social position nor profession keeps one above the fray, and the films express little sympathy for any of the cameras' victims. But each of these films also reflects greater self-consciousness—and anxiety—on the producers' parts about how their films disrupted their cinephilic crowds. *Photographer's Mishap* and *The Camera Fiend* sound sour notes in the burgeoning industry's song of itself by envisioning photographers making questionable judgments about what to shoot, even as the small coterie of "licensed" and independent film producers in New York were finding that their own such decisions missed with audiences as often as they hit. The photographer's attempt in *Photographer's Mishap* to recreate the Lumières' *L'arrivée d'un train* nearly leads to his own demise, implying that by 1901 it was already too late to expect short films that both produced and represented "shock" to pull patrons into the storefront theaters—including, perhaps, *Photographer's Mishap*. *The Camera Fiend* offers a more sinister allegory for the film industry's fascination with shock for its own sake. Its titular devil cares less about human life than about getting a good snapshot of human mortality, and, unlike such giddily violent offerings as British film pioneer Cecil M. Hepworth's *How It Feels to Be Run Over* or *Explosion of a Motor Car* (both 1900), the latter of which ends with body parts raining down on the unfortunate bobby who comes to investigate the accident, *The Camera Fiend* moralizes about the photographer's prurience. As the heroic diver attempts to resuscitate the boy, the Fiend, still snapping his shutter, finally gets what's coming to him: he falls into the water himself, and the hero dredges him out before returning to the child. For nearly the second half of this short film, the motionless Fiend lies at the extreme right of the frame while the hero revives the boy. Throwing up his hands in apparent disgust at the consequences of photographic obsession, the hero wheelbarrows the

Fiend away. The the photographers' fates in *Photographer's Mishap* and *The Camera Fiend* envision the industry's traffic in sensationalist images as a form of suicide. Rather than delighting in spectacle or titillation for their own sake, these films punish cameramen and cameras alike for disrupting social order.

The Story the Biograph Told and *Bobby's Kodak* scrutinize production as well, but expand their scope to include film reception, too, as if to give a full account of the unpleasant consequences of making prurient, exhibitionist moving pictures. The man caught with his secretary by the Biograph attends a vaudeville show with his wife, only to witness the office boy's little masterpiece of cinema verité. His wife thrashes him and pulls him from his seat, and in the final shot, she returns with him to the office to replace his stylish female secretary with a mildly effeminate man. In *Bobby's Kodak,* the long shots of Bobby's family that follow each slide image show Bobby's victims gesticulating or weeping histrionically in turn, while the rest of his captive audience laughs—until their own images appear on the parlor screen. The *Biograph Bulletin* dated February 10, 1908, describes the destructive powers of Bobby's camera to the film's potential exhibitors: "Again that peace-lacerating click. Oh, horror! Is there no help? Great Jove send forth thy thunderbolts and crush to smithereens this calamitous Pandora's Box; but, no, the fates do not intercept and Bobby takes his noxious negatives to have them made into Stereopticon Slides."[56]

Here the viewers rather than the producers suffer the immediate consequences of the show, but the producers do not escape judgment any more than does the Camera Fiend. At the climax of *Bobby's Kodak,* Father sees the final slide of himself with his secretary and stops the show by flogging Bobby. To put a finer point on where the blame resides, however, the final shot of the film displays Father, in a three-quarter shot, setting the Kodak on a table and demolishing it with an axe. Reprising the finale to *L'arroseur arrosé* (Lumière, 1895), in which the watered gardener lurches off camera to pull the bad boy back into the frame for his beating, Father knocks the camera off the table, lifts what's left of it back before the Biograph lens, and finishes it off. In early films, bad boys often get spanked in full view of the public, as if to offset their celebration of pranksterism with an act of retribution.[57] *Bobby's Kodak* is unequivocal about singling out the camera—and the medium it contains, which Father pointedly exposes before dispatching the Kodak once and for all—as the baddest boy in the film.

What binds together the self-reflexive turn of these films is a sensibility we could call *vitascopophobia,* in honor of the first widely used film projector in the United States.[58] In her discussion of the lesson that Uncle Josh teaches his viewers, Hansen argues that, "even if there were no empirical traces of autonomous public formations" during the emergence of film, "they could be inferred from the force of negation, from hegemonic efforts to suppress or eliminate any conditions that might allow for an alternative (self-regulated, locally, and socially specific) organization of experience."[59] Vitascopophobia is a subcategory of those efforts, a tendency that was not so much experienced by its producers as it was a function of films like *Uncle Josh at the Moving Picture Show* and *Bobby's Kodak*. My term is not meant to suggest that filmmakers were afraid of their own equipment but rather that these allegorical portraits of the film industry's woes distance the cinema of attractions from itself in such a way that they hold the *audience* accountable for the disruptions caused by "noxious negatives" like Bobby's. Presentational and semiscandalous films were signs of the industry's amateurish approach to filmmaking, not merely because the films traffic in prurience but because the production companies knew that, however much trouble such boudoir topics got them into, they had few clear options for attention-grabbing content available to them beyond sensationalism.

Thus *Bobby's Kodak* and *The Story the Biograph Told* distance "professional" producers from their product twice over: like *The Camera Fiend*, they bracket illicit behavior—the perennial subject matter of the cinema of attractions—within the moralizing framework of revealing and punishing the offenders; and they project the will to sensationalize that behavior onto photographic and cinematographic amateurs, ordinary people with cameras. As Nancy West has shown, "amateur" cultures that undertook aesthetic production and scientific endeavor had sprung up nationwide by the turn of the century, inciting great pleasure in some cultural arbiters and equally great discomfort in others. "Ours must not be a 'nation of amateurs,'" wrote an anonymous author in a 1903 issue of the *Atlantic Monthly*, "but a nation of professionals, if it is to hold one's own in the upcoming struggles—struggles not merely for commercial dominance [on the world market], but for the supremacy of political and moral ideas."[60] The problem with amateurism, it seems, was that it reduced highly specialized activities to hobbies that need not be mastered to be enjoyed; if it spread, the amateur impulse might reduce many serious professional activities to mere dilettantism, thus allowing other cultures to catch up with and invade the American cultural market. And after 1900, the year the one-dollar Brownie camera was introduced, few amateur cultures had more fervent aficionados than the cult of the Kodak. Although, under pressure from Eastman Kodak's relentless and brilliant marketeering, photography rapidly became associated primarily with leisure, at the time *Bobby's Kodak* was released that association had not yet entirely solidified. Amateurism in photography seemed to threaten desires for anything but practical knowledge of how things worked and anticipation of the result, a threat that registered in Kodak's world-famous slogan, "You press the button, we do the rest."

Thus scapegoating a bad boy for the industry's own quasi-pornographic sensibility seems at first a brilliant act of public denial. Many turn-of-the-century "camera fiends" were children, the same children who had emerged during the nineteenth century as "emotional assets that brought generosity, love, and vitality to the home" (West, 79). *Bobby's Kodak* cracks open such sentimental associations as surely as Bobby's father cracks open the Brownie at the film's conclusion, for Bobby functions not as guarantor of domestic bliss but as a literal and figurative aperture between private sphere and public life, all because a technology too powerful for him to handle responsibly (that is, in a way that parental authority would approve) has been placed in his hands. Yet for all the film's finger-pointing, it cannot dissociate itself from Bobby entirely because, after all, Bobby has caught his relatives thwarting social mores that he himself would no doubt be expected to espouse. Thus this little film seems stuck somewhere between indicting the film industry for its inability to "bring up" its medium into a respectable entertainment and congratulating itself for condemning vice in a delightfully immature, amateurish way: by making it look ridiculous before crowds. By 1908, of course, narrative had largely overtaken the sort of attractions offered by Bobby's lantern slides as the dominant filmmaking mode, but this fact only makes the vitascopophobia of *Bobby's Kodak* seem even more desperate, despite the pleasure it takes in the amateur's antics. It is as if the industry feared backsliding into producing the kinds of prurient scenes that so amuse the bad boy (and considering the presentational style of the film's series of tableaux, that fear seems well founded).

I would also posit that, by putting both Biographs and Brownies in the hands of cinematic "bad boys" who wielded mere water hoses and slingshots a decade earlier, the film expresses a certain nervousness that MPPA producers like Biograph—supposedly the early industry's beacons of virtue, at least comparatively speaking—had thus far managed to stabilize neither narrative strategies nor audience behavior. The *Biograph Bulletin* often had to fill in plot information that the films themselves simply could not communicate, and trade critics complained regularly that viewers could not follow the more complex story films.[61] The coveted hierarchical divide between screen and audience had so far failed to take shape, thus blurring in practice the ostensible divide between producer and exhibitor on the one hand and producer and viewer on the other. In other words, Bobby personifies both the power of an exhibitor to make "his" films tell his narrowly defined audience—his own family, an analogue for the communities that attended urban neighborhood theaters—the stories *he* wants to tell about his family's bad behavior, and the authority to posit and perhaps enforce their personal interpretations of films that viewers still possessed in the nickelodeons of 1908. Before filmmakers and exhibitors "programmed" more attentive reception into films and shows, respectively, viewers still felt entitled to articulate their responses to anyone who would listen.

The Critic, a wonderful Biograph film of 1906, criticizes the industry's amateurism even more obviously, even as it just as obviously displaces its autocritique onto the earliest years of the medium. *The Critic* follows critic Dalan Ale (a transposition of "Alan Dale," the famously acerbic theater critic of the time) into a vaudeville theater where he has his first look at a "continuous" show. Although the show is live, its structure and at least one of its acts explicitly parody the first Edison film programs. The first act, accompanied by a title card propped up on the stage, is "San Dowie," a chubby impersonator of the strongman George Sandow, who flexed his muscles for Edison kinetoscope loops more than a decade earlier. A juggler and a pair of fan dancers, the "Irving Sisters," follow him, and then the strongman returns to restart the cycle, like part of a living loop of short, exhibitionist films.

But continuous or no, the show is a complete flop. San Dowie, a performer of stunning mediocrity, labors tremendously to lift barbells marked "5000 1/2" and "5000 3/6" that his attendants then whisk away without breaking a sweat. The Irving Sisters dance so clumsily that they knock a flower basket into the audience, inciting the management to yank them off the stage with shepherd's crooks. Ale, sitting in the center of the extreme long shot of the theater and identifiable mainly by his bald head, actually gets into an altercation with San Dowie at one point, jumping on stage to protest when Dowie "lifts" a man suspended by an obvious wire. Back at his office, the thoroughly amused Ale writes the following review, which appears in an intertitle:

Last night I saw my first performance of a "continuous." The Irving Sisters ought to go back to washing dishes. Barrigan need not call himself a "Tramp Juggler" for he certainly is a "bum" juggler. San Dowie was so strong the audience knew he was in the theatre half an hour before he appeared. The entire tribe should be taken out and lynched.

In case we miss the subtleties of Ale's critique, the review ends with a stinger: "It was awful!"

Hilarious as *The Critic* is, its title describes not only the protagonist's job but also the reflexive function of the film. *The Critic* lambastes the omnivorous quality of many early films, in which anything the camera could photograph was considered worth screening. But it levels its complaints at decade-old films, which it characterizes as both crude (by emphasizing the performers' lack of skills) and somehow *live*. This is, after all, not a continuous film show but a continuous vaudeville act. In substituting live vaudeville for early film but retaining the content of the latter, *The Critic* avoids explicitly disparaging either present or past filmmaking. But the liveness of the "continuous" recognizes the continuing blurring of filmed and live registers of meaning in exhibition venues. It also reflects the continuing sense of copresence between stage/screen and audience fostered by the overlap of these registers. Because the film refuses to identify its subject unequivocally as "early film," however, it leaves open the question whether this critique is relevant to the present state of the industry. Could it be that film content and form still encouraged audiences to behave like publics rather than attentive, polite spectators?

The key to answering this question may lie in *The Critic*'s detailed representation of a gregarious audience. Throughout the "continuous," viewers in the small auditorium laugh derisively but good-naturedly, gesticulating to each other in response to the poor quality of the show. Patrons in neighboring seats even shake hands with each other after the intermission, seemingly taking much more pleasure in joking with strangers about the performers than they do in the performances themselves. *The Critic* misses none of this, because its only camera set-up during the theater sequence crowds the stage into the upper left quadrant of the frame, filling the rest of the screen with the convivial viewers. While the film makes short work of the cinema of attractions, it does so only via the proxy of a smart, well-dressed audience that shouts down the show as brusquely as any working-class audience might be expected to do. The respectable audience's ultimate power over the survival of film is personified most pointedly by Dalan Ale, whose column extends his complaints beyond the confines of the theater. When the fan dancers, San Dowie, and the juggler turn up at Ale's office to complain about the review, the critic and his assistant send them smashing through the office wall, then return happily to the task of talking back to urban amusements. First the critic pans the "films," and then he sends them packing. Who can blame him? And who can blame the upper-class audience—the very audience that the production industry most wanted to court—if they decided not to return? In the absence of any textual authority exerted by the show's exhibitors, the viewers take the reins of interpretation. They may not hold cameras, but they produce the ultimate meaning of the "continuous" just the same.

Uncle Josh at the Moving Picture Show deals with this kind of audience interaction quite differently, by placing the responsibility for excessively active spectatorship more squarely on the viewer than on attractions films or their producers. Josh, the stock vaudevillian rube, gets far too involved in his experience of films like the *L'arrivée d'un train* knockoff *The Black Diamond Express* (Edison, 1896) and a view of a Parisian dancer, which threaten and titillate him into jumping from his box to the stage and back. If we place the Camera Fiend's overinvestment in taking pictures alongside Josh's excessive involvement in responding to pictures, another strain of the film industry's vitascopophobia emerges from the amateur-photographer films I described at the beginning of this section: each of these films presents spectatorship as an amateur culture unto itself, in which nonprofessional critics join nonprofessional shutterbugs in a struggle with professional producers for the right to experience films according to their own interests and backgrounds. In other words, every amateur cameraman who gets hit by a train or becomes obsessed with violence and humiliation in an early film reflects simultaneously the amateurish experimentation of the film industry, which had not yet discovered the key to making the production business predictably lucrative, and the amateurish viewer (as described by Bush) who, like Uncle Josh, thinks *he* is master of filmic meaning and thus oversteps his (thus far only hypothetical) position as *consumer*.

At the same time, the amateur's camera is a derisive icon that casts its users' contributions as crude, less advanced than the moving images of film, with its (unkept) promise to present "life" in a manner that requires no interpretation. Three of the four films I've mentioned end with the poetic or direct punishment of the shutterbug for straying too far beyond the authority figure's limits on behavior; before Bobby's Kodak gets its just deserts, Father gives Bobby himself a thrashing, as if to punish the amateur for outing the limitations of the would-be patriarch of film's institutional "family," the Biograph company, for all to see. In *The Story the Biograph Told*, the outcome is different but the implication remains the same. The bad boy disappears after he shoots the film of his boss's flirtation, and all the punishment rains down on the boss instead. But we as spectators see the same film that the boss sees, displayed full screen, not matted into the long shot of the proscenium as Porter had done two years earlier in *Uncle Josh at the Moving Picture Show*. By aligning the audience's point of view with that of the boss, *The Story the Biograph Told* implies that the viewer could be next—that anyone could be filmed in a compromising position and displayed before a jury of their spectatorial peers. Perhaps this is even a "friendly" warning to viewers not to let their own productive impulses get out of hand. If the amateur film critics in the audience were ever to get their hands on actual film cameras, the film hints, no one's privacy would be safe.

This is not to say that these films do not suggest ways that film might shatter the interactive circuit of audience response that the cinema of attractions had so enticingly completed. At the climax of *The Critic*, nothing but a thick black line separates Dalan Ale's inner and outer offices. This caricature of a wall, crude as it is, nevertheless reflects an attempt to heighten the film's narrative complexity, for it allows the viewer to see into both offices at once. This earnest, if theatrical, stab at representing simultaneous events seems all the more self-conscious as a stab at pushing the medium forward when Ale and his assistant shove the personified "attractions" films through the wall, out of the frame, and out of *The Critic*. Thus the film concludes by making a show of banishing the very filmic past its continuous vaudeville act has reanimated. But the line is so rudimentary compared even to earlier attempts at representing simultaneous actions, such as the use of superimposition to represent a telephone conversation in *The Story the Biograph Told*, that it accentuates the crudeness of *The Critic* as a whole and underscores the unease the film expresses at cinema's failure to attract refined spectators. Instead of demonstrating *The Critic*'s sophistication by contrast with the Edison films, the line/wall provides yet another stage for vaudeville-style slapstick. At the same time, the final scene allegorically stages the attraction film's transgression of the threshold between screen and audience—a fourth wall that, if it could be patched up again, might convince respectable viewers like those in the diegesis to stay for reasons other than slumming.

Such moments where film steps down from the screen and into the world beyond the auditorium point to another serious destabilizing factor about which early films about film fantasize: film as an aperture through which the conventionally distinct spheres of public and private life might seep into one another. The classical cinema would later develop this notion of the screen as intersection point between the two spheres into a visual analogue to the realist novel, in which the screen provides a window into a complex private world that rewards public attentiveness to that world with emotional satisfaction.

Without producing a teleological account of an American cinema that fostered voyeurism from the beginning, I think I can fairly suggest that the first films about cinematic looking define filmic vision as a specifically social form of power. Many early films with plots that turn on cinematic or photographic evidence offer voyeuristic oversight as an authoritative position that is explicitly filmic without yet being classical. As Gunning argues, the trustworthiness of photographic evidence "rests less on [photography] as a simulacrum of perception than on the act of recording, the retaining of the indexical trace" by a purely objective, "nonhuman agent of truth."[62] But if films like Biograph's *Falsely Accused!* (1908) do not invite the audience to imagine that the camera stands in for their own acts of perception, they do claim for film a policing role over private indiscretion by portraying the moving picture camera collecting evidence that saves the innocent from criminal convictions.[63]

Even earlier films like *Grandpa's Reading Glass* (Biograph, 1902) and *A Search for Evidence* (Biograph, 1903), which offer the audience the pleasure of peeping for its own sake, unlock drawing rooms and cheap hotels and beckon viewers to indulge in a bit of judgmental ogling courtesy of the new community magnifying lens, the Biograph projector. *Grandpa's Reading Glass* riffs on a common theme of early films, in which a circular matte stands in for a diegetic lens and singles out a series of things, animals, and people within a flimsy narrative conceit about children (clear proxies for the audience) who delight in seeing how large the magnifier makes objects appear. In *A Search for Evidence,* a woman and a detective look through one keyhole after another in a hotel hallway, and the random events they see—an old man tripping over a chair in the dark, a doctor at a child's sickbed, a woman undressing for bed—are frankly displayed for the audience through keyhole-shaped mattes. The film displays so little interest in theatrical illusionism that once the investigators have moved through the hallway set from right to left, they reenter the same shot—not simply the same camera setup, but the same continuous take they have just exited—from right of frame to peep into two "new" rooms. The final shot of the husband's room, in which the wife, the philandering husband, and the mistress all hang their heads in sorrow or shame, seems merely a sop to psychology or moralization that the rest of the film either cannot or will not deliver.

However presentational and unsentimental these revelations may be, though, the tight analogy between the characters' peeps and the audience's views associates cinematic looking with public revelation and its consequence—shame—while allowing viewers to feel superior to the philanderers and other rapscallions if for no other reason than that the character has been caught while the viewers remain at large (and perhaps take the hint from the film to be more discreet about their *own* illicit liaisons). As the publicly viewed "story" in *The Story the Biograph Told* drops a bomb on the boss's home life, so these keyhole films stress the early cinema's voracious appetite for the most intimate and embarrassing aspects of the private sphere.

What makes these revelations especially relevant to cinema as a burgeoning institution, and not just to fantasies about film in itself, is the fact that the social impact of the moments of revelation depends upon the collective scrutiny of those moments, whether literally shown or only implied. Although in *A Search for Evidence* the "public" is made up of only two members, the detective and the wronged wife, *The Story the Biograph Told* reveals the bad boy's surveillance loop at the vaudeville show first by showing the "happy" married couple seated in their box, then filling *our* proscenium (rather than the screen-within-the-screen, as in *Uncle Josh at the Moving Picture Show*) with the telltale view. What Carol Clover writes of the trial film *Falsely Accused!* seems to fit this film as well, for *The Story the Biograph Told* spells out "the natural fit between [legal] trials and movies." Where *Falsely Accused!* places a film screen at the witness stand and thus "turns the courtroom into a movie theater and the jury into a film audience" (Clover, 246), *The Story the Biograph Told* converts two theaters—on-screen and off—into courtrooms of public opinion. Without the out-of-frame diegetic audience for which the actual audience stands in, it seems less likely that the husband would capitulate so rapidly to his wife's choice of a new secretary. When the audience-jury sees the evidence with its own eyes, plausible deniability evaporates.

Although they include no film cameras in the frame, films about railroad and streetcar passengers scrutinize the public-private transgressions of early cinema as well, for they focus on the accidental public spheres gathered together under the sign of technological modernity and a mobilized gaze. In *Streetcar Chivalry* (Edison, 1903), several men sitting against the wall of the streetcar make room for a young, attractive woman to sit among them, but when an older woman enters carrying a bucket, the men lift newspapers to their faces to block out this unwanted sight. Pretending to be jarred by the car, the older woman leans into the men and hits them with her pail, finally managing to clear a seat in the center of the frame. This scenario would have been familiar to contemporary streetcar riders and film viewers alike: "Unlike the extended encounters on a railway journey, the trip was brief and passengers were often jostled together. . . . The streetcar's interior made possible a new intimacy with strangers who could be by turns attractive, disconcerting, and disgusting."[64]

On a Good Old 5 Cent Trolley Ride (Edison, 1905) makes the passenger car's resemblance to film viewing more explicit by displaying the effects of technological shock on the travelers. The violent jolts and rocking motions of the small trolley car push the passengers—fourteen in all by the end of the film—into each other time and again, but the brunt of the jolts stems from inappropriate interpersonal confrontations both willful and accidental: the conductor uses a pistol to punch trolley tickets and steals a cigar and a plug of tobacco from his passengers; a woman with an enormous hoop skirt is pulled savagely through the car door; and a mammy figure in blackface drops a huge load of laundry, inciting passengers to fall on, bump into, or simply terrorize each other. Even time itself turns violent, as the hands of a wall clock spin out of control, as if measuring the train's annihilation of space and time, not to mention film's often-touted ability to do the same.

On a Good Old 5 Cent Trolley Ride represents the social heterogeneity of film exhibition spaces as a disaster in which films merely provide a vehicle for rude altercations. At the same time, the film cannot resist putting a utopian spin on that accidental publicness by providing a song slide at the climax: "A Ride on the Trol-ley is Jol-ly . . . / Whatever You Give Up is *Fair*; . . . *Air*." The early production industry may not have known exactly what to do about the sociability fostered by the cinema of attractions, but films like this one still recognize that publicness offers pleasures, too, such as singing along with a crowd of strangers or neighborhood acquaintances, and even being set equal to everyone else, ideally at least. After all, anyone sitting in full view of the screen had something approaching the best seat in the house.

While I agree with Hansen that *Uncle Josh at the Moving Picture Show* provides a negative example for audiences untrained in orderly theatrical behavior, I also think that it, too, bears witness to the persistently social character of exhibition. Judith Mayne claims that Josh's desire to enter the film frame makes him less a transgressor than a harbinger of the classical spectator. When Uncle Josh pulls down the screen at the end to pick a fight with the male half of the "Country Couple," she writes, his revelation of the projectionist behind it "stresses the importance of the threshold in cinema, the crossing over, the movement from one space to another. The rear-projectionist re-marks the separation that the film had fancifully put into question."[65] But I suggest instead that Josh's act of unveiling actually overcomes the artificial separation between auditorium and screen by awarding him what he seemed to want from the films all along: social contact on level social playing field. By tearing down the sheet and wrestling with the projectionist behind it, he breaks down the communicational hierarchy implied by pitting a single, enormous image against hundreds of spectators who face it in unison from a vertically inferior position. The screen comes down when he tries to fight the "farmer"—a social peer to Josh the bumpkin—and he winds up trading punches with the projectionist—a technological sophisticate and representative of the theater business—instead.

Josh channels his urge for contact into a force for social equalization and identifies the screen as a semipermeable membrane through which subjects confront each other in such spaces. In the process of making Josh the butt of a joke on credulous film audiences, Porter accidentally portrays him as the champion of a media utopia in which a sender of a message, represented by the projectionist-exhibitor and the filmmakers channeled by his film program, would be held accountable to its receivers. Whether he realizes it or not, Josh pummels the projectionist for not delivering the sociological connection to the people depicted on the screen that the medium, backed by a long line of prototelevisual fantasies, seemed to promise. But for Josh at least, a fistfight is the next best thing to being there.

Before we mourn the loss of the forgotten future of a pointedly public cinematic institution, or perhaps heave a sigh of relief at its disappearance, I want to underscore the possibility that this future resists its own eradication precisely because film screenings are still public events, at least during their theatrical release. Although pundits predicted the death of film over and over again throughout the twentieth century, films still screen before mass audiences, no matter how private the classical viewing experience is supposed to be. If the opportunity for social interaction had simply disappeared from today's theaters, theater chains would no longer screen trailers that remind the spectator to set cell phones on "vibrate" and keep our thoughts to ourselves. As Hansen might say, such friendly, colorful reminders (one of which, a trailer that identifies the theater as a variety of railway car, I analyze in the final chapter) recognize the structural opportunity for social interaction that theatrical exhibition constructs by negating that opportunity before it reappears. Thus it would seem more appropriate to call these "reminders" *forgetters*: ritualized spectacles that enforce our forgetfulness about the pleasures that cinematic publicness could offer.

Coda: Just His Imagination, or Must He Suffer?

The *Times* reviewer of the 1896 Edison program suggests that watching early films was an active and collective experience, structured by possibilities imagined by the audience—possibilities that producers struggled to place in the past tense through marking films and other visions within films as evidence or memory. But a residual trace of spectatorship as active fantasy appears in *Just Imagination* (Kleine, 1916), part of a series entitled "The Mishaps of Musty Suffer in Numerous Whirls." In *Just Imagination*, Musty Suffer (Harry Watson Jr.) wishes he had a good job and is immediately offered "work" by two lab-coated "Specialists in Imagination." In the course of this one-"whirl" film, food and water disappear before Musty can eat them, a table gives him what appears to be an electric jolt, a staircase levels off when he tries to climb it, a coffee pot changes into a goose, and a lit match melts a block of ice five feet square in just a few seconds. The film ends with Musty awakening amid the rubble of the wheelbarrow accident that opened the film. Apparently, his "job" was nothing but a dream.

But as the film ends, Musty picks up a wheel of the barrow and laughs, and an intertitle appears: "No, it wasn't a dream—just imagination!" As "whirl" teasingly replaces the more familiar term "reel" in the opening credits, Musty's wheel stands in for the dream that makes him laugh, and reminds the audience that they have not been dreaming at all but watching (or participating in?) cinematic magic performed by specialists in imagination who are still testing their technological legerdemain on more-or-less willing subjects. Musty's "imagination"—the film itself—has been no dream but a media project, as Musty himself recognizes when he picks up the barrow wheel and shakes his head at it as if addressing the medium of film directly and jokingly chastising it, then aligning his position as fantasist with the spectators as he leans against an anti-illusionist black backdrop that emphasizes his own status as a figment of the filmmaker's imagination. The viewers, like Musty, have been fully awake the entire time, subjects before a film packed with cinematic tricks that never disguise their unreality (the pixilation and edited substitutions are, it should be said, poorly executed compared to the tricks that Méliès regularly accomplished some fifteen years earlier).

One year after the stunning success of the epic *The Birth of a Nation,* then, the near-classical construction and emphasis on characters' minds and goals that Griffith achieved still had a rival system of audience-screen relations to contend with, a system made peculiarly visible in the distracting spectacle and slapstick of *Just Imagination.* But the film doesn't repress classicality altogether—far from it. Indeed, by focusing on Musty's continual disappointment—he gets no food or drink, no coffee, and no dream woman, only a broken wheelbarrow for his pains—it characterizes spectatorship circa 1916, on the cusp of full-blown classicality, as an alternately satisfying and frustrating experience. Forgetting the apparatus, as classical narrative encourages its spectator to do, leads Musty to mistake the world of "imagination" for his material world, only to have its phony plenty wrenched away from him once he has agreed to enter the world the experts have produced, and finally to be returned to his ramshackle life after he has consumed the fantasy. When compared to the visions of a gripping, illusionist cinema presented by *The Birth of a Nation* and *The Cheat,* this film offers an alternate point of view about film that takes the form of the question punned upon in its title: *Must* he suffer? Is there an alternative to a cinematic institution in which individuated viewers forget their suffering for a few hours only to be confronted with it once again, renewed and raw, when the lights come up?

The films discussed in this chapter rehearse similar questions about how the spectator can or should understand filmic address, even as they exhibit a persistently dialectical quality of media fantasy: they may blame film producers for allowing exhibition to remain a raucous affair, or heap shame on spectators for behaving "badly," but they can do neither without first envisioning exactly the kinds of interaction that concerned the producers most. While lambasting amateur production and undisciplined reception, both in jest and in sterner tones, these films overlap cinematic production with spectator activity time and again. Even Musty seems to have produced *Just Imagination* in his own head, under the influence of mechanical trauma. *Just Imagination* is thus couched as one spectator's response to being subjected to the medium (the whirls), a response he shares with his audience via this film, which temporarily plays the role of its spectators' collective imagination, a role it performs in a self-conscious, self-reflexive manner. Musty takes his figurative seat among the amateurs from other film fantasies who exploit the amateur status of the entire industry, from filmmakers to film viewers, by making a ruckus in theaters or trying their hand at filmmaking. Their unpredictable decisions—not choices among preexisting options but acts of sheer volition—produce a plurality of spectatorial *positions,* as if spectatorship were an array of dots scattered on a plane of social relations and production-consumption relationships rather than a point fixed on a line of seats in the auditorium. Indistinctness is the condition that makes fantasy possible, that leads the fantasist from fanciful speculation to an imagination of practice.

The cottage industry of early American cinema was in a dead heat with its publics in the race to stabilize production and exhibition practice, a race it would eventually win once narrative integration proved its suppleness, profitability, and cultural clout. But media fantasy films since 1917 reanimate that ambiguity about the relationship of spectatorship to cultural production, because they return media indistinctness to spectators as a thing to be worked out. In their drive to recast film in the reflected attention of new, interactive rivals, as I will show in the following chapters, media fantasy films invite that indistinctness to infiltrate the cinema again and challenge the perceived identity between classical Hollywood cinema and "film" per se.

But to call this negotiation a *race,* while descriptively useful for the moment, oversimplifies the process, which has been both hegemonic in nature and under continuous revision since the first decade of the twentieth century. In other words, there is no way for the film industry to "win" the struggle to define film, even with classicality on its side, because there is always another film, another topic, another historically specific set of audiences, and another interactive medium waiting down the road, inciting everyone involved in making, screening, or watching theatrical film to rethink the institution and its future against the backdrop of a range of media choices and reception paradigms that make "going to the movies" seem passive and old-fashioned by comparison. The reduction of the sociological interactivity of cinematic spectatorship—the act of fixing the identity of film in terms of a private-in-public experience of absorption into narrative—has not been a process of eliminating interactivity but of sublimating it.

The openness of turn-of-the-century films about this idea is good reason to suspect that critics, producers, and audiences were all aware of the change while it was happening. Knowledge of the change could well have been supplied by the intermedia landscape within which film emerged as a publicly screened entertainment. Uricchio argues that, "while it is impossible to reconstruct a full sense of late nineteenth-century 'liveness,' what nevertheless remains clear is that 'simultaneity' was both invoked by it and helps to distinguish its different forms" (119). I would add that the act of distinguishing between the two in technological terms would not necessarily keep viewers from imagining or wishing for a cinema that fostered social exchange, following the fetishistic logic of incredulity that Gunning describes as central to the earliest film shows, in which the illusion of the impossible taking place led to fanciful engagement with the event: "I know pictures can't move, but all the same . . ." is a response that runs parallel to "I know these pictures aren't live *transmissions* that I could speak to, but all the same. . . ." Nor would it have prevented them from mingling their *expectations* of an *interactive screen* that had yet to be invented with their *experience* of an *interacting audience.*

In fact, we might productively consider the possibility that classical spectatorship was founded on, among other things, an exceptionally successful fudging of the expectation with the experience, a process in which films continually deny the experience of sociological interaction with other spectators in front of the screen by displacing it onto an experience I will hereafter call *informatic intimacy*: an experience of copresence with the people and places depicted on the screen that sacrifices intersubjective exchange with other viewers for the opportunity to experience the private lives of characters. Obviously this is how Christian Metz and Jean-Louis Baudry have described classical spectatorship: as an illusion flickering on the wall of Plato's cave, a dream of subjective fulfillment and unification made possible by an all-empowering fantasy of optical superiority.[66] However, it is more than likely that, rather than a Manichaean split dividing active from passive spectatorship, a Lapsarian moment named Griffith or DeMille or Maurice Tourneur, the transitional period between the first story films and fully developed classical narratives was a lengthy one that offered abundant opportunities for viewers to enter, and revel in, the confusion between the sociologically interactive and informatically intimate spectatorship practices, to animate and reanimate the receding sense of "perceptual continuity between the space on the screen and the social space of the theater."[67] A glimpse of how one kind of spectatorship might have looked during that long transition appears in a 1908 *Moving Picture World* article entitled "Film Realism." An anonymous reviewer reports on a New

York screening of an unidentified film during which some spectators "involuntarily exclaimed, 'Don't drink that'" just as a character was prepared to sip a poisoned drink. "Surely manufacturers could not go farther than this in film realism," the reviewer wrote. "When they can induce those in their audience to warn characters not to do something they have accomplished what is most desirable. They have made the pictures speak."[68]

One cannot help but add: And in so doing, they have implored the spectators to speak, as well. Beyond the engagement of multiple spectators with the character's dilemma, and thus with the cinematic world they have momentarily exchanged for their own, a teleological sense that narrative integration automatically induced spectators to keep their responses to themselves cannot account for what would make the collective outburst "desirable" to a reviewer. Yes, everyone the reviewer describes as talking back to the image has more or less the same experience of the text at the same moment, at least as far as the reviewer is concerned; such spontaneous indicators of the success of unifying a subject position were rare and no doubt precious to the early industry. From the perspective of media fantasy, however, what is described is a waking dream of social interaction with the image that carries the charge from early cinema's electron cloud of self-conscious publicness into the era of narrative integration. I contend that this quasi-social attitude toward the screen is *still* desirable—albeit in subdued and qualified form—to the film industry. By honing that attitude into an experience of informatic intimacy, Hollywood makes the best of the bad situation engendered by the manifest publicness of theatrical exhibition; that is, informatic intimacy sublimates and commodifies the unavoidably public character of going to the movies. Keeping publicness part of the viewing experience, but only in this externally defined form, is at least as crucial now as it was a century ago, because the televisual, video, and digital forms of film presentation continue to leach into one another the private-in-public film experience and the distracted, collective, and vocal possibilities of home media consumption.

But if courting the audience's desire for publicness is desirable to an industry whose films appear first under the auspices of its institutional confines both physical and ideological—in other words, as expressions of the institution called "the cinema"—it's also an endless nuisance, because a real mass of humanity is always there, at least in the form of a living picture or a frozen moment in time, to model a sociological interactivity that could be just as fundamental to some unimagined future cinema as absorption is to this one.

The film industry has walked the line between social and asocial constructions of the spectator as the price of retaining its uniqueness and even its indispensability as a public media entertainment to the public that supports it. By maintaining this tightrope act for nearly a century, retaining public exhibition through the leanest of years in spite of profits to be made (with lower overhead, no doubt) by producing and releasing texts through other media, Hollywood has painted itself into a corner in which it must champion the sense that spectator-screen engagement has a social dimension—identification, somatic response, empathy—while simultaneously disciplining its audience, scuttling social interactions to the realm of imagination. Yet, no system of cinematic address, no matter how stable, can purge itself of the public nature of that paradoxical viewer position for good and all. It has to be accomplished film by film, public by public, media rival by media rival, over and over again. In 1926, culminating his potted history of human expression from cave drawings to Gloria Swanson movies, Terry Ramsaye revised the electrical metaphor of early cinema viewing for the classical era:

> Motion made the picture a language instead of a sign: made it the fundamental language [that pictures] set out to be in the beginning. . . . Motion in the picture cut out the transformers in the language expression circuit. The mind could now get its emotion juice from the re-created event direct. The transformer losses were eliminated. The juice was stronger, purer. The line noises, the static and squeals and howls of word perversion and attenuation, were gone. Automatic, photographic record supplied in full authenticity what before the individual had to conjure up for himself out of bits of memory and by really stupendous feats of intellectualization. (Ramsaye, lxvii)

Although Ramsaye equates moving pictures tout court with the elimination of "transformer losses" associated with media (such as phonetic, nonpictographic written languages) that excessivley mediate their information, a comparison of this electrical analogy with those of the *Times* reviewer in 1896 and Bush in 1909 suggests that what he is really describing is the triumph of classical narrative over an undisciplined audience. Moving pictures that disavow their opacity as mediators of the physical world replace the sparks of curiosity, wonder, and speculation that characterized audience response in 1896 with "emotion juice" supplied entirely by the screen and for which spectators provide nothing but Leyden jars that store the juice jealously, keeping it for themselves and themselves alone. Yet the fact that Ramsaye reaches so easily for the image of the electrical circuit implies that the collective energy that Bush had anxiously hoped to contain in 1909 could by 1926 still be recognized for the volatile force it was. As long as spectators still gathered to witness the stories the classical institution of cinema told, the industry had to keep one hand poised over the circuit breaker at all times.

As we will see, that hand begins to twitch most nervously when electrical entertainment media become the buzz of public discourse and engender the possibility, by way of energetic media fantasy, that they might draw something more sociologically interactive from their future subjects than "emotion juice" alone. By turns, Hollywood's screened media fantasies recognize these rivals as new business opportunities, as new elements to add to the armory of film technology, as economic and aesthetic rivals for audience attention, and as avenues to rethinking the forms and functions of mediated interaction, avenues about which audiences and producers are equally uncertain. When a new electrical entertainment medium is still new, Hollywood tinkers with it both materially and textually in ways that temporarily render the line between the production and reception of its own textual meanings nearly as indistinct as the qualities of the new medium.

The remainder of this book is something like a beast fable or, rather, a picaresque collection of the fables that the American cinema tells about interactive media beasts: amateurs who fool around with new media technologies before they have been fully tested and fully defined, and who thereby gain access to a public sphere where their voices, opinions, and desires can be expressed and even realized. Behind every amateur figure, however, lies a self-portrait of a film industry that new media, particularly media that both generate texts that amuse and entertain and couch their textual forms in the technology and ideology of *liveness,* perpetually threaten, not simply by challenging Hollywood's share in the mass amusement market but by promoting a more spontaneous and unpredictable paradigm for media consumption than the classical cinema can afford to reinstate. Such "new" media and their novel textualities cause both spectators and film producers to see themselves as amateurs all over again, fumbling to reconstruct the rules of filmmaking and the rules of spectatorship as if from scratch, and racing against one other to define the conventions of each practice.

2

A Cinema
without Wires

Michel Chion describes the invisible voice in sound film as singularly uncanny. For Chion, the cinematic voice-over, which he dubs the *acousmêtre,* is a sonic ghost that, merely by speaking, performs its absence from the image track.[1] Like the spectral-technological voice of the titular villain in Fritz Lang's *The Testament of Dr. Mabuse* (1933), the voice of the acousmêtre can arise anywhere at any time, thwarting the controlling gaze of the spectator by wielding its own unlocatable influence. Its powers include "ubiquity, panopticism, omniscience, and omnipotence," and films regularly exploit the radio as one of the "vehicles . . . of [that] ubiquity." Chion opposes this aspect of the acousmêtre to the radio of everyday life, a banal producer of invisible voices. If one cinematic acousmêtre is revealed, the frame always threatens the spectator with the possibility that more acousmêtres wait just beyond its edge; we cannot see the speaking subject, but it is not difficult to imagine it watching *us.* By contrast, the radiophonic acousmêtre lacks lack. We know we will never see the speaker over the radio, so its voice is more or less complete unto itself (21, 22).

But Chion's claim only holds for the dominant era of broadcast radio. A decade before the release of Lang's film, listeners still imagined radio as an occult technology that performed wonders as unfathomable as those of the cinema, the telephone, photography, and the telegraph before it. Even as late as 1933, the powers of its voices from nowhere drove raucous debates about values, sexual mores, politics, and the persistence of cultural traditions in a frighteningly democratized public sphere founded on thin air. Guglielmo Marconi first demonstrated his working wireless mechanism in 1896, the same year the Lumières premiered their Cinématographe. The disembodied telegraphic signals it snatched from the atmosphere reeked of the supernatural precisely because they lacked visible means of support; the medium's original name, "wireless telegraphy," refers directly to its surprising lack of a material bridge. Electrical experts and laypeople alike referred to the medium through which wireless signals traveled as "the ether" and speculated even into the broadcasting era that supernatural voices had a special affinity for radio waves. As Jeffrey Sconce has shown, the first wireless fantasies expressed anxiety that "spirits" and "aliens" would impose unbidden messages upon the earth-bound living.[2] Speculation ran wild: What would these unpredictable missives tell us? Could they be stopped or controlled?

The provisional answer was that they could not—not so long as wireless technology was easy to produce and the airwaves could not be harnessed and parsed out in measurable quantities like water, electricity, or telegraph and telephone service. As Susan J. Douglas puts it, by 1907 wireless was still "an invisible, mysterious realm, somewhere above and beyond everyday life, where the rules for behavior couldn't be enforced—in fact, were not even established."[3] Wireless devices could be constructed easily with household items like Quaker Oats containers and leftover wire—so easily, in fact, that by the early 1910s a group that was dubbed "the small boys" of wireless—young men in makeshift home laboratories—performed the most exciting and best-reported wireless experiments in America. "Every amateur 'felt that the world was his to explore,'" much to the consternation of federal regulators and the new wireless corporations.[4] They communicated with each other at will, formed national relay networks, developed transmission and reception circuits that left professional equipment in the dust, and even jammed navy and merchant marine signals (see Douglas, 194–215). These amateurs materialized the utopian wish first incited by the telegraph in the 1840s: the wish for a medium that would undermine the structure of privilege that kept telegraphy and cinema *public* media only in terms of their reception. Even the telephone limited its users to person-to-person conversations, rather than offering individuals a public forum, and its expense kept it out of the majority of homes until the mid-twentieth century.[5]

Like the amateur photographers who made mischief with cameras and projectors in cinematic fantasy films, wireless amateurs kept democratic fantasies alive in the discourse of the new medium. At the same time, however, the amateurs embodied the threat of media-supported lawlessness. For the navy and the corporations that stood to benefit from making wireless a scarcer commodity, the real and imagined pranks pulled by amateurs, whether they endangered ships at sea or merely irritated wireless telegram services, clinched the argument for strict regulation of access to the means of transmission. At bottom of these darker predictions were concerns that, if enterprising youth could trip up the navy with little more than a battery and a few coils of baling wire, other, more "alien" groups with more at stake in airing their voices and ideas might do even more to unbalance the circulation of cultural and financial capital.

Over the first forty years of wireless, from its beginnings as a two-way transmitter to its emergence as an entertainment and information medium, American radio fantasy films reflect both ends of this spectrum of public speculation: excitement that geographical distance and cultural difference might be abridged by radio, and fears that it would throw open the borders between white, Anglo-American ears and a heterogeneous mass composed of foreigners, the uneducated, and the uncouth who, like Marvin's telephonic grifters and miscegenists, would exploit the new medium for their own ends. Whether the films were utopian, dystopian, or somewhere in between, they acknowledged radio's potential to revise the definition of media interactivity that the institution of classical cinema tried to defend. These media fantasies also express the compromises that Hollywood struck with radio in the former's crusade to curtail the reception practices that threatened to undermine classical cinema, practices like talking back to the text and using films as vehicles for remembering, collecting, and expressing political interests in the midst of a crowd.

Another Kind of Wireless

Two kinds of utopian fantasies were promoted with particular intensity during the emergence of American wireless: free, open, and universal communication and robust, remote-control imperialism. The former fantasy praises wireless for opening new channels of sociological interaction. Like telegraphy before it, wireless seemed to promise universal access to the means of transmission and reception. In practice, however, Western Union had monopolized the telegraph network, restricting access and charging exorbitant rates for sending telegrams, while the government stood sentinel. But how could any state or commercial enterprise regulate wireless telegraphy? A pay-per-message structure seemed at best impractical. Marconi's first attempts to develop wireless on this model failed, because the propagation patterns of radio waves proved difficult to track and nearly impossible to control.[6] The image of a chaotic ether, in which anyone with a receiver might catch a stray signal from anyone anywhere, made a spiritualist of many a wireless enthusiast, and vice versa. Arcane predictions made by such respected inventors as Edison, Marconi, and Nikola Tesla lent expert authority to fantasies that interstellar aliens were trying to communicate with Earth via static or that the dead used radio signals to speak with the living.

Early cinema's representations of wireless represent its exciting powers in more mundane terms. *Caught by Wireless* (Wallace McCutcheon, Biograph, 1908), the earliest wireless film I have seen, dispatches wireless to catch its melodramatic villain, a corrupt land manager who throws an Irish family off their farm, falsely accuses the husband, and steals money from his boss. Like the errant husband of *The Story the Biograph Told,* this apparently upstanding citizen is revealed for the rogue he is by a highly presentational unveiling of wireless technology. As the farm wife and her children flee their homeland for the United States, the wife walks in front of a large shipboard wireless set, complete with a flashing spark-gap, and picks up a telegram dropped by the operator (apparently played by D. W. Griffith, just before his directing career at Biograph began). The telegram reports that the crooked manager has also left for America and booked passage on the same ship. Once alerted to this news, the operator signals the American coast, leading to a final tableau in which the thief is caught as he steps off the ship, while the family reunites with the father who awaits them in the New World.

By demonstrating how wireless works, *Caught by Wireless* offers the new medium as a blank slate to a public that associated such didactic displays with the public "ownership" of new technologies. The thick atmosphere of display culture that collects around the film's wireless scene would have reminded some viewers of the first demonstrations of film projectors, which foregrounded the medium over whatever content it might project. The March 21, 1908, number of the *Biograph Bulletin* nearly equates the film's narrative thrills to its status as a demonstration of wireless by paralleling the two media in the notice's "stinger" sentence: "The film is replete with stirring situations of a thrillingly sensational character, and the Marconi device, which is accurately reproduced, is most interesting and novel."[7] *Caught by Wireless* maintains film's reputation as a medium that interconnects its viewers, this time by granting them collective access, purely visual though it is, to the newest wonder of technological progress.

By participating in this democratic fantasy of access, however, *Caught by Wireless* showcases a wireless fantasy that runs counter to the film industry's hopes for its own future. By 1908, social reformers and nativist politicians found interaction in the theater the most perplexing aspect of film viewing. The darkened theaters, the slack policing of unchaperoned women, the psychically shocking and often "blue" tinge of the short films all allowed spectators to use the nickelodeon's giant screen as a catalyst for activities that ranged from heated discussions to playing hooky to inappropriate displays of affection. Although *Caught by Wireless* does not allow anyone but the uniformed operator to touch the huge Marconi set, the spectacle scene turns the farm wife into the agent of the film's electrical hero. When the operator carelessly drops the all-important wireless missive, the desperate wife picks it up. Unlike the trained authority figure, the agrarian immigrant—from all appearances a stranger to technology—grasps the personal urgency of the message and acts upon it, using it to solve both her private crisis and the public crisis caused by the murderous thief. In an important way, this scene speaks to two separate audiences in the same voice: it rewards the "typical" film viewer, the female immigrant, for not sitting passively by while media shuttle messages among the elite and educated; and it implicitly hails the wireless amateur, who had just entered the public consciousness, by shifting the limelight from a Naval operator—symbol of the inept "authorities" to whom amateurs were to yield the airwaves—to an ordinary citizen.[8] While Griffith's operator stands stiff and straight, as if on display himself, the farm wife's personal stake in the proceedings makes her a more active, and effective, receiver of the message.

Thus a film that rather innocently exploits the new medium as a topic for fiction films produces sympathetic positions for spectators who might most distrust the hierarchies of message sender and message receiver that the wireless and film industries alike labored to construct. However, the film also reflects a competing model of media interactivity favored by critics of each of these media: the fantasy of imperialism by remote control, a fantasy that required keeping "novices" away from the transmitters. While the immigrant woman makes use of a wireless message here, she does not actually *use* the wireless. The resolutely unidirectional wireless this film portrays is less democratic than democratizing, a kind of megaphone that the technocrat uses to signal other technocrats who then (if they are doing their jobs properly) pass the information on to the public. Electrical experts of the nineteenth century had "styled themselves as the continuing link in a cultural tradition charged with preserving Western civilization for future generations."⁹ This tradition would be difficult to maintain if the technological and cultural elite lost exclusive control over the sending and receiving stations of both wired and wireless telegraphy.

What the experts touted as inclusive media use, however, was in fact a combination of cultural imperialism and intercultural prophylaxis, disguised as a missionary endeavor. In news stories, editorials, and literature, they constructed wireless as the ultimate propagandist for Western civilization. As Marvin relates, experts regularly told nineteenth-century readers that "contact with other cultures [via media] would reveal people like those at home." With its potentially limitless field of influence, wireless promised to trump even the most bombastic promises of wired telegraphy or electric light; it was sure to bring "world peace, freedom from the [telegraph] cable companies, a democratized communications system, [and] transcendence over space and time."¹⁰ Relying on the confusion between technological advancement and higher "truth" that had dogged technologies of representation and communication at least since photography and telegraphy,¹¹ experts adduced the exciting new technology as proof of the Western world's advancement and its worthiness to instruct the backward "heathen." At the same time, they imagined it firing off cultural ideals, capitalism, and democracy like long-range cannonballs into the heathen's midst, thus eliminating the physical and cultural risks of face-to-face imperialism (Douglas, 7–8). This mythology only grew stronger over the following decade. In "A Song of Wireless," a poem by V. C. Jewell published in the American Marconi Company's *Wireless Age* just as the United States entered World War I in 1917, the personified medium sings the familiar chorus of electrical democracy, but the song concludes on a refrain of imperialism and isolationism:

> My messages are broadcast—seek not a chosen few,
> But fall alike upon the ears of Christian, Pagan, Jew.
> I span the raging oceans,
> Safe from their wild emotions,
> And I flout the booming breaker as he rages far below;
> I join the hands of nations,
> In firm, newborn relations;
> I unify the universe; I'm king—King Radio.¹²

Jewell's King Radio equates its listeners to one another, then expresses relief that he need not endanger himself by setting foot in the more feral nations of the empire. This vision of "firm, newborn relations" among "wild" states bears little resemblance to democracy, nor does it envision interaction among the objects of this inculcation process beyond the vague congeniality the fantasy demands. Indeed, Jewell's wireless fantasy resembles much more closely the spectatorship model of what I have been calling informatic intimacy—attention to and identification with the situations and emotional states expressed by characters in a fiction—which classical film form installed to displace interaction among spectators. In each case, the medium in question requires undivided attention *to the medium,* and specifically to the texts it transmits, to the exclusion of actual spectators or wireless users with whom they might otherwise engage. No longer, Jewell's poem implies, will wireless remain a technology that *mediates* between or among its users, in the etymological sense of "media"; instead, it will offer that sense of mediation only in the sense that all *share* the same text, even as they consume it silently and separately.

One might say that Jewell's poem announces the closing of the wireless frontier of sociological interactivity; put better, it denies the real possibility that radio's future would be as interactive as its past. What still separated wireless from telegraphy, long institutionalized as an information network by 1917, and film, recently institutionalized as an entertainment medium, was the amateurs, who were living proof that wireless could provide inexpensive, uncensored, two-way communication that doubled as a form of entertainment. Between 1907 and 1912, the press praised the "boy" amateur for his enterprising creativity in the mysterious new field. Several periodicals and a supply industry sprung up to meet the needs of this culture as they negotiated the medium's capabilities.[13] The amateurs' reputation as enterprising, young populists gave American culture an opportunity to debate the entry of individuals into media transmission in a relatively uncontroversial fashion, for these "small boys in radio," as Commerce Secretary Herbert Hoover called them, were expected to become the engineers and inventors of the future.[14] Affirmative as they seemed, however, the amateurs undercut the experts' promises of an orderly ether. As the United States edged closer to war with Germany, the press turned against the amateurs for (supposedly) pranking a navy that needed to keep the airwaves clear for waterway reconnaissance and defense. The newly politicized amateurs argued that the government was framing them for the navy's wireless mistakes, and eliminating them to clear the path for corporate development.[15]

Wireless fantasy films of the late teens refract this pivotal moment by centering attention on "official" radio heroes. Granted, films of the previous decade had been as quick to laud Naval operators as unexpected amateurs. *CQD, or Saved by Wireless: A True Story of the "Wreck of the Republic"* (Vitagraph, 1909), a lost film about the famous "boy" navy operator Jack Binns, showed the hero using his skills to avert disaster after his ship collides with a freighter filled with Italian refugees. His widely reported act infused the stock amateur with some authority, balancing the image of the inattentive operator in *Caught by Wireless*. By the mid-teens, however, the balance appears to have tilted to the official operator's side. In the Edison short *One Kind of Wireless* (Saul Harrison, 1917), Tony (J. C. O'Laughlin), an Italian laborer who speaks in heavily accented intertitles, loses his job at a railway yard and gets revenge by agitating for a strike. After kidnapping the foreman and learning that strikebreakers will arrive via the number 20 train, the strikers cut the telegraph wires and plot to "let [the number 20] run into the river!" At last, Jack Orr (Albert Mackin), "boy" telegraph operator of *The Dude Operator* (Saul Harrison, 1917), comes to the rescue by transmitting a wireless message to his father down the line: "STOP NO. 20/AT JCT." Reversing the class identification of *Caught by Wireless, One Kind of Wireless* racializes and vilifies the immigrant character and characterizes the working class as a mob against which the wireless protects the railroad's interests.

Where the earlier film envisions even the unskilled citizen-to-be as a potential agent in the new world of wireless, *One Kind of Wireless* marks the foreigner as an anticapitalist rabble-rouser, worthy only of being represented by wireless—as a threat to security—but not fit to represent himself. The film performs a neat trick of superimposition that the preclassical photo-amateur films never managed with any consistency: it projects the ideal of media pioneer onto a screen hero who quells the expression of a technological nonprofessional (in this case, a railroad saboteur).

One Kind of Wireless looks forward to a cycle of broadcast radio films that would liken the wireless to the unidirectional classical cinema. Like telegraphy films before and after it, the film posits an analogy between the coded message and the flickering photographs that converge to produce the message of moving pictures. In fact, no wireless telegraphy equipment appears in the film at all. Instead, *One Kind of Wireless* visualizes the unvisualizable—the coded signal itself—by revealing the titular wireless to be Morse code flashed via electric light, calling out of obscurity the first technology given the name "telegraphy"—the optical system that relayed combinations of opened and closed shutters between large, highly visible stations, used first by the French military in the eighteenth century.[16] Three separate intertitle breaks recreate the stuttering effect of "telegraphic" reception for the spectator by adding to the messages one letter at a time. Jack's makeshift signaling device explicitly parallels wireless and cinema: It is, after all, a flashing light that requires no medium but photons and a clear view between sender and receiver. The caboose lantern Jack rigs up, the title tells us, is one *kind* of wireless—the kind that presents a message to someone who must act upon it, not the kind that waits for an answer. Its key function, like that of narrative cinema, is to *represent* in the sense of creating a text *about* someone or something, rather than to foster subjects who represent *themselves.*

The narrative function of this message hints at how the wireless-film analogy supports, but also overdetermines in curious ways, the classical model of spectatorship. Rather than inviting the audience to imagine film viewing as literally interactive, the letter-by-letter trickle of Jack's messages onto the screen follows Griffith's lead in using electrical media to train viewers to follow narrative editing. Knowing about the space-annihilating power of telegraphy allowed the viewers to watch electrical messages being sent and received with an assured sense of the spatiotemporal relations between one shot and the next.[17] They might also have felt gratified to be addressed as an audience who understood the exciting new world of electrical communications, which were increasingly the bar by which modernity was measured. This scene, like other crosscut scenes from the early story-film period (roughly 1905–1912), engages the spectator's knowledge of wireless and telegraphy by metonymizing the instantaneity of wireless in the immediacy effect of narrative suspense—the intense emotions it produces in the viewer.

At the same time, such scenes invite the audience to accept wireless or telegraphic communication and cinematic representation as similar processes. When *One Kind of Wireless* overlays the temporal linkage between shot A and shot B with the temporal instantaneity of quasi-telegraphic communication (a category in which I include the letter-by-letter pixilation of the message itself), it implies quite forcefully that narrative editing is itself a code, like Morse code or the visual signals that Jack sends, and it encourages spectators new to this development to learn that code and thus unlock the pleasures of narrative and character identification. The editing accelerates as the film closes in on its endlessly delayed climax, changing back and forth among shots of the train running, Jack signaling, his father squinting in the dark to discern his son's message, and the letter-by-letter intertitle displays.[18] The viewer gets the best of both worlds: the wireless world of immediate reception and the newly varnished cinematic world of story-bound shocks and thrills—no matter how simulated the former might be.

Elsewhere I have referred to the collusion between electrical media knowledge and the narrative-bound experience of informatic intimacy as *communicative realism*, a late attractions mode/early classical mode of mediating between the audience's residual interest in the cinematic apparatus for its own sake and the film industry's imperative to refine film viewing into an experience less like a World's Fair electrical demonstration and more like an upper-middle-class theatrical entertainment (Young, 250–57). In the communicative realism paradigm, when electrical media play diegetic and narrational roles simultaneously, they function to shift the spectator's imagination (at least for as long as she sits in front of the screen) of "media" and how they operate from electrical media to film, that is, from communication among subjects to communication from screen to spectator, to which the spectator "responds" not by interacting with others but by engaging mentally with screen information. To use Roman Jakobson's terminology, communicative realism gently exchanges sociological interactivity, and even the overarching sense of a national and/or local community united simply by gathering around a new technology (an important overtone of nineteenth-century technological displays), for a sense of interaction founded on the *phatic* function of the film, its mechanized "act" of addressing the viewer and supplying her with images that may be pieced back together into a story.

This superimposition of media experience, however, risks turning the clock back to before classical subjectivity was stabilized. Whenever classical cinema represents a new instantaneous medium, the trick it has to perform is to exploit the public's curiosity about that medium without reanimating the distinctly unclassical subject position that dominated the American cinema's first decade. By overlapping qualities of wireless with those of film in such direct yet messy ways, *One Kind of Wireless* invites the cinematic subject to imagine herself as a wireless subject in whatever way she likes—an open invitation when wireless was still a fad for the basement tinkerer, attracting the attention of many onlookers but only a smattering of civilian users. If the wireless user of press and science fiction fantasies expected two-way exchange *through* the medium, what would prevent a socially engaged cinematic subject from expecting such exchange as a *result* of media reception? After all, the cinema of attractions had guaranteed precisely such interactions only a little over a decade before. To make the film's aura of film fantasy even less stable, Jack plays on the amateur implications of the title of *One Kind of Wireless* by engineering his signaling device on the spur of the moment. He signals only to save the company's property, true, but his ability to do so depends on his knack for *reimagining* a technology, that is, scraping off the ideology of its conventional functions (a caboose lantern is for signaling simple messages to switching-yard attendants from the rear of a train) and turning it into a medium that serves the necessity of the moment.

One Kind of Wireless works to stave off such a response to the medium of film by linking telegraphic instantaneity to narrative continuity, but also by rewarding the viewer's attentiveness with a sense of the judge's prerogative. The attentive, silent, privatized gaze of the classical spectator receives information about both story and characters that she can only receive by way of ubiquitous, voyeuristic *oversight,* and when the spectator accepts that point of view, she accepts a position of social adjudication, a simulation of the agency enjoyed by the *sender* of wireless messages. The film's visual "wireless" models this definition of spectatorship. As Jack's wireless disciplines unsanctioned social interaction—the strikers' organization against the institution and in turn against modern industry, metonymized by the train and the electrical telegraph—so the visual "wireless" of the film disciplines *its* assembled masses by setting the pleasure of film equal to the pleasure of narrative resolution and making both hinge on the reversal of a social disturbance. The film hangs unsanctioned, active media use in effigy as surely as the hyperbole of *Uncle Josh at the Moving Picture Show* attempts to shame its viewers out of interacting with one another. The audience of poor, working-class, minority urban dwellers, the same audience that made film a successful entertainment medium to begin with, becomes by the teens a regular target against which unified, goal-oriented, ultimately law-abiding protagonists define a "universal" form of Americanism—Anglo-Saxon, middle class, and devoted to order in law, romance, and family—which is synonymous with a unified and "universal" form of spectatorship.

An undated Éclair film from about the same time, *The Telegraph Operators,* folds wireless utopianism into classical cinematic reception more explicitly. Two professional operators foil a heist and save themselves from the thieves who have trapped one of them when she secretly taps Morse code on a window to her beau, the second operator of the title. Like Jack, these ingenious amateurs patch together a wireless medium for themselves, but here the analogy between the ether and the film screen is much more obvious. The tapping travels only in one direction because a second set of taps would draw the kidnappers to the window; the receiver of the message can only look longingly at his lover through the window while she signals, then run to get help. Success in the film industry's crusade to privatize cinematic experience—despite its public nature—depended on its ability to produce films that, like the window-as-wireless "medium" showcased by *The Telegraph Operators,* suffused the screen-viewer relationship with *intimacy* without sacrificing *attentiveness.*

The exchange of heroic amateurs for official bricoleurs across these films reflects the xenophobia of wireless discourse during the late teens. The Russo-Japanese War and World War I pushed wireless colonialism from prognostication to practice, though not for the purpose of converting the rest of the world to Americanism. The U.S. Navy relied on wireless to synchronize military activities, send coded information, and coordinate sea strikes (Douglas, 144–45). Released just as the government rescinded amateur wireless licenses and began recruiting amateur operators, Metro's *To Hell with the Kaiser* (George Irving, 1918, lost) represents wireless as a one-way watchdog, not a two-way network. According to the AFI catalog description, after Kaiser Wilhelm rapes Alice's (Olive Tell) sister and has her inventor-father killed, Alice uses her father's special "noiseless" wireless to inform her lover where to find the killer. In captivity at last, the German prince, who earlier sold his soul to the Devil, commits suicide and finds himself spirited off to the lowest, hottest frequency of the ether.[19]

Irving's film acknowledges the universal access that amateur wireless promised, by allowing a young woman to use an experimental wireless set, but this aspect of the film is less subversive than it sounds. Telegraph and telephone operators were often young women, paid little for skilled labor but lauded (in gendered terms) for their patience and soothing voices. Like Jack the "dude operator," Alice employs Daddy's wireless to defend (and avenge) both father country and patriarchal authority.[20] Her example celebrates the waning of the amateur against a rising tide of foreign invaders, real or imagined. The cover subheading of the December 1918 issue of *Wireless Age,* "How Science Beat the Hun," parallels *To Hell with the Kaiser*'s affirmative wireless fantasy. Both texts exchange the dream of global empathy for a fantasy of disciplining the world.

The first chapter of the Mollie King serial *The Mystery of the Double Cross,* "The Iron Claw" (William Parke, 1917), reflects the widespread acceptance of this xenophobic fantasy by expressing a subtle distaste for the idea of universal wireless access. An intertitle reports that the "immigrants" "make merry!" as a mysterious submarine approaches (even as the United States was entering World War I after the submarine attack on the *Lusitania*), while belowdecks the shipboard Marconi operator casually transcribes a message for the protagonist, unaware of any danger. When the passengers learn of the crisis, the immigrants begin to fight the upper-class passengers for lifeboats and floats. Unindividuated by close-ups, the immigrants resemble a pack of self-interested animals, reversing the *Titanic* mythology in which the rich monopolized the means of escape at the expense of the poor. Considering the presence of the wireless—not to mention the lingering long take of the signaling set, which dwarfs its operator—and the fact that ship-to-ship and ship-to-shore signaling was the most important practical use of the technology during its first two decades, it's surprising that the wireless does not save the day here.

But the scene's tone regarding citizenship and social class produces a textual explanation: lose the populism and gain a kind of wireless that could save the day in a heartbeat. As the *Titanic* disaster unfolded in 1912, some wireless amateurs relayed the ship's distress signals to the navy, while a few others jammed signals and impersonated official operators. When the press overreported the latter's hijinks, the amateurs lost much of the public goodwill they had enjoyed over the previous five years (see Douglas, 226–39). Had wireless been regulated from its inception, commentators argued, more *Titanic* deaths might have been averted. *The Mystery of the Double Cross* implies that wireless itself may have lost its clout as a trustworthy medium thanks to the interference of rabble like the people cavorting on deck. The scene recalls the "terrors of technology" films of the cinema's previous decade, in which electrical media tease characters with their inability to do anything to help their family and friends as they suffer at the other end of the line, but with a twist: the wireless simply stays out of the fray altogether, despite the prominence of the operator's cabin in this scene. The heavy crosscutting does not even piggyback on wireless transmission, since only one transmitter-receiver is depicted.

By missing this golden opportunity to exploit wireless for narrational purposes, *The Mystery of the Double Cross* addresses the viewer as a subject who does not simply consume the wireless's image in order to access the logic of classical narration. Rather, it addresses her as a critical observer of new media, engaged in a discussion of the wireless's current uses and how its uses—and users—ought to be regulated in the future. Film, the medium that shapes the spectator's interpretations of and ideological position toward the wireless, doesn't even try to compete with wireless's then-current functions. *The Mystery of the Double Cross* does not report an *actual* sea disaster as it happens, nor does it pretend to. Instead, it marks itself redundantly as a fiction; the chapter opens with Mollie King agreeing to appear in the serial and projecting herself into a novel called *The Mystery of the Double Cross* by means of a process shot. But it does allude to the historical crossroads to which wireless had come regarding who should and should not be granted licenses. When faced with this populist medium that it nonetheless claims as a media sibling, film casts itself not as the enemy of radio but as an ally in radio's "development" into an affirmative, managed media institution, as film had been retooled into the affirmative institution (so its producers liked to claim) of classical cinema.

If we align this film with the other wireless fantasy films I've described, their aggregate definition of film up to 1917 might be stated this way: film is a medium that, among other things, analyzes the development of wireless in a way that the latter can never accomplish on its own; only a storytelling medium can take such a position, by unfurling a "past" story in present tense without ever leaving the restoration of order in doubt. Unlike the blinkered wireless operator of *The Mystery of the Double Cross,* the classical spectator gets a good look at the big picture from his omniscient and omnipresent viewpoint with the help of editing, which bridges (fictional) time and (fictional) space as rapidly as any wireless and with a clearer purpose—and, in this case, refuses the assistance of wireless in doing so. By presenting wireless populism as a problem to be solved before an assembled audience—that is, by outlining the terms of the contemporary wireless debate—classical cinema bolsters its status as a performer of public service, not just a conjurer of sensationalist images or a gatherer of mobs (though the film makes the most of the spectacle of immigrants rioting on the ship).

This manifestation of wireless simply could not compete with film's claim to edify the masses. Indeed, the public nature of cinematic spectatorship set the conventional definition of film against a persistent fantasy in which the solitary nature of wireless use made the medium dangerous. Wireless operation was a solitary task partly due to technological necessity. Before amplification was developed for radiotelephony, wireless operators had to use headphones to hear the electrical pulses. Wireless discourse turned that necessity into a symbol of rugged individualism on the part of its operators, as I have noted; the boy amateurs who "borrowed" kitchen utensils to concoct better receivers in their bedrooms or attics turned domestic space into a conduit that opened into a world of diverse voices. But a wireless housed in domestic space threatened to subject the private sphere to unwanted voices that could not be shut out. Ribboning through the campaign against universal wireless access lay a pervasive xenophobia: How to stanch the flow of foreign voices and un-American ideologies into the private sphere if no textual structure exists to shape interpretation and no expert (except perhaps parents who were unlikely to share their children's skills) "explains" to the amateurs what they hear? And who will regulate the amateurs' own invasive behavior?

The broadcasting craze of the 1920s ignited a wave of fantasies about radio waves "invading" helpless homes (Hilmes, 14), but a science fiction story by Harle Oren Cummings, "The Space Annihilator" (1902), shows that even the earliest wireless speculations feared such electrical trespassing. Its narrator tells of a reporter named Martin Bradley who built an experimental wireless device he calls the "seismaphone," which will send the sounds of the Boxer Rebellion from China back to the narrator in the United States. Like the amateurs who followed him, Bradley spouts the rhetoric of free communication when describing his figurative earthshaker: "They can put restrictions on the press, the telegraph, and the cables, but they can't restrict Martin Bradley's seismaphone."[21] But when the Chinese capture Bradley, the narrator can only recoil in horror as Bradley tells him of his torture and the anguish yet to come, and at last they punish him by pouring hot wax in his ears. Their "howls" of triumph, mingled with the amateur's cries of pain, travel instantaneously back to the narrator's own ears as he sits, helpless, in his own home.

Although the Chinese never threaten an actual invasion, nor do they *intend* to transmit anything by wireless (apparently they never find the reporter's transmitter), the idea of their "wild emotions"—victory cries following the torture of an American civilian—hitting the ears of a home-bound American like so many drops of hot wax reverses the terms of Jewell's "King Radio" fantasy completely. The problem with wireless imperialism, it seems, was that, no matter how civilized and civilizing the messages sent by the West nor how sweeping the regulation of the airwaves, some anonymous group thousands of miles away might still make its voices heard with impunity. If the amateur could not have the last word on the wireless future, another, more alien culture might yet get to speak it. Gayatri Chakravorty Spivak's famous question "can the subaltern speak?" leads her to the conclusion that the subaltern cannot speak under contemporary conditions of global political discourse—when she wrote her essay, at least—because the colonialist will not recognize it *as* speech unless it makes use of that discourse and speaks from a position defined by that discourse as authoritative.[22] "The Space Annihilator" derives its tension from the chance that wireless offers bestial foreigners to represent themselves—as warriors, as speakers—instead of being represented by the West, their images and voices reconstituted and preinterpreted for general consumption. The story lays open a structural opportunity for subaltern speech to gain authority, if not discursive fluency, via wireless in that it places the bourgeois narrator, curious about the rebellion but happy to listen from a distance, in the position of the wireless *colonized* to the Chinese torturers' wireless *colonizer.* Although he cannot understand the language he hears, he would be wrong to interpret the situation as anything but a defeat for the American fantasy that technological progress instantly triggers universal understanding and peace.

Although the Chinese win this fictional battle, however, the story symbolically removes their tongues. "The Space Annihilator" engages in the usual stereotyping to give its white reading public exactly what it expects to "learn" about Chinese culture: its barbarity, bordering on absolute savagery. The narrator even describes one of the oldest and most sophisticated languages on the planet as a cacophony of "howls." By divesting the heathens' voices of humanity, Cummings makes them threatening in narrative terms but less powerful in terms of Orientalist fantasy. The point here is that, while wireless, the instantaneous medium, forces an intercultural confrontation on the invader's terms, *narrative* mitigates the blow. The arrangement of events and the narrator's commentary together divest the radio signals of their autonomy by casting the Chinese in the most racist light imaginable. The reader experiences the "howls" by linguistic proxy, but the narrative tells us exactly how to interpret them. Compared to the cinema, and even to the telephone, Cummings's wireless is an open window through which alien voices could slip into anyone's home without waiting for an invitation.

Caught by Cinema: Spying on the Overgrown Amateur

The cinema came to the rescue by staging an invasion or two of its own. D. W. Griffith and Cecil B. DeMille both staked their early careers on melodramatic narratives in which private indiscretions were brought to light, first by the omniscient camera, then by heroes who race to the rescue in the nick of time. George Loane Tucker's remarkable film *Traffic in*

Souls (1913) sets its sights on rescuing the unsuspecting from new, privately owned electrical media. Trubus (William Welsh), a seemingly respectable philanthropist, lives a secret life as a white slaver. His "identity remains unknown both to the police and [to] the other traffickers precisely because his connection to the trade is purely technological."[23] Thanks to an audio surveillance hookup and an electric stylus device that allows him to receive the day's tallies via wire, Trubus remains hidden even from his own gang.

In the meantime, his men join him in crooking technologies to serve their purposes. Two of his henchman pull the wool over the eyes of a distracted wireless operator, who hands them a Marconigram that instructs them, in a rather slapdash secret code, where and how to abduct two Swedish ingénues who have just arrived at New York Harbor (Figure 2). All the while, Trubus eavesdrops on the operatives who do his dirty work a floor below his office. But the anonymity Trubus enjoys only lasts until Mary (Jane Gail) finds his listening device, hears his go-between (Howard Crampton) discussing prostitution profits with the man who kidnapped her sister (whose voice she instantly recognizes), and follows the wire to a window through which she peers at the culprit

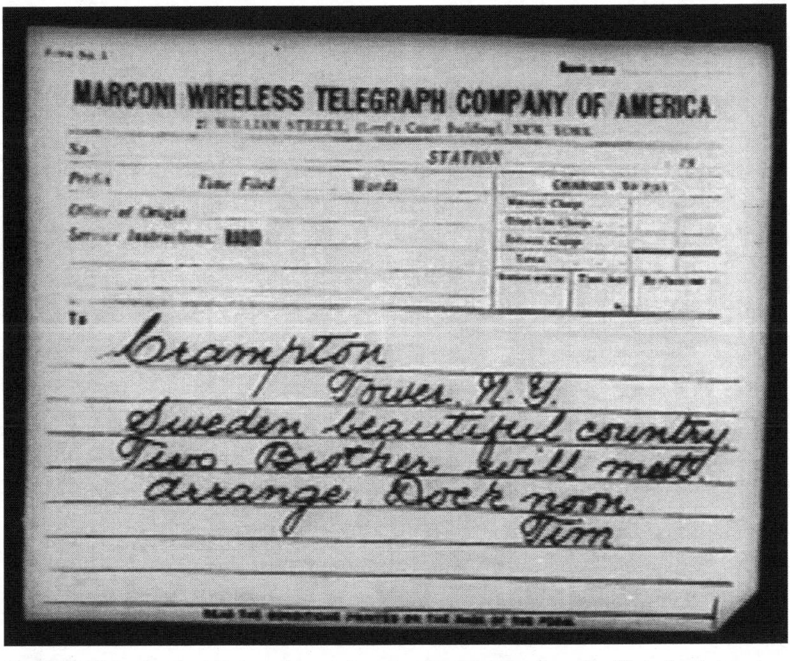

Figure 2. The encoded Marconigram. Frame enlargement from *Traffic in Souls* (1913).

without being seen herself. Once Mary informs her friend Officer Burke (Matt Moore) about Trubus's secret life, the police quickly break up the ring, and the public that once revered Trubus for his philanthropy nearly tears him to pieces outside the courthouse. Kristen Whissel calls Mary's intervention a clever use of electrical media to rehearse the melodramatic convention of the "reversal of fortune": the right to privacy may protect Trubus at first, but the very wires that connect him to his cronies can be turned against him.[24]

What has not been recognized in the many discussions of *Traffic in Souls* thus far is that the slavers' technological ingenuity references a privately accessible wireless culture that had just lost much of its democratic luster. The navy and the press took advantage of the *Titanic* disaster to call for immediate regulation, and the federal government responded by passing the Radio Act of 1912. The Act decreed that all amateur operators must be licensed, it established high fines for "malicious interference," and it outlawed amateur use of much of the spectrum by increasing the number of wavelengths dedicated to navy business (Douglas, 234). Now, Trubus is scarcely a small boy, and wireless makes only a cameo appearance at the harbor. But by "appropriat[ing], transform[ing], and thematiz[ing] the structural features and effects" of media in general (Whissel, 3), *Traffic in Souls* invites the much-discussed wireless to haunt the film in various forms. In the electric pen, a device that Edison had briefly marketed for stenography, Tucker appeals to the audience's curiosity about media that had not yet been weighed down by definite social functions; Trubus's headphones closely resemble those sets worn by little boys in upstairs bedrooms all over America, and the white slavers' misappropriations of Dictaphones, telephones, and the shipboard Marconi set mark them as amateurs who have graduated from overpowering navy signals to strong-arming delicate girls into lives of sin.

Considering the noisy press reaction to the amateurs after the *Titanic* incident, it seems odd that *Traffic in Souls* does not put a wireless set in Trubus's hands; no other medium could have better served its association of bad behavior with unvarnished technologies. It's certainly possible (if unlikely) that no one thought to fit a homemade wireless set into the mise-en-scène, but it is equally true that giving Trubus a wireless surveillance device would have made the plot's denouement impossible. Without the wires that lead from Trubus's office to the go-between's lair below it, Mary could not discover the face behind the disembodied ear. Thus the film accidentally, or rather by negation, associates wireless with the kind of mediated secrecy that the cinema's concern with public oversight can't even acknowledge. The dialectical message: no wires, no return to bourgeois normalcy! *Traffic in Souls* marks amateur wireless as the epitome of media decadence precisely by *not representing it*. It makes the phenomenon present by absenting it where it's most expected.

By doing so, the film implies another intermedia lesson, one that pits recording devices against media that leave no record of the information they communicate. Mary and Officer Burke gather enough evidence to put Trubus away by using a Dictaphone modified by Mary's father to "strengthen sound waves." The film does not specify how they have been "strengthened," but it does imply that *strengthening* is a euphemism for *inscribing* (considering that the lack of amplified microphones hindered the inscription of phonographic grooves until the 1920s). If nothing else, the device strengthens the law's ability to use media as evidence, for Trubus and his gang rely on the ephemeral quality of live transmission: his electrified mystic writing pad erases its accounts as quickly as they appear, he burns his written records, and of course his eavesdropping leaves no trace. Mary's phonographic cylinder alone exposes his guilt by capturing its impression, as the chief reminds us when he chastises the newly captured slavers one last time: "Your conversations are on these records in your own voices." But imagine if Trubus's profit records had reached him via radio, or if Mary had been forced to use a wireless to report Trubus's activities to the police. For all the progress and wonder it signifies, the wireless would have preserved neither fingerprints nor vocal patterns—only an abstract dot-and-dash code transcribed by the hand of an operator to whom all messages are anonymous. As if to emphasize the impotence of recording media when faced with the menacing new media that crackle around the edges of *Traffic in Souls,* the bored Marconi operator and unwitting accessory to sexual assault was apparently played by director George Loane Tucker himself.[25]

By portraying the recording device as the white slaves' salvation, the film alludes to the self-reflexive films of the previous twenty years, which regularly awarded film itself the prize for catching crooks and exposing them to public scorn. Like Mary with her father's Dictaphone, *Traffic in Souls* has figuratively recorded "evidence" of white slavery, giving the spectator the jump on even Officer Burke from the beginning. But Burke the listener also models a specific behavior for the viewer: attentiveness to the "secretly" recorded representation. Freed from the contingency of *live* media by the Dictaphone, he can listen carefully to these voices from the past and, with time on his side, plan an elaborate strategic attack on the bordello. Patriarchal science and the law come together to reinstate the hierarchy between technological masters and technological consumers that the bad patriarch, Trubus, brought crashing down with his "boy amateur" shenanigans. The fact that Mary realizes Trubus's deceit when she peers past the edge of a neatly framed window makes a modest but unmistakable case for the *Traffic in Souls*'s role in this (Figure 3). As Mary and Burke rely on recording media to monitor the behavior of the guilty, so *Traffic in Souls* allows the viewer to stand in judgment over those private citizens who conceal their true intentions behind masks of respectability. The angry crowd that swarms Trubus as he descends the courthouse steps is a proxy for the film's spectators: many and diverse, but united in their rage and identical in their reactions.

But *Traffic in Souls*'s fascination with insidious and beneficent media alike mucks up the unity of that subject position. To borrow Whissel's metaphor, Tucker does everything he can to direct the traffic of information passing before the viewer. Throughout the film he exploits and interweaves telephone conversations and Dictaphone surveillance to clarify

Figure 3. Mary discovers the Go-Between and one of the Cadets of the white slavery ring. Frame enlargement from *Traffic in Souls*.

the spatial and temporal relationships between one shot and the next: "When the film resolves its narrative crisis through a technology [the Dictaphone] that arrests dangerous mobility and converts fragmentation into unity and wholeness, it thematizes the cinema's own technical solution to the formal and structural problems associated with the multi-reel feature film" (Whissel, 17).

At the same time, Tucker misses few chances to ogle its strange technologies, reminding us that film still retained its place of prominence among modes of technological display. It visualizes the pure fantasy of Trubus's writing pad via pixilation, cuts back and forth between eavesdroppers and eavesdropees as frequently and rapidly as its editor dared, and even uses framing to instate a visual shorthand by which to distinguish *Traffic in Souls*'s beneficent, official media users from its evil, experimental ones. When Trubus and his gang communicate via their "amateur" media, they face (and inhabit) the right side of the frame across the cuts between their respective hideouts, while Mary and the chief of police face the opposite edge when operating benevolent media like the telephone and the "strengthened" Dictaphone.

Under these representational circumstances, where every medium is a potential attraction, it is not difficult to imagine the film's impossibly complex editing turning into an attraction by default, as if the film cannot bear to tell its engrossing story without hinting at the technical labor that went into turning film from an opaque technological display into a carefully polished window.

While most of the images of amateurs I've discussed keep affirmative, proto-professional operators distinct in class and ethnicity from the seamier amateur types, *Traffic in Souls* does no such thing. By making Trubus an upstanding citizen during daylight hours, Tucker's film acknowledges that the wireless promise of free communication might just attract someone more respectable than thugs, howling foreigners, or bad little boys. Trubus is an Other who looks, talks, and acts like the bourgeois Self that classical narrative courted as its ideal subject, a position to be either shared or identified with by the spectator: white, male, moneyed, respected, sexually and paternally successful, his home a Victorian castle fortified with tchotchkes and velvet sashes. Despite all its indications that the cinema was entering a period of formal and institutional stability, *Traffic in Souls* keeps the future of film as a medium open to possibilities beyond narrative suture. Film and wireless had each hit a similar historical crossroads by the mid-teens. Like the discourse of wireless, media fantasy films acknowledged that playing the amateur remained an attractive possibility for the cinema's own audiences.

This open-endedness did not get past the film industry, including the producer of *Traffic in Souls*. Whissel reports that on the eve of the film's release, Universal chief Carl Laemmle bemoaned the loss of the sociable and distracted cinema of the prior decade. When viewers could still wander in and out of nickelodeons at will, Laemmle thought, they were enjoying an entertainment that aligned with the fits and starts of urban culture in ways that long, complicated feature films like *Traffic in Souls* could not (Whissel, 22). If Trubus rehearses the scandal of a cultural authority who moonlights as an irresponsible media amateur, Laemmle, it seems, lived the scandal of the *film* authority who dreams of returning to a more interactive, more amateurish version of film viewing. Although Laemmle could not reanimate the interactivity fostered by early film reception, *Traffic in Souls* does offer the spectator the structural possibility of a more distracted, more intersubjective media experience.

Of course I don't mean that the medium of film could send or receive messages. But *Traffic in Souls* still gestures back to the preceding decade, when the cinema was still an interactive *media institution*. Few films this side of *The Lawnmower Man* fantasize so feverishly about other media as Tucker's does; it makes them such intriguing, dangerous attractions that they manage to compete with white slavery for the viewer's attention. In so doing, *Traffic in Souls* recasts the classical cinema's spectatorial position of media oversight as a perch from which to scrutinize what the slow roll to classicality is making of film, and what repercussions that novel identity will have for the future of the cinema's interactive past, the past that Laemmle mourned. As long as people sat together in the auditorium, classical cinema's noninteractive reception practices could always be reversed, just as Trubus's miniature network gets reversed back on him. *Traffic in Souls*'s media sensibility controls the potential chaos of its editing scheme as carefully as its editing disciplines the human traffic of New York City, as Whissel suggests; the film behaves like a kind of traffic cop, producing the spectator as "the trafficked individual . . . [who] see[s] what the imperiled protagonists fail to see—a position described by [Shelley] Stamp as one of recuperated surveillance, by Gunning as that of the detective, and by Lee Grieveson as omniscient" (20–21).[26] Yet for all the brilliance with which the editing of *Traffic in Souls* keeps the characters moving efficiently through New York City's seamier side, it is not difficult to imagine such tight control as a textual hedge against another sort of chaos: the threat of a readerly text becoming, through ambiguity or distraction, a writerly one.

If the logic of melodrama depends on last-minute reversals of fortune, *Traffic in Souls* shapes communications technologies into vehicles for those reversals by their own potential "reversibility" of the information pipeline, as Whissel convincingly argues: "the same technologies that initiate a dangerous mobilization of bodies and technologies . . . [could] return detoured bodies to their proper place" and fix, at last, the ambiguous identities of people like Trubus, whom the media have allowed to operate anonymously (Whissel, 15). Perhaps this is the most significant "anti-message" offered by this wireless-less wireless fantasy: a medium without wires would offer an opportunity for yet another reversal beyond the affirmative reversal that Mary achieves when she finds the telltale wire—auguring a wireless imperialism characterized by infinite rebounding. With no wires showing to allow "us" to snoop "them" out, or vice versa, the final word over access or interpretation would belong to no one. Foreign/savage and civilized, unlicensed amateur and official operator would all operate on the same playing field of the ether. If wireless was to become an institution—and indeed, if the cinema was to be safe from the intervention of its *own* amateurs—free-thinking media users would have to go the way of the distracted film viewer.

Building on this discussion of the emergence of wireless and the silent films that tracked its fantasy life, the next chapter works toward an intermedia theory of how early sound films positioned their spectators. As Donald Crafton has shown, Hollywood and the companies that engineered synchronized sound exploited radio fantasies to promote talking pictures as a new medium: "Playing up the talkies as radio capitalized on its aura of mystification, scientific complexity, and cutting-edge technology. . . . The intention was probably not to trick people into thinking that they were watching radio-plus-pictures [i.e., television], but to tap into the audience's awareness of radio's program format."[27] But the more film invited the radio imagination into the theater, the more it undermined its own format. To help it contain the threat to classical reception inherent in the act of grafting a medium with interactive connotations onto its own, Hollywood called upon a mass-cultural form that attracted even more controversy than had the little boys of wireless: jazz and its African American heritage. By *picturing* one of broadcasting's most notorious acousmêtres, the black jazz musician, Hollywood cinema presented sound film as a kind of inoculation—for the spectator and for its own institutional conventions—

against the intercultural transactions anticipated by broadcast radio fantasies. Indeed, the discursive position left open by the extinction of the bad-boy wireless amateur was taken by the fantasy of dangerous black music. Contrary to classical impulses, however, the radio fantasy films I will discuss skate dangerously close to imagining a "live" cinema—a radio-inflected experience of film in which public exhibition acts as a visible and present equivalent to radio's imaginary, fragmented public, and in which black voices press the limits of representation.

Eating the Other Medium:
Sound Film in the Age
of Broadcasting

> I'll be glad when you're dead, you rascal you
> I'll be glad when you're dead, you rascal you
> I brought you into my home
> You wouldn't leave my wife alone
> I'll be glad when you're dead, you rascal you.
> —*Louis Armstrong, in* A Rhapsody in Black
> and Blue *(1932)*

By 1918, continuous-wave transmission entered the serious testing phase, and it was clear that the spark-burst wireless set would soon give way to radiotelephony—the transmission and reception of articulate sounds. Sound radio had been under development at least since Marconi's first public demonstration of wireless telegraphy in 1899. But the utopianism surrounding the amateur movement had subsided, due in no small part to news reports and published "expert" opinions. As early as the sinking of the *Titanic*, the press "unanimously denounced the amateurs . . . for interfering with 'legitimate' message handling"[1] and argued that the ether needed to be "freed" *from* individual users so that free enterprise might determine its future usefulness. The federal Radio Act of 1912 wrote that attitude into law by forbidding amateurs from transmitting unless they obtained licenses and deferred to commercial and military radio traffic. Amateurs survived the turning tide for a while by lobbying Congress through the American Radio Relay League (established in 1914) and by shifting their emphasis from signaling prowess to "DX'ing" contests, in which they competed to collect coherent signals from the longest distance away. They also began to broadcast speech and music as soon as they obtained the necessary equipment and garnered such appreciation from listeners that AT&T and RCA took notice of the practice. Ironically, the switch from telegraphy to broadcasting became the bludgeon that the growing radio industry used to beat amateur culture to within an inch of its life.

Yet the image of amateurs as bricoleurs with loud voices was so firmly fixed in the collective imagination that the wireless outlaw loitered in mass culture for decades following their extinction. The hero of Ralph Milne Farley's science fiction novel *The Radio Beasts,* serialized in *Argosy All-Story Weekly* in 1925, resembles an older, buffer version of Tom Swift, bricoleur-hero of boy's fiction a decade earlier. Myles Cabot, whose very name broadcasts his penchant for DX'ing, picks up radio waves from outer space and uses his own experimental transmitter to beam himself, bodily, to the planet Venus. As the manly, oft-naked Myles battles a race of gigantic ants called Formians (from *le formi,* the French for, well, "ant") to save the planet's humanoid race, it becomes clear that he is a man out of time, living a wireless future that never happened. Cabot's souped-up radio transmitter and his artificial antennae mark him as a muscular amateur who has grown up to resemble less an engineer or inventor than a Formian, right down to his French surname. Had he attempted to broach the broadcasting boom of the mid-1920s, he would have seemed as alien to that radio culture as an eight-foot ant.[2]

Of course, Cabot's alien status does not prevent him from bearing the standard for the romanticism of amateurism, any more than his fascistic individualism and the equally fascistic physical culture fantasy he embodies undermine his iconic status as a radio *speaker.* But it does suggest the degree to which the dreams of radio self-expression went underground with the rise of broadcasting. Cloaking these dreams so thoroughly in fantasy allowed the utopian dream to linger in a more or less affirmative, if impotent, form. But the longer media fantasies persist, the greater the likelihood that they will acquire new relevance, particularly when other media, old or new, mobilize them for the purpose of constructing their own identities.

This chapter is a story about how two not-so-new media, wireless and film, were transformed by technological and institutional changes into novel media once again and how the practitioners of each medium siphoned off practices—and fantasies—from the other. Their efforts to formulate standard modes of address for sound radio and sound cinema necessitated these friendly acts of theft, but in Hollywood's case, as I will demonstrate, inviting the broadcasting imagination to set some parameters for cinematic spectatorship meant opening the gates to the "barbarian" that classical cinema was supposed to bar from the theater for good.

Amateurs and Other Radio Beasts

As the burgeoning radio industry cultivated the legal and economic means to develop broadcasting into a marketable commodity, it helped to reshape the utopia of universal communication into a less interactive fantasy. The revised dream fit the broadcasters' needs perfectly: only a few authoritative sources would transmit signals, uniting the public in what it collectively heard and learned from the transmissions. In this, it resembled the "universal language" myth of early narrative cinema, in that both fantasies embraced cultural imperialism rather than self-expression and debate as the telos of media progress. In 1923, *Literary Digest* reported that Westinghouse had introduced a shortwave system that "makes it possible for a speech or concert delivered at a central point to be received clearly by radio listeners with even the cheapest instruments in the area which is at present bounded by the Panama Canal Zone, Bermuda, the North Pole, and the Hawaiian Islands." The President of the United States—more than simply a convenient example—could now speak from Washington to "an audience estimated up to 200,000,000. In time, it is predicted, he will be able to speak in this way to the entire world. . . . With such a marvelous device to serve it, civilization ought to progress as never before, with the world made more interesting as well as wiser."[3] Broadcasting—a word that once meant the scattering of seeds—promised to pollinate the nation, and eventually the world, with middle-class American values and mores, "achieving," as one commentator wrote in 1924, "the task of making us feel together, think together, live together."[4]

It was easy to postulate that broadcasting would refine and assimilate a nation of diverse class, ethnic, and regional identities by means of a centrally determined cultural message, but disciplining the audience to receive that message in a uniform way was another matter altogether. The audiences of the cinema of attractions were difficult to discipline because they gathered in public for an event that promised maximum pleasure without requiring the spectator to concentrate on the screen. Classical cinema persuaded its viewers to face forward through multiple disciplinary means: telling long and involved stories, rewarding attention to small details (and enforcing that attention via close-ups and other visual means), the "high culture" pretensions of picture palace design, rules of behavior enforced by uniformed ushers, the darkness of the auditorium space, and habitual exposure to identical conditions on each visit. By contrast, radio audiences were difficult to discipline in part because they were neither gathered together specifically *as listeners* who knew and adhered to institutional rules, nor were they isolated from nontextual factors or even other people. They listened to broadcast programs of music, news, drama, and comedy in the private sphere, where they were subject to distractions of a more domestic sort—doorbells to answer, children to care for, cleaning and entertaining to do, and so forth—that could not always be set aside for the sake of the radio program.

A comic strip published in the 1925 issue of *Wireless Age,* reprinted from an unspecified issue of the *New York World,* illuminates the worrisome variables that home listening inserted into the equation of consuming the radio. Entitled "The Refining Influence of Radio," it tracks a husband's evolution from cad to gentleman as he listens to "Aunt Kutie" telling her "kiddie" listeners the story of "the three darling little daisies that lived in the green, green meadow" (Figure 4). The story "refines" him both physically and behaviorally; six panels after slapping his wife and telling her to shut up, his five o'clock shadow, cigar, and sizable girth have all disappeared, leaving a dapper fellow who raves to his wife about the "precious" daisies from the story. Unfortunately, the program works a little too well. The final panel reveals not simply a gentleman, but a mincing fop. With one hand on hip and the other delicately raised, he tells his wife (who looks even more horrified here than she does in the first panel) that the fairy tale made him "so very, very excited I almost screamed!" The joke here is not on the radio per se or even on the kiddie program but on the contingencies of private listening practices. While the film industry promoted individual films to specific audiences who physically entered a specific movie theater to confirm their choice, broadcasting stations had no control over who would happen to switch on a program designed for a given demographic. Silly as the cartoon may be, it ties unexpected listening experiences to the unmanning of the man of the house. By penetrating the home so insidiously, Aunt Kutie has relieved him of his authority to control the information flow between public and private spheres without his even realizing it.

The burden was on the radio industry to use broadcasting content to manage the effects of such chance occurrences through broadcasting content. Unsurprisingly, RCA used the Hollywood cinema—the most commercially

The Refining Influence of Radio

By H. T. Webster

Figure 4. Cartoon by H. T. Webster, *Wireless Age* 11, no. 12 (September 1924): 68.

successful mass-media institution in America by the end of the teens—as a template for shaping the parameters of radio experience. David Sarnoff, the former Marconi operator who was now commercial manager for RCA, proposed in 1920 that Marconi's periodical *Wireless Age* stop printing mechanical plans and other specialized information pitched specifically to amateurs and address instead the growing market of casual radio listeners. Up to this point, *Wireless Age* had been "Devoted to the Highest Form of Electrical Experimenting," as its masthead slogan proclaimed. But Sarnoff proposed that it should "perform the same mission as is now being performed by the various motion picture magazines," listing programming schedules for stations nationwide and reporting on radio personalities, trends in popular programming, and listening habits (Barnouw, 79).

Sarnoff's reorganization plan for *Wireless Age* was realized in May 1922, and the magazine's slogan abruptly changed to "America's Foremost Radiophone Review." Instead of photographs of radio innovators, amateurs, and distinguished Naval operators, its covers now sported Norman Rockwell-esque paintings of families, dreamy-eyed women, and dancing couples "listening in" attentively from domestic settings. The new magazines *Radio World* and *Radio Broadcast* (both launched in 1922) held to the paradigm of amateur culture by addressing their target female audience both as consumers and as experts at determining how to choose and tune their own receivers. But by 1923 the *Wireless Age* formula dominated the radio periodical market. Even amateur wireless guru Hugo Gernsback "feminized" his own magazine, *Radio News,* in similar fashion, replacing ads for variable capacitors and tools with pitches for radio sets encased in chestnut cabinets.[5] *Wireless Age* sold radio not merely as a medium but as a lifestyle choice for an upwardly mobile middle class. The Marconi-era reports and poems lauding the medium's interactive qualities had given way in its pages to an eminently *cinematic* vision of interaction, in which famous people "visited" the radio-age parlor not to be spoken to but to be heard and worshiped like movie stars. And each issue now opened with photographs of Hollywood stars and other celebrities posing with radios or microphones. Dorothy Gish (February 1923) and Norma Shearer (July 1924) used stock platitudes to praise radio for bringing the world closer together. An article titled "Why I Became a Radio Fan" (February 1924) answers its own question in a way that echoes the earliest of the wireless fantasies: radio means "a bigger world!" But the article's mobilization of the term "fan" points up how much *Wireless Age*'s construction of radio depended on the adulation from afar that the Hollywood star system, an institution with enormous press presence by the mid-twenties, inculcated in its spectators.[6]

Broadcasting itself emulated classical cinema's appeal to undivided attention by constructing a theatrical discourse of intimacy, and implementing it in an eminently cinematic way, by constructing stars and cultivating fan culture. When the first announcers addressed their audiences, listeners felt that they and they alone had been addressed. The most popular announcers were suddenly swamped with embarrassingly personal letters—perhaps the inevitable outcome of packaging radio broadcasting in the discourse of fan culture (Barnouw, 164). To radio producers and performers, this invisible public increasingly resembled an organized *audience,* but not a theatrical one as the liveness of radio might suggest. For radio performers, like film actors, played to the individual:

> In 1922 performers still imagined themselves in a vast auditorium "where rear seats are hundreds of miles from the stage," but by 1925 a cozier image was established. Many artists liked to imagine the audience as a "single person." Letters encouraged this; no other medium had ever afforded an audience this illusion of intimacy shielded by privacy. (Barnouw, 164)

But the discourse surrounding radio liveness could not muzzle the contingency that liveness implied. Indeed, liveness posed a set of problems that were only exacerbated by broadcasting's relative powerlessness over the conditions of reception. What if someone said or did something completely unexpected in front of a microphone? What if an anarchist or an African American expressed a controversial opinion to thousands or millions of listeners? Not even the most tightly controlled radio play, variety show, or musical performance could eliminate the unexpected intervention of material inappropriate for home listening—that is, material that undermined the fantasy that Americans were a unified and united audience, or that they ever could be united simply by listening to continuous streams of "real" American culture and values.

As I have discussed, radio fantasy films contrasted two of film's technological qualities with the qualities of wireless: they celebrated the power of *recording* to restore social order and emphasized the power of the *image* to unite spectators in voyeuristic judgment. But radio fantasy films were not alone in presenting the invisibility of electrical media as a serious liability; radio fantasy in general also defined visibility as a quality that the new medium lacked. Now, to say that any medium "lacks" some quality or another smacks of the Bazinian ideology of cinematic evolution, in which film develops new appendages (sound, color, and so on) on its inevitable path toward representational transparency. Such theorists of radio drama as Bertolt Brecht, Walter Benjamin, and Rudolf Arnheim took a much different tack. Like the silent film theorists Hugo Münsterberg, Vachel Lindsay, and Arnheim himself, who argued that "silence" forced film-makers to develop an intricate aesthetics of images in time, radio theo-rists characterized the medium's detachment from the visual world as an opportunity to invite listeners to participate in, or even to resist, the meanings produced by the radio play.[7] However, when anxieties arose about the potentially negative effects of broadcast programming on the Americanization project undertaken by radio, expert opinion repeatedly pointed to the facelessness of radio as a general seat of blame. Over the radio, Arnheim argues, whatever noise one is hearing at a particular in-stant is the most important thing—indeed the only thing—that exists in that constructed world: "In a broadcast dialogue, only the person who is speaking exists acoustically." Unlike film with its power to frame and edit images in multiple ways, radio cannot single out people unless they speak, nor can it induce listeners to attend to mute objects or other elements of setting. Thus, the radiophonic subject effectively owns the listener's atten-tion for as long as she or he is speaking.[8]

Arnheim articulates in media-specific terms the power that radio fan-tasy in general attributed to the acousmêtric voice. In the wireless era, Morse code rendered all signalers anonymous, allowing pranksters to impersonate Navy officials and young women to enter the ether without fear of reproach (133). But audio transmission made subversive voices even more threatening, because they could manipulate vocal inflections and discursive framing to create even more convincing masquerades. Groups normally granted little authority to speak to a national public, such as African Americans and women, might sneak into the airwaves and spring themselves on the unsuspecting, breaking the imaginary barrier between public and private life and crossing the lines of sexual and/or interracial taboo in the process.

When blacks spoke or played musical instruments on the radio, for example, the possibility that they might not speak at all or even mimic white minstrels' vocal caricature of black slaves' English (in an audio twist on what Arthur Knight calls the "black blackface" in a few Hollywood films) "had the potential to increase the confusion of racial categories to intolerable levels."[9] Knight reprints a 1936 cartoon from the Chicago *Defender* satirizing a white "race-hater" who listens appreciatively to a classical pianist only to become enraged when the announcer reveals that he has been enjoying "George Johnson, the inimitable *Negro* pianist." The race-hater's rage over the invisibility of black speaking and performing subjects, however, is only symptomatic of a deeper struggle over who gets to decide what those sounds *signify*, the listener or the speaker; lacking an image of the pianist to trigger the race-hater's prejudice, the performance tricks him out of using that prejudice to "evaluate" the pianist's skill.

With its impartial distribution of authority to any and every voice, "radio's ability to escape visual overdetermination had the potential to set off a virtual riot of social signifiers" (Hilmes, 20). Hilmes suggests that blacks and women on the radio proved so irritating to radio experts and social critics because they escaped the objectifying male gaze that visual mass culture had constructed to contain them. I would add that these complaints had as much to do with the speakers' self-representation as they did with visualization and that these two categories were practically interchangeable in radio fantasy. When the station manager at station WJZ complained in 1926 that women's voices have "*too much personality.* A voice that is *highly individual and full of character* is aggravating to the audience that cannot see the face and expression," he implied that seeing the female body behind the voice would mitigate the anxiety of a (male) listener who objected to the structural authority that radio granted her. Labeling her attractive or unattractive, like labeling a voice or instrumentalist black or white, would allow the listener to call up prejudices associated with those labels and thereby "evaluate" the message while maintaining his sense of superiority to a voice that carried much farther than his own.[10]

The fantasy that unites these racialized and gendered complaints is the fear that subaltern voices could use radio to grab the nation by the ear and thus sabotage radio's solemn project of homogenizing culture. Presiding over this fear was the specter of race music, particularly "hot" music or hot jazz, which radio had granted a shot at invading the white private sphere. Even *without* radio waves to carry it, the "monster" of African American jazz, as white critic Henry O. Osgood called it, floated through the American atmosphere like a virus that instantly "corrupt[ed] . . . untrained minds."[11] This "swarming, foreign invader" would be the weapon of choice in an anti-American coup that was as political as it was cultural: "jazz was seen as a harbinger of literal revolution. This meaning made sense given jazz's association with social unrest embodied by race riots and ethnic immigrant labor activism."[12] In an infamous article from 1921, Anne Shaw Faulkner spins jazz as a threat to capitalism itself: jazz is "that expression of protest against law and order, that bolshevik element of license striving for expression in music" (quoted in Evans, 102).

But if jazz *tout court* was a threat to Anglo hegemony, *radio* jazz was simply an unstoppable force. Even the most utopian rhetoric about broadcasting portrayed radio programs as invaders that penetrated "doors and windows, no matter how tightly barred."[13] Radio simply expanded the range of the jazz plague infinitely in all directions. In 1924, an essay by Bruce Bliven invents a hypothetical young girl, "little Elizabeth," who "gets control of the instrument [of radio,] . . . moves the dials until (it is usually not a difficult task) she finds a station where a jazz orchestra is playing," and finally "sinks back to listen" with cheeks reddened by a "precocious flush." Bliven's jazz ravishes the most stereotypically vulnerable inmate of the private sphere, right under the patriarch's nose. Even worse, the power of choice granted her by the simple radio dial seems to relieve her of both her shame and her will to resist the sensuous power of jazz (Hilmes, 15–16).

This nightmare of unsupervised reception resembles the castration disaster of the *Wireless Age* cartoon, except that Elizabeth is portrayed as a willful consumer who knows what she wants and knows how to get it. It's no wonder the cultural pundits began to worry: the user-friendliness of radio and other musical media threatened their authority to shape the listening habits of the nation. The "talking machines" and "mechanical music" of the turn of the century, from player pianos to radios, democratized musical experience but at the risk of "increasing access to rubbish"—that is, nonclassical music—"and inattentiveness to everything."[14] "We are in danger of becoming a nation of piano-pumpers, radio-rounders and grafonola-grinders," Peter Dykeman wrote in 1922. "Those mechanical instruments, *if unwisely used,* are dangerous to the musical life of America" (Hilmes, 49; emphasis added). In this respect especially, radio was "more threatening than the movies in its potential for detrimental influence on impressionable members of the public. . . . [Its] invisible, omnidirectional, and pervasive messages . . . challenged the listener to recreate an imaginary mental picture from the aural stimulations transmitted. Consequently, radio programming did not simply deliver the public sphere into the private realm"—it also encouraged listeners' imaginations to wander in ways that the literalness of cinema's visual register did not. "The interplay between these two processes made radio a powerful force for the possible disruption or reaffirmation of the . . . imaginaries cultivated by mainstream religious, political, and social institutions."[15]

If in *Traffic in Souls* the reversibility of electrical media saves the day, these fabulists worry that reversibility is not an inevitable means to a happy end but rather an infinite feedback loop that not even the centralization of transmission could block. The jazz invasion of domestic space—and the construction of that space as escaping the kind of scrutiny necessary to teach the Elizabeths of America that such music was beneath their contempt and act accordingly—was infused with a specifically foreign connotation. Israel Zangwill, author of the play *The Melting Pot* (1909), called Americans' irresistible attraction to ragtime music a species of "musical miscegenation" that flouted the "scrupulous" and "justifi[ed]" ban on black-white intermarriage (Moore, 157). In the two decades that followed, racialist music critics and composers made hot music quite literally their bête noire. They portrayed it as uncivilized because it undercut the Viennese classical music tradition in fundamental ways that threw the body of the listener into a partly savage, partly mechanical frenzy: it leaned so heavily on syncopation that it distracted the listener from traditional metrical stress, and it encouraged and even rewarded improvisation and independence on the part of individual musicians, against the hierarchy that placed the highest value on the integrity of written score and orchestral conductor.

Once it had broken cardinal rules of rhythm and authority, hot music rendered both its players and its listeners monstrous, caught somewhere between human and ape or, rather, between American citizen and "African" savage. Shaw Faulkner connects jazz to forces from an African prehistory more primal than U.S. slave culture's "bizarre dances and cakewalks," which she calls the "natural expression of American Negroes": "jazz originally was the accompaniment of the voodoo dancer, stimulating the half-crazed barbarian to the vilest deeds" (Hilmes, 47). The idea that hot music was all "monkey talk, jungle squeals, grunts and squeaks and gasps suggestive of cave love," in Henry Ford's equally infamous words, meant to racialists that its musicians and fans alike were "as bad as the voodoo worshipers of darkest Africa," as Peter Dykeman put it in 1922.[16] A 1925 poem entitled "The Jazz Cannibal" satirizes this line of reasoning without diverging from its moralizing point:

> My Phillida, before the jazz
>> Began its devastating boom,
> My thoughts of you were as gentle as
>> The tunes that whirled us round the room;

> To perfect harmony with grace
>> We moved, delighted and content
> To smile into each other's face
>> With meanings kind and innocent.
>
> Alack! my Phillida, to-day
>> The music does not sooth[e] my mind;
> In truth I am compelled to say
>> My dreams are horrid and unkind;
>
> For, while the bawling niggers biff
>> The drums that agitate our feet,
> I'm gravely speculating if
>> You're really nice enough to eat.[17]

According to the poem's logic, the moment that jazz enters the ears of even the most cultured Anglos (note the exaggeratedly correct diction), it devolves them into cannibals who crave physical pleasures and blurt out forbidden desires. And these desires might lead white listeners to cross *physically* the strict boundaries of difference that jazz, particularly when carried by the radio, had violated *aurally.* The problem with jazz on the radio wasn't merely that broadcasting slipped it through the chinks in the armor of white domesticity but that no experts were on hand to train listeners to ward off the "demoralizing influence of the persistent use of syncopation, combined with inharmonic partial tones," which Shaw Faulkner claimed would render the listener "incapable of distinguishing between good and evil, right and wrong" (Hilmes, 47–48). If white audiences enjoyed hearing jazz, all the better reason to wipe it from the ether: "If education is to be the aim of radio broadcasting," Jerome Kerwin wrote in *The Control of Radio* (1934), "it is absurd to talk at the same time . . . of giving the public what it wants. . . . Education must come from above at all times" (quoted in Smulyan, 135).

When the white public itself became carriers of the jazz plague, however, radio blurred the boundaries of distance even more distressingly. Anglo and Jewish composers, arrangers, and conductors who experimented with the form usually "sweetened" it with classical style and regularity. Their results were accompanied by the cheers of critics who argued that hot music, if properly scrubbed and primped for the orchestra hall, gave the Western tradition access to primal energies that would relieve the enervations of modernity. Paul Whiteman, the bandleader whose premier performance of George Gershwin's *Rhapsody in Blue* at New York's

Aeolian in 1924 made him a star, garnered praise for making "an honest woman of jazz," as an announcer in the Whiteman revue film *The King of Jazz* (John Murray Anderson, 1929) puts it. Even the nativist music critics lauded Whiteman's achievement, claiming that he had "refined" the "jarring polyphonies" of jazz and "taught it the manners of Vienna."[18]

But white jazz musicians also seemed to put themselves in harm's way by attempting to tame a beast that might transform *them* more completely than they transformed *it*. Bing Crosby, Rudy Vallée, and other young male "crooners" of the 1920s struggled against virulent complaints that crooning feminized them, while at the same time stirring up erotic urges in their female listeners, turning domestic space into a "romantic, sexualized space." The intimate style of crooning, as Alison McCracken shows, was itself a product of radio. The new electrical microphones, engineered to improve recording and broadcasting fidelity, amplified the voice so that singers no longer needed to project their voices to be heard. This technological-historical accident made crooners as dangerous to radio fabulists of the late twenties and early thirties as any black jazz "primitive."[19] The crooner's excess of intimacy led to excessive engagement with the listener's body, an act of war that pierced the private sphere with the force and stealth of broadcast black jazz. Indeed, the invisibility of his skin color tinged the sexual indiscretion of the crooner's voice with shades of black.

The ambiguous figure of the white male jazz musician—a subversive cultural producer masked by a normative, authoritative identity—ushered the specter of the "boy" wireless amateur into the broadcasting era. For critics, jazz musicians who drifted into the waiting ears of women behind their husbands' or fathers' backs reanimated the amateur's double threat: the misappropriation of a culturally affirmative technology to subvert authority—in this case, patriarchal authority as it inhered in the private sphere—and the ability to exchange one identity for another, which white musicians did by performing the music of "savages" without even the benefit of a blackface image to racialize the sound as redundantly as possible. In the critics' worst-case scenarios, white jazz musicians acted as mere hosts for the virus of jazz, which vitiated their whiteness and allowed secondhand black voices to "spread" through the airwaves. It seems only appropriate, therefore, that "hot" music (from either race records or the first disks cut by the white Original Dixieland Jass Band) and "sweet" orchestral jazz first hit the airwaves thanks to amateurs, who began playing jazz recordings on their makeshift stations around 1920–21 but were soon stopped despite the popularity of their selections. The Commerce Department banished phonograph records from the ether when commercial broadcasters protested, arguing that records defeated the purpose of "live" radio and further claiming (contrary to fact) that the public was tired of jazz.[20]

A radio scene in *The Big Broadcast* (Frank Tuttle, 1932) packs all of these fears—black jazz sneaking through the ether, the effeminacy of the crooner, and the dangers of unsupervised listening—into a single scene. After Bing Crosby loses his job singing on a show sponsored by the Griptight Girdle Company, the comically depressed crooner invites his new acquaintance, the effeminate Leslie McWhinney (Stuart Erwin), to his apartment. Unlucky in both work and love, Bing lights candles and contemplates suicide when suddenly the radio switches on by itself and lets loose with the Louis Armstrong standard "I'll Be Glad When You're Dead, You Rascal You." Within a few seconds of this admonition, Crosby and Leslie turn on the gas stove and wait to die, but they interrupt their own attempt when they light a match to share a final cigarette and accidentally blow up Bing's kitchen. Already susceptible to suggestion thanks to Bing's contagious case of the blues, the twosome follows the song's instructions so faithfully that they seem to have wandered off the set of *The Manchurian Candidate.* The extent of their transformation by the voice of jazz, however, does not become clear until the next morning, when the mincing millionaire "Leslie" awakens in bed with Bing and asks, "Are we married?"

However comically, these scenes replicate the logic of the crooner fantasies that dogged Crosby's radio persona: the radio beast of jazz has sapped their will to live and even their will to patriarchal, heterosexual self-control. Those who *watched* the film, by contrast, could consume African American jazz in the very visible form of the Mills Brothers, who sing a technically proficient and unimprovised number—"Hold That Tiger"—from the confines of a radio studio, framed a second time by the film screen and a third time by the theater that allowed spectators to enjoy African American voices without inviting them into their parlors. And even if one did have the urge to end it all during the movie, the picture palace contained too many witnesses who might put a stop to it, and provided no oven in which to stick one's head.

All in Fun, until Someone Loses an Eye

Sound film took to defusing the threat of jazz as quickly as it took to *playing* jazz. When film began to make noises of its own, some of the first tunes it eked out were jazz numbers, or at least, they purported to be. The first feature film with synchronized dialogue sequences was called, after all, *The Jazz Singer*.[21] Krin Gabbard has criticized Michael Rogin for claiming that there is no authentic jazz in *The Jazz Singer* by recalling the historical meaning of the term "jazz." Gabbard argues that "jazz" was, in fact, a wide-open term, and Nicholas M. Evans concurs by showing that the term "could indiscriminately denote virtually any commercial popular music" in the 1920s. To a certain degree, musicians themselves considered the term derogatory or simply the wrong label for the musical genres they performed. Richard M. Sudhalter argues that "serious professionals" referred to the heavily syncopated and improvised music most often played by African American combos as "hot music" or "playing hot," reserving the term "jazz" for the "sweet," toned-down popular music most often heard in white dancehalls and ballrooms.[22] If this is the case, Jolson's role is precisely that of a "jazz" singer, a minstrel who adds to the already sizeable catalog of white revisions to black music. As a jazz singer who also performs in blackface, he also draws a direct line backward from sweet jazz to minstrelsy and contributes to the construction of a false American memory founded by minstrelsy's masquerade: a nostalgic vision of a carefree slave culture that never existed.

But Rogin's argument about *how* the Jolson film expropriates the "black" voice reveals much about the intermedia significance of sound cinema's jazz discourse. For Rogin, Jolson's minstrel persona limits the self-actualized black voice by appropriating that voice through caricature and sentimentalism. In effect, Jack's climactic, blackface rendition of "My Mammy" at the Winter Garden acknowledges African American suffering past and present only to claim that same suffering as nothing more than a signifier for his *own* suffering as an immigrant's son, torn between family tradition and the new "religion" of show business.[23]

At the same time, Jolson's minstrel numbers perform a prophylactic *media* function for white viewers who share their homes with a swarm of diverse and potentially hazardous radio voices. Phonograph recordings of "coon" songs had raised the alarming question "What happens to the 'love & theft' of blackface when there is no face?" for the nineteenth century, and radio had expanded the range of that faceless voice to supernatural proportions (Gitelman, 124). *The Jazz Singer,* however, reattaches to coon songs the soothing face of black impersonation. In the act of stereotyping race at the level of the image, *The Jazz Singer* reduces the authoritative power of the otherwise disembodied "black" voice of hot music and vitiates the residual barbarism of even the sweetest orchestral jazz.

I propose that this understanding of *The Jazz Singer* was available to contemporary spectator-auditors in order to suggest, in turn, that spectators perceived early sound films like *The Jazz Singer* as supplementing broadcast radio and even aiding it. By appending images to broadcasting's slippery and all-too-autonomous "alien" voices, sound film provided a means by which those voices could be objectified and their threat tempered. Such a supplementary function fit well among the multiple ways in which the film industry (and its partners in developing sync sound) pitched film and radio as technological complements to one another. Advertising for the competing processes—Warners' Vitaphone, Fox's Movietone, RCA's Photophone and RKO Productions (founded in 1928, RCA's upstart studio took the "new trade name, Radio Pictures, and a corporate logo with suggestive flying bolts of electricity" in early 1929)[24]—encouraged the public to consume sync sound films in terms of the technologies of recording and amplification that made telephony, phonography, and radio possible: "While today it is difficult to see any similarity between radio and movies, evidently in the late 1920s the dividing line was not so sharp."[25]

Indeed, by 1920 radio seemed the most obvious means by which to synchronize sound to image and distribute that sound to theaters. In 1922, the tiny Rothacker film company of Chicago demonstrated a radio-film sound system, which the movie-conscious *Wireless Age* dutifully reported:

> A device has been perfected whereby any number of motion picture theatre projection machines can be operated in synchronization with a master projection machine at the radiophone broadcasting station. . . . At the broadcasting station the movie actors re-enact the drama, speaking out their lines . . . but watch the film very closely . . . to synchronize the spoken words with the pictures.[26]

Although this process proved impractical for obvious reasons, Hollywood was eager to surround its own sync sound experiments with the *aura* of radio.[27] To do so allowed the studios to siphon off some of radio's "mindshare" in "the electrifying spirit of the twenties"; although its connection to the technological capabilities of radio was merely figurative, its promoters promised that sound film was like the Rothacker sound-on-radio system in that it would "bring performer and auditor together in the space of the virtual performance" (Crafton, 10, 63).

In effect, the film industry founded a new and thrilling identity for its thirty-year-old medium on the discourses of electrical sound recording, amplification, and transmission. In spite of the contemporary label of "talking pictures," however, early reviewers observed that the pictures played second fiddle to the talking. It was practically a truism among producers and critics that the majority of sound films merely illustrated performances that were more or less autonomous as audio performances. The short subjects that premiered along with *Don Juan* (Alan Crosland, 1926) and *The First Auto* (Roy Del Ruth, 1926), the first two features using Warners' Vitaphone sound-on-disk system, were soon marketed to exhibitors as "a commercial library of recorded performances—phonograph records with visual accompaniment—that could be rented in various combinations and replayed on an ongoing basis."[28] *Exhibitors Herald* described *The Jazz Singer* as "scarcely a motion picture," but rather "an enlarged Vitaphone record of Al Jolson in half a dozen songs" (Crafton, 110).

One reason for these conceptions seems to be that sound film, particularly the shorts programs and part-talkies like *The Jazz Singer*, borrowed forms and formats from the recording and radio industries. Unlike the soundtracks for *Don Juan* and *The First Auto*, which mimicked live accompaniment practice by employing semi-synced music and sound effects for purposes of narration, the Vitaphone shorts employed direct address to the camera and a variety format familiar from vaudeville, live prologues to movies, record-playing parties at home, and radio broadcasts. For an industry that had long worked to perfect the supple, readerly flow of classical narration, such self-conscious hybridization of film with other media offered the notoriously fickle film audience a paradigm within which to understand and take pleasure in their favorite actors' newfound ability to speak and sing.[29] As indicated by the *Exhibitors Herald* review, however, the same gesture toward other media muddied the viewer's ability to think of a part-talkie like *The Jazz Singer* as a "motion picture" any longer. The definition of film was under siege from within its own ranks. Indeed, the variety format of these programs follows the evolving format of radio variety so closely that it seems to have shaped not only Warners' choice of entertainers and genres but also its mode of combining their performances into *texts*. The most obvious example of this is the fact that Warners reconstructed a famous broadcast revue for the first Vitaphone program (see Altman, 119–20). But the similarities run even deeper. At least as early as the *Fleischmann's Yeast Hour* (1929), hosted by crooner Rudy Vallée, programs were constructed to acknowledge the distracted behaviors of their home listeners and to use that distraction to the advantage of their sponsors by constructing entertainment programs of various genres—whether dramatic, musical, comedic, whatever—around commercial breaks. As Michele Hilmes argues, even the radio drama format that Hollywood co-created, exemplified by *The Lux Radio Theatre* (1934), constantly interrupted its stories with advertisements and self-reflexive gestures that were anathema to classical film narration. But the radio drama made the most of listeners' unfocused attention by strategically weaving the "frames" of plot, Hollywood glamour, and product—Lux soap—together to foreground the metatext of "golden age" radio: listener awareness of the sponsor's product (Hilmes, *Hollywood and Broadcasting*, 90–91, 97–100).

The Vitaphone programs bear scant relation to the specifics of the *Lux* format, and it indeed would have profited Warners little to establish such a tightly wound structure; exhibitors could program discrete Vitaphone shorts in any combination they liked. But Hilmes's *Lux* summary seems to me an uncannily close description of the multiple registers juggled by the part-talkie format, which was the basic form for the sound feature through 1930. As a largely dialogue-free film with only four live-synced segments of Jolson singing and talking, *The Jazz Singer* seems more a gaggle of Vitaphone shorts than a conventional narrative film, as the *Exhibitors Weekly* crack that the film combines several illustrated Jolson records suggests. The technology of the talkies encouraged this format. Recording sound live on phonographic disks while the cameras rolled made editing both sound and image next to impossible. The only way to edit the image track according to presound classical conventions was to film a scene from multiple angles and camera distances at the same time and cut that footage into the master shot without flubbing the synchronization of words to mouths. In other words, whereas live performances of music and sound effects had once served the image track, now the image had to defer to the indelible sound track. Limiting synchronized vocal performance to a few scenes allowed Warners to use classical editing conventions to tell the *story* of *The Jazz Singer*.

While these technological determinants explain why *The Jazz Singer* looks and sounds the way it does, they cannot provide an account of how the film might have been experienced from within the matrix of radiophilic discourse that situated sound film for its audiences. But Hilmes's description of the multiple frames of radio narrative can be usefully imported to help describe three separate textual registers that *The Jazz Singer* juggles in quite self-conscious ways: the plot of the film, supported by nondiegetic music that helps to narrate dramatic peaks and valleys; the star power of Al Jolson, whom critics praised for shedding his character and becoming "Jolson" in his song performances; and the ultimate product this first talking feature puts up for sale—the wondrous Vitaphone. The equivalent of the *Lux Radio Theatre* switching discursive registers comes in the transitions between (silent) narrative and (synchronized) songs, such as when Jolson begins to speak at Coffee Dan's before his first number. These moments break from the plot as surely as a commercial message does during a radio program, but as in the multiply determined radio program, Jolson retains a dual identity as both character and star, directly addressing the audience *within* the film and the audience *of* the film at the same time (Jack's boast at Coffee Dan's, "You ain't heard nothing"—Jolson's "signature tag line" as a stage performer—confirms that "Jack Robin" is *really* Jolson).[30] As distracting as they may be, these very noticeable jumps from one mode of address to another could also function to keep the viewer acutely aware of the Vitaphone as a technology, thus enabling her to enjoy the show as a kind of technological demonstration, a (sonic) display of cinema's ability to stay current with the progress of media modernity.

This encoding shows through most obviously in the direct-address songs I have already discussed, but another, less presentational scene helps to demonstrate how thoroughly the film is itself convinced that it *is* radio, right down to its construction of the spectator-auditor. In one of the film's most lauded scenes, Jack Robin flirts with his mother (Eugenie Besserer) before singing "Blue Skies" to her. Jolson proffers "the theatrical illusion . . . that the film actor [is] overheard," as James Agate put it twenty years later (in 1946). "Overhearing," a term used in the twenties along with "listening in" to describe radio listening, well describes the radio effect this scene seems designed to replicate—the effect not of eavesdropping, as Agate's review implies, but of intimacy laced with a dramatization of exchange. Staged in the Rabinowitz parlor, the mother-son reunion synthesizes the voyeuristic thrill of watching domestic scenes from one's theater seat (as one did during silent narrative films) with the sense of being addressed directly by a radio announcer.

In Mrs. Rabinowitz, the film envisions a hybridized radio-film consumer to fit its hybridized radio-film aesthetics, what might be called a radio spectator. As she sits enraptured, as solitary in her enjoyment as if she were listening to Jolson on the radio, the singing star gazes at her just as he gazes into the audience during his minstrel numbers. At the same time, she rehearses the conventional behavior of the silent film spectator, viewing in public: silence, or at most soft murmurs of appreciation—never vocal articulation. While Jack addresses his mother rather than the camera, the recording reduces her response to her son's japes to appreciative mumbles. If the talkies—or broadcasting, for that matter—had intended the consumer to speak, the scene implies, they'd have supplied her with a microphone of her own. In other words, *The Jazz Singer* actually *pictures* its viewer as a cross between an intimate *home auditor* and an attentive *public viewer*. Thus *The Jazz Singer* borrows back the discourse of informatic intimacy that broadcasting had expropriated from classical film form, and mobilizes listening and watching quietly in the comfort of one's own home as a metaphor for the private-in-public mode of viewing that Warners, Fox, and the other early adopters of sync sound hoped to reestablish in this new cinematic era.

Yet the same structural trappings of radio that supported a sense of continuity between radio listening and the unfamiliar experience of *film* listening also challenged the paradigm of attentiveness modeled for the spectator by *The Jazz Singer*. I have hypothesized that early sound films prefigure the techniques of radio drama by calling on their primary product, the Vitaphone, to bind their somewhat contradictory registers together for the viewer. Ironically, however, the more the talkies fed into expectations created by radio listening, the harder the Vitaphone was to sell. Assessing the critical response, Crafton remarks that *The Jazz Singer* "was represented as a triumph for Jolson, and for Warners in hiring him, but not for talking cinema" (110). I would submit that the very talking cinema Warners tried to peddle with this film disappeared, ironically, behind the window dressings of radio. For by importing radio practices into its production and radio fantasies into its promotion, Warners encoded *The Jazz Singer* so heavily as a radio text that its familiarity to audiences *as radio* undercut the novelty of the Vitaphone.

If the talkies were sometimes not visible enough, at other times they made themselves *too* visible. Prior to talking pictures, the film industry had struggled for twenty years to force live sound performances to "serve the image" by sending musical cues and eventually full scores to exhibitors, often to no avail. When musicians played what they liked or played music appropriate to the ethnic audience's tastes but inappropriate to the producers' intentions, the "bond between performer and audience" created through site-specific musical selections produced, "to the consternation of manufacturers, [a] community [that] often came together at the expense of the film" (Lastra, 112–13). When sound cinema put these decidedly nonclassical, radio-furbished conventions into play, it may have allowed movie studios the luxury of evacuating live shows from theaters, but now it built the challenges to continuity presented by those same live shows into the films themselves. The first Vitaphone program begins with Motion Picture Producers and Distributors of America (MPPDA) President Will Hays introducing the new technology while standing before stage curtains that must have looked, despite their colorlessness, uncannily coterminous with the screen curtains. He looks directly at the camera and bows in multiple directions as if he were facing a live audience, causing titters in some venues. The audience no longer had live performers to bond with against the film; it no longer needed them. Films now alienated audiences with their technological missteps and accidental moments of self-reflexivity quite well on their own.

This is exactly the problem with promoting private-in-public spectatorship through discourses of "home" (i.e., "home" iconography, distracted listening practices, and the like): public viewing involves a different set of choices than does private listening. When radio textuality loses its cohesion or flow (as between programs, or between a polished network broadcast and a locally produced sustaining program), or when one gets distracted from listening, the listener can choose to do any number of other things without interrupting others' pleasure. But in a theater, when a film juggles its discursive frames in a noticeable and distracting way (today this kind of juggling usually takes the form of a projecting accident, such as a misframed or out-of-focus image), one either tries to stay focused on the film—which involves cutting the film a lot of slack for not living up to the viewer's expectations of a unified narrative experience—or one turns to talk to someone. A few infamous sound features, such as the first all-talking feature, *The Lights of New York* (1928), and *Tenderloin* (1928), a dramatic vehicle for the comically lisping Dolores Costello, poorly reproduced the distracting voices of stars who once had only to *look* affecting.[31] *The Lights of New York* made big money as a novelty, but the unintentional comedy of its actors' awkward line readings broke an already brief film into even tinier bits of unsustained melodrama and made reviewers as self-conscious about the relationship of (static) image to (distracting) sound as the actors themselves appeared to be (Crafton, 117). The position of radio spectator meant that one had to be prepared to exchange absorbed attention for recognition of "the talking picture" as an apparatus at a moment's notice. Too often, radio-flavored spectatorship was a license to laugh at how the grown-up apparatus of classical cinema had reduced itself to a technological toy again overnight.

Let me offer the intermedia stakes of this situation in a nutshell, or rather, a mouthful: in 1926, the talkies were a public medium that imagined itself as a private medium (broadcast radio) that imagined itself as a public medium (silent classical cinema). Hollywood had locked itself into the terrifying position of trading a single, stable medium dogged by a few residual distractions from the attractions era (such as the contingency of live musical accompaniment) for two distinct media—the talking picture and the "silent" picture—each of which would develop along its own path. One scenario projected the development of the unspoken language of expressive gesture and omniscient narration founded by silent classical film, while sync voice would be reserved for variety shows, spectacles, and fantasy films.[32] I'm not suggesting that Hollywood would have rejected out of hand the idea of throwing out classical film and its trimmings, if the studio moguls thought it would make the business more profitable. The problem with grafting radio onto the cinema, rather, was that it haunted classical cinema with its preclassical skeleton in the closet, the self-conscious interruption of entertainment, as if technological "progress" moved in a Viconian spiral rather than from link to link in an endless diachronic chain.

The King of Jazz recognizes the destabilizing effects this worst-case scenario might have on spectatorship. In a musical number called "On a Bench in the Park," the face of Paul Whiteman appears in the moon in

Figure 5. Whiteman in the Moon. Frame enlargement from *The King of Jazz* (1929).

homage to *Le Voyage dans la lune,* the 1902 Georges Méliès film that continually interrupts its own rudimentary plot with moments of pure spectacle (Figures 5 and 6).[33] Though Whiteman's man in the moon doesn't sacrifice an eye to the "kiss" of a Terran rocket, his appearance recalls the earlier film's figurative assault on the eye and links the vignette format of *The King of Jazz* to Méliès's promotion of visual shock for its own sake. This return of classical cinema's repressed has chilling implications for the continuity of what had been a reproducible, reliable entertainment form for the studios who had worked diligently to conventionalize it at every stage, from production and distribution to the positioning of seats and the requirement of silence in their theaters.

The film defends the vestiges of classical spectatorship from these attacks of formal atavism by imagining a complicit audience that is at the same time too sophisticated to allow visual or episodic jolts to devolve it into a vaudeville crowd. Whereas the Méliès in the Moon gets enoculated by a new technology that assaults his vision as pointedly as film did the eyes of early viewers, the Whiteman in the Moon merely winks of its own volition. "On a Bench in the Park" also features a young man offering a ring to a young woman and various synchronized and relatively tame courtship rituals; unlike the mashers of the nickelodeon era, the men refuse even to

Figure 6. Méliès takes it in the eye. Frame enlargement from *Le Voyage dans la lune* (1902).

pet in the park without getting engaged first. Later in the film, a barber-shop group sporting plastered-down hair and handlebar mustaches sings "Has Anybody Seen Our Nellie?" and leads an offscreen audience through the final verse. This number not only indexes the relationship between the variety format of many new talkies and the early cinema's multiple registers of meaning—it stares the relationship straight in the face and derides it. The horrible singing voices, the too-tight suits, the alternately prissy and terrified affects of the barbershop quartet, and the poorly projected lantern slides that illustrate the song congratulate the modern spectator on her purchase of a ticket to a thoroughly modern revue, complete with two-strip Technicolor, sound, and the presence of an avant-garde conductor who helped win for jazz the adulation of thousands of high- and middle-brow Americans. In the end, however, "Has Anybody Seen Our Nellie?" degenerates into a cinematic primal scene when one of the closing song slides enjoins the film audience to sing along—in Hebrew! (Figure 7). Try as it may to project participatory viewing into a naive past, this scene links the vignette format of *The King of Jazz* to communal interaction in the present of public spectatorship, while its nostalgic good humor and unwillingness to banish such recognitions of spectatorial difference as a

Figure 7. Hebrew song slide (quickly replaced by an English translation). Frame enlargement from *The King of Jazz.*

Hebrew lantern slide registers that lost community *as lost*—a form of inter-active viewing that early sound films, their dual registers fused by the new technology yet made strange by the novelty of the combination, had every chance of bringing back from the preclassical dust heap.

If *The King of Jazz,* produced by Carl Laemmle Jr., reiterates Carl Laemmle Sr.'s melancholy at the passing of the nickelodeon, Warners' *The Show of Shows* (John G. Adolfi, 1929) negatively acknowledges this monstrous birth by means of an on-screen execution. As described by Charles Wolfe, *The Show of Shows* opens by staging the execution of "Prologue" (in the effigy of an actor dressed as an eighteenth-century "French aristocrat"). Before the axe falls, the executioner mounts a devastating eulogy: "You've wasted hours of our times. Wasted years. You're useless . . . we intend to stamp you out forever." The mob cheers as the executioner beheads his prisoner and says, "Prologue is dead. On with the Show of Shows!" (61). This scene lets slip the ferocity of Warners' desire to be rid of the expensive live performers who introduced and accompanied feature films. But like all public executions, as Foucault would have it, this act of discipline is indistinguishable from an act of public coercion. What is secretly being killed—or at least warned of its mortality—is the specter of Uncle Josh and the sociologically interactive audience for which he stood. Act like an individuated and polite audience, the film mutters under its breath, or suffer the consequence of giving up cinematic pleasure the way Hollywood will construct it forever after. The problem with such a proclamation, of course, is that it reveals the weakened position from which the cinema issues it. I doubt that *The Show of Shows,* another radio-style revue film much like *The King of Jazz,* would threaten to destroy its "aberrant" spectators had its producers known how to silence them by textual means.

Congorilla Strikes Back

By 1932–33, the studios had acheived a balance between silent classical narration and the episodic forms initially taken by the talkies. While it would be tempting to attribute this balance to technological "improvements," such as the editable sound-on-film systems engineered by RCA and Western Electric, Lastra has demonstrated that the development of sound conventions in Hollywood film depended on a shifting ideology of sonic realism. Sound engineers like Carl Dreher adhered to a fidelity model of sound space, in which the volume and reverberation level of sounds depended on the camera's distance from the sound source, as late as 1931. Eventually, as camera blimping (i.e., soundproofing), mixing, and postdubbing made the talkies more editing-friendly, the engineers reformulated their model to keep acoustic effects from diverting attention from the plot. The new sound paradigm placed the highest value on the intelligibility of dialogue and subordinated all other sounds, and even spatial fidelity, to achieving that goal.[34]

In this section of the chapter, I will narrate the redevelopment of classical narrative in the early sound era from a different angle, as a struggle to purge the talkies of the same devil of radio fantasy that Hollywood had just ushered into its sound-wired theaters with the talkies. This struggle left the deepest impressions in films that chronicle the persistence of the "amateur" threat into the broadcasting era. In the xenophobic mythology of jazz as invader, the unidirectional structure of broadcasting reversed the excessively democratic nature of wireless, but could itself be reversed if hot jazz were to establish a place for itself in the "respectable" airwaves. That mythology well served Hollywood's gambit to reinvent the classical subject position by example, for however small the audience assembled to watch any given film on any given evening, the structural possibility existed that an "amateur" spectator—many of them, in fact, one or more in every theater—could become just such a loud speaker him- or herself.

Let me begin by returning to a scene I've already discussed, only this time I want to look at it as a fantasy in which classical film plays savior to the distracted audience, rather than executioner. The "suicide" from *The Big Broadcast* reiterates the lesson of *Traffic in Souls* that the *pastness* of film—that is, the lag between the profilmic event and the time of spectatorship—is an asset to the viewer, not a sign of film's inferior powers over space and time compared to the instantaneous radio. While radio jazz muscles its way in uninvited and starts telling men what to do, *The Big Broadcast* offers the viewer a critical, satirical distance from which to consider the consequences of radio-jazz invasion. Bing and Leslie cannot resist the seductions of the radio voice, but the viewer can, thanks to this elaborately staged joke. Although the scene's racialization of the radio-jazz threat is hardly progressive, it portrays broadcast radio for what Brecht knew it to be—"purely an apparatus for distribution"—and enframes it with a medium that, by negative example, seems to know "how to let the listener speak as well as hear, how to bring him into a relationship instead of isolating him."[35] Although the spectator-auditors could no more talk back through the radio on the screen than they could strike up a conversation with the screen image of Bing Crosby, the film offers them an imaginative space in which to indulge their trepidations about radio's effects without being distracted by character identification or even cajoled into making a specific judgment about the "message" of the scene. While I tend to read the scene as antiradio, Leslie and Bing capitulate to the song's "orders" so quickly that it might just as easily have come off as a parody of antijazz hysteria, or radiophobia, or both.

But *The Big Broadcast* offers no answer to the more pressing problem for classical cinema: how can Hollywood produce sound films that would appeal to an audience used to loose, disjointed radio forms without sacrificing the disciplinary power that classical narrative exercised over that audience? Films could hammer lessons in cinematic reception into the spectator's head but could not do so for long without becoming more didactic than entertaining. Hollywood knows that it can't rely on simply showing films in public to keep its audiences in check, because publicness was itself the essence of the problem faced by early cinema: publicness leads to sociological interaction, unless textuality can be employed to stave it off.

Early talkies offered a solution to this conundrum, but the solution was less formal than it was overtly disciplinarian. Hollywood coexisted with the monstrous radio spectators it helped to create by scapegoating black jazz for boisterous and antisocial activity and ritually portraying its segregation from whites on the screen. Like radio discourse before it, Hollywood of the early sound era follows the lead of radio discourse in making "jazz" synonymous with sonic otherness, which, once visualized, can be more easily distinguished—and thus distanced—from its potential victims. Early sound film does radio not one but two better on this count: it reifies and segregates the black bodies playing jazz at the level of the image, and it models uninvolved but appreciative reception by white viewers. Many early sound films did, in fact, feature black musicians and singers. As Alice Maurice has demonstrated, critics praised the black voice as perfect for sync-sound film due to its resonance and depth. But Maurice also argues that Hollywood mobilized the black voice to distract audiences from the strangeness of sound film.[36] *Hallelujah!* (King Vidor, 1929) goes so far as to project its all-black cast into a near-timeless past of southern agrarian life and restricts them to singing spirituals and sorrow songs, as if to prevent the spectator from associating the film with anything "modern," be it sound-film technology or jazz.

When blacks played or sang jazz, however, radio discourse taught that they could not help but threaten the "refined" ear with corruption. For viewer-auditors concerned about "musical miscegenation" of this sort, sound films with jazz themes offered the screen as a kind of spatio-temporal cage with the medium-specific limits of the frame and the pastness of the profilmic event. In addition, they produced spatial and ideological frames within the frame, redundant systems of containment that replicated or exceeded radio's less definite frames.

The most obvious frame of segregation was the proscenium arch. The climactic performance of the Dudley Murphy short *Black and Tan Fantasy* (1929) brooks no integration between black performers and white listeners. It locks Duke Ellington's orchestra up in a jungle-themed proscenium, flanked by cartoon palm trees, replicating the "African" motif of the whites-only Cotton Club where Ellington's orchestra was the house band. *Check and Double Check* (Melville W. Brown, 1930), the film debut of blackface radio comedians Amos 'n' Andy, once again cages Ellington between the curtains (Figure 8). The camera frames his orchestra in long shot from behind the tables, making the proscenium as two-dimensional as a postage stamp—or rather, a movie screen—compared to the audience, which is staged in considerable depth.

By recalling the space of film exhibition so directly, this last scene in particular recommends the cinema and the traditional attentiveness

Figure 8. Ellington and his orchestra enclosed in the proscenium. Frame enlargement from *Check and Double Check* (1930).

of spectatorship as protection against musical miscegenation. Rendered absolutely immobile as Ellington leads an eminently danceable number, these spectators have no trouble resisting the urge to dance, let alone the urge to eat someone, as expressed by the "Jazz Cannibal"; they do not engage with jazz so much as consume it, dumbstruck. The scene calls on spectators to discipline themselves, under threat of the panoptic oversight of the classical cinematic audience: like the audience enjoying(?) the live performance in the diegesis, the spectator *can* resist the call of the jungle drums, and the urge to become subject to the "African" usurper of King Radio's throne. Don't panic, the scene whispers subliminally to its audience, just listen politely. If you don't enjoy the spectacle, or you find it offensive to your racial sensibilities, wait a few minutes and Amos 'n' Andy will make you forget both black skill and black self-expression. There is safety in public consumption, and strength in numbers.

If caging black jazz in a proscenium arch wasn't protection enough for all audiences, some films increased the geographical range. One of the most fascinating aspects of jazz-themed films between 1926 and 1933 is that they express an exuberance about representing space and distance that borders on giddiness, as if sync-sound film were expanding its imaginative relationship to radio to include the ability to picture the space that radio broadcasting annihilated. As in the case of film's "addition" of images to the sounds made by African Americans, however, these representations transform distance into a signifier for otherness. They produce "space" not as a category that radio or film has dissolved but as a cage for the vocal black subject. Compare the use of "I'll Be Glad When You're Dead" in *The Big Broadcast* to its appearance in the Betty Boop cartoon named for the song (Max Fleischer, 1932), in which Louis Armstrong appears as a disembodied head among cartoon cannibals,[37] or the Armstrong short *A Rhapsody in Black and Blue* (Aubrey Scotto, 1932), named, ironically, after Armstrong's anthem of black frustration "(What Did I Do to Be So) Black and Blue?" One answer to that musical question might be that he agreed to appear in this short, for Armstrong's brilliant cornet performance and improvised scat break are quadruply contained: by an all-black cast (enclosing it in the generic confines of the "race" picture); by a dream sequence attributed to a lazy black man who listens to race records; by the proscenium in which the dreamer, clad in a drum major's uniform, sits in the royal throne of "Jazzmania"; and by the inevitable jungle imagery. Armstrong stands center stage in a leopard-skin tunic that could have been lifted from Tarzan's wardrobe (Figure 9).

Figure 9. Louis Armstrong as the official bandleader of the Kingdom of Jazzmania.
Frame enlargement from *Rhapsody in Black and Blue* (1932).

Other films of the early sound era claim refinement rights over jazz
somewhat differently by tagging it as foreign and then "discovering" it. In
her book on the "tourist gaze" as constructed by mass culture since the invention of the picture postcard, Ellen Strain summarizes the Heideggerian
concept of the "world picture" this way: "to see the world as a picture is to
'get the picture,' to understand the world as a uniform totality, and to take
up a subject position in relation to an objectified world . . . [that] attain[s]
the illusion of mastery through . . . aestheticized representation."[38] In a
similar vein, Donna Haraway has developed the "camera-gun" trope to
summarize the colonialist violence signified, and perpetrated, by this
form of visual mastery. As Cynthia Erb defines the trope in her discussion
of *King Kong* (which I will pick up in this context shortly), when "paired
with a weapon, the camera becomes rhetorically contaminated by the violent properties of the gun it purportedly resembles," and collaborates with
the weapon in a semiotically violent project to reify the foreign body.[39]

The *King of Jazz* opens by employing the camera-gun trope as the crux
of an origin myth for jazz. After a spoken introduction that promises to reveal how Whiteman "came to be crowned the King of Jazz," the film segues

to a cartoon animated by Walter Lantz (later of Woody Woodpecker fame) that portrays Whiteman hunting big game "in darkest Africa." Although cartoon-Whiteman carries not a camera but a gun, his journey to shoot a lion summarizes the overarching project of *The King of Jazz*'s narrating camera: to appropriate black jazz as a commodity. To characterize the "African" voice as an object of exchange—a material good that must be harvested—rather than a radio signal is to claim that committing it to film renders it sterile, powerless to speak for itself. Cartoon-Whiteman does exactly this when he produces jazz by "playing" a cartoon lion with his shotgun, recalling the slavers' safaris of past centuries and imbuing slavery and jazz alike with a guilty, white fantasy of interracial collaboration; the lion, after all, raises his own skin for Whiteman's buckshot to hammer his ribs like marimba mallets. After the jazz-bwana decides to soothe the savage beast with indigenous American music rather than violence—including a chorus of the black spiritual "My Lord Delivered Daniel," stripped of any reference to its slave history by cartoon-Whiteman's whiter-than-white Irish tenor voice, and a bit of down-home fiddling (Figure 10)—the lion then drops to one knee, spreads his arms wide, and says "Mammy" (Figure 11). This bit clinches the "authenticity" of Whiteman's jazz burden by implying

Figure 10. "Music hath charms, though it's classic or jazz . . ." Frame enlargement from *The King of Jazz*.

Figure 11. The lion does a spontaneous Jolson impersonation. Frame enlargement from *The King of Jazz*.

that Jolson channeled his plantation songs directly from the African prairies and that African American hot music perverts the original African. Hollywood transforms jazz from a forced imposition of uncivilized behavior on the white private sphere to a beast on display in a cinematic zoo.

After the cartoon, the film displays the spoils of Whiteman's journey to save "authentic" jazz from its black practitioners in several forms: in extreme close-ups of clarinetists and other instrumentalists who display incredible technical skills (dexterity and accuracy, not improvisation, dominate the display); in its many decidedly nonsyncopated and often inexplicable "jazz" numbers (which include a "south of the border" fandango sans Mexicans and a Louis XIV court wedding wrapped in the whitest of white tulle); and in its culminating fantasy of jazz bubbling from a "melting pot" of white folk culture. The bwana of jazz stirs a diverse group of Euro-Americans into his jazz mélange, which amounts to a country club swimming pool that doesn't even allow black servants to enter the service door. *The King of Jazz* only admits the blackness of jazz once, when Whiteman proclaims that jazz was "born in the African jungle, to the beating of the voodoo drum."[40] Cued by Whiteman's announcement, the dancer Jacques Chartier appears atop a gigantic "voodoo drum" clad in a grass skirt and headdress and covered in ebony body paint. The extreme long shot reduces him to a synecdoche for savagery as he dances with head bowed, dwarfed by his own black shadow (Figure 12). But if the film can only acknowledge blackness as an absence that structures the ideological process of refining jazz, at least it is honest about the economic imperative that motivates its expropriation. The white "folk," stripped of their kilts and other ethnic costumes, emerge from the pot dressed in tuxedoes of gold.[41]

Even ethnographic films got in on the act of scrubbing jazz white, by discovering traces of jazz littered all over various jungles. Merian C. Cooper and Ernest B. Schoedsack's quasi-documentary *Chang: A Drama of the Wilderness* (1927) uses intertitles to "interpret" the speech of its Siamese subjects according to Western stereotypes of ancient speech patterns, and like *Grass: A Nation's Battle for Life* (Cooper and Schoedsack, 1925) before it, it imagines the people as timeless and beyond politics, subject only to the vagaries of weather, vegetation, and wild animals. Yet when "Bimbo" the monkey "speaks," she speaks (via intertitles) in jazz age idioms. Her happy ending comes when a "big butter-and-egg monkey from the middle wilderness" takes her for his bride—an explicit reference

Figure 12. Jacques Chartier dances on a "voodoo drum." Frame enlargement from *The King of Jazz.*

to the Armstrong standard "Big Butter and Egg Man from the West." These discoveries of jazz indulge in a process of captioning that Fatimah Tobing Rony has called "ethnographic ventriloquism," in which "the film-maker speaks for native peoples. . . . Ethnographic ventriloquism *assumes* the inarticulateness of the native," and so "the West's own narratives of evolution [and] loss . . . are expressed" instead.[42]

The function of these ventriloquisations of jazz is not to express regret at the West's "lost" primitivism, however, but to envision a geographical and racial buffer between white America and the black voice. While critics of hot jazz imagined radio waves transmitting black voices straight from the jungle into the American home, these ethnographic fantasy films throw the "black" voice overseas and into an unchanging past that film itself—the media object that objectifies its subjects—refines for American eyes and (racializing) minds, then imports as a physical commodity for display only in movie theaters. Martin and Osa Johnson's African explo-ration "documentaries" brim with jokes that attempt to naturalize the connection of jazz to the jungle. Their silent feature *Simba, The King of Beasts* (1928) refers to monkeys and humans alike as "flappers," and in the introduction to their first sound film, *Congorilla* (1932), Osa holds her ear in mock pain behind the back of an African performer playing a stringed instrument, while Martin's voiceover tells us we will witness the "first pic-tures in natural sound ever made in the jungles of Central Africa—the next best thing to being on the Dark Continent itself. . . . The natives will sing for you and dance to the beat of the tom-tom." The Johnsons promise a spectacle of fully embodied, fully visualized, authentic black music while simultaneously undercutting its authenticity compared to "our modern music," which plays on a phonograph later in the film as Osa leads the Mtubi in a "jazz" dance.

Each of these images supports the idea that savagery well becomes jazz and that "the jungle" is not only the obvious source of its barbaric music and movements but the best place to grab it and set it on the road to re-habilitation under civilization's guiding hand. The imperialist character of the project could scarcely be more obvious; as Ella Shohat and Robert Stam characterize it, the Johnsons' camera "penetrated a foreign and fa-miliar zone like a predator, seizing its 'loot' of images as raw material to be reworked in the 'motherland' and sold to sensation-hungry spectators and consumers, a process later fictionalized in *King Kong*."[43] In the process of refining not only native images but native sounds, the acousmêtric cap-tions duplicate the work of the supposedly unifying voices of broadcast authority that promised to flatten out American identity through a combination of didacticism and the will to typify, deride, and silence groups that did not fit the "universal" definition of that identity. As "experienced vaudevillian performers" who mounted their various tales and "prizes," animal and human, as entertainment spectacles as well as moving pictures, the Johnsons knew enough about the conventions of vaudevillian racialization to stage the Mtubi in "situations guaranteed to produce laughs among white American audiences"—and if contemporary reviews are accurate, they met with gut-busting success.[44] Martin even tells us that because the pygmies stop growing physically at a very young age, they never "grow up" at all. Even if they had any authority to speak, the film assures us, they would have nothing to say. In one long take, a pygmy speaks for several minutes without any translation whatever; as far as the Johnsons are concerned, his voice is an exotic curiosity, not a signifier of agency.[45] When a Mtubi sings a song in her native language early in *Congorilla,* the all-knowing Martin refers to it as "Yes, We Have No Bananas."

Each instance I've mentioned implies that the jazz "discovered" in the jungle is *already white.* In other words, this is a doubly racist joke, for it both roots African *American* music forms in an Africa fraught with fantasies of timeless savagery, and it claims that coon and plantation songs created by white minstrels, like "My Mammy," are the "original" jazz. When *Congorilla* stages its tableau of pygmies bobbing up and down to a jazz record, Martin plays the role of benevolent acousmêtre: "Let's give the boys and girls some modern jazz! . . . It was remarkable how quickly they caught the rhythm of our modern music," he says, though "sometimes they got out of time." For the Johnsons, jazz is "our modern music," a triumph of progress over atavism. It is both an import and an export to the natives who grinningly consume it in a safari parody of a white living room, while Osa hops up and down arrhythmically at the edge of the frame. When *Congorilla* inspired a song and a dance craze of the same name, the sheet music cover displayed a stylishly tailored "jazz age" white couple dancing, backed by the obligatory cartoon-tropical foliage and a photograph of Osa and Martin standing before a squiggling line of Mtubi, their hands at chest level in imitation of Osa's "modern" dance pose.[46]

The Cohens and Kellys in Africa (Vin Moore, 1930), a feature-length episode in a Universal series about two globetrotting piano salesmen from New York, projects this fantasy of America exporting jazz to the jungle directly onto a jungle-dwelling black body. It ends in a jungle jamboree in an unspecified part of Africa, led by a piano salesman and ivory seeker from the Bronx named Sam Ginsberg (Eddie Kane), who has gone native to become chief of the "Zulus." As humans and animals alike bang on pianos, the camera pans over to two gorillas in a tree, one of whom listens appreciatively to the other's piano playing until, just as the film fades to black, he, like Whiteman's cartoon lion, spreads his arms and says "Mammy!"

In all these ways, jazz and jungle films both emulate the radio, by traversing time and space to rehearse the fantasy of jazz coming from "darkest Africa," and quell the invasion of these savage amateurs by reversing the direction of the invasion: rather than black voices invading through the airwaves, the recording technology of film "takes" the audience to their palm-lined doorstep.

But these images do a much better job of containing *jazz* than of containing their own *hysteria.* The hysteria projects itself most revealingly onto an animal that racist eugenics fantasy always kept close at hand: the gorilla. As a containing metaphor for hot jazz, the gorilla seems to have everything going for it. It is as familiar as Jolson in blackface, or Amos 'n' Andy in blackvoice, as a derogatory figure for blackness in general and hot music in particular, and no one, white or black, wants to identify herself with a jungle beast who can never swing from vine to vine fast enough to catch up with evolution. By putting "Mammy" in an African gorilla's mouth, *The Cohens and Kellys in Africa* rehearses the old saw that white jazz is real jazz. The reason it resonates with paranoid fantasies about *radio* jazz is that, unlike the Jolson lion in *The King of Jazz,* the gorilla keeps turning up on American territory as both a cause and a reflection of domestic upheaval. When it appears on Anglo territory, the gorilla signifies a hostile invasion by hot jazz and its "primitive" sensibility and constructs jazz as an escape artist, able to slip the geographical and discursive bonds with which cinema tries to confine it. In Josef von Sternberg's *Blonde Venus* (1932), Helen Faraday (Marlene Dietrich) has to raise money to save her scientist husband's life, so she returns to her profession as a chanteuse. But by dressing her as a gorilla for her first appearance at the club, the film constructs her as a jazz beast simply for leaving the house—even before she sells her favors to Nick (Cary Grant). After terrorizing the audience a bit and straining slightly against the chain that collars her, Helen ambles onto the stage (Figure 13), removes her gorilla suit in strip-tease fashion (Figure 14), and sings "Hot Voodoo," a song that runs through nearly every stock nightmare connecting jazz to miscegenation, cultural and otherwise:

I'm beginning to fe-eel like an African fe-e-eels. . . .

. . . and the whole night long, I don't know the right from wrong . . .

Hot voodoo, black as mud!
Hot voodoo, in my blood!
[Her eyes widen]
I'd follow a caveman right into his ca-a-ave . . .

That beat gives me a wicked sensation
My conscience wants to take a vacation. . . .

Hot voodoo, burn my clothes!—
I'm going to blazes, I want to be bad!

Dutifully playing its role in a familiar racialist narrative, the gorilla suit acts as both a sign of and a scapegoat for the newly willful sexuality of the white hausfrau.

Illicit sexuality also appears under the sign of gorillahood in the short *Sing, Bing, Sing* (Babe Stafford, 1933). This scenario plays even more like a transcription of a paranoid jazz-radio fantasy, in which the jazz singer blows radio kisses over the patriarchal walls and flushes the cheeks of an

Figure 13. Helen Faraday (Marlene Dietrich) makes the most of an unusual wardrobe choice. Frame enlargement from *Blonde Venus* (1932).

Figure 14. Frame enlargement from *Blonde Venus*.

innocent "girl." Bing Crosby, again playing himself as a radio crooner, woos his beloved Helen (Florine McKinney) by remote control, because her unsympathetic millionaire father ("Marrying a radio singer!" he blusters) has turned his absurdly large private sphere, a palatial estate with its own zoo, into a cage that restricts his daughter along with the animals. Bing invades the estate twice, first virtually (by singing a coded invitation to elope during his evening broadcast) and then in the flesh. When he sneaks through the daughter's bedroom window, he materializes the fantasized threat of the radio crooner who steals the hearts of young and vulnerable "girls" from under their fathers' noses. If the film had left the cast of characters at these three, plus the bumbling detectives hired to enforce the Law of the Father, Bing's return of the radio to its past of one-to-one communication would be simply a symptom of healthy Oedipalism; we are confident that he only wants to become patriarch of his own personal private sphere. But things get more complicated once the gorilla escapes from the father's zoo. Once loose, the gorilla (Charles Gemora) charges the father and his detectives, grabs the wheel of the detectives' truck, and drives it into a pond with all three killjoys inside. This diversion gives the happy couple just enough time to steal the millionaire's private plane and reenter the ether from whence Bing came. The hot jazz beast acts as a beast of burden for fantasies of public-private liaison, both utopian and dystopian, that contemporary definitions of radio and cinema forbade. The film masculinizes Crosby in part by contrasting him to the gorilla that stands for primal emotions and the hot "jungle" music that Bing does *not* sing. The appearance of the gorilla not only makes Bing look more white (and less dangerous) by contrast; it takes the rap as the *truly* dangerous jazz body and leaves Bing looking more like an affirmative, run-of-the-mill classical spectator who simply watches in disbelief as the gorilla de-authorizes the patriarch and turns the private sphere upside down. *Sing, Bing, Sing* scapegoats a bestial black body for the sexual and media desires of the young white crooner, then lets Crosby reap the benefits of those desires while all the gorilla gets is wet.

But King Kong is the ultimate jazz-radio beast of early sound cinema. The name "Kong" flashes back to Congo Square in New Orleans, the place where slaves were allowed to hold traditional celebrations through the nineteenth century,[47] and fantasized references to "the Kongo" as the birthplace of jazz, where "witch-doctors and medicine-men . . . used [the term 'jaz'] at those jungle parties when the tom-toms throbbed and the sturdy warriors gave their pep an added kick with rich brews of Yohimbin bark."[48]

But just as Whiteman and nearly every other white jazz historian of the time conveniently forgets the New Orleans and Chicago jazz scenes (as if jazz evolved in a two-stage process beginning with slave spirituals and ending with Irving Berlin), *King Kong* (Merian C. Cooper and Ernest B. Schoedsack, 1933) projects the home of jazz onto Skull Mountain, Kong's prehistoric island lair. The dinosaurs and treacherous precipices of Skull Mountain kill nearly as many people as Kong does himself, making it the perfect stereotypical soil for sprouting a lawless musical form. Claudia Gorbman asks a rhetorical question about the implied source of the music in this scene of intercultural contact:

> If a microphone and a soundman were accompanying Denham, what would the mike pick up? Would it record the drumming, the chanting, and the RKO orchestra? We know the "obvious" answer to this question, but this scene [of the sacrificial dance that introduces Kong] seems to test its very obviousness in eliminating, on the diegetic level, a soundman along with Denham and his camera. It is as if sound in a film has no technological base, involves no work, it is natural . . . just like the spectacle Denham witnesses. . . . Sound is just there, oozing from the images we see.[49]

Whereas Gorbman obviously describes classical sound film's newly minted ideology of effortlessness—images just automatically "make" the sounds appropriate to them—the film also offers further "proof" that the original "voodoo drum" of jazz was the black body itself. Kong and the natives of Skull Island are creatures of sound, inseparable from "savage" percussion and music. The first sign of life that Denham (Robert Armstrong) notices on the island is the sound of drums, and Kong makes his initial appearance only when summoned by a gong struck by the native chief (played by man of a thousand races Noble Johnson, formerly a star at the Lincoln race film company). Kong even turns his own body into a drum by beating his chest, perhaps the next logical step in turning black bodies into instruments after Chartier's human drumstick act in *The King of Jazz*; in fact, sound designer Murray Spivack created the chest-pounding sounds by miking a man's chest while tapping his back with a drum mallet.[50] Even the steps he takes "make" music, thanks to Max Steiner's mickey-mousing score.

By bringing gorillas to America rather than leaving the jazz-spouting beasts where they are, these gorilla narratives rehearse the threat of musical invasion that radio fabulists had feared since the beginning of the wireless age. The character of Helen Faraday takes Bliven's fable of "little Elizabeth," the woman made a monstrous tramp by jazz, to its most forbidding conclusion: entering the public sphere to sing "hot voodoo" songs for money, she quickly switches professions from singing to (apparently) sleeping with another man to get the cash Ned (Herbert Marshall) needs for medical treatment. When Ned learns of her liaison and threatens to take their son, she grabs little Johnny and flees without a cent, sneaking rides on hay trucks and roaming the Southern countryside in search of food and work.

But her secret life as a gorilla reminds us that she, too, is an outsider, little different from the fearsomely authoritative voices of the female radio announcers that critics complained about so bitterly a few years before. Rony points out that Helen's entry into civilization closely resembles King Kong's: both are extracted from natural settings overseas (Helen from a forest pond in Germany where she swims naked with her troop of chorines, Kong from Skull Island where he runs naked through the jungle wrestling dinosaurs and eating natives) to New York, and both have exotic bodies that become highly prized commodities based on their value as spectacle (173–74). The jungle stage setting, the blackface chorines that stamp and sway behind her, and Helen's own to-be-looked-at blonde afro wig and the pre-Code costume that sets her legs free and her breasts aglitter, all place her squarely at the "intersection of male and imperial gazes."[51] Pictured as an object of sexual-colonial conquest instead of an ephemeral sound wave, she lacks the anonymous acousmêtre's structural autonomy.

But whatever chance this scene has to inoculate the spectator—and the cinema—against the threat of radio invasion evaporates when Helen removes her ape suit. As with Jolson in *The Jazz Singer,* Dietrich's star persona switches on the moment the mask slips past her face. Her triumphant stance on stage, the slyness of her guttural voice, the low camera angle (which is only scantly attributed to Nick's point of view, and thus allows her to tower over even the ostensibly omniscient shots), and the song she sings about sending her conscience away on vacation all mark her as full owner of both her body and her sexuality. The power she exerts through her voice allows her to overcome even the image's power to define her. If jazz has cannibalized the white woman here—as if the suit were a real gorilla that had swallowed her whole, or a jazz-crazed dance partner who suddenly found her "nice enough to eat"—Helen emerges from her monkey-fur chrysalis as a speaking subject defined by her own volition: "I *want* to be 'bad.'"

Helen's jazz-charged expression of desire in "Hot Voodoo" represents the first and most bombastic indication that she, not Ned, will determine how her desires will be fulfilled. Ned may have (grudgingly) granted her permission to get out of the house and into public to hunt and gather for the family, but as Gaylyn Studlar writes, even when Helen "is reinserted into the imprisonment of marriage" at the film's conclusion, "Ned's revenge fails" because "mother and son are reunited"—and at the narrative direction of the son, Helen's primary love object, not the father; "the superego is functionally dead."[52] Considering this point, we might describe "Hot Voodoo" as the point at which she remaps the patriarchically defined territory separating private sphere from public life as a kind of evolutionary narrative space, one in which the radio fantasy of jazz invading the home gets reversed, in terms of both the direction through that territory which jazz "moves" the subject, and the phylogenetic degeneration that such invasions were supposed to provoke. Her lumbering gorilla walk from dance floor to stage traverses multiple boundaries of both geography and identity: from mass to individual, spectator-auditor space to performing space, passive silence to defiant speech, stereotype to subject. Helen peers confidently down from the top edge of the *plan américain* framing, surveying her new kingdom with a self-assuredness she never exhibits until exactly this moment. Rather than being raped by the black body, *she* has entered *it,* and wears it as one sign among many of her power over the masquerade of femininity. Her de-evolution as re-evolution stems not from the phylogenetic determinism of musical miscegeny but from an ontogenetic decision that becomes available to Helen only when she has to engage with a public that allows and even encourages her to speak for herself, whatever the disguise (entertainer, gorilla, "Blonde Venus").[53]

Lest we see the gorilla suit merely as a form of blackface, a means of appropriating subaltern suffering for one's own ends without having to experience it, recall that Helen does not begin to speak/sing her (or rather Dietrich's) "primal" mind until she takes the suit *off*. Although the eroticism of striptease depends on the possibility that the stripper might leave her clothes on, and equally on the number of clothes the stripper does leave on, the political force of Helen's performance depends upon her claiming the stereotype of blackness as a kind of stealth disguise or a carrier wave that signifies not only exoticism but also difference as power: the power to cause grown men to stand back as she ambles through the crowd, allowing her to take her place at the center of attention and broadcast her voice throughout the space. For Helen, the gorilla costume functions like a stream of blackened, hot (voodoo) jazz carried over the radio that conceals her identity as a woman just long enough for her to take control of the performance space. If Helen-Dietrich uses the stereotype of black musical primality to her advantage, she does so quite self-reflexively. She deconstructs the stereotype by revealing the suit as exactly that and revealing nothing but another costume underneath, this time the costume of eroticized and exoticized femininity.

In the self-consciousness of this striptease, we begin to see traces of a cinema still nervous about its own noises and self-conscious about the residual affinities between talking film and broadcasting. For if not even the filmic image can reify the excessive subjecthood that the sound of jazz connotes, what could stop the classical spectator from discovering the pleasurable autonomy over mind and body that the myth of little Elizabeth works so diligently to conceal? She need not even make the literal trip through the no-woman's-land between private and public spaces to do so. She's already there, watching the movie and thinking whatever the ambiguous spectacle of Dietrich, the Blonde Venus, invites her to think.

Jane Gaines writes that, "if the cinema is . . . an othering machine, a machine that stages the face-to-face encounter between entities in search of identity, it must offer some satisfaction of the desire to overcome differences" (85). Gaines echoes Fredric Jameson in arguing that even the most racializing cinematic representations of such encounters must offer a little utopia with their reification—in this case, the notion of encounter as driven by curiosity and the possibility of reconciling oneself to mutual difference rather than obliterating it in the Other—or risk being rejected or ignored.[54] Considering the otherness that Hollywood cinema struggled with in the form of its own dual identity as both a teller of stories set in the past and a dead ringer for the contingent, disjointed, and invasive radio, it seems to me that the "Hot Voodoo" number stages an intermedial encounter that stands watch over all the others I have discussed in this section: an encounter between the othering machine of film and the radio it had tried to cannibalize by swallowing the latter's fantasies and claiming them as the cinema's own. The fact that the encounter takes the form of a vignette, a performance that breaks away from the plot as cleanly as do the sync-sound numbers in *The Jazz Singer,* only admits more loudly that classical cinema is having trouble overcoming even its own construction of the voice as a highly visible, not to mention audible, medium within the medium. No matter how hard its technicians work to phase out its novelty, the soundtrack resists serving the image and the story in unreflective "silence."

And if the gorilla *suit* functions in *Blonde Venus* as a kind of radio, what of King Kong, who *is* a gorilla? Mark McGurl argues that Kong is the ultimate manifestation of RKO's trademark title card of the early thirties: "A Radio Picture." In McGurl's reading, *King Kong* reflects the desire of RCA, corporate parent to both NBC and RKO, "to be seen, and to see itself, on the big screen. Taking visual possession of its own 'vivid,' 'glamorous' body on screen, RCA responds to the anxiety of invisibility."[55] The body of Kong is more vivid than glamorous, but as a towering monster who makes his most famous screen turn high above New York City, he seems to support McGurl's claim that Kong fulfilled RCA chief Sarnoff's desire to produce a vivid marriage between radio and cinema, one that would reverse the standard promotional hierarchy between cinema and radio while at the same time proving RCA's mastery over both media. But I submit that if Sarnoff wanted the film to give RCA a visible presence on the mass cultural scene, he shot himself in the foot rather severely, for the ape embodies nearly every myth of black savagery and monstrous miscegenation that racially paranoid critics of broadcasting fired off at radio jazz.

McGurl, then, is half right: Kong does visualize radio, but like the bestial effigies scattered throughout wireless and broadcasting fantasy, he pictures the ultimate stage of the amateur's devolution, in which the doppelganger figures of Bing, the crooner-as-amateur in *Sing, Bing, Sing,* and the gorilla that acts out Bing's id, reunite in the form of a larger-than-life jazz beast. This identity expresses itself most intriguingly through the resistance of Kong's voice to civilization and the constructs it erects to contain difference. His alinguistic but surprisingly expressive growls and grunts, and the terror his voice strikes in the natives and the crew, cannot be blocked by the wall the natives have built; his roars reach every corner of the island. Indeed, in large measure he is a pictured voice that ducks perpetually out of sight, like the elusive faces that lurked behind black and female radio voices in radio criticism. Before the film reveals him as a visible creature on Skull Mountain, it produces him for the audience via his voice. Eventually the image track marks the bestial threat as black and apelike. But like Chion's acousmêtre, Kong appears only to disappear again in his first scene in New York, roaring from out of frame as press photographers look up at him, longing to take his picture.

Although Noël Carroll cautions against taking *King Kong* too seriously as an allegory about film, he usefully underscores the self-referentiality of such scenes as his screen test of Ann, in which he directs her to scream as she plays with her fingers "like Lillian Gish," and how the film continually reviews itself, directing its spectators how to receive it, whenever Denham refers to events on the island or to Kong himself, who happens to share a name with his film, as nearly indescribable spectacles that will make them all millions: "Holy cow, what a show!" he says as the natives perform their sacrifice ritual, long before Kong appears before the astonished theater crowd in New York.[56] My only disagreement with Carroll's remarkable article on *King Kong* is that I see its self-reflexivity as the hub of the film's media unconscious, an indication of the film's impulse to purge itself of the jazz-radio beast that the cinema had willingly invited in. The voyage of Denham's "moving picture boat" fulfills, in a blatantly allegorical way, the radio fantasy film's goal of taming radio beasts by recording their images as well as "transmitting" their sounds. The gigantic wall the natives have built to protect themselves from him can no more contain him than the private household can block the radio, particularly when a blonde Venus in the form of Ann Darrow (Fay Wray) stands just beyond its confines. Denham, like a slave trader who also happens to be a film director, brings the once-distant black voice to the United States on the boat, importing "black music" in the form of the giant ape that lies tranquilized until his arrival on civilized shores.[57] Kong's importation to New York as a commodity, a "show for your amusement" as Denham puts it, only confirms the lesson this director of ethnographic films should have learned back on Skull Island: the jazz beast is not merely a comical animal that blurts out Jolson lyrics at the drop of a hat but an unrefinable threat to white sexuality and civilization.

When Kong kills scores of his own black "subjects" on the island, the film places their king at the center of an allegory about the white man's burden, in which the civilized must save the savages from their own hearts of darkness lest they destroy themselves and each other. One need only watch Fredi Washington dancing herself to death in a jungle-jazz fever in *Black and Tan Fantasy,* or read the remarks of an Osgood or a Seldes about the need for the West to take the reins of jazz from its black keepers, to see the colonialist implications of Kong's abduction: Denham protects the natives from further harm and in the process secures a mammalian mass cultural goldmine.[58] All he need do is take the monster home in chains to accomplish both ends.

Like *Blonde Venus, King Kong* makes no bones about racializing the jazz-radio beast. It goes without saying that substituting a gorilla for an African or African American body reflects the worst kind of Spencerian Darwinism, in which the evolution of nonwhite races simply stops before they can reach the point where they might civilize themselves.[59] But like Helen-Dietrich's gorilla number, the gorilla figure in *King Kong* and the other films I've mentioned always acknowledges itself, however sublated the acknowledgment may be, as a sign of cultural appropriation as *play,* an expression of curiosity about the strenuously othered other. What happens when the colonizer's cinematic frame traps the other in a beast's body and reduces its actions to silence, goofy violence, or a few words from "My Mammy"? With few exceptions, the cage produces the same narrative result: the revolt of the colonized—and not only that, but also an invitation to the spectator to identify with this object of broadcast colonialism and cinematic imperialism alike. The kinds of resistance pictured by these narratives need not be realistic in the slightest; Jenny Sharpe notes that the "success" of the postcolonial critic depends not only on recognizing the subaltern's speech but also on recognizing that it may be not only "irreducible" but also "irretrievable" to the language of the colonizer.[60] But, as I will show, these gorilla narratives offer culturally colonized spectators a means of resistance, in the forms of anger and the recognition that there's a *media*-generated barrier between them and their colonizers to be resisted in the first place.

Wherever the ape lurks in these films, in fact, not only active spectatorship but also active hostility toward the performance hides behind it, waiting to pounce. At the climax of the cartoon that opens *The King of Jazz,* after a full-out jungle jamboree that reduces the human residents of "darkest Africa" to a kinetic wallpaper of rubbery black bodies slinking in unison far behind the animals, a disgruntled monkey, just soaked by an elephant with a trunkful of pond water, beans Whiteman with a coconut. The blow produces bumps on his victim's head in the shape of the "crown" of the "King of Jazz." It's tempting to see these long, skinny bumps as stigmata, simultaneously the price Whiteman pays for his colonial risks and a manhood dividend that pays off in multiple pink phalluses. That is, this *would* be a tempting reading, if the cartoon portrayed Whiteman's mission as honorable or noble in any way. Instead, it paints Whiteman as the Elmer Fudd of cultural imperialism—a rotund figure of derision armed with a shotgun that flops in front of him in an alarmingly flaccid way. The record he brings back from his cinematic safari is not a sound recording or even a film but a set of scars, a cartoon crown consisting of bruised flesh. This fleeting image, however comical, pictures the possibility of counter-colonial resistance. The offending monkey doesn't care to have the raw material of his home "harvested" to fuel fantasies of cultural imperialism any more than Kong enjoys being harvested himself.

This lesson in jazz geography locates the *authenticity* of sweet, orchestral jazz in the heroic risk that Anglo-American culture takes by appropriating it. Like the angry monkey, hot jazz might turn on its keeper, forcing listeners to hear—and allowing them to enjoy—the voices and talents of African Americans without realizing how much credit they give to an "inferior" race by taking pleasure in it. The informatic intimacy model could thus be broken without broadcaster or listener noticing it, because unwanted "values" would make it into the bourgeois household in coded form through the indissoluble form of jazz itself, which always—or so these films attest—bears the traces of its hot music past. The Whiteman cartoon does not necessarily imply this because of some oppositionality intrinsic to jazz. Rather, the work that early sound cinema does to "master" radio's racial threat cannot escape the contradictions of the other, twin desires these films express: white desire to engage African American identity through jazz and the cinema's desire to capture the thrills of radio listening and make them part of cinematic pleasure, but on Hollywood's own, classical terms.

Rony, however, proposes a tactical response to ethnographic film's world picture, a response that suggests how the jazz-jungle-radio subjects might reverse the one-way channel of Anglo media culture. Ethnographic film accidentally generates a "third eye" that the spectator can appropriate under the radar of the classical gaze that the films construct. This third eye is, effectively, the gaze that the colonized turns back on the colonizer, whether this reversal takes place on the ethnographic screen itself or in the minds of viewers who know the context of the colonized from which the ethnographic image springs. The possibility of this third eye

> turns on a recognition: the other perceives the veil, the process of being visualized as an object, but he returns the glance. The gesture of being frozen into a picturesque [sic] is deflected. In a circulating economy of seeing and representation, there are moments in early ethnographic cinema that halt the flow of the evolutionary narrative: the Historical collapses into the Ethnographic, the Savage parodies the Civilized. (Rony, 213)

The Third Eye's returned gaze resonates with W. E. B. Du Bois's "double consciousness" dilemma but transforms its chilling scrutiny of oneself as both (private) self and (public) Other into an act of resistance (4), allowing the spectator who turns the tables to "see the very process which creates the internal splitting" in the viewing—or listening—subject.

What the coconut-wielding monkey does to Whiteman is enact that splitting in full view. If representation can't literally civilize the jungle, it can mobilize stereotypes to "protect" (white) America from accepting mediated African American voices as anything but lion's roars or monkey's grunts. But showing a monkey making a monkey out of the King, explicitly airing his dissatisfaction with the invader's rule, reverses the cartoon's visualization of film as more successful at media colonization than radio had been. And by giving the monkey the last "word" and pretty clear justification for broadcasting that word in the form of a missile instead of a "Mammy," the cartoon opens a channel for even the Anglo spectator to split into two contradictory subject positions at the same time—well-trained viewer/listener versus unruly amateur—just as the radio-jazz amateur has so often been split in wireless fantasy films since the beginning of the century. Social stability has its merits, but when cultural expropriation exposes itself as a front for spectatorial coercion, somebody has to talk back.

In similar fashion, *Sing, Bing, Sing*'s gorilla, a doppelganger for the positive and playful broadcasting amateur, is less Bing's subterranean opposite than his acknowledged reflection. In terms of their relationships to the white patriarchy, at least, the two figures mirror each other, particularly if we think of them both as playing the role of vanishing media amateur in the age of broadcasting, and teaming up to undermine bourgeois privacy and patriarchy. If Crosby leads the charge for young white bluebirds who are curious about the blackbirds' culture and wouldn't mind a radio that allowed for freer exchange between the home and a more inclusive public sphere (to riff on Bing's number with the Rhythm Boys in *The King of Jazz*), then the gorilla envisions those same black radio voices as righteously malicious—stereotypes that escape their ventriloquists' control by exercising righteous wrath and forming liaisons on the run with a white radio boy who has a similarly unnerving ability to slip free of expectations projected upon him from without. If the audience roots for Bing-as-gorilla to commandeer technology—literally the truck, figuratively the radio—to help the lovers escape (and who in the film's audience would not?) while Bing as Bing does the same—the radio, the airplane—to fulfill his sexual desire, they inevitably root for a mobile "black" identity to undermine the mass cultural patriarchy.[61]

Bing's id-gorilla breaks not just the hermetic seal of the private sphere but the ideological principles that support it, by articulating in the most physical terms not only Crosby's but the daughter's common political cause with the gorilla—her status as just another animal caged in the father's menagerie, a role that Dietrich's love goddess had turned on its head the same year by trading her domestic cage for a gorilla costume that "trapped" her into saying what she really wanted. All this is to say that *Sing, Bing, Sing* makes the ideal of private sphere as protectorate immensely unappealing. The walls of Home are here raised so high that it seems more an isolationist nation with a population of two or a maximum-security prison than the foundation of public subjecthood. In this collaborative revision of minstrelsy, where one lives happily ever after in the public sphere of the ether rather than the private zoo of home, Bing supplies the love, while the gorilla supplies the theft.

But this very act of ventriloquism upends the entire project of purging the beast of radio jazz from the newly classicalized sound cinema's definition of film and its spectatorial address. My favorite such cinematic ventriloquist act of this period is set in a jungle but features no gorillas, only a bona fide puppet that blurts out a few unexpected admissions of its own about the voice-throwing act that radio fantasy films stage again and again. *Africa Speaks . . . English* (Roy Mack, 1932) is a freestanding Vitaphone short that features Charlie McCarthy and his "uncle" Edgar

Bergen as castaways in yet another unspecified jungle. As radio stars who have touched down in "the heart of the African jungle," as Bergen says, their castaway narrative exhumes the aging wireless fantasy that "our" broadcasts would someday act as missionaries, spreading Western culture throughout the world. Like good representatives of the mass culture that spawned them—and indeed, like radio stars who are also good film spectators—they employ their fantasies of black "presence" as fostered by media culture to defend themselves against the other. "I'm pretty well informed" about Africa, says Charlie, "I've seen all the African movies." When Bergen struggles to transmit an SOS on their wireless set, Charlie asks whether they can "get *Amos 'n' Andy* on there," and relentlessly pursues this running joke when the inevitable black natives appear in grass skirts and war paint, calling them "Congorilla" and "the Mills Brothers." To Charlie, as to many of his listeners and viewers, there is no Africa outside the jungle of representation that broadcasting and Hollywood cinema rule side by side.

But the fantasy that virtual travel via radio would keep the West "safe from . . . wild emotions" doesn't stand a chance, at least not in this sound-stage Africa. Charlie and Edgar's plane has crashed, and the natives immediately identify themselves as cannibals. But the masterly joke of the film—much funnier than Charlie's shrill and condescending japes—is that the cannibals have already "consumed" plenty of Western culture: Western education (the cannibals had previously eaten an Oxford professor, whom the lead native, speaking in a comically refined British accent, dubs "the best we ever tasted"); religion (the leader declines to eat Charlie and Edgar because "It's Friday—we only eat fish today!" revealing his apparent conversion to Catholicism as both success and failure, and simultaneously cracking a sacrilegious joke about the cannibalistic overtones of the Eucharist); and an oil-driven economy (the natives have a gas pump which the stranded duo wants to use to refuel their downed plane; we have to wonder whether the pump is planted there as bait for oil-addicted Westerners).

Africa speaks English, all right. Like the puppet who has inadvertently paid them a visit, the natives mouth what an avuncular mass culture industry makes them say. But the "natives" retain their particularity in spite of their "refinement." *Africa Speaks . . . English* reveals that the inculcation of cultural particulars (like eating fish on Friday) has no necessary connection to "civilized" ethics or values. In fact, these trappings can be detached from values altogether, as Homi Bhabha argues in his discussion of the colonized's reading of the colonizer's texts, and incorporated into a patchwork of creolized social rituals just as easily as Westerners appropriated and transformed jazz to fit Western expectations of (mass) culture.[62] Like postmodernist cultural cannibals a few decades later, these ostensibly unwashed heathen have not ingested the body of middle-class mass culture so much as taken bites of the parts they liked, only to use the resulting pastiche to take control of the castaway situation—a control all the more dangerous to the notion of civilization as an informational preserve of Western culture in that it saves the castaways' lives—for now—and is utterly self-assured. The chief, played by black comedian F. E. Miller (who was paired that same year with the infamous Mantan Moreland in a more gratuitously stereotyped Vitaphone short, a bug-eyed and superstitious ghost story called *It's Got Me Again,* also directed by Mack), looks silly in his grass skirt, but his overplayed and skillfully timed performance nearly takes the film away from the irritatingly one-note Charlie.

The scenario undermines the utopianism of cinematic and radiophonic imperialism at the same time, because it admits the possibility of context-dependent consumption, even if its specific images of context and consumption never escape the racist truism that African Americans carried the jungle with them wherever they went. Considering the tangled logic of subject-object overlap these films locate in contaminated colonialists who traipse through contaminated jungle settings, the fact that the mass cultural "body" doing the invading here is a *wooden* body—a body no cannibal could fully consume—is no coincidence. As Bill Brown argues, Charlie McCarthy has a long and rich history as a medium for consciously intercultural subjectivity. Although (painted) white and dressed in a vaudevillian mockery-homage of upper-class New York, Charlie nevertheless speaks only through the intercession of his various masters, doubling for them no matter what color their skin. Charlie's uncanny "life" at the hands of anyone who learns the needed skills animates the possibility of acculturating oneself via mass culture without losing the edge of hybridity and critique that immigrants, including Bergen himself, might find necessary to the project of inscribing themselves, of entrenching themselves against the gravitational pull of American's massive melting pot.[63]

But sound cinema is also a form of ventriloquism, sharing the same perpetual crisis that Edgar Bergen had to deal with constantly (unless, of course, he was "appearing" on the radio): convincing the audience that the image, the "figure" sitting on his knee, is the one doing the talking:

[Synchronized speech] displaces our attention 1) from the technological, mechanical, and thus industrial status of the cinema, and 2) from the scandalous fact that sound films begin as language—the screenwriter's— and not as pure image. . . . The ventriloquist's problem is exactly that of the sound track—how to retain control over the sound while attributing it to a carefully manipulated lifelike dummy with no independent life of its own. Indeed, the ventriloquist's art depends on the very fact which we have found at the heart of sound film: we are so disconcerted by a sourceless sound that we would rather attribute the sound to a dummy or a shadow than face the mystery of its sourcelessness or the scandal of its production by a non-vocal (technological or "ventral") apparatus.[64]

During the transition, sound cinema built the prototype for a future cinema that would make its electrical ventriloquism act the central attraction. It built that prototype not simply with speakers and wires and a projector synchronized to an enormous phonograph but with specific kinds of texts that supported that definition, the shorts programs and musical revue films that basked in the capabilities of the technology. Focusing on the radio and its mythology allowed early sound films to project their own reflexivity onto another medium that was itself institutionally committed to noticing its own artificiality and acknowledging its audience. What we find in Charlie, the failed radio imperialist, is a haphazard, hysterical conglomeration of three failed acts of ventriloquism: first, the throwing of a white radio voice into a black body, hoping to steal its right to animate itself; second, the throwing of the voice of radio fantasy into the cinema, in hopes that radio's connotations of liveness and intimacy would rub off without threatening the unitary message of classical narrative or upending the audience's own fantasy of private voyeurism; and finally, the throwing of a mechanical voice into a lifelike cinematic image. All three ventriloquism acts fail, for the spectator at least, for the same reason: Charlie. His very presence as a dwarfish, cartoon-like puppet outs the other dummy acts as acts, discursive maneuvers that are no longer meant for the spotlight.

The radio fantasy films I've discussed attempt to *contain* hot jazz, the radio, and their own sync-sound ventriloquism tricks. But containment, as Bhabha argues regarding racial stereotypes, requires repeated public performances of the containment process in order to naturalize the boundaries they both presume and produce.[65] In the case of the jazz-jungle films, containment requires staging media reception as an interactive activity over and over only so that blacked-up figures for amateurish sending and receiving—that is, for the production and consumption of jazz—can be scapegoated for the chaos that ensues or be squelched altogether.

The stereotypes mobilized by *King Kong* function to this end, as I have suggested, and further, they imply that sound cinema has mastered this process of containment. Kong's big debut on Broadway does not simply inject another self-reflexive joke into the narrative. In effect, it restages the primal scene of sound film's origins. As Will Hays had done when introducing the first Vitaphone program, Denham introduces what we are about to witness as something never before seen or heard, an astonishing nexus of progress, power, sacrifice, and human ingenuity. And he delivers his introduction from a proscenium that dwarfs him in long shots, interspersed with cut-ins that mimic Hays's introduction to the Vitaphone when Denham looks left and right at the audience of the film as well as the one within it.

As if he senses the disaster of publicness that could break out as a result of presenting not just a pure spectacle but an actual Other for its audience to confront, Denham redoubles his controls over Kong's "performance" with shackles and chains and of course the proscenium itself, the Rubicon between black performance and white reception in *Check and Double Check*. Ever the film director, he does everything in his power to limit the contingency of the event. One of the women in the New York audience expects a Cooper and Schoedsack film featuring "those darling monkeys and tigers and things"; she is clearly a good classical spectator in that she wants the exotic, faraway space to unfurl before her, but only if it's heavily captioned to make its monkeys appear "darling," like Bimbo the flapper-monkey from *Chang*.[66] But she acts disappointed when the usher tells her that this evening's show will be "more in the nature of a personal appearance," and in fact she has a right to be disappointed, for what she gets is neither the narrative she wants nor the live show she doesn't but something other to them both, something that addresses her only *in the nature* of a personal appearance: Kong as the ghost of talkies past, glaring directly into the audience and the camera, roaring his rendition of "you ain't heard nothing" in the form of a prelinguistic roar. It scarcely seems coincidental that behind Denham, caged by the proscenium until the curtain rises to reveal him (Figure 15), stands not "Kong" but a *film*—a rear-projected, pixilated animation like the many projections that appear behind and in front of profilmic figures in the Skull Mountain segment of *King Kong*. Such is the price of mounting an untested medium, it seems; Denham, like the first directors of talkies, must use very noticeable bonds

Figure 15. "Ladies and gentlemen, look at Kong." Frame enlargement from *King Kong* (1933).

to keep the beast in check. Denham's introduction to Kong even summons the ghost of the attractions cinema's self-reflexivity and scopophilia for its own sake, in language that sounds suspiciously like the lead-ins to Smith and Blackton moving picture shows of the 1890s. He promises a "story so strange that no one will believe it. But ladies and gentlemen, seeing is believing. . . . I'm going to show you the greatest thing your eyes have ever beheld. He was a king and a god in the world he knew," Denham bellows, "but now he comes to civilization merely a captive—a show to gratify your curiosity."[67]

The allegorical referent for the chained Kong is a little more specific than just early sound film, however, for the noisy image of the inarticulate monster gets enframed, both visually and discursively, just as black jazz had been framed since the talkies' inception. Cooper and Schoedsack stage Kong precisely as *Black and Tan Fantasy, Check and Double Check, A Rhapsody in Black and Blue,* and *Blonde Venus* had staged their decadent performances. This time, the filmic construction of Kong himself— the two-foot-tall pixilated puppet whose sounds *must* be manufactured and synchronized in postproduction, since he could scarcely offer a "live" performance to record as the cameras rolled—has done half the work of containing him already. The proscenium is a literal prison for the black body and the black voice, but the body in question is the ultimate discursive prison for black jazz, for Kong rolls the bestial, utterly embodied voice and a key icon for jungle monstrosity into the same figure, thus naturalizing the captioning function usually performed in jazz scenes by papier-mâché palm fronds and imitation leopard skin. By placing the gorilla smack in the center of the movie stage-screen, the film underscores Maurice's insight that sound film was founded upon the *presence* of a black body as surely as sweet orchestral jazz, with its overtones of minstrelsy, was founded upon its *absence*.

Kong's stage debut, then, functions as an origin myth of sound film. It also acknowledges the specter of broadcasting that haunted the early talkies. As I've suggested, that ghost gets summoned in several early sound films by way of the dangerous ape, the master trope that symbolically arrests the invisible hordes of invading African Americans for which broadcast hot jazz was supposedly a carrier wave. At the same time, through Denham's efforts as the director of the "film"—or rather, the ethnographic documentary as "live" narrative—within the film, *King Kong* works to contain the radio monster in the same fashion that Hollywood sound engineers contained the distracting aspects of sound: by subordinating all noises to the story. From the moment that he directs Ann to pretend to see a giant monster and "scream for your life"—foreshadowing the performance that Cooper and Schoedsack demanded of her for the remainder of the film—Denham is determined to impose a classical Hollywood plot on the proceedings. He blames his "public—bless 'em," for demanding that even documentaries must generate romantic stories, but he stays on task because he, too, is a creature of cinema, a mouthpiece for the institutional desire to stuff the cinema of attractions back into the cave from which the Vitaphone accidentally called it out. When the photographers begin "shooting" Kong in New York, their flashbulbs ablaze, Denham bellows, "He [Kong] thinks you're attacking the girl," and as Kong lies dead at his feet after falling from the Empire State Building, his captor intones, "It wasn't the airplanes. 'Twas Beauty killed the Beast," fulfilling the expectation set by the "Arabian proverb" from the film's opening intertitles. If the plot of *King Kong* kills Kong with classical retribution for wrecking the El, pulling people out of buildings, and kidnapping Ann twice, it's only following the script that Denham has imposed upon his prize.

Indeed, in the figure of Denham, the jazz musician as bumbling imperialist on display in *The King of Jazz*'s animated jungle transforms into the sound film director as tyrant. Unlike Whiteman, the amateur bwana, Denham is a professional, a pro explorer and a pro filmmaker, modeled after codirector Cooper himself, and a daredevil who would risk anything for his moving picture—scores of shipmates, tons of explosives, and even the pleasure of the I-told-you-so moment that should accompany the voyeuristic, racist pleasure of showing what "really" lies at the heart of radio jazz, as *Chang* and *Congorilla* had offered before *King Kong*. Denham has objectified Ann as well, having picked her up for the price of a sandwich and coffee on the streets of Depression-era New York. When Denham directs her, he does so as if he were indeed Griffith directing Gish, filling in the "soundtrack" with his own narrative commands: "Scream, Ann! Scream for your life!" Kaja Silverman argues that male desire for the female voice in classical film amounts to a desire to reduce it to screams that offer no affront to his linguistic mastery.[68] I would only add that Denham reduces Ann's voice to screams specifically in the interest of flexing the narrational power of the camera over any "wild beast"—vulnerable woman or jazz monster—that might cross its path and attempt to express itself. Denham epitomizes the classical imperative to force cause-and-effect narrative on both female voice and black voice, and manipulates them both like the pixilated puppets they are in profilmic reality (Ann as often as Kong, at least when the Kong-puppet has "her" in its clutches).

Denham's narrative "interpretations," however, undercut the objectivity promised by ethnographic ventriloquism, and indeed mock the power of narrative to restrain the talkies from stirring up their spectators. To say that Kong thinks the flashbulbs are "attacking the girl" seems a forced reading at best, after we've seen Kong spend several hours on Skull Island fending off invaders with flashing rifles—why wouldn't his roars at the shutterbugs represent his desire to protect *himself*? And as he lies dead and the crowd behind Denham grinds out his "Beauty killed the Beast" line just before the final fade to black, I, at least, no longer try to stop myself from grumbling at the screen, "No, 'twas *Denham* killed the beast." Had the shyster ethnographer not chased him down for a trophy, shot him with gas bombs, and dragged him across the ocean and onto the stage, Kong and his hundreds of human victims would have survived the film.

In addition, Denham's voyage calls the slave trade to mind a little too easily, right down to the ship, the return he expects on his backers' investment, and the "auction block" on which Kong appears on stage, in chains, at the film's climax (Snead, 21). This resonance might reduce even a conservative white audience's fledgling identification with Denham (though it would surely have warmed the hearts of white racists to see the black/jazz monster dispatched this way in an age of race riots and lynchings) and can hardly help but increase our sympathy for Kong, who behaves more like a well-meaning if irritable child than a monster and exhibits both gentle curiosity and heroism as he saves Ann from threat after threat. James Snead persuasively argues that the film fragments the spectator's sympathies almost to the point of incoherence: Denham (as narrator figure if not an attractive hero), Ann (as victim), Jack (as Ann's love interest and accidental action hero), and Kong himself, who never asked for any of this and treats Ann more gently than Jack does, however strongly the attraction plays out a miscegenistic fantasy of black virility and lust. While Snead comments that Kong's sensitivity suggests that he has "absorbed all aspects of otherness: not only the black male, but the female," he also behaves, as Carroll argues, much more like a kid playing superhero, saving Ann from pterodactyls without a thought to his own safety, than a savage rapist unable to contain his libido.[69]

And contrary to Denham's descriptions of Kong only in terms of bestial lust, destructiveness, and commodification, the "monster" shows enough sentience to become curious about life—not physical life but cinematic life, specifically the use of synchronized sounds to imbue the illusion of life upon Kong, Denham, and all the other cinematic ventriloquist's dummies who populate the film. After killing the tyrannosaurus rex, he gingerly plays with its jaws while making low grunts that seem to express curiosity, as if he expected sounds to come out and is fascinated by its silence (Figure 16). By fiddling with the puppet, he mimics the profilmic manipulations that animator Willis O'Brien and sound designer Murray Spivack had performed on both the dinosaur and Kong himself. Unwittingly (though O'Brien and Spivack themselves could surely have been thinking of nothing else while assembling this scene), Kong is also teasing the classical audience with the reality of sync sound—that voices do *not* naturally exude from moving cinematic lips. The puppet is dead unless electrified by the mechanism of sound film. This is Kong's coronation as king of a dying civilization in the classical era—call it the Lost World of Astonishment—a ritual in which a puppet fools with a puppet, wonders at what makes it talk, and invites the audience to contemplate these questions along with him. He republicizes the cinema by begging the question of where those noises *really* come from, and not just in technological terms but also in terms of the mass media's ventriloquisms of difference.

Figure 16. Kong experiments with ventriloquism. Frame enlargement from *King Kong*.

But Kong's lesson in ventriloquism doesn't stop with the dinosaur dummy, for *King Kong* pulls blackness out of sync with its sound film stereotypes, too. Charlie McCarthy's African detour provides the necessary groundwork for understanding how this works in Kong's case. In *Africa Speaks ... English,* Charlie does not wear his signature top hat, apparently because it has migrated to the cannibal chief's head instead. Dressing the "native" in the puppet's clothes pulls back the curtain that conceals the ethnographic ventriloquist of (sound) cinema and shows the cannibal characters for what they are: a white fantasy about the black voice and what "it" has to say, which *Africa Speaks!* (Walter Futter, 1930), the ethnographic film from which this short takes its title, portrayed as little more than noise.

Bhabha argues that "the stereotype is at once a stereotype and a shadow. By acceding to the wildest fantasies (in the popular sense) of the colonizer, the stereotyped Other reveals something of the 'fantasy' (as desire, defence) of that position of mastery."[70] F. E. Miller and his fellow "cannibals" in *Africa Speaks ... English* expose the desire lodged in broadcasting fantasy that the will of the non-Westerner might be mastered by (mass) cultural imperialism; but their frank seizing of the means of

ventriloquization marks their accomplishment as a bit more radical than
the structural revelation that Bhabha discusses. These natives from central casting have colonized, if not the colonizers, then at least the process
of their own colonization. By appropriating the trappings of civilization
to capture and charm their guests, they perform "Westernness" as high
farce. In particular, their exaggerated social graces satirize the radio he-
gemonists' expectation that the darker races would inevitably trade their
culture for civilization, when in fact they have kept both and now wear the
sign of their puppethood, the top hat, as a crown that signifies their self-
actualization, the triumph of the speaking subject over the fantasy that
radio will ultimately speak *them*.[71]

In a serious drama, ethnographic film, or adventure narrative, the natives might have stood in for the captive radio listener, as the pygmies do
in *Congorilla* when they dance obediently to the records Osa has imported
from civilization to give them a dose of modernity. They might also have
functioned as polite spectators of sound film, for Charlie the dummy wedges
cinematic ventriloquism into this equation as yet another soother of savage beasts. Instead, however, it is Charlie—the radio voice who now finds
himself reified, stuck in the enemy's territory like a film dropped from the
sky rather than a voice thrown safely from Radio City—who is held captive
to what his unbound, African (American) audience wants *him* to consume.

If King Kong(orilla) is the real king of jazz and prince of puppets,
at the moment he works the jaws of the T-rex, he is also the last of the
radio-cinema amateurs—a radio beast in the manner of the rogue science fiction hero and part-time antman with whom this chapter began,
Myles Cabot. That is, Kong pictures the radio body as a half-othered white
amateur—both sympathetic and dangerous, humanlike and ape, thrilling and destructive—gone native. The technological feats performed by
the small boys of wireless symbolized the future of radio colonialism and
an alarming surplus of independent voices at the same time. In similar
fashion, Kong, the savage beast who nevertheless has every right to sing
the blues, tinkers with an avatar for the technology that makes him speak
and thus refers the film's spectator to sound film as machinery, no more
natural than Kong himself. The review of *King Kong* in *Variety* cuts no
corners in expressing how obviously its special effects are just that: "There
are times when the plot takes advantage of its imaginative status and goes
too far. On these occasions the customers are liable to laugh in the wrong
way." While the reviewer says that "the picture, as a whole, got them," he
makes it clear that what "got" them was not the strength of its story:

King Kong is "chiefly an exhibition of studio and camera technique, but packs an entertainment punch. . . . It seemed that . . . a few details were too strong to swallow." Once "accustomed to the phoney atmosphere" and the "machine-like movements" of the monsters, audiences, "while not believing it . . . will wonder how it's done."[72]

A bad boy amateur framed for taking vocal liberties, guilty of fostering disbelief and distraction in the talkies' spectators, and eventually executed for it, Kong makes his final stand atop the Empire State Building, gesticulating like an anthropomorphic radio antenna in the thick of the ether that carries his roars. In the end, of course, *King Kong*'s directors complete director Denham's fairy-tale narrative by momentarily breaking into the diegesis and shooting Kong down themselves.[73] But before Kong falls, he rains radical acts of uncivil disobedience upon the "civilization" that hoped to exploit him. Just before the curtain opens, Denham announces, "Look at Kong"—but soon the audience is forced to do a lot more than simply look. The barrage of photographic flashes sends Kong into such a rage that he tears away his chains and rushes the audience. Once he has torn himself down from the "screen," he turns Broadway into a virtual Skull Island, wringing the neck of the elevated train as if it were a charging stegosaurus. True to the radio critics' worst fears, he then turns his energies to penetrating the private sphere—in the flesh. Peering through a window into a woman's boudoir, he pulls her out and drops her to her death before discovering Ann at last (Figure 17).

This scene tells us much more about the chanciness of the transition to sound for the film industry than does, say, *Singin' in the Rain*. Letting Kong jump from the stage into the crowd sets up another ritual execution of a too-live cinematic experience that his primal body marks as much more behind the technological times—and thus all the more worthy of extermination—than "Prologue." His act of breaking the fourth wall also recalls—in an unsurprisingly racializing way—the recent history, and for Hollywood the unpleasant memory, of black jazz musicians playing unsanctioned hot music during silent features in Chicago's African American theaters instead of the narrational accompaniment that white viewers would have heard in "their" picture palaces.[74] But precisely as in *Show of Shows*, Kong's escape recognizes, along with the virtual liveness of the early talkies, the *literal* liveness of the *crowd*. Suddenly they have to act, interact, escape themselves—and listen to Kong's warning instead of the platitudes barked by his unasked-for mouthpiece.

Of course, the film's racial hysteria will only allow this return of

Figure 17. Kong discovers Ann (Fay Wray). Frame enlargement from *King Kong*.

interactive cinema to be staged as a mob scene, but by doing so it only admits what it fears most: unpredictable responses, even before a redefined version of film in which the producers controlled both the image and its accompanying sounds. *King Kong* here casts the new technology as a monster of the sort its keepers neither understood nor anticipated: a monstrous technology for turning spectatorial gold into film industry lead, that is, for turning happily antisocial, classical spectators (or so the industry worked to position them) into a theater filled with Uncle Joshes of all ages and both genders, embodying themselves as individuals and as masses by running like hell from a "screen" that no longer casts a spell of informatic intimacy. Kong's rage at being photographed within the film insists upon the right of spoken subjects to speak for themselves, against all efforts to manipulate their identity through image or narrative; on the lower frequencies, to paraphrase Ralph Ellison, he speaks not only for himself but for the spectators as well.

　　King Kong is, finally, a staged and choreographed battle between two conflicting registers of signification in the sound cinema, not fidelity and narrative—the dueling paradigms that *King Kong*'s actively narrational musical score attempts to synergize—so much as sociological interactivity and informatic intimacy. Interactivity is associated in *King Kong* with spectacle, with counterproductivity, and with a dangerous kind of radio. But this is surely a more interesting radio to *watch* than the only other radio I have found in the film, the police radio that announces that Kong has climbed the Empire State Building and bows out with a phrase that admits its relative impoverishment: "That is all" (Figure 18). This radio is a dead ringer for the freestanding "civilian" tuners that inhabited parlors all over America, but all it offers is what classical cinema and its recording technology siblings had promised would protect against monstrous media interactivity since *The Story the Biograph Told* and *Traffic in Souls*: surveillance. And in this case, surveillance leads to the death of the only character imbued with enough personality to make us sorry to see him die, a fate earned by committing crimes he would never have imagined had he been allowed to chart his own path.

If the classical cinema worked to retain Hollywood's authority over film interpretation, it still conjured the *image* of that contingency of otherness-as-reception through the many fantasies of jazz production, retrieval, and reception I've discussed. None conjures this image more open-endedly than *King Kong,* where Kong, the object-subject of Western refinement, vocalizes his abjection under the radar of narrative, as both black film

Figure 18. Radio to spectators: "That is all." Frame enlargement from *King Kong.*

performers and all spectators, no matter what race, could only do at risk of being silenced by the usher, by other spectators, and—of course—by the film. The conscious intermedial "lesson" of all this, regarding the identity of cinema, is product differentiation. RKO's representation of Kong does not criticize *radio* per se as atavistic. Rather, it warns against the discursive mixture of a historically private medium, broadcasting, with a historically public medium, cinema. For Carroll, the very term "monster" implies interstitiality; like Frankenstein's monster or the Creature from the Black Lagoon, there is no parent and no offspring (though, as it turns out, both *Kong* and Kong gave birth to a sequel, *Son of Kong*, the same year *King Kong* did boffo box office). As Rony has added in her own discussion of *King Kong*, the monster's "existence threatens cultural boundaries. . . . The Ethnographic [subject/object] is seen as monstrous because he or she is human and yet radically different."[75] But while Rony argues that "monstrosity is essentially visual," a claim that jibes with the root it shares with the verb *to demonstrate*, it is Kong's monstrous *voice* that threatens the perceptual, technological, and cultural borders the film would like to presume between (white) human and (black) animal, screen and spectator, and (black) image and (externally supplied) sound.

If we take it as a crossroads text where all these problems of sound-era border crossing smash against each other, *King Kong* urges the viewer to consume this noisy image of "Sound Cinema, Eighth Wonder of the World" as proof of the talkies' evolution since 1926. *King Kong* is no crude beast like the live gorilla-minstrel show at its climax, whose star roars his defiance and bursts out of the auditorium and into the streets. At the same time, *King Kong* is a cautionary tale from the home of Radio Pictures to the rest of the industry, a warning that too much radio discourse might awaken an exhibition paradigm in which every space of strictly rule-bound public activity, from theater to elevated train, becomes undeniably public space. And, as Kong's civilian victims would say if they had not themselves been silenced, public interactivity can *hurt*. This fantasy of the return of early cinema as civic disaster, a natural force that knows no civilization, acknowledges a much more benign signified of that pain, but only by acknowledging its life and death consequences. This signified is a self-consciously interactive arena of spectatorship in which an unofficial public could argue, playfully or seriously, about the stereotypes of African American images and voices that *King Kong* undercuts in the act of maintaining them—a spectatorship that resembles the sort invited by early ethnographic films as described by Alison Griffiths, in which viewers were "instructed" in the wiles of the cultures depicted by stentorian lecturers but were never entirely certain which parts of the travelogue were "real" and which were staged.[76] The Hollywood anxiety buried deepest beneath the audiovisual cacophony of *King Kong,* the sensation that still compels viewers, despite its failing as a classical—and even an ethnographic— ventriloquist's turn, is that perhaps spectators already interact with one another along those painful lines and may do so no matter how hermetically this quasi-classical film tries to seal off its reception.

The public's engagement with sound film, jungle films from *Africa Speaks . . . English* to *King Kong* suggest, does not necessarily end in the spectator's head any more than had the consumption of silent film. Each spectator takes the film back to her own jungle and remakes it as she will, just as surely as she consumes radio outside the spatial parameters that regiment reception. Not even sync sound and the effigy execution of "live prologue" can silence the restless poacher of cinematic meaning. The foundational ventriloquist act that *King Kong* exposes, once it has revealed all the others, is sound cinema's disguise as a media institution whose products preconsume themselves via their classical, textual construction and the removal of distractions from the viewing experience. Under the disguise lurks a vision of precisely the transnational—and more to the point, national—audience that Hollywood feared most, one that made up the meaning of its texts as it went along, imbricating a naive and "faithful" reading of the colonialist's broadcasts with their own exigencies. If the spectator begins to think about the puppet as a puppet, she has begun to reconceive the leviathan ventriloquist puppet of cinema as something that lets you tell someone—many someones—something. This possibility is structural only; no content is suggested, no guarantee made of the effect reconsideration might have, if any. But the idea of collective control over the means of expressive production is also, always, a media fantasy with the potential to jolt the ossified conventions of the medium back to imaginative life.

King Kong is nothing more or less than just such a fantasy—an example of the monstrous sort of sound film that the movie itself fears the most. Ironically, it also presages the action movies of the New Hollywood, peppered as it is with attractions "numbers" that, for all the narrative glue that strings them together, invite as much spectatorial distraction as the song slides in *The King of Jazz.* No matter how diligently early sound film worked to contain its radiophilic connotations, it seems, there were as many new kinds of amateurs waiting to be born in the theater as there were as-yet-unknown media waiting to be grafted onto film.

The Glass Web: Unraveling the Videophobia of Postwar Hollywood Cinema

Only MGM had an official mascot, but by the 1950s all the major studios had adopted television as a scapegoat for their economic misfortunes. So strong was television's power as an icon in the corporate imagination that Harry Warner issued a short-lived but passionate edict that TV must never appear in a Warner Bros. film.[1] TV fantasy films of the fifties portray television as an electrical alchemist that transmutes objective reality into lies. Sometimes the lies are little and white, as in Billy Wilder's *The Apartment* (1960), where lonely C. C. Baxter (Jack Lemmon) waits eagerly with his TV dinner for *Grand Hotel* to begin, only to have his spectatorial coitus infinitely interrupted by the sponsor. Other fifties TV fantasies "expose" more dire prevarications. In Jack Arnold's 3-D film noir *The Glass Web* (1953), a murderous TV writer (Edward G. Robinson) uses his true-crime reenactment show to frame his cowriter (John Forsythe) for a killing. Although Robinson takes the rap in the end when he accidentally admits his guilt in front of a live camera, TV's sensationalism and air of being "on the scene" do damage that cannot be easily contained. Throughout the film the viewers at home believe that the "Crime of the Week" show has given them more in-depth information about the murder than any other source. To them, Forsythe is guilty until proven innocent.

As media fantasies go, however, videophobic films like *The Glass Web* came later in the "new" medium's history than the films I have discussed in previous chapters. Excited technophiles speculated about far-seeing machines before the first moving picture cameras rolled, and researchers had some success with mechanical image transmission (that is, using moving parts rather than electronic scanning) and rudimentary facsimile transmission by the early 1920s. RCA began promising electronic TV by the early 1930s and kicked off the medium's emergent era in earnest by unveiling a working model at the 1939 World's Fair in New York. Dozens of books and many more popular press articles about television were published throughout the 1920s and 1930s. The opening montage of a television fantasy film from this period, *Murder by Television* (Clifford Sanforth, 1935), displays four shots of piles of such articles, followed by a shot of the door of the "C. M. P. Television Corporation" around which the narrative revolves, as if to position the film as the latest in a series of purely speculative but invigorating prognostications. From its first scene, which takes place behind the closed doors of C. M. P., *Murder by Television*'s characters discuss TV as if it were indeed worth killing for; corporations already spy on one another in the race to file the first working patent.

If this film is any indication, the struggle for media identity begins in earnest in the thirties rather than the fifties. By 1953, the year that *The Glass Web* was released, both Hollywood and its audience knew the competitor all too well. The total number of TV sets owned in the United States jumped by more than 1200 percent between 1947 and 1948. The major studios could do little to shape its institutional future, for TV had been *labeled,* as Lisa Gitelman would put it—that is, granted a resilient and function-defining title—much more rapidly than radio.[2] Christopher Anderson writes that Warner Bros.' "legendary antagonism toward television did not begin until this moment [circa 1953]—when it became clear there was no hope of integration on any terms other than those dictated by the networks" (Anderson, 45). Thanks to Federal antitrust suspicion of the film industry and the FCC's willingness to maneuver radio broadcasters into the driver's seat, the institutional identification of television as a homebound medium preceded its appearance in the American living room: "With the exception of theater television . . . nonbroadcast uses of television did not receive general public recognition or debate after the 1920s."[3] Without a truly speculative media fantasy culture to engage, TV fantasy films of the 1950s provide little insight into Hollywood-TV relations except that the film industry had been reduced to taking jabs at an enemy that had already won the war to define television.

Or so it would seem. Certainly Hollywood saw TV as an economic competitor, particularly after 1954, when NBC and CBS first turned profits. Negative portrayals of television, however, are not simple expressions of Hollywood's abhorrence for the medium. Most of the studios profited from leasing or outright selling theatrical releases for broadcasting, and they converted their B-movie units into factories for producing filmed programs—practices without which Hollywood might not have survived the downward spiral of ticket sales that began in 1947–48.[4] Videophobic fantasy films thus could not have been intended merely as anti-TV propaganda. What industrial interests, then, might the fifties films express? What continuities and disjunctures in the history of media fantasy did they access, and how does the emergence of TV as Hollywood subject matter develop into the videophobia expressed by *All That Heaven Allows, Network, Poltergeist, Videodrome, The Truman Show,* and *EdTV*? Answering these questions will get us closer to understanding Hollywood's vitriolic response to a similarly contentious media wave—the rise of interactive digital media—under similarly compromised circumstances for the film industry, and to determining the functions performed by videophobic films in the endless process of defining the classical Hollywood cinema.

Surprisingly, this line of questioning has been followed only spottily up to now. Drawing on arguments made by Carolyn Marvin, Colin MacCabe, and others on the ideological functions of media fantasy, for example, Anderson writes that films like *A Face in the Crowd* (Elia Kazan, 1957) "construct a preeminent position [over television] for the cinema" by representing the medium's "epistemological superiority over television," that is, "reporting" (in fictionalized form, of course) on the crass gambit to turn viewers into consumers that goes on behind the video cameras (Anderson, 18). In *A Face in the Crowd,* Andy Griffith plays an opportunist who turns his hillbilly "Lonesome Rhodes" persona into a goldmine for his equally opportunistic sponsors. One scene portrays Rhodes preaching to his potential sponsors, shaping his rhetoric to appeal to down-home "common sense" while making an unremarkable over-the-counter analgesic sound like an elixir more potent than the Fountain of Youth.

The *epistemological* superiority of cinema over television: this provocative phrase deserves to be unpacked theoretically as well as historically, for it denotes the ideological dimension of *A Face in the Crowd*'s intermedia gambit, a branding of cinema that ties spectatorial point of view to culturally and socially informed knowledge of the new medium at a moment when television threatened to redefine the practices of audiovisual spectatorship in general.

As Anderson writes regarding television "exposés" like MGM's *It's Always Fair Weather* (Gene Kelly and Stanley Donen, 1955), where a TV variety host proves to be less of a humanitarian than she appears, "the movie industry has a stake in differentiating the two media" despite its eventual position as a mere supplier of programming to TV. Hollywood needed to inflate the cinema's "intrinsic" value and justify charging admission for entertainment when TV appeared to offer it for nothing. Such antitelevision tracts, then, function as fictional investigative reporting: "As cinema spectators . . . moviegoers are able to recognize [TV's] dissimulations because the movie narratives provide privileged access to the characters' motives, revealing the hidden schemes that are masked by commercial television's obsession with surface detail."[5]

I would like to work a slightly different angle of Anderson's "epistemological superiority" concept by suggesting that Hollywood media fantasy defined film in the emergent age of TV much as it had in the 1930s, during the emergent age of broadcasting—not simply by stressing film's technological differences from its new rival but by constructing television as a technological-institutional nexus of domesticity and liveness against which film's public address would have to construct itself anew yet again. In fact, a number of the "TV fantasies" I will discuss in this chapter are as devoid of television sets as Harry Warner wanted all his films to be. If studios were so frustrated by the early fifties that they hesitated even to display the new technology for fear of accidentally advertising it, during TV's truly emergent decade—the 1940s—its absence was equally significant. Throughout the forties, and particularly as World War II ended, Hollywood and the radio industry wrestled each other for economic control of the new audiovisual medium that Americans had considered imminent since the late nineteenth century. During that period, as the major studios stumbled over the obstacles radio and the FCC placed between Hollywood and the video future, films did not shout televisual dreams and worries; they whispered them. Instead of using the new technology as a rudder to steer their explorations of media discourse, forties TV fantasy films approach television from the other direction. That is, they begin by exploring the *discourses* associated with TV and thereby construct it as a discursive phantom, made present only by the variations on the themes that dominated public debates about television: the rise of postwar consumer culture, the economic and political uncertainty of the postwar era, and the shifting relationship between the domestic sphere and public life.

Film noir, the cycle of films in which hard-boiled detectives, icy criminals, and deceitful femmes fatales sneak through Expressionist city streets, will be my tracer bullet for discerning Hollywood's screened responses to the emergence of television. Many critics describe film noir's fatalistic tone as an expression of anxieties that postwar American culture could only admit to itself in its movies, via encoded visuals and knowing silences. Technology, when it is discussed at all as an ingredient in this cycle, generally gets characterized as an externalization of the Oedipal undercurrents fueling noir's full-blown gender wars. Take, for example, the moment in Billy Wilder's *Double Indemnity* (1944) when Phyllis Dietrichson (Barbara Stanwyck) attempts to start the getaway car after her co-conspirator Walter Neff (Fred MacMurray) has strangled her husband. Frank Krutnik reads the unresponsive car as an agent of the Lacanian Law of the Father and argues that Walter's unyielding drive toward his own doom, a drive summarized by his comparison of the murder plot to a railway journey "straight down the line," signifies his need for assurance that the Law of the Father has retained its potency.[6] J. P. Telotte interprets such mechanical and metaphorical breakdowns as allegories for a grander pessimism regarding the possibility of productive communication in a culture atomized by the war.[7] From this perspective, *The Glass Web*'s representation of television as an agent of fate could be read as another noir manifestation of the long arm of the patriarchal Law, a story in which the villain, try as he might to "crook the wheel" (to borrow a phrase from Walter Neff) of the justice system using his TV show, finds himself cornered by the same technology he used to do the crooking. As Henry Hayes (Robinson) holds Don Newell (Forsythe) at gunpoint and prepares to kill him for what he knows, a live TV camera happens to catch him in the act of describing all his crimes. At the moments when noir crooks look most likely to get away with their crimes, technology conveniently misfires; or, to put it better, technology dutifully does the bidding of its economic and political masters, like any good agent of the Law.

While such interpretations have helped shed a great deal of light on postwar gender relations, and in particular Americans' backlash against the same women the government beckoned to the factories during World War II, film noir's recurrent images of desperate people wrestling with machines have something to say about a different sort of historical struggle. Edward Dimendberg describes technology and its uses, whether criminal or official, as crucial aspects of film noir that resonate with transformations in consumer culture after the war: "the culture of late modernity . . . explored throughout the film noir cycle is perhaps best understood as a response to the new experiences of space, time, and social control brought about by the convergence of cinema with television, the automobile, and surveillance technologies."[8] To this I would add that one of the respondents to those new experiences is the film industry. The *technological* changes in exhibition that we often think of as Hollywood's initial responses to TV, such as anamorphic widescreen, 3-D, and stereo sound, actually represent the culmination of a decade-long rivalry between cinema and television. That rivalry began on *institutional* grounds rather than technological ones, as a struggle between Hollywood and broadcasting for the right to define television in the public imagination. The ultimate stakes were even higher, for Hollywood's very construction of the spectating subject of moving-image media was at stake. The "media noirs" I will discuss express the parameters of this struggle in terms that should be familiar from the media fantasy films of earlier decades: debates over the concepts of liveness, intimacy, and interactivity, inflected by the rise of consumerist culture and by growing concerns about the fortification of the social and spatial boundaries that separated private experience from public life—concerns that Hollywood shared with its dwindling audience, and that it used both the idea and the fact of television to ponder. Seen through the lens of media fantasy, Walter Neff and his cohorts in technological crime represent the new, postwar face of the media amateur.

Moving Images Come Home

The domestic installation of television was as much an ideological process as a literal one. Initially, television was expected to become a public mode of information dissemination. Although image transmission was impractical until the 1920s, as I discussed in previous chapters, the lifelike movements of moving pictures fulfilled some of the expectations produced by the contemporary fantasy of electrical image transmission, while the rambunctious spectatorial conventions that leached into moving picture shows from fairs and vaudeville helped buttress the impression that the experience was interactive.

In its first years on the market, television acquired a public character to complement its literal liveness. Anna McCarthy has shown that, in the mid-1940s, bar patrons experienced TV as an organizer of social space, rather than as a domestic apparatus that addressed the individual directly, like the radio.[9] McCarthy's observation suggests an alternate future for television as a public communications device that, in a saloon setting, might have provided (and perhaps still does) a sociologically interactive outlet for the experience of a "flow" of distinct images, sounds, and morphemes that television provides in any venue, whether public or private.[10] The attempts by the Paramount-Scophony collaboration and other Hollywood initiatives to bring "theater TV" to the picture palaces also point to this future that never happened. The hybrid, nonstandard-ized theater TV technologies might well have caused radio and cinematic reception practices to mingle with one another in still stranger ways than they did during the transition to sound.[11]

As far as media fantasy films of the thirties were concerned, television was best understood as a subset of film. In the Paramount short *The Musical Doctor* (Ray Cozine, 1932), for example, infamous radio crooner "Dr." Rudy Vallée turns on a monitor in the operating room of his hospital and views the effects of his voice on multiple male patients who need his soothing jazz to heal them (Figure 19). No cameras or other apparatus are shown; as Richard Koszarski points out about other films of the thir-ties that feature televised performances, the images seem to have been "grabbed right out of the air."[12]

But admitting that any machine beyond the cinematic apparatus was needed here would undermine a key fantasy underwriting informatic inti-macy: that one experiences something at the same moment that the screen

Figure 19. Rudy Vallée in *The Musical Doctor* (1932).

figure experiences it. For classical cinema to portray an instantaneous audiovisual medium always entails at least a bit of risk, for to do so is to peg instantaneity as the property of a *different* medium, some "not-film" technology, and thereby undermine the fetishistic liveness that spectators attribute to the film they watch. *The Musical Doctor,* however, portrays "television" viewing as so similar to film spectatorship that, rather than undercutting the illusion of shared time between viewer and screen, the "Televisor" finale affirms it. Whatever kind of television this Televisor is, it constructs the radio crooner Vallée as an empowered film spectator who looks on from afar with the distanced eye of the expert. "Visualizing" listenership within the public (health) edifice of the hospital mitigates the threat of radio jazz in general and of crooning in particular. Although these patients are men, and thus might bring to mind the perverse crooner-listener relationship envisioned by *The Big Broadcast,* they lie in clinical beds, their relationship to their "doctor-crooner" legitimated by the clear positions taken by speaker and listener within the institution. By rendering camera technology invisible while replicating the hierarchal relationship of speaker to spoken, *The Musical Doctor* manages to produce a strong sense that what film does is already a kind of TV—one that both grants voice and copresence to the spectator, and protects him from an apparent epidemic of male fragility.

The catch to this reading of the film's training function for the classical viewer, of course, is the film's reversal of classical *seer* and classical *seen,* in which the *viewer* (Vallée) owns the voice that makes meaning. But in fact this televisual allegory breaks classical subjectivity into its component parts, its active and passive elements. If the enraptured patients mirror the quietude of the ideal audience, Doctor Vallée reflects the actively engaged, informatically intimate dimension of the spectator position, secretly monitoring others' sleep with a privileged but sympathetic eye. If we restitch these halves back together into the whole subject position that the film idealizes through Vallée, we have a telling image of a self-scrutinizing spectator, his position as overseer enforced by his identification with the ultimate overseer—the camera—on the one hand and by his identification with multiple spectators who constitute the separate but equal space of exhibition on the other. The patients are edited together by lap dissolves into an organized mass, like spectators who each inhabit their own well-demarcated spaces, the close-up headshots in the frame-within-the-frame. The sequence declares Vallée the überspectator, a mirror for the camera's powers of seeing that both materializes the audience as a public united in perceptual mastery and dematerializes their presence to each other.

Such tactics cheer on both media at once, particularly film, which looks more up to date whenever it draws such flattering comparisons between itself and a thoroughly modern medium. When television plays narrative roles that resemble the wireless amateurs' behavior, however, the rules of the fantasy change dramatically. While Koszarski remarks that "television's dark side" was primarily aired in pulp serials like *Flash Gordon,* which "plac[ed] it in [an] arsenal of evil assembled by science run wild" (132), A-films imagined plenty of sinister types exploiting the untested medium for selfish or demeaning purposes. Fritz Lang's *Metropolis* (1927) portrays Joh Frederson, the Master of Metropolis, communicating with his plant chief over a two-way television transmitter the size of a phone booth and operating fairly intricate (though purely fanciful) controls. A decade later, Chaplin's *Modern Times* (1936) parodies Frederson's surveillance over his plant when a monumental image of the boss's face appears on a giant screen in the men's washroom to interrupt the Tramp's smoke break.

Unlike *The Musical Doctor,* these films portray television as a futuristic intercommunication medium like the wireless was expected to be. By portraying it as a surveillance device, they manage the difficult trick of granting both TV and film the power to look in secret, while avoiding the pitfall of constructing TV as a rival entertainment medium. Indeed, the spectator might take umbrage at the image of an instantaneous audiovisual medium that makes her the object of the gaze rather than subject of the gaze and object of fictional address; one can scarcely identify pleasurably with the Tramp's position as an overworked, neurasthenic laborer whom the stern face on the enormous, filmlike screen will not allow even to smoke. As Garrett Stewart sees it, Chaplin uses this screen to excoriate the talkies he so despised: "such an abyssal effect as the [company] president's talking screen is stationed not to replicate but to *throw into relief* the superannuated purity of the film as a whole."[13] The thrill of simultaneity loses much of its attraction when the machine threatens to reverse the classical sightline and discover the viewer peeping through the keyhole.

These films exemplify an overarching trend in Hollywood film's intermedia functions that seems especially prominent during the emergence of TV: when a new medium provides simultaneous access to other people— that is, when media interactivity is cast as a *technological* difference, an advance over film's merely photographic simulation of liveness—Hollywood responds by foregrounding one of its own *institutional* aspects, in this case the prophylactic voyeurism enjoyed by the cinematic spectator. Privacy-in-public and the pastness of classical storytelling implicitly protect the viewer from being discovered while enjoying the privileges of oversight and judgment. Other TV fantasy films of the 1930s do not necessarily disparage video surveillance, but they similarly pit surveillance against entertainment as functions that properly belong to television and film, respectively. In *Murder by Television* and *Trapped by Television* (Del Lord, 1936), inventors introduce TV as an entertainment technology. The content of *Murder by Television*'s inaugural broadcast is a vocal solo performed by the inventor's daughter, while in *Trapped By Television,* a starry-eyed inventor (Lyle Talbot) and his devoted partner cart their television camera to a baseball game in an effort to prove its viability.[14] And viable it is—so much so that the inventor in the former film is literally murdered by television thanks to a "death ray" rigged into the camera by a corporate spy, while in the latter another inventor's assistant kills his boss and attempts to steal Talbot's camera and receiver to sell to the highest bidder.

In each of these films, TV's most useful benign function is to catch criminals in the act—the same function that early cinema attributed to photography. But even in this, film tends to outdo its electrical sibling. Echoing early cinema's argument against amateur cinematographers, these films present instantaneity as a value in itself but also tag it as an unstable pleasure at best. Television's only contribution to civil society, here, is to clean up its own messes. Its lack of institutional boundaries, made clear by the struggle between inventors and thieves to control the technology, under other circumstances might have freed its inventors to test it imaginatively, like the far-seeing machines in William Cameron Menzies's 1936 film *Things to Come* (which Stewart reminds us are also cinematic devices that automatically develop and project films of speeches, much as the Paramount-Scophony theater TV system would soon do).[15] Instead, however, its instantaneity and freedom from institutional definition combine to keep the medium off balance. As both producers and consumers of the emerging medium, the inventor-amateurs are simultaneously well-meaning Dr. Frankensteins and blindly ambitious entrepreneurs who would have been better off tinkering with innocuous shortwave radios. In *Murder by Television,* the professor is murdered, and in *Trapped by Television,* the crooks would not have existed without the attractive technology. In the guise of pinning the poor quality of the entertainment on the amateurs' lack of production skills, these TV fantasies dream of scratching "entertainment" off TV's to-do list.

The media unconscious of these films, like that of early films about film and films about wireless, paints private media control as anathema to the powers and pleasures of cinematic spectatorship. But this portrait ran counter to the media fantasies marketed by the early TV industry, which promised a live amalgam of entertainment and quasi-social contact with a widening world. At the "Century of Progress" 1939 World's Fair, factory machines, new forms of transport, labor-saving appliances, and TV were pitched as signals of the beneficence of progress. Only wartime rationing and the priority given to combat materiel manufacture kept television off the market for the time being. By 1944, television developers RCA and manufacturer-broadcaster Allen DuMont had already begun to prepare ration-weary Americans to buy their share of the technological golden age that would arrive, it was claimed, as soon as the war ended. In their print advertising campaigns, they defined TV as a *household* technology that functioned like a picture window, allowing the private viewer to enjoy the public world from a distance, as a source of intrigue, and as a kind of décor that put the very notion of the private sphere as privileged safe haven on display.[16]

This fantasy of private media consumption as a safety valve against public encroachment was managed carefully by TV manufacturers and radio broadcasters, which were the FCC's chosen midwives for the new medium. "The media discourses" of television "as a staple home fixture," Lynn Spigel writes in her discussion of television ads in women's magazines, "did not so much reflect social reality; instead, they preceded it" (Spigel, 39). The networks consciously worked to avoid a reprise of the "intense debate in the 1920s about the proper social uses of broadcasting" and lobbied Washington and the American public hard into fantasizing television as radio with pictures—a one-way medium that would provide entertainment, news, and advertising without dragging its public down a tumultuous river of amateur experimentation first.[17]

In the interest of shaping the collective imagination, corporate chiefs filled the roles played by the electrical experts of the previous century. In 1942 and 1943, the mass-market digest *Predictions Likely to Come True* published predictions of how the war would end side-by-side with essays by RCA chief David Sarnoff and others that "predicted" a televisual future of unsurpassed sophistication and amusement. The confluence of televisual and war-related prognostications was not simply coincidental. Print advertisements for television also associated the exciting new medium with the wartime know-how that would eventually let the technology of everyday life recede into the background and provide cozy, Victorianesque evenings on the sofa around the machine that Cecelia Tichi has aptly named the "electronic hearth." Put another (and familiarly postmodernist-Marxist) way, the element of choice placed the televised public world in the position of a consumable good, rather than a consuming machine like the bombs, tanks, and automatic weapons that ravaged loved ones during the war.

The biggest marketers in the business thus envisioned TV as a visual upgrade to radio, particularly for the housewife. Like its predecessor, TV would supply information and entertainment to pass the time, and doubled as a piece of high-status furniture. Magazine advertising anchored these qualities in a science-fictional fantasy of bourgeois omnipresence. In the words of one DuMont ad, TV augured an "America . . . linked through television with the remote peoples of the earth."[18] One ad reprinted and discussed by Tichi (which also appeared in the May 24, 1944 issue of *Variety*) inverts the radio fantasy of the outside world paying a titillatingly inappropriate visit by hailing the viewer as an "Armchair Columbus!": "in peacetime," the ad says, home viewers will "travel" to see history in the making ("You'll sit at speakers' tables at historic functions, down front at every sporting event").

Yet these promises keep spiraling back to a version of liveness that, like the address of early broadcast radio, owes much to the classical cinema's version of interactivity. DuMont promises "the world actually served to you on a silver screen," as if the movie theater had come to pay a visit and conveniently left its other patrons behind.[19] Moreover, like broadcast radio before it, TV promised its viewers more arresting translations of the cinema's informatic intimacy into the private sphere. Another 1944 DuMont ad proclaimed that television was

> a force of unparalleled power. Television will carry new thoughts, new hopes, new products into millions of homes. It will stir men's minds and hearts in a matter of moments. We will watch the truly wonderful tomorrow take shape before our eyes.[20]

Accompanying this ad copy is an image of the family viewing the Earth from a sofa perched thousands of miles above it, as the planet projects images on the sky via a beam of light (Figure 20).

This ad speaks to a powerful fantasy in which television automatically produces community, a dream that predicts both Marshall McLuhan's concept of the global village and the utopian rhetoric used by TV drama critics less than a decade later. Television's new definition of audiovisual media spectatorship contained two key differences from that of classical Hollywood cinema: its (eventually) primary presence in the private

ARE YOU READY FOR TELEVISION?

The time is here for America to revise its concepts of its living-rooms, its classrooms, its town halls. The time is here to become familiar with new measurements of human progress...economic, political, scientific.

For full-scale Television is near...a force of unparalleled power. Television will carry new thoughts, new hopes, new products into millions of homes. It will stir men's minds and hearts in a matter of moments. We will watch the truly wonderful tomorrow take shape before our eyes.

DuMont will provide you with the finest in Television reception...sight and sound. DuMont quality will be assured by impressive prewar pioneering in Television, by vigorous wartime development, by highly specialized production "know how," by advantageous patents.

Indeed, the world stands on the threshold of an astonishing age...DuMont Television is ready...Are You?

Copyright 1944, Allen B. DuMont Laboratories, Inc.

DuMont *Precision Electronics and Television*

ALLEN B. DuMONT LABORATORIES, INC., GENERAL OFFICES AND PLANT, 2 MAIN AVENUE, PASSAIC, N TELEVISION STUDIOS AND STATION WABD, 515 MADISON AVENUE, NEW YORK 22, NEW YO?

Figure 20. Advertisement for DuMont Laboratories, *Atlantic Monthly*, November 1944.

sphere, and its liveness—the very qualities that underwrote radio's claims to spontaneity and intimacy, only now those qualities were infused with the authority of the image. Of the two qualities, the *liveness* of the televisual transmission poses difficulties for classical cinema's ongoing labor to substitute informatic intimacy for social interaction. William Boddy writes that, according to the first television writers of the 1940s, "the essential technological feature" that distinguished video from film was video's "capacity to convey a *simultaneous* distant performance visually."[21] Early experiments in live TV drama were touted by critics like Jack Gould of the *New York Times* for inciting audience participation in a way that film simply could not. As veteran media critic Gilbert Seldes put it in 1952, the viewer "tune[s] in one station or another according to whom you want in your room at any particular moment" (Boddy, *Fifties Television,* 82–83). Live television, and particularly live drama, was thought to provide a thrilling union of seer with seen in which "both the player in the studios and the audience at home have an intrinsic awareness of being in each other's presence." Gould explicitly used the cinema to clarify the temporal distinction between the experiences produced by each medium. He argued that liveness set television miles apart from "cut and dried" drama—that is, the "canned" narratives of Hollywood film and the prefilmed material the studios were by then supplying for network broadcast and syndication—with its "feel of the past" (80, 81).

Granted, this copresence was, for all its technological backing, no less ideological than the classical film spectator's illusion of voyeuristic intimacy with screen characters. In his effort to debunk the claim that live theater automatically induces a sense of participation in the event, Philip Auslander defines televisual liveness and theatrical liveness as discursive experiences that parallel one another. In each case, the viewer's sense of "community" extends to other viewers only in the abstract, but not to the objects of the most intense desire for interaction that live, naturalist theater induces in the spectator: the actors on stage.[22] I think Auslander is right, except that he leans his argument too heavily on the determining power of the text over audience experience. Perhaps "desire" as he describes it speaks to a historically repressed desire to engage with others in the theater, a desire that, as in the movie theater, was gradually displaced onto the proscenium without ever being effaced entirely. Indeed, the unrequited desire to interact with performers—a key aspect of the fetishistic power of the star, the object of desire that is both knowable and unattainable—would seem likely to benefit from the parallel ban on interacting with other spectators. Perhaps, too, domestic televisual spectatorship invites a more emphatically public reaction—that is, interaction within the space of the "crowd"—than live theater does. While the playgoer consumes plays within a system of social codes that forbid some responses and demand others, the television viewer only restricts her social urges out of respect for other TV viewers in the household (a rare sort of respect, to be sure), not out of respect for the performers.

Even these fantasies, however, carried the guarantee that such virtual guests as actors or newsmakers would come to call by invitation only. The premarketing of television attached domestic connotations to the medium in part by representing viewer choice as a boundary against undesirable elements from the public world. The DuMont ad's image of the family watching TV in outer space is a particularly telling allegory for the antisocial character of what Lynn Spigel calls the "sanitized" worldview promised by TV (Spigel, 121). The ritual celebration of the new machine staged here exudes as much relief at the absence of others proclaimed by the images on the "silver screen" as it does excitement at this new channel of others' presence. The family's ludicrously safe distance from Earth analogizes and imaginatively extends the distance between peaceful suburbs and dangerous cities, and between America and the foreign threats from which U.S. servicemen would soon be safe.

In the mid-forties, not only TV but technology in general was a central rhetorical figure through which consumer culture negotiated a newly armored, newly detachable definition of private experience. In this definition, new technologies enabled the consumer to inhabit under any and all circumstances the kind of private-in-public, consumption- and pleasure-oriented subjectivity provided by classical cinema. At the same time, technologies both old and new inverted the terms of that subjectivity from private-in-public to public-in-private, either by locating that subjectivity in a home filled with wondrous new appliances that freed up time for leisure and delivered entertainment or by producing an iconography of pleasure that always alluded to "home" as a privileged space. This image of technology overtook even the oldest of modernity's new and earth-shattering technological networks: the railroad. A 1944 ad for the Association of American Railroads portrays a passenger who looks as if he's reclining in his living room, while the copy promises future travelers—again, after the war is won—"All the Comforts of Roam!" (Figure 21). If the ads for TV envisioned viewers as far from the madding crowd as they could get, this image subordinates the railroad engine, the master icon of technological progress in all its wonder and violence, to the lower corner of the page along with the technologically aided violence of World War II; instead of the conventional headlight, the face of the once-wild iron horse bears the words "BUY MORE WAR BONDS."

ALL THE *Comforts* OF ROAM!

The day is coming when a train trip will again be something to look forward to eagerly — something to be enjoyed at ease, in spacious comfort — and all at moderate price. That of course will be after the war is won. It will be when the armed forces no longer need nearly half of all our passenger equipment to move fighting men. It will be when many coaches and Pullmans now busy in war service can be honorably retired to make way for new cars with comfort, convenience and thoughtful appointments beyond anything the past has known. That will take money — vast sums of money. It will take time. But we believe that it is worth while today to tell you what we plan for tomorrow — to help you realize that the wartime service we are able to give today is by no means a sample of what's in store for the future.

ASSOCIATION OF
AMERICAN RAILROADS
ALL UNITED FOR VICTORY

Figure 21. Advertisement for Association of American Railroads, *Atlantic Monthly*, April 1944.

Rather than denying out of hand the negative connotations technology inevitably acquires in wartime, ads that presell television (and postwar railroad travel, for that matter) function hegemonically. They acknowledge the negative connotations, then transform technology itself into a sign of the unprecedented autonomy soon to be granted the private sphere: visual knowledge of a world that grew larger and more bewildering as the war continued. They also promise that all (rail)roads lead back home, where the real recliner (of which the passenger berth model is merely the simulacrum) waits to cushion the subject against the slings and arrows the ad associates with something other than the technology it cannot avoid—that is, other people. On this issue, the AAR ad concurs nearly point for point with the ad for DuMont televisions. By evacuating all other human presence from the image, the railroad ad equates home and comfort with isolation, while at the same time it offers the smiling passenger the option (which he simply happens not to exert at this time) to interface with the outside world in motion through the shielding frame of the train window or through the phone, a media conduit here made simply another icon of domestic security.

This ideology of technology protecting the individual also characterizes film noir. Here, however, technologies form not shields but weapons, active rather than passive barricades against the outsider. In *Double Indemnity,* Walter and Phyllis plan to kill her husband and cash in on the insurance policy that Walter himself sold to Mr. Dietrichson for precisely this purpose. Throughout *Double Indemnity,* Walter "shows [his] ability to recognize and traffic in a world of uncertain and qualified communications" by wresting control of technologies and media large and small away from their makers and regulators.[23] At every stage, he implements this meticulous plan using—and mastering—familiar technologies that range from the car he hides in to commit the murder, to the train he rides while disguised as Phyllis's husband to harvest witnesses to Dietrichson's faked accidental death, to his own doorbells and telephone ringers. By slipping business cards between clapper and bell of each of these crude machines, he effectively reinvents them as surveillance devices: if the cards have dropped to the floor by the time he returns, he'll know he needs an alibi that places him away from home. Both the placing of the cards and the checking of these makeshift "traps" are marked by close-ups (apparently shot from masterful Walter's point of view) that heighten the importance of these actions as signs of Walter's devious intelligence, his ability to see and use machines as something other than the labor-saving gadgets they were manufactured to be (Figure 22).

Other noir antiheroes use similar acts of mechanical subversion to realize their desires. In *Sorry, Wrong Number* (Anatole Litvak, 1948), Leona (Barbara Stanwyck), an invalid pharmaceutical heiress the press has nicknamed "The Cough Drop Queen," continually uses the telephone, not to

Figure 22. Walter Neff turns his door buzzer and telephone bell into signalers of other information entirely. Frame enlargement from *Double Indemnity* (1944).

gossip as contemporary stereotypes would have it, but to subvert the restrictions placed on women's power. Like Phyllis Dietrichson, Leona clearly finds no satisfaction in fulfilling the stereotype of subservient wife to her working-class husband Henry (Burt Lancaster), but instead of killing her husband, Leona uses a machine to "crook" the position forced upon her and maintain her position as the central force in the relationship.

In *White Heat* (Raoul Walsh, 1949), Cody Jarrett (James Cagney), the members of his gang, and his fellow prisoners are masters at setting up their own networks: Cody is aided at one point by his partly deaf cellmate Reader, who gets information from a blockmate in the cell above by reading his lips in a mirror; the news of Cody's mother's death is relayed through the mess hall via whispers passed from person to person; and Big Ed (Steve Cochran), who "inherits" both Cody's gang and his wife Verna (Virginia Mayo) after Cody's incarceration, installs a small bell on the front door of the gang's hideout to alert him if the escaped Cody tries to sneak in. Cody himself does Big Ed one better, however. When Verna warns her husband of Ed's trap, Cody dampens the bell with his hand on his way in and then rings it purposely to draw his enemy into a deadly snare of his own.

Perhaps the most ambiguous and vivacious version of this technological ingenuity plays out in Joseph H. Lewis's *Gun Crazy* (1949). Bart (John Dall) and Laurie (Peggy Cummins) are both crazy about guns, which they operate with such accuracy that their revolvers become like extensions of their bodies. They depend no less on automobiles, the postwar symbol of an independent mobility that the two outlaws embody beyond the wildest fantasies of any automotive advertising campaign. The film's celebrated three-and-a-half-minute bank robbery sequence shot is filmed from the back seat of the getaway car, as are other scenes in the film, emphasizing the degree to which technology has become the defining medium though which Bart and Laurie understand the world (see Figure 23).[24] Laurie and Bart's gun love gets linked to the more quotidian freedom associated with the automobile. In a consumer-age parody of the star-crossed lovers' backward glance and the inevitable, fateful erosion of their pact to part, they look at each other from their cars and "run" back to each other's arms on four wheels apiece.

Instead of the bizarre new media that bad boys and girls of earlier media fantasies hijacked for their purposes, Walter and his fellow rogues use machines primarily associated with "ascetic," pragmatic consumption

Figure 23. The sequence shot from the back of the getaway car. Frame enlargement from *Gun Crazy* (1949).

to achieve their own personal *jouissance*.[25] Together these characters represent a new breed of media amateur in Hollywood cinema. They share the ingenuity and social deviancy of camera fiends and radio beasts, but differ from their ancestors in that media fantasy noirs cast them as the dispossessed of technological progress—the little people of America's deteriorating cities whom DuMont television would leave behind to sort out rampant class and gender inequities on their own, while the bourgeois family fantasizes its own media-aided happiness and watches the earth turn. These postwar amateurs are deeply dissatisfied with their class and/ or social positions, and they are in every instance not only the central characters of their films but the most sympathetic ones as well; imagine a remake of *Traffic in Souls* that investigates Trubus's motivation for entering the white slave trade. What does it mean for a classical film to portray an amateur engineer as simultaneously a threat to social order and the only figure in the film with the chutzpah to escape an unsatisfying life?

An unexplored answer to this perennial question lies in the postwar film industry's identification of both itself and the majority of its audience with bright, discontented characters like Walter and Leona. In a curious twist of history, Hollywood's own pet techno-utopia—its hopes to dominate the future television industry—crumbled at roughly the same time. As Timothy R. White puts it, "The failure of the studios to establish themselves as forces in television broadcasting was a result of FCC policy, not studio incompetence" (White, 146). The FCC favored NBC-RCA and CBS's interests at every turn, as it had in the twenties and thirties when it gave the networks carte blanche to insinuate commercialism into every pore of radio programming and to define "public interest" to suit their own interests.[26]

To make matters worse for the film industry, the FCC kept a watchful eye on Hollywood's attempts to get in on television's ground floor. By 1944, the Big Five were almost certain to be convicted of breaking antitrust laws in the *Paramount* suit filed by the Justice Department in 1938 but postponed due to the war. *Variety* was already reporting the rising fortunes of independent film producers now that the majors would soon be forced to divorce themselves from their theater chains, the wellspring of their profits. Paramount in particular had not given up on TV; the studio had purchased a major interest in DuMont Laboratories. But the radio interests had already gotten cocky about their impending victory over the film industry. In March of 1944, two months before it published its first section devoted exclusively to television, *Variety* ran an article entitled "'Produce Pix for

Tele or We'll Make Our Own,' Trammel Tells Hollywood." It reports that
NBC "prexy" Niles Trammel's "frank statement that 'if Hollywood won't
make pictures exclusively for television we'll do it ourselves,' rumbled
through the studios like a blast from Washington." The explosive simile
that concludes this sentence makes the image of television producing "pix"
sound as ominous as the Justice Department's threat of divestiture.[27]

The studios thus faced the possibility that they would wind up competing with television from a weakened economic position. The extent to
which the studios already felt they were backed into a corner is evident
from their radio policies. According to a March 8, 1944 *Variety* article, the
major studios banded together earlier that month to "discourage the guest
starring practice," the use of film actors in radio programs. Cost per film
script for broadcast adaptation was increased by a factor of six (from $500
to a hefty $3000); contract players had to be officially requested by a letter
from the sponsoring agency; programs "held to be of questionable value"
to a studio's players were to be "blacklisted"; and the networks were asked
to relinquish actor and story selection to the studios. The broadcasting industry interpreted these "edicts" as an expression of Hollywood's intent to
get the upper hand on the television industry any way it could: "Through
[the new edicts'] thin disguise [radio advertising and production] agency
men could discern . . . a thoroughgoing and concerted attempt to 'weaken
the radio structure so that its position will not be too impregnable with
the advent of television.'"[28]

Since Hollywood's chances at making a killing on video looked bleak,
the entertainment press recommended that it compete with TV via subject
matter, by speaking directly to troubled Americans rather than glossing
over their concerns and risking emptied theaters. Robert Gessner, "N.Y.U.
Professor of Pix Dept.," wrote an article for the January 5, 1944 *Variety* entitled "Film Industry to Mature—or Else," predicting that escapism would
lose its attraction for an audience that had lived through a long foreign war:

> For the first time in the history of the motion picture industry escape
> films will not be enough. . . . [T]here will exist a wider interest in the
> realities for their own sake, for such realities cannot be worn off [sic]
> the next morning like a reluctant hangover. In other words, there will
> be more people who will be more interested in the human equation of
> how we got this war and where we are going. Films for this audience
> won't be propaganda and they needn't be in color, but they can make a
> sizable profit nevertheless. . . . If Hollywood should fail to undertake the
> assignment, . . . others will satisfy that market. There will be the danger

of Government intervention, possibly a crusade, or the excitement of private production elsewhere than in Hollywood. . . . What are these realities in which people will be interested? Without giving away any free plots, I can say that they are simply the common ordinary truths about the way people feel and think.[29]

Gessner exaggerates Hollywood's "escapist" tendencies—the previous decade had generated hard-nosed social-problem films like *I Am a Fugitive from a Chain Gang* and "fantasies" like *Golddiggers of 1933* and *King Kong* with their images of showgirls sleeping three in a bed and a starving Fay Wray nearly stealing an apple from a street vendor. But he well represents a trend in industry thinking of which film noir is perhaps the best proof: the need to relate narratives to everyday experience, including festering resentment that wartime cinema, and public life in general, had repressed. Gessner's "common ordinary truths" are those of "the stomach and the brain, simply because those two organs have made their existence more widely known. Not only the rationing of food, gasoline, tires, and the limitations of public and private services, but also the wherefore of the war and the peace—these are the realities that have been imposed from above and below."

One reality that Gessner does not specifically mention, but that surely weighed on the minds of many Americans who had worked in factories before or during the war, was technology's reputation for ruining Americans' futures rather than burnishing them. Public expectations of technological progress lost much of their glitter during the Depression. Soon after the Crash of 1929, "the latest technological marvels of industry and agriculture lay unused or underused, and technological unemployment was becoming a widespread source of concern." This situation spread throughout the country, "sour[ing] many Americans on purely technological solutions to economic, social, cultural, and political problems."[30] According to one 1939 Gallup poll, a majority of Americans blamed "technological development" for reducing the job pool at the very moment that Americans most desperately needed jobs.[31] The sourest of these citizens belonged to the working class. As Amy Sue Bix shows, labor unions and left-leaning economists pegged technological development as a straw man—albeit a reasonably chosen one—for the perpetuation of the employment disaster. Assembly-line tasks once performed by human hands were being mechanized one by one, making automation look like little more than a tool for enforcing class hierarchy. Though automation probably played only a marginal role in actual unemployment, so many people believed that technological unemployment was imminent that the fantasy shaped their writings, thoughts, and actions regarding technologies of all sorts.[32]

In making the machine the lightning rod for their frustrations, workers and labor leaders generated a counterdiscourse to the capitalist fantasy that technology offered only universal benefits without human costs (except in the form of collateral damage—a steep rise in unemployment that would, the industrialists promised, work itself out eventually). As long as capitalists praised automation, loudly and lavishly, for reducing their overhead by making many human laborers redundant, workers' suspicions that automation and rampant unemployment were somehow connected kept their currency (Bix, 146). Workers worried they might soon find themselves permanently replaced by mechanical parts that made no material demands, and thus reduced to the status of spectators not only in the movie theater during leisure time but all the time, no matter what the venue, without the financial means to participate in America's glorious technological future.

Individual agency, of course, was a major stake of the technological development that TV symbolized, but working-class viewers had little reason to place their faith in the ability of television (or any other shiny domestic appliance) to help them achieve that agency. While the image of the nuclear family floating on an interstellar sofa metonymizes the postwar ideology of agency, few Americans had cause to appreciate technology any more after the war than they had before it. Although nearly every American labor union signed a no-strike pledge in late December of 1941 and vowed to work at home for "Victory through Equality of Sacrifice," and some factory laborers suddenly felt like valuable commodities rather than machine parts, so many laborers also believed the unions had given away their only leverage for making demands—the strike itself—that "the second World War . . . saw more strikes than at any other time in the history of the American working class," in the form of wildcat strikes and walkouts. Laborers organized these work stoppages as much to protest the union's abandonment of their interests as to protest unfair practices and wage freezes.[33]

As George Lipsitz writes, wartime workers found little comfort in a vision of "progress" that excluded them no less than it had before the war: "Mobilization for war and postwar reconversion during the forties permanently altered economic and political power relations within American society, producing a potentially totalitarian oligarchy of the major interest groups—big business, government, and labor. . . . The individual worker, consumer, or citizen had little recourse if he or she objected to the priorities set by big business."[34] Nearly five thousand documented strikes and other stoppages took place in 1944, an average of twelve per day during the first quarter alone, sparking another huge "strike wave" in 1945 and intensifying workers' anxiety about the postwar job market (Lipsitz, 87 and chapter 4). Matthew Smith, the socialist leader of the Mechanics Educational Society of America (MESA), said at a 1945 congressional hearing on work stoppage that, while all laborers would say they were committed to making the war winnable, "just below the surface [they are] very apprehensive as to what is going to happen to [them] when the war is over."

> For the first time [i.e., during the war] he is getting wages where he can feed his wife and kids and buy some luxuries. . . . [Then s]omebody comes along and says that, "What you ought to do is to concentrate on finishing this war . . . in order that you can go back to the bad old days of peace when you could work 3 months a year. You could be laid off. You could exhaust your unemployment insurance. You could go down to the welfare and plead for a basket of groceries. You could be kicked off the lawn of the White House, perhaps. All these things could happen to you." (Glaberman, 91, 90)

The Depression's language of lack and frustration had survived in response to this labor dread, adding to the sense that the corporations sacrificed nothing to the war effort, not when compared to the rights that unions had sacrificed without consulting their members and to the resource rationing that made even decent wages useless.

To make matters even bleaker for technology's reputation, the United States experienced an economic tailspin immediately after the war that temporarily gave the lie to the official promise of postwar prosperity. Through the war, consumers eagerly saved their relatively generous wages in anticipation of having something to spend them on; rationing forced them to treat once-quotidian commodities as luxuries, and few leisure-time activities beyond the movies and radio or phonograph listening were even available on a predictable basis. In the meantime, RCA, DuMont, and the whole of the manufacturing industry used their ads to presell commodities that only the end of their wartime production obligations would allow them to supply. To generate as much consumer desire as they could, they pitched the postwar era as one of tremendous prosperity, ease, and comfort, as we have seen. Even the Association of American

Railroads made the train, the most dangerous and tenacious symbol of modernity, look like a den. And as soon as the war was over, consumers began to spend money they didn't have on that constellation of long-promised goods. Elaine Tyler May writes that, although the majority of the population fared much better economically in the last half of the 1940s than the first, a 1945 poll revealed that a large majority was also very nervous about inflation, unemployment, and the postwar political economy: "Americans were only slightly more hopeful about the economic future in 1945 than they had been in 1937 at the depth of the depression. Fears of another depression were widespread, and one-third of the population was still in poverty" (May, 165).[35] Even affluent postwar consumers were nervous about how much money they would have left over at the end of the month and how long their higher wartime rates of pay would last, and yet their spending patterns far outstripped their actual "discretionary income," with money spent disproportionately on household items like appliances rather than food or clothing.[36]

To understand the contradiction at the heart of purchasing practices—people buying TVs on credit at prices they never would have dreamed of paying for a leisure device six years earlier—we have to recognize that economic uncertainty came wrapped in a discourse in which national and personal security were inextricably linked, a discourse that lingered after World War II and rapidly caught its second wind in Cold War rhetoric and policy. May argues that, because the U.S. government portrayed consumer goods as signs that the Soviets ran behind in the race for technological dominance, consumers bought cars, homes, and household furnishings to "strengthen their sense of security" (May, 165). The security associated with such purchases derived from their perceived connection to a future centered on home and family, prosperity in the most patriarchal and privatized sense.

But noting the various noir articulations of such themes as isolation, pessimism, insatiable desire, and violence in this context adds another shade of meaning to May's theory of security through consumption. The antiheroes of noir generally begin their stories in relative comfort and security—think of Walter Neff, a door-to-door insurance salesman who seems to enjoy his bachelorhood, not to mention his freedom to circulate through the class-stratified geography of Los Angeles—but are quickly compelled to grab everything they can by a nagging irritation at the uneven distribution of wealth that they repress until suddenly desire is born, usually catalyzed by sexual attraction but never limited to eroticism alone.

Walter's fall is a telling example of a noir protagonist who is less converted to crime on a sudden whim than he is convinced, finally, to enact his
long-running fantasies of cheating the system to reap what he feels is his
share of its fruits. Neither Walter nor Phyllis has any reason to associate
autonomy with home; Walter's dank apartment resembles a dorm room,
cluttered with sports trophies and pictures of boxers that imply both ar-
rested development and decrepit dreams of glory, while the house Phyllis
shares with her husband and stepdaughter is less a home than a cell, its
walls splayed with the shadows of Venetian blinds, where Phyllis "sit[s]
and knit[s]" and tries to forget how much she hates her fellow inmates.

This loss of home as haven resonates sharply with postwar media's
tightly controlled *interactive* turn. In 1953, Twentieth Century Fox head
Darryl F. Zanuck touted Fox's CinemaScope process as a "recreation"
technology as opposed to the traditional studio ideal of "entertainment":
"Entertainment . . . is something others provide for you, while recreation is
something you provide in some measure for yourself—something in which
you participate."[37] The studios experimented with different technologies
in a self-conscious attempt to satisfy audiences looking for more participatory, more interactive pleasure seeking (Belton, 76). But "participation"
here is, as I've already suggested, as discursive a notion as "liveness" in
official mid-forties fantasies about TV. The notion of the "global village"
prefigured by the DuMont ad campaign (fifteen years before McLuhan
published *Understanding Media*) depends upon the transmission and reception of news and current events as they happen, not just live theater.
But TV's simulation of the classical public sphere is already compromised
by its reification as a theatrical medium. TV prognosticator Robert E.
Lee imagines a show he titles "BACKSTAGE!" as the ultimate statement
of televisual education—showing what goes on behind the scenes at "a
slaughterhouse! a steel mill! an aircraft factory!" Why businesses? Clearly
not to investigate their labor practices but merely to instruct the folks at
home about the ways the world works by providing "truthful analysis of
the 'why' of world events, revealed full scope by responsible spokesmen as
soon as security permits."[38]

Television's first fabulists praised it as a new, postclassical public sphere,
but there was a clear revision, and a cost, to the version of "the public" that
home television would construct. The social cost of this public-in-private
viewing schemata was already on display among the many fearful images
of mentally deadened children—and adults—in a constant state of hypnotic suggestion or simple obtuseness because of their antisocial relation-

ship to a screen that offered "reality" as if it were a film and reduced even the highly constrained publicness of movie viewing to a grouping of silent, familiar coviewers. Before the viewer even had the opportunity to decide what to watch, experts would filter out the dross and stage the important materials for a grateful audience. Lee argues in 1944 that TV will allow "us" (i.e., Americans) to understand everything and everyone by taking viewers behind a metaphorical theater curtain that usually obscures the underlying nature of the little planets outside their picture windows: "No condescending 'tourist-photographer,' the iconoscope [i.e., the television receiver] . . . will help us to understand the other two billion people with whom we must learn to live in this postwar world." But Lee does not give up the imperialist rhetoric of radio's fantasy project of Westernizing the rest of the world. He recommends broadcasting programs that will teach "Basic English, or whatever international language is adopted as standard in the exchange of ideas" (136).

What I want to suggest is that film noir, and especially the media fantasy variety I have discussed, was well on its way to constructing an informatic version of spectatorial participation as early as 1944. These commercially produced, often A-list narrative films sacrifice any number of classical conventions, including the ethical protagonist and the link between successful romance and satisfying narrative conclusion, in the interest of following Gessner's advice to publicize the material realities of its most uneasy spectators.

Coming at the cycle from this intermedia—or rather intertechnological— perspective, what strikes me as most remarkable about forties film noir is the war it wages against progress, at least as defined by mid-forties consumer culture. This ideological war stages its skirmishes explicitly on the discursive field of media fantasy. Media fantasy noirs take a consistent tone of boredom and frustration with respect to the conventional wisdom about what machines could and would do to make life easier, and its tacit acknowledgment that war-era ambivalence about progress exceeded the containment strategies of corporate propaganda. These films continually enact an unethical but undeniably vital version of what Benjamin called the "mimetic faculty," the receding human propensity to both "recognize and produce" correspondences between objects that exceed the uses and meanings imposed on them over time.[39]

If such technological correspondences, in which mirrors become media and doorbells tell tales, seem all too instrumental compared to Benjamin's allegorical, critical form of mimesis, they nonetheless make the objects visible again as products of history, not natural secretions of progress. Once noir characters come across them, any and all "machines"—even objects we don't normally categorize as technological at all—can be broken out of their old identities and used as media if need be. Heidegger defines technology as any tool, whether mechanical or mental, used to extend human agency—precisely the way these characters redefine lots of things as technologies, and more, as *media*. Aping the wireless amateurs who made off with Quaker Oats cylinders to use as coil cores, Walter uses fully institutionalized, benign machines (doorbells are for telling you, politely, that someone waits at the door) for purposes of signaling what he wants to signal, against the intentions of its designers and its conventional users. In fact, Walter's act is even more radically amateurish than those of the small boys of wireless because he has to reach back much farther than they did into media history. He must effectively conjure up a forgotten moment when doorbells and phone bells were new and strange enough that their "proper functions" did not accrue around them like an aura.

The sheer determinedness of Walter's counterinstitutional tactics and the strange quaintness of *Double Indemnity*'s master allegory, the train, point an intermedia interpretation of the film in this relatively radical direction. Walter does not merely use a train to produce false evidence that will suggest Mr. Dietrichson died accidentally; in fact, he descries his entire scheme as a railroad trip "straight down the line," with every wheel and gear of his plan meshing perfectly to produce the desired outcome. In fact, railroad lines ribbon through all the noirs I've discussed. Cody's first heist in *White Heat* is a train robbery. In *Gun Crazy*, a train runs past Laurie and Bart's desperate hideout where they plan their last big job, and they secretly hop a boxcar to (successfully) escape the police. The thugs who murder Leona in *Sorry, Wrong Number* coordinate their break-in with the train timetable so that the noise will drown out Leona's screams. In each case the train is associated with battles over agency, whether fleetingly or directly. When Cody stops a train engineer at gunpoint during *White Heat*'s opening heist, he says sardonically, "You're fifteen minutes late! We just put in a new engineer!"

The appearance of the train carries a special weight among the possibilities for technological appropriation, for the railroad is the metafantasy that backs all democratic fantasies about communications media like a gold standard. The most intriguingly mimetic aspect of noir reimaginings of the train as a tool for individual expression is that, within the logic of technological fantasy, they reanimate the long-lost moment when the steam engine, the first symbol of progress in its technological and social ineffability dating back to Daniel Webster and before, could yet have taken American culture down a different path. Symbolically, the railroad was the template for democratic media fantasy. It stitched together the experience of millions of riders all over the country, engaging them to imagine their national community as one linked by progress and speed and the shortening of spatial boundaries among them. Materially, the earliest railroad cars lumped everyone together from all classes and ethnicities and thus synechdochized the nation in every single carriage everywhere at any time.

If trains stand for progress, and Walter jumps the train, then, win or lose, the dominant dream of progress no longer looks so invulnerable or so ineffable. Amateurs in early films and radio fantasies are dangerous because they are either inept or antisocial. Film noir portrays amateurs as downright apocalyptic figures, bent on destroying those who stand in their way and themselves if need be. When Walter and Cody take over trains, they're metaphorically hijacking a fantasy of technological progress that left that idealism behind, in all but its most imaginary sense, the moment that railway moguls set up the means to monopolize freight and travel and kept their laborers as poorly paid as possible. Like their counterparts in the other films, these two amateur engineers—in both senses of the term— attempt to make the train work for them materially and symbolically. In each case, the protagonists seem to run after a technology so old that no one thinks much about its early implications as modernity's shocking killer, the very image of modernity's technological bewilderment. These films transform the tamed train of postwar America back into a leviathan, a bringer of war against the constraints placed upon individuals even at the level of desire by capitalism and the law.

By adding the train to their list of mechanical conquests, Walter and Cody access the possibility of remaking the technological world by eschewing the institutional restrictions that limit not only their actual uses but also what can be thought about them. The accidental runoff of this tactic is the production of a horizon of spectatorial self-consciousness that allows the audience to do the crooking itself in terms of re-envisioning the qualities and functions of film. If media fantasy noirs represent and stage media publics as publics akin to the viewers of early cinema, they seem inexorably drawn by this recognition to reflect the cinema's interactive primal scene by way of the image as well. Note the opening shot of the credits of *White Heat*, which replicates the Lumière brothers' *L'arrivée d'un train* right down to the dynamic diagonal composition of the shot

(Figures 24 and 25). Although by 1949 a filmed image of an onrushing steam engine would have shocked no one, *White Heat*, like Cody himself, injects some shock value into nearly invisible filmic conventions. When Cody leaps from the railroad bridge to the freight cars below (Figure 26), the object of his desire suddenly expands from the diegetic hijacking of the train and the symbolic seizure of an unequal and unstoppable Progress to a self-reflexive takeover of the cinema. By flinging himself into the first film seen by many a viewer—call this remake "L'arrivée d'un gangster"— Cagney links his maniacal, ambiguously sympathetic, sketchily classical star persona to the era in which films were identical to maniacal shocks. He then hits the metaphorical reset button on film history by shooting the train's engineer and fireman and blowing up a freight car in a twisted but unmistakable reflection of Porter's *The Great Train Robbery* (1903). At this profoundly troubled moment when Hollywood was sure its number was up, *White Heat* dreams longingly of an amateur *film* engineer who saddles up the slowly chugging train of classical cinema and rides it back to its volatile past like the wild mechanical horse it once was, and secretly still is.

One way noir's working-class audience, living in a less-than-ideal relationship with technology and progress, might have experienced these

Figure 24. Opening credits from *White Heat* (1949).

Figure 25. The charging iron horse from *L'arrivée d'un train à la Ciotat* (Louis Lumière, 1895).

Figure 26. L'arrivée d'un gangster. Frame enlargement from *White Heat*.

characters is as object lessons of another sort: rather than attempting to reconnect to others and make good on the technological fantasies grandfathered by the train and projected upon the instantaneous media that followed it, from telegraph to wireless and now welcoming the entry of TV, Neff and his ilk all blow their chances at criticizing "the system" in anything approaching a systematic, communally beneficial way by using the tremendous potential that their fantasies unleash for purely individual gain. They seem so overtaken by the ideological equation of progress with heightened consumerism that every technology they reimagine ultimately gets pounded into a sword for their use and their use alone. After their packing plant heist, Bart finally articulates the regret that through much of *Gun Crazy* he can only express via grimaces of pain: "Two people dead, just so *we* can live without working" (emphasis added). It's as if the communalizing vision granted to the railroad passenger, as she sits securely in the knowledge that the railroad line will connect her to faraway places, has been fully reversed by what Dimendberg calls the centrifugal orientation of the car and the highway. A centrifugal logic, driven by the aggressive marketing of automobiles and the equally aggressive postwar campaign to expand the national highway system, pulled Americans away from the city and transformed their traveling selves into Henri Lefebvre's "abstract subjects," instrumental passersby on road surfaces leading away each other.[40] Bart and Laurie represent media fantasy noir's negative object lessons about the perils of privatized consumption.

Considering Hollywood's own struggle with the radio industry's federally supported TV fantasies, perhaps the antagonist here isn't bad amateurs but bad fantasies, especially precooked ones like the TV fantasies of the forties. TV cast domestic ensconcement as a positive value by linking the fortified, technologically sophisticated home to vaguely defined ideals of freedom and security. Those ideals are characterized by the films as both overly constraining for the users and individualist in a way that sacrifices the characters' social conscience to a solipsistic notion of "freedom." In other words, Walter, Leona, Cody, and the rest have managed to slip past the specific fantasies projected upon television and the all-electric dream world it symbolized, but they have not escaped the hunger for product consumption at any cost that underwrites the postwar edition of "official" media fantasy. In an era that accepted corporate heads like David Sarnoff as the most knowledgeable and objective electrical "experts," the nineteenth-century experts' desire to retain cultural capital for the educated classes gives way in the culture of media fantasy to a desire to profit as much as possible by constructing unattainable desires for consumers that no amount of purchasing power could fulfill. The ubiquitous dreams of extending democratic media access in all directions papered over the fact that television supported the continuing exclusion of "private-domestic or personal familial matters . . . from public debate" by "personalizing," "familializing," or "economizing" them—often through the content of the programs themselves, which frequently pictured homes and families but consistently envisioned those families as tightly knit units whose troubles stemmed from external complications. As Stephanie Coontz so succinctly states, "'Leave It to Beaver' was not a documentary."[41]

By contrast, media fantasy noirs not only admit but also embrace longings for other identities and other forms of social contact that push beyond the borders drawn by the domesticity/isolation and security discourses of early TV ads. These films cultivate remarkable empathy for women's domestic frustrations and the possibility that technology could offer a more functional key to freedom than the washing machine's promise of saving time or television's promise to make time fly. Sylvia Harvey writes that representations of family in film noir negate the usual functions of family in Hollywood film—"the mechanism whereby desire is fulfilled, or at least ideological equilibrium established"—and instead make domestic life "the vehicle for the expression of frustration."[42] The desires of the femme fatale contradict the ideals of family and home with a directness that might have shocked 1940s audiences. *Gun Crazy*, perhaps the most excessive statement of noir subversion produced in the forties, decimates those ideals altogether. Not just Laurie's life with Bart but also the harassed domesticity of the "good" woman, Bart's sister Ruby, bears only satiric relation to postwar fantasies of home. Her private sphere reads as an exposé of what the idealized, video-era private sphere conceals, that is, the falseness of its claims of connecting the home to the world, of making the living room a locus where private experience could make new and productive connections to a larger public. By contrast, Laurie's criminal life seems an understandable attempt at autonomy.

In each of these noirs, women like Ruby jump on the bricoleur's train to escape from domestic conditions that look and feel like prisons. Leona is a conniver, but what we remember most about her is her helplessness and her frustration at being homebound, a problem that the telephone only exacerbates; her invalidity and confinement to the house concretizes the condition that she struggled against when she was ambulatory, too: wanting some autonomy from men but having no alternative but to achieve an attenuated version of autonomy *through* men, her father and her ultimately haywire trophy husband ("I, Leona, take thee Henry").

Leona's failure to enter public life clarifies Ruby's function among *Gun Crazy*'s media fantasies. Consistently dressed in an apron, Ruby answers a telephone call from Bart early in the film while gasping for breath after a grueling act of housework and crossly tells her children to be quiet. Once the grimy but gleefully irreverent Laurie meets Ruby face to face, the contrast could not be more evident, and Laurie looks upon her doppelganger with a mixture of pity and contempt. Domestic(ated) appliances have done no more good for Ruby than cars and guns have done for Laurie, but at least Laurie has escaped the prisons of gender and domesticity, no matter how desperate and doomed her freedom may seem.

The very existence of the femme fatale—as well as her male counterpart, the disaffected anti-engineer of dominant progress—undercuts the claim that official public discourse represents everyone's interests, what Negt and Kluge describe as a foundational myth of the bourgeois public sphere, *"the rejection of the proletarian context of living as it exists"* with which the "production public spheres" of film and TV have largely complied.[43] The femme fatale's primary sin, indeed her defining quality, is her disdain for the boundaries of home and family drawn around her by cultural and political norms. She represents a threat not only to conventionally imagined masculinity but also to the exclusion of private life from public discourse. Despite the misogyny inherent in the characterizations of Laurie, Leona, and Phyllis, and in film noir's insistence on the inherent perversity of female desire, these complex figures hint at the truths obscured behind the caricature: "the suppression of the bourgeois family and centrality of women in the male world of action [in noir] produces female representations outside family definition and dependency," representations that give the lie to the bourgeois family ideal.[44]

A couple of films from the decade's turn provide sharp expressions of these connotations in a most literal mode. These films focus on the industry in transition as itself a fatalistic noir landscape, and indirectly recognize the implications of noir self-reflexivity for Hollywood cinema as an institution. The first rumbles of the self-redefinition I'm suggesting occur in two noirs from 1950 that set aside general technoskepticism to focus much more directly on the cinema than *White Heat*: Nicholas Ray's *In a Lonely Place* and Billy Wilder's *Sunset Boulevard.* Each of these films frames Hollywood as an industry in trouble. Both Dix Steele (Humphrey Bogart) and Joe Gillis (William Holden), struggling screenwriters in an industry facing a drop in number of tickets sold from 1948's 90 million-per-week high to a mere 60 million,[45] suffer losses as devastating as those faced by earlier noir antiheroes, but their fates also have metaphoric implications for the film industry. Dix, subject to Cody-like bursts of rage and violence, alienates his fiancée Laurel (Gloria Grahame) for good when he loses his temper because she suspects him of murder and tries to strangle her; and when Gillis tries to walk out of aging silent film diva Norma Desmond's life and shrug off the dead weight of Hollywood's past, Norma (Gloria Swanson) shoots him in the back. As characters "from" Hollywood, their success intertwined with that of the industry, Dix and Gillis's twin declines plumb the depths of personal disempowerment and, by association, Hollywood's general despair.

First and most obviously, these films hook fatalism explicitly to the fate of cinema as its audiences and its industry knew it. The industry these films show us is scrambling to redefine itself. *In a Lonely Place* characterizes contemporary Hollywood's backstage as an apocalypse of out-of-work writers and epic madness, where time-honored textual and economic strategies no longer meet spectators' needs. Like the historical Big Five, which hedged against this disaster by simply making its stories and budgets bigger than ever, *In a Lonely Place*'s movie executives place their chips on historical, musical, and Biblical epics like *Samson and Delilah* (Cecil B. DeMille, 1949). Mildred (Martha Stewart), the coat-check girl at Dix's favorite Hollywood eatery, calls an epic "a picture that's real long and has lots of things going on," and her sensationalistic description of the novel that Dix, the disillusioned Oscar-winning screenwriter, begrudgingly agrees to adapt confirms her definition—much to his chagrin.

Intriguingly, the battle for Hollywood's right to define film on its own conventional terms, rather than capitulating to the pressures of a "recreational" spectatorship culture led by television's example, plays out allegorically in terms of sexual politics, with Dix cast in the role of Hollywood's stubbornly classical traditionalism. When Mildred is murdered, circumstantial evidence makes Dix the prime suspect. He is eventually exonerated, but the film leaves open every possibility that Dix might have killed Mildred in one of his fits of rage had he had the opportunity. On the way to its unusually unhappy ending, in which Dix nearly chokes Laurel to death just as she prepares to tell him he's in the clear, *In a Lonely Place* emphasizes the incompatibility of "his" Hollywood—a Hollywood that intrinsically favored artists over hacks, a Hollywood that never existed—with the epic-addicted Hollywood that the film derisively associates with "mass culture as woman," that is, the factory for cranking out easily consumable, eye-pleasing, three-hanky yarns—the Hollywood in which Bogart, Grahame, Ray, and the rest of *In a Lonely Place*'s cast and crew had always done their work.[46]

Rather than simply mirroring the fatalistic worries of an industry in trouble, however, the conclusion of *In a Lonely Place* exposes the antisocial consequences meted out by the unexamined, hermetically sealed life sketched out by official television fantasies, less in the sense of mere prurience for the spectator's sensationalist pleasure than in its representation of an all-too-common instance of the agonies to which a "sheltered" private sphere can lead. The film's unbearable revelation is not that Dix murdered Mildred, which he (apparently) did not, but rather that his lead-lined solipsism and explosive temper erupt regularly in the form of domestic violence in both its psychological and physical forms.[47] This conclusion metaphorically addresses the industry's stagnation and frustration, but at the same time it admits that the film industry itself may be to blame for not connecting with its audience. Whether accidentally or purposely, Hollywood here produces an allegory for its failure to respond to Gessner's criticism of mid-forties Hollywood. Dix's inability to distance himself from the idealized, chauvinistic professionalism he associates with prewar Hollywood forces him to leave a private sphere to which he has no means to relate. In similar fashion, the cinema was figuratively cast out by suburbanites who now sought entertainment not at the picture palaces but in their own neighborhoods and rumpus rooms—not simply because many former cinephiles had migrated to suburbs, the film hopefully implies, but because the film industry, like Dix, no longer knew how to address home life in a way that lived up to the more complex expectations of its dwindling postwar audiences.

The dual interpretive paths of TV fantasy noirs—the parallel tracks of a critique of simulacral media intimacy, on the one hand, and industrial self-flagellation for film's inadequacies regarding the private sphere and representation, on the other—cross arrestingly in *Sunset Boulevard*'s mausoleum of film history. Norma Desmond's mansion on Sunset is filled with awards, outdated knickknacks from the silent days, and a bunch of cronies from that period who never say a word when they come to play cards—a veritable dustbin of Hollywood history, or rather, Hollywood's prewar history envisioned *as* a dustbin. The dead atmosphere of the place suggests that film's classical past is a thing best left behind by an industry that hates radical change but has no choice but to begin afresh. It's hardly coincidental that Norma's home screen circa 1950 is not a TV but a movie screen, on which she shows Joe her old films and makes unselfconscious remarks about film history that nevertheless express the height of historical consciousness for Wilder and Brackett, the scenarists: "They had faces then," in the silent era, she says, but the coming of sound cut many of those faces off at the neck and compelled the studios to restructure classical form around the demands of dialogue. Unwittingly, Norma directs *Sunset Boulevard*'s viewer to consider the forgotten futures of film, such as the slip of a chance that silent narrative might have continued to evolve alongside the talkies, at a moment at which Hollywood's institutional introspection hit a peak higher and more visible to the audience at large than any since 1927.

But the film succeeds at addressing home as a crisis space of postwar culture. The film, though fictional, "take[s] the rooftops off" to display "what dark shapes issue from amidst their homes," the narratorial plaint that Raymond Williams cites as an expression of Dickens's purpose as an activist novelist, the revelation of "real and inevitable relationships and connections" among citizens that the "sheer rush and noise and miscellaneity of this new and complex [urban] social order" make impossible to see.[48]

While the Hollywood-centered noirs don't poach another medium's tropes for "intimacy," nor do they deal with Dickens's nineteenth-century city, they do suggest one option available to the cinema as a way of maintaining film's place in the televisual age, that is, a compromise with the promised effects of TV: to broaden the myth of intimacy itself to include the cinema's narrative involvement in private lives, and implicitly place this kind of intimacy above television's mere "liveness" as a fuller, more incisive instrument for knowing and understanding the feelings of others.[49] Like *Double Indemnity* and the other quasi-televisual noirs, *Sunset Boulevard* and *In a Lonely Place* represent the private sphere as deceptively benevolent and make prurient attempts to lay that truth bare. Dix Steele, upbraided by friends and police alike for his deceptive coolness—"He's hiding something," one police detective says, "I've a feeling it isn't the proverbial heart of gold"—buries homicidal tendencies that repeatedly erupt into violence, leading both the police and Laurel to suspect him of murder. As Telotte writes of Dix, who seems innocent, then guilty, then most guilty after his innocence is proven, *In a Lonely Place* "reveals . . . a basic discrepancy between the public and the private, between what one seems and what one really is" (193). *In a Lonely Place* beats TV at its own game of connecting the home firmly but safely to the rest of the world. The preselling rhetoric of the television industry claimed that TV would open that channel, but the channel only allowed information to flow in one direction—from "outside" to "inside." Television offered only a simulacrum of interaction that was literally less social than the informatic "exchange" that Hollywood had to offer, for at least when one went to the movies one *went* somewhere and mingled with others. TV aided homebound viewers in "sharing" the sorrows and joys of (largely fictional) others, but did not guarantee them access to anyone with whom to share their responses. Ray's film recasts the cinema as Bobby's Kodak for a dawning feminist era.

Looking back from this perspective toward the forties films with which I began, *Double Indemnity* becomes more than simply an object lesson about disregarding the dominant order. To see this, we must realize that Keyes's counterallegory to Walter's—a tale of the inevitable path from murder to execution in which the railroad becomes a "trolley" and the "last stop is at the cemetery"—acknowledges exactly the same situation as does Neff's allegory of the train: progress circa 1944 demanded passivity and acquiescence to whatever changes it brought in tow. According to this version of progress, Walter's happiness would require that he be satisfied with what he has, but we find nothing but open dissatisfaction and disappointment in *Double Indemnity,* and these feelings are not limited to Walter and Phyllis. Even a bit character in the grocery store where Phyllis and Walter meet to make plans complains, "I don't know why they always put what I want on the top shelf," after asking Walter, ever the overreacher, to hand her a package of baby food.

This line, practically thrown away but for the bit actor's adamant delivery, takes on a special irony when considered in the context of wartime scarcity, which most Americans experienced in the form of food rationing. *Double Indemnity* is set in 1938, before the war and war rationing, and so the market scene required that the shelves hold much more food than Americans were used to seeing in stores by 1944. Naremore notes the conspicuous absence of rationing here, adding that throughout the film "the Los Angeles locales are free of any sign of military activity."[50] Richard Schickel's monograph on *Double Indemnity* reprints a publicity photo of armed Los Angeles policemen in the market behind Stanwyck and MacMurray; the caption states that the police were there to guard the food from theft. While the abundance of food implicitly refers to both past and (imagined) future plenitude, the female extra's line—and the shooting history of the scene—infuse this moment with the leaner reality of 1944, as wartime ideology of sacrifice wore thin and literally had to be defended by threat of force.[51] Even if the guards were part of a publicity stunt, which was very likely the case, the fact that this stunt was chosen over other possibilities reflects Paramount's awareness of the "common ordinary truths" of the "stomach and the brain" that Gessner implored Hollywood to acknowledge—the public frustration with scarcity of resources that coexisted alongside dreams of deferred material wealth and homes so "modern" and well supplied with moving images that one need rarely interact with strangers thereafter.

Indeed, the market scene, in which a large crowd of anonymous people slide past each other like theatrical spectators knocking knees with other patrons on the way to their seats, sketches the ideological preconditions for reimagining the public's relationship to each other through acts of collective consumption. Not only does *Double Indemnity* "advertise" dresses and other goods as Hollywood films had done since the twenties, creating market desire simply by displaying the goods and allowing viewers at least to fantasize about owning them, it also salts the wound of want by showcasing *food* as yet another an unattainable consumer luxury.[52] Between the images of the food—food become nothing but image, denuded of its use value, circulated primarily to reproduce the image of an era, with its surplus value being to create a sense of lack at the gut level—and publicity pictures of its being defended against the public gathered around to watch the shoot (not to mention the underpaid extras milling about Jerry's), the film may as well invite the audience to experience discomfort, even fury, at the fact that this surreal food stands stolidly unreachable. Cinematic technology shows them food without feeding them. Unlike advertising discourse, however, *Double Indemnity* allows the anonymous baby food customer to vent exactly that rage.

If we place this scene next to Walter's soliloquy to the Dictaphone, in which he confesses his sins to an indifferent recording technology that emits an irritating buzz, the two scenes examine the limits of cinematic interactivity as technology and as institution. Think of this market as a figure for a classical public, a literal agora that nevertheless hosts individuals as monadic as those in the theater. The public subject portrayed here is a hyperindividuated subjectivity—one disempowered by being squeezed into this role. Is going to movies like being surrounded by goods that you can't obtain? And is it all right to ask for help? The scene hails the public film viewer as a consciously, presently unsatisfied voyeur, a consumer in a perpetual state of envy and looking for a literal public. Fittingly, Walter and Phyllis's trip to the market would be enough to give anyone agoraphobia, at least if one were looking for a public to aid one's political needs. They meet to communicate rather than to buy, but they do so precisely because no social exchange happens there beyond Walter's robotic retrieval of the baby food. Only in the consumer-culture manifestation of the crowd, a public only in the most literal sense, could a couple of soon-to-be-murderers be so alone as to plan their crime without fear of being overheard.

The film circumscribes this scene with a mediated, more public marketplace—ironically, an empty insurance building. By contrast with the chilly visit to Jerry's, Walter's trip to his building to use the Dictaphone inverts the literal agora. But the inversion yields a similar inversion of the dispersal of consciousness seen in the market, for the Dictaphone—a recording medium—produces the opportunity for exchange. His home communications technologies become putty in his hands, but only for instrumental purposes. But the recording technology he must leave home to use transforms into a machine through which he can air his feelings. Walter tells a Dictaphone how much he loves Keyes and even what he did and why, and this leads to a one-on-one final moment in which Keyes, who has overheard Walter, expresses his love for Walter as the latter leans, bleeding, against the doorjamb of their depersonalizing insurance company.

The film offers a public airing of grievances as the ingredient missing from the cold, strictly market agora. It superimposes a structure of exchange onto the use of a one-way, recording technology. *Double Indemnity* thus demonstrates how "interactive" media fall prey to a monadic and one-sided institutional vision, while an institutionally public medium could provide both intentional and accidental airings of the subject's speech. The conventional logic of media determinism is thereby reversed: public recording technologies express the individual's interests while private instantaneous/interactive technologies lock the user into a spiral of isolation and antisocial behavior. Reimagining media, indeed. By using the Dictaphone to represent himself, Walter Neff defies the individual's normative relationship to technological progress even in the act of capitulating to it.

These media noirs often display quite literally the social limits past which a homebound technology cannot push. Ruby in *Gun Crazy* has to pretend enthusiasm when Bart calls on the phone, for, as the film's audience (but not Bart, obviously) can plainly see, childrearing and housework have left her haggard. When Sally Lord (Ann Richards) in *Sorry, Wrong Number* uses the phone to warn Leona of the trouble her husband is in, Sally's husband shouts to her to bring his partner a beer. She has no privacy in the private sphere, from husband or child, from which to examine her past identity (Leona's husband Henry was once Sally's beau) or discuss it with others; the apartment is so small that she must duck into her son's bedroom to speak to Leona, with nothing but a tacked-up blanket separating the bedroom from the living room and efficiency kitchen. Her conversation with Leona is so proscribed by the presence of her husband— another federal cop, casting the shadow of the *Paramount* decrees over yet another film noir—that she must disguise the intimate and empathetic nature of the discussion by pretending to exchange recipes with Leona. All the while, as her lists of phony ingredients render her reason for calling utterly incomprehensible, her husband looms behind her in an exquisite deep-space composition, working with his partner at the same table where he takes the meals produced by his devoted wife. Frustrated and in danger of Leona ringing off, Sally makes up a story about picking up more beer, then goes to use the pay phone at the drug store—ironically the only place where she might speak freely.

In their examination of the consequences of confining media "publicness" to the domestic sphere, media fantasy noir keeps the screen/window open to public consideration of film's social and political functions, how it might be appropriated from the studios' intentions by the spectator herself. They portray the "nature" of privatized media and technologies as a function of the relationships they foster among their users. Calling the central subject of these examinations by its name—television—would upset the key political function, accidental or otherwise, of media noirs' negative dialectic: to keep the medium's future uncertain, unstable, and unwritten, for to make it literal is to capitulate to the TV wrought by RCA-NBC and CBS with the assistance of the FCC and the Justice department and foreclose the possibility of fantasizing one's way—Hollywood's way and the spectator's way at once, whether they resemble one another or not—out of the institutional form that gripped TV as tightly as a pistol in a federal cop's fist.

Extending the Screen

If *Sunset Boulevard* and *In a Lonely Place* bring the film industry's concerns about representing the private sphere into alignment with its concerns about Hollywood's survival *tout court, White Heat* takes those concerns out to the movies. After the Feds descend on the Jarrett hideout and force the gang to scatter, Cody and his wife and mother hold a spontaneous gang meeting while hiding out in one of the major studios' least favorite spots on the American map: a drive-in theater. As Mary Morley Cohen has argued, the popularity of the drive-in theater after the war attested to an "overt preoccupation with privacy" that extended to film spectatorship itself and showed how little Hollywood's idealized image of its audience, the "'average' or conventional spectator," related to present reality (if it had ever reflected the reality of spectatorship at all). The drive-in materialized postwar audiences' understanding of themselves as individuals or groups with diverse interests, willing to watch films in an "unpredictable, distracting, and somewhat irreverent atmosphere."[53] The drive-in exploited the automobile's postwar connotations of individuality and recreation to construct a new definition of spectatorship, generated not by Paramount or MGM but by independent exhibitors who saw urban audiences dwindling and decided to retool exhibition to fit suburban leisure trends. Drive-in owners reconstructed viewing space into an outdoor extension of living space, transforming it into a hybrid of a laundry room (on-site washers and driers), a backyard (picnic tables), and a community center (beautiful baby contests) as well as offering a privacy-in-public that resonated with long-standing "inappropriate" theater activities (petting in the backseat of a car).

One way to read this scene is as a limit case to media noirs' gesture toward revisiting the original cinematic public in the postwar here and now. *White Heat* gets specific about the implications of this for film spectatorship. Cody, Ma, and Verna hide from carloads of Treasury agents in a venue already as familiar a sight to film audiences by 1948 as television was a familiar thorn in Hollywood's side. The same year the film was released, the total number of TV sets in the United States jumped by more than 1200 percent over the previous year, and the Hollywood studios found themselves divorced from their theaters by the *Paramount* decision.[54] In addition, 1948 saw Hollywood blocked from obtaining TV broadcasting licenses for four years, a move that assured the radio networks, who already owned and operated the majority of TV stations, primary authority over the development of the medium.[55] Although television would not reach all regions of the United States until 1955, the first boom in broadcasting and receiver sales was already well under way (Spigel, 32).

For the film industry, the swing toward suburban, self-styled (rather than merely supplied to spectators who could not control its consumption conditions), interactive leisure meant that consumers began leaving the old neighborhood movie theaters behind along with the cities that filled their breadwinners' workweeks. Instead, they spent their leisure hours in more participatory and family-oriented activities like board games, going for drives or picnics, getting together with neighbors, and puttering around in the garage in a reprise of the bricolage that defined young manhood and its rosy future for the early wireless era, only this time the bricolage was defined as inutile and even foolish play, undertaken primarily for the sake of relaxation. Cody and family, under the influence of "privatization" at the drive-in and elsewhere throughout the film (as Cody crooks every little technology in sight), appropriate and tinker with spectatorship itself. The actual audience in the theater watching *White Heat* could conceivably model itself after this one, with *White Heat* itself playing the parallel role to whatever nameless movie they're watching.

By the time the industry augmented cinema's technical apparatus with 3-D and widescreen, it was in fact literally contaminated by TV, a situation preferable only to missing out on television profits altogether. When the FCC lifted its four-year frequency allocation ban in 1952, it was clear that the networks and their corporate sponsors controlled the structure, advertising, and programming of television. The best an ailing Hollywood could do was to raise what money it could by supplying TV with old films (long considered but not attempted until RKO's sale of its pre-1948 features in July 1955, with other studios quickly following suit by either leasing or selling their catalogs)[56] and newly produced "telefilms." The studios broke into television production most earnestly beginning in 1953, a move that Hilmes attributes to the convergence of such events as the end of the station freeze, "the resultant shift of advertising money to television, the drop in theater revenues and the final throes of divestiture," and perhaps most important, the merger of Paramount's divested theater chain, United Paramount Theaters, with the young ABC Network, which reignited the imaginations of studio heads looking to control film exhibition via television as they had done with theaters before divestiture.[57]

Yet TV fantasy films continued to fight for public film exhibition's right to exist, even as Hollywood reached for new means to compete with the various public-in-private models of spectatorship postulated by TV viewing practices and drive-ins. By mixing a series of filmic cocktails that mingled new technologies with satire, Hollywood pleaded with its audiences to appreciate what media critic Charles A. Siepmann, discussing film and TV explicitly as "rival media" in 1950, called "Hollywood's advantage" over television, "the *inherent* attractiveness of moving pictures on a *full-sized* screen."[58] Innovations like 3-D and widescreen processes had been available to Hollywood for many years before 1952, but few studios saw fit to risk serious experimentation until television had garnered a national market.[59] Unusual (if not new) technologies helped to establish the cinema's difference from TV at this troubling juncture, when the industry weathered devastating legal actions as well as new competition. William Paul summarizes the industry's logic for pushing 3-D and widescreen as follows: "If the government insists that the movie companies release their products to television, then the movie companies . . . can answer with movies that cannot be shown on TV, movies that materially inscribe themselves as unalterably theatrical. The ontology of the photographic image is thus rewritten and redefined by its essentially theatrical nature."[60]

As Belton has argued, television is only part of a "larger field of cultural transformation" that damaged Hollywood's popularity after the peak box-office year of 1948. This field is defined by the rise of the American suburban culture after the war, which emphasized home activities like cookouts, garage work, and evening drives that were more convenient than shuttling into town to see a movie (Belton, 70). Although they did not explore the economic implications of television's claims to liveness, fifties television fantasy films explicitly debunked liveness as a fabrication, a stage show concocted to sell products to a credulous audience. *It's Always Fair Weather*'s plot revolves around a television show called "Midnight with Madeleine" whose star (Dolores Gray) exudes the personal intimacy associated with live shows in the 1950s; she introduces one segment by alluding to her "personal" feelings about it, saying it's "the part of the program that's my favorite because it *means* something." But the minute the video cameras switch off, she slumps at a table and bellows, "Gimme a club sandwich and two cans a' beer—make it three!" Not only does she care little for her "constituency," but her supposed fans, it turns out, object strenuously to what Angie (Michael Kidd) calls her "phony sentiment and corn." If, as Jane Feuer writes, the Hollywood-centered "backstage" musical *Singin' in the Rain* (Kelly and Donen, 1952) responded to declining cinema attendance by suggesting "that making musicals can provide a solution to any crisis of technological change,"[61] this television-focused backstage musical makes an identical argument—regarding the cinema again, not television—by proving film's ability to warn us of the false claims that technological change carries in tow.

Films that satirized television often intensified this kind of insult by marking widescreen and color as unmistakable signs of film's superiority. *Will Success Spoil Rock Hunter?* (Frank Tashlin, 1957), for example, effectively castrates TV by comparison to the width of the CinemaScope frame (an appropriate tactic for a film so concerned with its titular character's virility, his ability to keep his "pipe lit"). Rock (Tony Randall) at one point asks the audience directly whether it would prefer a tiny, black and white TV image to what it's getting, while the image readjusts briefly to realize this worst-case scenario. As Rock elaborately praises the pleasures of the new machine, the image of his face, nearly swallowed by the blackness of the remainder of the 'Scope image, begins to flip, twist, and stretch in imitation of poor TV reception. In a more connotative vein, the preponderance of high-budget, widescreen, and color epics like *The Robe* (a genre ridiculed three years before by *In a Lonely Place,* through Mildred the star-struck coat checker and future murder victim, as "a picture that's real long and has lots of things going on") and musicals like *It's Always Fair Weather* and *Brigadoon* in the mid-fifties presented cinema as a sophisticated entertainment for which money was no object, in direct contrast to the cheaply produced, commercial-riddled, close-up-laden entertainments provided by television.

But the film industry's new emphasis on technology and spectacle also allowed Hollywood to construct versions of "presence" and "liveness" that were no less ideological than those of television. Fox patented CinemaScope in 1953 in the wake of Cinerama, a three-camera widescreen process owned by independent producers. According to Belton, Cinerama resembled a fairground attraction more than it resembled classical cinema. As the cumbersome multiple-camera setup made close-ups and rapid editing nearly impossible, Cinerama productions were generally travelogues, reminiscent of the train or boat panoramas of early cinema in their concentration on movement and exotic locales.[62]

Belton rightly argues that "the model chosen by Hollywood for purposes of redefining its product was less that of the amusement park, which retained certain vulgar associations as a cheap form of mass entertainment, than that of the legitimate theater,"[63] but early 'Scope films also engaged with television discourse, both in their residual allegiance with Cinerama's particular mode of attractions and in their pretensions to theatricality. Fox's single-camera, anamorphic CinemaScope process, nicknamed "the poor man's Cinerama" by the critics, repeatedly mimicked Cinerama's ideology of presence. Even the narratively conservative comedy *How to Marry a Millionaire* (Jean Negulesco, 1953), the second 'Scope feature after the quasi-biblical epic *The Robe* (Henry Koster, 1953), shifts generically between travel film and star vehicle. A trailer for the film promises "the glamour of the world's greatest city [New York]. . . . The thrill of Maine's ski-slopes. . . .

The dazzling beauty of a fashion show!" along with the glamour, thrill, and dazzle of Lauren Bacall, Betty Grable, and Marilyn Monroe. The film itself fetishizes these scenes as much as it fetishizes female bodies, with prolonged takes, sweeping pans, and a long take filmed from the front of a landing airplane. While television played its liveness/simultaneity card to the hilt with news shows like *See It Now,* reporting from the warfronts of Korea and other points of historical or cultural interest, CinemaScope ushered a physical experience of presence into the theater that rhymed with televisual presence, even if it could not exactly reproduce it. If television promised to bring the world closer, 'Scope was to put the viewer "on the scene" by filling even the periphery of vision with images of distant lands.

To complicate the tautology further, widescreen musicals and comedies celebrated the "unique" experience of new cinematic technology while mirroring the live television spectacle and the variety show. *How to Marry a Millionaire* puts its own slant on theatrical verisimilitude with "Street Scene," an orchestral overture to the picture play that follows (Figures 27 and 28). Like the Warners-Vitaphone shorts of the early sound era, the 'Scope framing is relatively static and emphasizes the sprawling width of the orchestra. The overture also gestures toward an aesthetic of "live" theater by unfolding continuously in time; there is no cut-in or reframing even at the beginning of a loud solo by a cornetist buried deep in the orchestra (although the camera does eventually track in a little). At the end of the overture, as if to replicate Vitaphone's radio-theatrical ideology of "presence" or the theatricality of TV, composer-conductor Alfred Newman bows deeply to his "audience." Here film presents itself as live but does so by cloaking itself in the same theatricality that television used to produce its own ideology of liveness and promote its difference

Figure 27. The curtains part on Alfred Newman's "Street Scene" prelude. Frame enlargement from *How to Marry a Millionaire* (1953).

Figure 28. Can you find the cornetist in this picture? Frame enlargement from *How to Marry a Millionaire.*

from the cinema. "Street Scene" displaces television's claims to media singularity—especially liveness, copresence, and temporal realism—by proffering cinematic analogies to those very claims. The point is, for this film, that "liveness" is not, or should not be, merely a matter of feeling close to an actor or identifying with an event. Rather, it should be backed by a guarantee of the event's contingency, a guarantee that doesn't depend solely—or perhaps at all—on the liveness of the performers but rather on the presence of the audience. As Auslander argues, "liveness" in theater may be palpable, but that liveness cannot only be a matter of shared time and space between performers and spectators, because the play is more or less the same every time.[64]

The other relatively unexplored basis on which Hollywood took on TV, also related to the media noirs, was on the grounds that the "intimacy" offered by television is a trap that prevents private experience from finding some means to express itself. Events like "Street Scene," as well as the videophobia promoted by *Will Success Spoil Rock Hunter?* and *It's Always Fair Weather,* may seem banal and calculated compared to the negative invocation of TV in media fantasy noir. But the critical possibilities of noir technoskepticism still hide in these films, in the form of accidental overlaps between the newly renovated cinematic apparatus and fantasies of televisual intimacy that had all but dissipated by the mid-fifties. At one point in *It's Always Fair Weather,* Ted Reilly (Gene Kelly) and his now-estranged army buddies Doug (Dan Dailey) and Angie dance "together" via a tripartite matte shot that recalls Cinerama, the earlier three-projector system (Figure 29). Unable to rekindle their Army friendship on their own, they get a little help from the new, recreational cinema. The 'Scope framing expresses their longing to get back together even as it stresses their

Figure 29. Dan Dailey (left), Gene Kelly (center), and Michael Kidd go into their virtual dance. Frame enlargement from *It's Always Fair Weather* (1955).

isolation. But this moment is also an allegory for cinematic spectatorship, in which individuals sit alone together in the theater, watching the same film and thus sharing a horizon of experience, if not necessarily the same reactions (the film repeatedly stresses the fundamental personality and class differences among the three men).

Initially this moment seems a fairly cheesy bit of foreshadowing in which CinemaScope flexes it sinewy muscle to preview the reconciliation among lapsed friends that the plot will surely sanctify in the end. But the film's impetus to debunk the intimacy myth of live TV shades this scene as a comparative statement about media identities as well—a plea to acknowledge the discursiveness of TV liveness and see its promise of community for the informatic construct it is, rather than an ineffable, interactive reality. Interestingly enough, however, the framing of this long-distance dance shot can only pull off such a shrewd critique by calling attention to the equally discursive "participation" generated by the widescreen image. For like this fantasized *image* of community that recognizes no boundaries of space or time, CinemaScope brings no one in the theater any closer to anything or anyone shown on-screen—not that this fact would have surprised any viewer in 1955, but the suspension of disbelief on which even the first projected films depended for their thrills takes an anticlassical beating at this moment. The punches only hit harder thanks to the fact that this moment appears during a dance number, the Hollywood musical's unique throwback to the disjunctive mode of attractions cinema. 'Scope artificially limits *participation* to an imagined link between spectator and screen—a unity as imaginary as the use of optical printing to stitch the three friends together into a single 3:1 frame.

At fleeting moments like this one, Hollywood fantasizes film as not intrinsically public, in the sense that it harbors social connection and engagement through the screen, but contingently *public-forming,* more or less so depending on the mix of strategic, tactical, and utterly accidental effects of Hollywood's need to convince its viewers that it, like a new medium that seems to hold the patent on an era's ideas about what social exchange is and what it means to the culture, has some kind of interactivity to offer. In this case, what the CinemaScope film offers is a basis for recognizing how isolating it can be to accept a mass-produced simulacrum of social interaction as if it *were* that interaction itself.

If curved-screen CinemaScope musicals like *It's Always Fair Weather* enveloped spectators while striking balletic blows to their collective classical gaze, 3-D pulled no punches whatsoever. It pummeled viewers with a hail of rubber balls, chairs, knives, falling wax figures, and even spit; in perhaps the weirdest and most irreverent scene in 3-D's short history, an infantryman spits tobacco at a rattlesnake in Gordon Douglas's *The Charge at Feather River* (1953), hitting the spectator's eye instead. In such scenes, Hollywood reminds its patrons that they are no longer sequestered in the suburbs but are instead subject to a few cinematic surprises that no TV could supply. *The Glass Web,* the 3-D film with which I opened this chapter, provides a version of this reminder that speaks directly to the *institutional* differences between (3-D, public) film and (tiny, homebound) TV. The problem *The Glass Web* has with TV extends beyond the corrupt sensationalism of its "true crime" programs. It represents the entire televisual institution as a lost cause for viewers seeking information about real events. The "true" crime show folds its tent of integrity before the sponsors' demands for sensationalism, as demonstrated by a long take of an actor sycophantically delivering a cigarette ad between puffs, which imitates the centered framing and lack of cutting of early fifties TV spots all the while. The irony of shooting a man holding a cigarette with an elaborate 3-D camera is, of course, that it's a boring thing to watch as well as a mock-up version of intimacy, as phony as the cheap wooden desks that looked like mahogany on newscasts before HDTV. But the crowning irony of this scene is that, perceptually at least, a 3-D *film* of a man smoking carries an unsettling impression of presence—a visual depth that *The Glass Web* allegorically links with the greater investigative depth it attributes to film as well. The opening scene briefly fools us into thinking a real murder is being committed, but then the camera tracks back from the narrow purview of the "viewers at home," allowing the film's audience to see the boom mikes and soundproof glass. A few moments later, in the supremely privileged space of the control booth, we overhear Hayes complaining that the producers paid no attention to the facts of the murder that he'd so painstakingly researched.

Like the media fantasy noirs of the forties and early fifties, *The Glass Web* criticizes the dominant logic of media progress and argues implicitly for the authority of the recording medium that, however fictional its "reports," allows the potted (and self-interested) media critics who just happen to work in the movies to assemble their case against TV with painstaking accuracy (or so the film would probably like us to think). But like the thin stream of 3-D horror shows that preceded it during the short life of the process, *The Glass Web* also imbues film with an edginess that in turn suggests *possibility,* supporting at the haptic level its claims for the cinema's insight into hidden realities while at the same time stressing the technological transformation of film. The most conspicuous 3-D effects are the outward explosion of a television screen (during the opening credits, no less) and a series of attractions at the center of the film, when water from a hose, an avalanche of broken concrete, and a huge truck barely miss the distracted Newell as he wanders down the street and instead fly straight out at the equally distracted audience. These effects catch us in a cinematic web of visceral experience that renews the cinema as a medium that produces unexpected effects of liveness, just as earlier noir reinfused technology in general with random fantasies of technological possibility.[65] By punching the viewer square in the eye, *The Glass Web* picks a fight with the idea that TV intimacy could fill in the gaps of community left by suburban emigration and urban decay.

The dialectic of media shock and media possibility on display in these last few films echoes the forceful ambivalence of earlier noir, but none of them quite matches film noir's energy in this respect. By 1955, Hollywood had lost its battles to govern TV but had won the war to install classical spectatorship in the home rumpus room via the growing dominance of the "canned" programs that both critics and the broadcast networks had once thought anathema. In *It's Always Fair Weather* and *The Glass Web,* TV simply *is*—a natural element to complain about, like the weather that Kelly and Donen's film assures us is always fair under film's giant, curved umbrella, but not a "new" medium any longer. Its institutional glue has set. But the revisions Hollywood made to its own media parameters at this moment, when the concept of "TV" was nearly indistinguishable from that of commercial broadcasting and fantasies about it turned on the possibilities of entertainment and commerce, bore witness to the fact that film's "qualities" were as subject to external redefinition as they had ever been.

In an important way, however, both *The Glass Web* and *It's Always Fair Weather* hang onto the amateur-maverick standing of the noir brico-leurs in that they each reduce television's benign functions in the public sphere to exactly one: live surveillance. The simultaneity of TV saves the day by surreptitiously transmitting Hayes's guilt to *The Glass Web*'s con-trol room, and by displaying Ted's tangle with a gangster to the entire American viewing public in *It's Always Fair Weather* ("You've just given a nice, clear statement to about 60 million people!").

These moments delineate a tamed media fantasy in which television does its best, most honest work when it takes advantage of its liveness to report events as they happen, instead of attempting to entertain. These commandeered TV cameras revive the radicalism of media fantasy noir's amateurs by renewing the demand that TV either fulfill its promises of material, unilateral change or prepare to be boarded. The liveness of video, the films suggest, could still form accidental constituencies around common problems or goals, but that potential has less chance of develop-ing in the hothouse of commercial broadcasting than it does if handled by an outsider. Ted is no media professional, just a mediocre fight promoter who happens to figure out at the spur of the moment that he must direct the gang boss for the TV camera if he hopes to get out of the mess he's in without losing his teeth.

In other words, Ted is an amateur through and through, and even has a job that sounds familiar from any number of film noirs. But only the amateur with a specific worry would think to replace the *central* screen in a bank of monitors with the image of what worries him most (Figure 30).

Figure 30. Culloran (Jay C. Flippen) unwittingly confesses his crimes, flanked by dancing commodities in *It's Always Fair Weather.*

This tripartite framing of the three TV monitors neatly parodies the wish image of human contact produced by the matted, CinemaScoped dance number, implying the superficiality of a televisual "contact" that regularly interrupts its own intimate address to display dancing boxes of soap and cigarettes. As it turns out, what Ted has to communicate—the confession of a dangerous gangster who might otherwise remain at large—is both much more intimate than Madeleine's artificially sweetened condescension and much more crucial to public well-being than a tribute to "little people" like Angie, who immediately grasps the insincerity of the entire affair and matches Ted's impromptu public service announcement by inviting Madeleine, on behalf of all the so-called little people whose happiness supposedly depends on her, to kindly step off. Even if *The Glass Web* or *It's Always Fair Weather* can't imagine TV's future potential beyond the narrow definition of social stability promoted by *The Story the Biograph Told* and *Caught by Wireless,* they still foreground alternative practices that would allow individuals to transmit images themselves, images that might communicate something of critical importance to them rather than turning them time and again into terminus points for images they cannot even request outright, only choose between by changing channels.

Postscript: The Eternal Return of Videophobia

Unlike the cinematic radio craze, which was limited to the emergent era of broadcasting, Hollywood's videophobia appears to be chronic. Sidney Lumet's *Network* (1976), Tobe Hooper's *Poltergeist* (1982), and Joel Schumacher's *Batman Forever* (1995, discussed in chapter 5) represent a tiny percentage of films from the past forty years that cast TV as a deceitful houseguest. *Network,* scripted by 1950s live-television dramatist Paddy Chayefsky and featuring *Sunset Boulevard's* William Holden, reanimates the media amateur in the figure of Howard Beale (Peter Finch), a fired network news reader who starts speaking his mind on live TV at his farewell broadcast. His ratings leap to such stratospheric heights that he's given a second chance, and he soon uses his newfound charisma to convince a large portion of the global village to throw open its windows and yell his infamous motto: "I'm as mad as hell, and I'm not going to take this anymore!"

But while he attracts much support from the populace and is even allowed to condemn the network on the air, he's soon reduced to the flavor of the month. Thanks to a hypnotic pep talk by the chair of the multinational conglomerate that buys the network in mid-film, Beale's criticisms become so subdued and arcane that his fans no longer understand, or care, what he's talking about. Yet however ridiculous he becomes, the film sides with his perspective on televisual deceit and against network executives like Diana Christensen (Faye Dunaway), who exploit Beale mercilessly to boost the network's market share—ironically at the expense of the network's news division, which is promptly swallowed (as most actual broadcast news divisions have been since then) by the entertainment division. When Beale's aimless philosophizing finally renders him useless to them, the executives have him assassinated, making him, as the voiceover informs us, "the first known instance of a man who was killed because he had lousy ratings." By portraying the titular network as willing to exploit transformative moments of collective empathy and rage to sell the TV audience to the sponsors, the film blames the television industry for bungling television's fantasy charter. Yet even while stressing the institutional nature of the disaster, *Network* molds TV itself into a symbol for both TV's alternative possibilities and its actual, nightmarish effects.

How does this *Glass Web*–style tirade about a long-standing media structure function in a televisual fantasy produced so long after TV's emergent period? When *Poltergeist* represents TV as a conduit between the suburbs and the world of the angry dead, does it simply take an easy swipe at a tried-and-true straw man? Considering the historical specificity of forties and fifties TV fantasy films, I suspect that these "belated" manifestations of videophobia are not merely anachronistic. Technoskeptic and videophobic constructs left over from the forties and fifties provide Hollywood with ready-made tropes for positioning the cinema with respect to new developments in media and, in the process, afford audiences much-needed (un)reality checks with respect to the entire media landscape, opportunities to map that landscape anew rather than blindly accepting its current form as identical with TV's nature as a medium. Taking a step back from the Vietnam reports of the early seventies and continuing reports of student protests and other "radical" activities, *Network* reminds us to consider both as carefully framed representations rather than intrinsically true missives from the front. *Poltergeist* picks up its nervous energy from the fears ignited by HBO and other cable channels that began to pump movies into the private sphere, much to the chagrin of studios who hadn't yet cut deals with cable concerns. At the same time, it offers a hysterical, and partly ironic, affirmation to parents who felt that allowing R-rated films into the family room might just signal the end of Western civilization.

In each case, however, the institutional necessity of fixing media difference—and the contradictions inherent in that necessity—continue to render cinematic representations of TV semiotically incoherent and thus, I think, simultaneously as utopian about media intercommunication in the most accessible sense as they are (or purport to be) dystopian. In *Network,* counterpublics unite less *around* Beale, at least at first, than *through* their dissatisfaction with their meager impact on politics. In *Poltergeist,* a graveyard full of dead souls, their burial sites desecrated by a suburban subdivision, enter the neighborhood through a television and start exacting their revenge. In the guise of a horror tale about channeling the undead, *Poltergeist* manages to envision TV as a medium that airs long-trampled histories at last, allowing young suburbanites to see past their consumerist tunnel vision long enough to pay homage to pasts both ancient and recent that they had chosen to ignore.

Reprising its 1950s role as investigative media reporter, Hollywood cinema in the video age stands watch over these uncanny intersections between public and private experience, but it also reanimates the lost imaginary of TV, the idea of "seeing far" contained in the word *television* that Adorno identified in 1953 as the machine's receding but still palpable utopian possibility.[66] Unlike the hyperprivatized institutional form that television has taken, Hollywood cinema gives its public a chance to react *as* a public, *in* public, to the vexed and fungible media identities that its films take apart and put back together on the screen. Like Cary (Jane Wyman) in Douglas Sirk's *All That Heaven Allows* (1955), we are continually asked by TV fantasy films whether network and cable television's prepackaged versions of "life's parade" might turn the private sphere into a more heavily armored trap, reflecting dim images of ourselves back at us, with all trails leading from the global village to the home but none leading out.[67]

To counter this fearsome possibility, which *All That Heaven Allows* explicitly pictures in its most famous scene, the film projects a fantasy figure for the cinema screen, the picture window at the Thoreauvian home of her lover Ron (Rock Hudson) through which she gazes upon the landscape as the film draws to a close. The laughably stereotypical landscape, complete with a gregarious deer that always prompts a huge laugh in my classes, is not so important here as the fact that this figurative screen represents the experience of "nature" she and Ron have come to share, an ideal around and through which she learns to express her sexual desire against the community's sober expectations of elder widowhood.

This fantasy is crammed to the breaking point with contradictions; as

Laura Mulvey argues, there's little subversive in Cary's repositioning as caregiver for the injured Ron, which seems merely to trade one form of domestic servitude for another.[68] But the allegory nevertheless re-publicizes (in the sense of rejuvenating self-conscious publicness) the cinematic sphere as an alternative to the washed-out image of TV's "community," which for Cary would simply fulfill her fear of being walled up in a pyramid like a widow of an ancient pharaoh. As with the exuberantly contradictory, even antisocial amateur scenarios of the media noirs, such contradictory futures residing in the same image could spark productive confusion about where and how *All That Heaven Allows*'s oscillations between utter joy, abject disappointment, and making do with what one must intersect with the viewing experiences depicted in the film, not to mention the viewing experience of various spectators before this alternately cartoonish and subtle melodrama. In the end, the overdeterminations of media films after the emergence of television stretch to the limit the powers of Hollywood cinema to claim the last word on either its rival medium or the nature of cinematic experience itself.

The Negative Reinvention
of Cinema: Late Hollywood
in the Early Digital Age

Trailer: Come (Back and) Ride the Movies

This is where I come in. I lived through the emergent era of the Internet, (fortuitously) while in graduate school, and it was my first screening of *The Lawnmower Man* that alerted me to the possibility that interactive media were putting pressure on Hollywood to defend and revise the identity of film. The Internet's emergence may be fading now, but its movie legacy, a newly refined version of the cinema as an interactive experience, is apparent wherever we look. I drove to Lawrenceville, Georgia, one Saturday evening to see *The Truman Show* (Peter Weir, 1998) at a third-run decaplex housed in a segment of suburban Atlanta's endless line of strip malls. The ticket cost me a buck—approximately the per-play cost of the video games sitting in the theater lobby. By the time I sat down, the trailers were already running, but I didn't miss any of my favorite: an animated Regal Cinemas trailer asking patrons to refrain from smoking, talking, and leaving garbage in the aisles (which didn't stop two little kids in the front row from tossing ice cubes at the older spectators behind them), and reminding us to buy all the popcorn necessary to compensate Regal for its ridiculously low admission charge. The trailer was structurally identical to every other of its kind, with the exception that it aligned my point of view with that of a roller coaster passenger, speeding over celluloid tracks into a dark tunnel of spectatorial pleasures. Though not a postmodern "ridefilm" of the sort Lauren Rabinovitz describes, those amusement park and Vegas spectaculars accompanied by kinetic effects and thundering stereophonic sound, the trailer made the same connection—a connection as old as cinema itself—between the somatic experience of travel and the simultaneously embodying and disembodying experience of viewing a film.[1]

But where Rabinovitz rightly finds in contemporary ridefilms a means of mediating cultural unease about the technologically produced image in the digital era, the fact that I was invited onto a roller coaster in order to reach *The Truman Show* switched me onto a different track. Rabinovitz writes that full-blown ridefilms perform a nostalgic function in that they root knowledge and certainty in bodily experience at a time when digital representation technologies sever image from referent in wholly new ways, thus throwing the very possibilities of knowledge and certainty into pronounced doubt. In this nostalgic function, ridefilms resemble the Hale's Tours films of the cinema's second decade, which "responded to the newness of cinema's autonomization of vision . . . by grafting the process onto a bodily sensation of motion" (Rabinovitz, 135). However, as I settled into my window seat to view a film dedicated to giving the medium of television a good discursive thrashing, I couldn't help but think that the nostalgia contained in this trailer was a nostalgia for the cinema's infancy, a time when the medium of film had no absolute conventions of representation, address, or exhibition to contain or define it—when every film and every viewing experience was a point of self-definition, and no other technology of vision could touch film for sheer novelty or possibility. This belated Phantom Ride, by contrast to Hale's Tours, was transporting me to yet another intimation of narrative cinema's advanced age: *The Truman Show*. Long drained of its initial novelty, Hollywood film has gotten accustomed to implying its singularity and superiority by use of negative media examples, and television historically has taken the full force of the blow. *The Truman Show,* like such memorable anti-TV Hollywood films as *The Glass Web, A Face in the Crowd, Network,* and *Broadcast News* (James L. Brooks, 1987), knocks TV for its ideology of liveness, intimacy, and truth. TV's primary victim here, Truman Burbank (Jim Carrey), suffers the realization that his entire life has been fictionalized without his knowledge by a video production company that beams his every move to millions of enraptured viewers.

A film like *The Truman Show* might seem a pointless exercise in the age of digital media, its anti-TV message a voice that barely rises above a whisper in the din of global telecom and its decidedly uncinematic agendas of interactivity (versus voyeuristic classical spectatorship), collective engagement (versus spectator individuation), and information consumption (versus narrative consumption). Indeed, one wonders if any contemporary antimedia film can be anything but pointless, a magnetically taped whistle in the digital dark of technological progress, during which the entertainment market is increasingly overtaken by experiences related to the PC and the Internet. It is this very appearance of pointlessness, however, that requires us to take a closer look at the mediaphobic films produced by Hollywood since the emergence of the personal computer and the modem. Not surprisingly, perhaps, digital fantasy films continually invite their distracted audiences to glance into film's equally distracted ancient past in order to glimpse its present and its future, for in that past of distraction and spectacle for their own sake lies Hollywood's best chance for competing with the new media institutions and the interactive publics they gather. Mediaphobic films are certainly nothing new, as I have shown in the previous chapters. Here I will focus on cyberphobic films, a recent cycle of films with digital media themes that makes particularly fervent—and questionable—claims about what the contemporary Hollywood cinema is not.

Opening Credits: The Mythical Strategies and Anxious Misreadings of Cyberphobia

Long before the Internet and the World Wide Web were household words, films about electronic media like *Tron* (Steven Lisberger, 1982) and *WarGames* (John Badham, 1983) helped to establish a paranoid discourse about computer communications. Granted, each of these films expressed wonder as well as anxiety about the emerging landscapes of virtual reality and computer communications; in *Tron,* Flynn (Jeff Bridges) is sucked into a computer and forced to take the position of video game avatar—surely a favorite fantasy of any American kid plunking endless quarters into video arcade games like *Defender* or *Robotron* in 1982, not to mention the highly successful *Tron* tie-in game—while *WarGames* makes computer whiz kid Matthew Broderick both villain and hero when he accidentally entices a childlike defense department computer named Joshua to play a war "game" with the nuclear warheads under its control, then proves through his clever questioning of that same computer that no machine ought to be given sway over the entire population of Earth. Although the computer in each film makes faulty and even dangerous decisions, both *Tron* and *WarGames* capitalize on the thrills of electronic discovery.

But by the 1990s, when the digital revolution began to capture larger portions of the market and of the public imagination, the paranoid tendencies of digital media films began to overwhelm their good-humored fascination. Brett Leonard's *The Lawnmower Man* (1992) epitomizes Hollywood's strategies for representing the digital media's dominant phase. In the film, the mentally handicapped Jobe (Jeff Fahey) gains superintelligence through a combination of psychotropic drugs, computer learning tools like CD-ROMs, and, most important for the film's status as a special effects extravaganza, VR simulations in which Jobe tests his new abilities.

As his intelligence and electronic dexterity increase, however, the influence of digital technology makes him detached, self-serving, and feloniously dismissive of others' autonomy. Jobe's transformation narrates the film's concern that digital media's promises of more intimate long-distance communication are ultimately false. About halfway through the film, Jobe straps his lover, Marnie, and himself into datasuits, headgear, and gyroscoping harnesses that will allow them to experience VR as a fully sensory, fully shared experience. He coaxes her to try VR by presenting it as a haven where their minds can interact through electronic avatars, free from the contingencies of real life: "In here," Jobe says, "we can be anything we want to be. Nothing can hurt us in here." Subsequent shots of their virtual tryst, represented by animated computer graphics, portray VR eroticism as a transformation of two consciousnesses into one. However, these shots are intercut with shots of the flesh-and-blood versions of the lovers, embracing their own bodies in corners of a huge testing room. They may be melded together in cyberspace, but in physical reality they're literally wrapped up in themselves, more alone than together (Figure 31). The film peers into the backstage area of their digital unity, and finds only an electronically induced delusion.

But if some promises that digital media will close the distance between subjects prove false, others come a little too true. Telling Marnie "This is what you really want," Jobe transforms his avatar into a monstrous cartoon predator and penetrates her with beams of mental force that leave her with the mind of a child. His previous, compassionate identity is replaced with that of a megalomanic psychic rapist once his mind is shot through with the new media. By the film's end, Jobe leaves his body behind entirely; it actually dissolves, leaving nothing but a smoking datasuit. He then attempts to take over the global telecommunications network—computers, telephones, and all—from the inside. "I am God here," cries the virtual (and all-too-actual) fascist, and the film extends Jobe's claim to encompass the real world he claims to want to save from itself.

Figure 31. Though linked in cyberspace, Jobe and Marnie grasp at air in the material world. Frame enlargement from *The Lawnmower Man.*

Despite its obvious references to Mary Wollstonecraft Shelley's *Franken-stein* (with Dr. Angelo cast as the postmodern Prometheus), it would oversimplify matters to say that the film merely updates Romantic notions that science and technology extend the human race's reach beyond its grasp; nor may the film's glitzy paranoia be explained away in terms of an ahistorical technophobia. Films about digital technology consistently and specifically address computers *as media,* exploring their capabilities as transmitters of images, information, and ideas. *The Lawnmower Man* and other early 1990s films about digital media choose their terms carefully, culling themes from the contemporary social, cultural, and critical discourse about such computerized mass media as video games, computers, the Internet, and VR. In this sense, digital media films are not simply technophobic but specifically mediaphobic.

The Lawnmower Man makes its most overt nod toward preestablished media fantasy circa 1992 by distilling the various digital media currents down to a single, representative medium: virtual reality. In theory, VR is a fully computer-generated environment connected to the user via 3-D eyephones, datagloves, and datasuits, all of which are supposed to feed multisensory information to users and thus enhance their sense of presence in a metaphysical electronic environment. The first full flower of VR as the defining medium of the future came with William Gibson's 1984 cyberpunk novel *Neuromancer,* in which the electronic sensorium was famously dubbed *cyberspace,* a "consensual hallucination" shared by millions of users, a habitable space nearly complete unto itself—a universe in a hot-wired microchip.[2]

But discursively, *The Lawnmower Man*'s representation of digital interaction refers less to VR than to the more familiar technologies of personal computers and modems. We are led to this unspectacular referent for spectacular cyberphobia by the media metanarratives that have arisen alongside the Information Superhighway. In particular, *The Lawnmower Man* exploits two PC-centered anxieties that have gained the status of dominant mythology in the 1980s and 1990s, thanks to their redundant representation in other media from science fiction novels to newspapers, news and entertainment magazines, television, and academic utopias and dystopias of life in a media-saturated world. Each of these anxieties revolves around the problem of media interactivity, and specifically the new opportunities for blurring the boundaries between public and private experience that digital media represent.

First, the film appropriates what I will term the *hacker myth*: the idea that computers offer unearned and uncontrollable power over the real world to irresponsible subjects like children. Hollywood had already discovered the narrative possibilities of this myth with *WarGames,* in which teenager Broderick accidentally hacks the United States into a thermonuclear crisis by using his 1983-model PC and modem (already near-omnipotent according to the film) to enter the Pentagon's missile guidance computer. This same myth colors journalism about digital culture, as evidenced by Katie Hafner and John Markoff's *Cyberpunk: Outlaws and Hackers on the Computer Frontier* (1991), which describes young computer thieves not only as inherently criminal but as politically naive mutants who are always already caught in the act of creating a technological underworld fit for them to inhabit.[3]

"The term *hacker* has had an unfortunate history," cyberpunk novelist Bruce Sterling writes in *The Hacker Crackdown,* his admirable nonfiction attempt to shed light on computer hackers' interests and the nature of their "crimes" without either lionizing them or judging them according to the laws governing physical property rights, as the FBI had so often done by 1992.

> The term can signify the freewheeling intellectual exploration of the
> highest and deepest potential of computer systems. Hacking can describe
> the determination to make access to computers and information as free
> and open as possible. Hacking can involve the heartfelt conviction that

beauty can be found in computers, that the fine aesthetic in a perfect program can liberate the mind and spirit. This is hacking as it was defined in Steven Levy's much-praised history of the pioneer computer milieu, *Hackers,* published in 1984.[4]

To put the larger themes of Sterling's book more succinctly (and in less sympathetic terms), hackers were—and are—primarily young men who use modems and the preexisting channels of global telecommunications networks to bypass every firewall and other virtual boundary explicitly erected to keep them out, just to show that they can do it, that they have self-taught skills they picked up by fooling around at all hours of the night, hanging out on the Web and trading information with their friends. Obviously hackers are no strangers either to emergent media cultures or to Hollywood media fantasy films. Sterling compares them to the boys and young men who "sauc[ed] off" to customers and crossed wires when Bell Telephone hired them as cheap operator labor in the 1870s (14). Although the analogy is certainly apt, media coverage of hackers, both fictional and journalistic, consistently constructs them as the wireless amateurs of the digital age. For official media culture, hackers perform essentially the same cultural function that bad boys and girls of all ages, dating back to Bobby the camera fiend, the "small boys in radio" who made the *Titanic* disaster even more difficult, and Trubus the electric pen aficionado did in previous eras of media fantasy: they portray unregulated use of live, interactive media as disruptive and even destructive to the official social order.

In keeping with this stereotype as updated for the hacker era, Jobe in *The Lawnmower Man* turns into a fascistic monster in part because he is too mentally immature to understand the implications of the powers he wields. Jobe the hacker "god" has only omnipotence and omnipresence going for him, not wisdom, and thus his domain turns from a "consensual hallucination" into something much less than consensual, as Marnie discovers; possession or lack of instrumental knowledge is all that stands between innocent people and the infiltration of their property, minds, and bodies.[5] These motifs of theft and terrorism ribbon through other 1990s films dealing specifically with hacking, such as Robert Longo's *Johnny Mnemonic* and Iain Softley's *Hackers* (both 1995). But despite their heroic representations of dissident computer users, these films only harden the myth in the mold that *The Lawnmower Man* so histrionically casts. Each film reverses the terms of Hafner and Markoff's myth by making the hacker kids essentially good and the corporations they run up against essentially evil, but the terms of the myth—the normal and healthy versus the electronically freakish or monstrous—are the same. There are no politics here, according to these films, only bad kids and good kids, soulless anarchists and defenders of democracy—and of "good," nonexploitative capitalism.

Aside from the critique of capitalistic media practices such narratives provide, siding with good hackers and associating bad hackerism with corporations seems a shrewd maneuver for Hollywood, a way of exploiting public distrust of capitalism and the technologies that serve it (from being put on eternal hold to "computer error" misbillings) despite the film industry's involvement in the technology business.[6] Aficionados of media-phobic films will recognize a similar linkage of hacker invasion fears and individuated corporate avarice in *The Net* (Irwin Winkler, 1995), but because it focuses less on the invaders and more on the experience of being invaded, this film might be better explicated in terms of a second phobia that media films also exploit.

I will call this myth a *myth of total media*: the fear that computer media, since they allow (relatively) unmonitored input and afford users a unique sense of "presence," will inevitably lead to disastrous invasions of privacy; in effect, there will soon be no space private enough to preserve individuals from media's total penetration of reality. The myth of total media might be described as a cross between André Bazin's myth of total cinema, the "guiding myth" that pushes visual technologies toward "a recreation of the world in its own image," with Jean Baudrillard's procession of simulacra, in which nothing can be distinguished any longer from its own representation.[7] Many early visions of VR blurring the distinction between "real" and simulated experience take an unsurprisingly Bazinian, utopian tack. In a 1991 *Smithsonian* article, journalist Doug Stewart tests three-dimensional VR simulations of lung tumors and architectural space and discusses the future with experts like William Bricken—"Virtual reality eliminates the distance between you and the computer"—and Randal Walser—"People will enter cyberspace to work, to play, to exercise, to be entertained. They will enter it when they wake up in the morning and will have no reason to leave it until the end of the day."[8]

But the narrative arcs of media films nearly always terminate on the darker side of the myth of total media, in shadowy dystopias where physical life becomes as cheap as the virtual existence of a video game avatar. *The Lawnmower Man* mobilizes this myth to elicit sympathy for Jobe as a victim of VR's encroachment on the real, rather than a victimizing hacker pure and simple. Jobe's telepathic/telekinetic powers are narratively linked to his virtual experiences, but the film provides no explanation of their origin, a move that exudes paranoia regarding the technologies that made his experiences possible and the unfathomable parallel universe they construct. Although corporations and evil hackers sponsor the intrusions into the private sphere (up to and including the body itself) in *The Lawnmower Man*, ultimately the technology provides the conduit and powerfully determines its own use; human input is neither requested nor desired.

The coexistence of the hacker myth with the myth of total media in *The Lawnmower Man* points to the fact that these myths share a common enemy: the PC as an omnidirectional medium, an instantaneous connection to information stores and individuals worldwide. The greatest sin a protagonist in a cyberphobic film can commit is to put blind faith in the progressivity of these connections; indeed, according to the films, the very limitlessness of digital networks guarantees their destructiveness. In *The Net,* Angela Bennett (Sandra Bullock), a computer software consultant, is so acculturated to—and isolated by—the Internet that she prefers anonymous newsgroups to personal contact. However, she soon realizes that for all the perks of on-line existence, the traces of identity one leaves behind in all phases of an information society—credit card numbers, identity records, server accounts, consumer profiles—invite disaster by allowing anyone with the right skills and equipment to manipulate those traces. Among other disasters, the terrorist corporation transforms Angela into a fugitive prostitute named "Ruth Marx" by vandalizing her identity records, and arranges the death of her only friend. *The Net's* lesson is that all things digitally communicated exist to be sabotaged and that the effects of that sabotage flow easily through the unstable boundary between virtual and actual.[9] The crowning glory of the terrorist's deadly smear campaign against Angela is their decision to name her *Marx,* thereby translating her self-identification as a Netizen, one who takes pleasure in anonymous, category-leveling Internet chat for its own sake, into a sign of the reddest and most un-American of politics.

At the most immediate level, cyberphobic films stage the myth of the hacker and the myth of total media as means to define VR and the Internet as *criminally* interactive, even politically subversive. *The Net's* gangsters use the Internet to play cat-and-mouse with an innocent woman, but even they are merely extraruthless capitalists compared to Angela's pinko nerdiness. If this is the case, however, Hollywood's discursive response to new electronic media carries strikingly different connotations from its material, industrial response to the possibilities of digital representation. The film industry appears to have little to lose and much to gain from the success and mass proliferation of digital media. Hollywood studios and their parent companies are directly involved in the development of digital media from computer animation to interactive technologies, just as they have taken a hand in developing other media forms since the advent of commercial radio. One recent practice brings home the effects of Hollywood's media diversification on its theatrical releases: As Janet Wasko has shown, action-film screenplays are now routinely altered to make their plots easier to adapt into video games, and actors' bodies are sometimes three-dimensionally scanned for use in these games.[10] As studios like Warner Bros. viewed television as a postdivestiture method of controlling distribution in the 1940s and 1950s, so all the contemporary Hollywood studios utilize their many media outlets to ensure the profitability of their "software," as Hollywood management and marketing branches are now wont to call their films (Wasko, 60, 148).

The cinema also finds in electronic media a plethora of new opportunities to arrest the eye. Hollywood has continued to benefit from the new media by developing them in directions that help keep films visually attractive and interesting to audiences who might otherwise stay home with the TiVo or Sony PlayStation on Friday nights. Two of the busiest companies producing special visual effects for Hollywood films—Industrial Light and Magic and Digital Domain—earned their reputations by producing computer effects for such films as *Terminator 2* (James Cameron, 1991), *Jurassic Park* (Steven Spielberg, 1993), *Forrest Gump* (Robert Zemeckis, 1994), and *Titanic* (Cameron, 1997), effects that helped ensure the blockbuster successes of these films. Besides attracting record crowds, digital effects carry the added ideological bonus of displaying the cinema as an institution in synch with the technological times, despite the fact that its basic machinery—the camera-projector-screen triad—is strictly nineteenth century.

Yet in spite of Hollywood's love affair with the digital at the levels of economics and production, films that follow *The Lawnmower Man*'s phobic path seem more the rule than the exception. Of course, nothing requires Hollywood to celebrate any technology. Hollywood films simply exploit what the industry perceives are the interests and concerns of its target audiences. But I suggest that Hollywood's disproportional use of dystopian digital media myths to hail those audiences produces an illuminating allegory of the compromised position in which the American cinematic institution finds itself regarding its own reception by the increasingly diverse, mass-mediated publics of the '90s. Cyberphobia narrates digital media as horrific to the degree that they are literally social and interactive, or to put it in intermedial terms, to the degree that they do not foster an experience that resembles classical film spectatorship. In other words, cyberphobia does not simply construct a menace to society out of media myths; it constructs an Other to cinematic experience. In order to construct difference, however, it must address VR and Internet intersubjectivity fantasies that might be very attractive to film audiences or video game and computer mavens who may find themselves less than satisfied by the directives of silence, attention, and contemplation that still constitute the ideal film spectatorship experience.

The Lawnmower Man, The Net, and *Virtuosity* confront these fantasies head-on, arresting consideration of the cinematic institution in cyberspatial terms by legitimating the social anxieties about electronic communications inherent in the hacker and total media myths. The force of this legitimation process depends upon implicit contrasts these films draw between computer media and the cinema, in which the cinema comes out on top primarily because it *isn't* VR or the Internet. As we sit in the theater (before the film we watch makes the institutional/media leap to cable or home video), our feet gummed to the floor, physically and ideologically far enough from the screen to suspend our disbelief without forfeiting our ability to look elsewhere or walk away, these films repeatedly rehearse the notion that there is no hope of living harmoniously with digital media because they extend the concept of "interactivity" too far beyond the voyeuristic rush of widescreen or the semiautonomy of changing TV channels from the sofa.

Spectacularizing new media, however, can only compromise any attempt to keep external influences out of film production and conventions. In this contradictory strategy for confronting the cinema's digital media others, cyberphobic films manifest the multimedia equivalent of Harold Bloom's anxiety of influence via the tropes they use to engage (or to pretend not to engage) other media texts to which they might be compared: "Every act of reading is an act of belatedness, yet every such act is also defensive, and as defense it makes of interpretation a necessary misprision."[11] No poem, according to Bloom, can signify anything outside the discourse of poetic precedents, despite its defensive misreading of other poems. Neither can the cinema avoid using the terms and possibilities of its media competitors when it comes to constructing an image of itself, even an implied or negative image—especially when it drags those very competitors right into the path of its arc light.[12]

In the process of constructing digital nightmares, cyberphobic films transform digital media myths in ways that inevitably return us to discourses that once surrounded the cinema. Fredric Jameson has written of mass-culture narratives in general that they "cannot be ideological without at one and the same time being implicitly or explicitly Utopian as well: they cannot manipulate unless they offer some genuine shred of content as a fantasy bribe to the public about to be so manipulated."[13] Before a utopian myth can be toppled, it must first be built, represented at the height of its power. While films like *The Net* and *Virtuosity* condemn the digital at the immediate level, they also portray these new media as potentially limitless and globalizing, heirs to such nineteenth-century technologies as the railroad and the telegraph in their power to overturn previous conceptions of time and space, and perhaps equally volatile in their implications for the future of political involvement.

It is the persistence—and persistent energy—of these fantasies that cyberphobic films tap into in their search for an audience, but their dystopian retoolings of media myths can only ever be retoolings, for the utopian leanings of these myths remain remarkably resilient. The imaginative energy of media fantasies tends to taper off once new media become matters of convention, their purposes "naturalized" in terms of their economic value as business or entertainment technologies. But, as I have suggested throughout the book, media fantasies take on lives of their own, often serving individual needs and desires that have nothing to do with the intent of those who produce and police them. The ambiguity and volatility of digital fantasies threaten to release them from the restrictively critical narratives of cyberphobic films, and thus might allow these fantasies to foster not just paranoia but also more purely curious speculation about digital media, and threatens to open out that speculative energy onto the medium that stages the horrors while itself bearing the marks of digital transformation: film.

San Francisco musician and programmer Marc de Groot perfectly epitomizes the paradox of Benjamin's wish image, in which a new technology is imagined in terms of older technologies and their uses and yet is expected to transform human life utterly:

> Virtual reality is a way of mass-producing direct experience. You put on
> the goggles and you have this world around you. In the beginning, there

were animals, who had nothing but their experience. Then man came along, who processes reality in metaphors. . . . Verbal noises stand for experience, and we can share experience by passing this symbology back and forth. Then the Gutenberg Press happened, which was the opportunity to mass-produce symbology for the first time. . . . And virtual reality is a real milestone, too, because we're now able for the first time to mass-produce the direct experience. We've come full circle.[14]

There is no end to the historical blind spots one could list in this VR creation story, in which printing "happens" sui generis and VR merely represents the next logical phase in the development of human communication (here inseparable from the evolution of a production economy). But De Groot's Genesis narrative of VR as a system of "symbology" returns us directly to turn-of-the-century fantasies of film as a universal language that would obviate verbal and written language and thus unite the world,[15] as does virtual guru Terence McKenna's linkage of VR to psychedelic experiences: "If you look at the evolution of organism and self-expression and language, language is seen as [a] process that actually tends toward the visible. . . . We may be moving toward an evolution of language that is beheld rather than heard."[16] De Groot and McKenna, for all their ahistorical claims, drag progressive, long-forgotten dreams of media as democratic art forms back into the landscape of present-day media, confronting older media institutions like Hollywood cinema with their own "forgotten futures."

The fact that digital media films mainly invoke the new in phobic ways suggests not Hollywood's dismissal of new media but rather its intense engagement with them. While digerati like de Groot and McKenna construct VR out of leftover cinematic ideals, current Hollywood production has done exactly the opposite: it uses fantasies of new media to rejuvenate its own self-image. Although *The Lawnmower Man* might be called a film about postmodern anxiety, we must also consider how it reflects the cinema's cyberphobia (to return to the Freudian implications of the term I invoked in the introduction): its postmodern anxieties about its own future, anxieties that contain and repress the terms of "late" cinema's possible reinvention as a medium more closely resembling digital interactive media.

Scott Bukatman has argued that recent science fiction texts from all media display intermedia influence insofar as they "construct a new subject-position to interface with the global realms of data circulation, a subject that can occupy or intersect the cyberspaces of contemporary existence." Bukatman describes this "terminal identity" as fragmentary, keyed almost exclusively to the postindustrial, multimedia version of modernist shock rather than the sequential flow and psychological depth of the traditional literary, theatrical, and cinematic narrative (Bukatman, 8–9). Similarly, Anne Friedberg postulates that the "simulated experiences" of cinematic and televisual spectatorship have progressively "derealized" the concepts of presence, identity, and time, producing a postmodern subjectivity that Friedberg characterizes as a fragmented, "mobilized virtual gaze."[17] I take Bukatman's and Friedberg's cues to make a claim specific to the American cinema as a historical institution: the narratively absorbed position offered the spectator by classical filmmaking is approaching some kind of end, and cyberphobia acknowledges this disappearance and envisions it as a threat to Hollywood's institutional future. In effect, films like *The Lawnmower Man* create cinema's most threatening media Other in order to protect the cinema's traditional mode of address. But in denying the influence of the new and trumpeting the continued relevance and novelty of the cinema, cyberphobic films subtly recast the cinema in the very terms set by the new media and the discourses that collect around them.

The Plot Thickens: The Cinema and the Virtual Audience, or Hollywood's Optical Nerves

Classicality, as Christian Metz was among the first to argue, constructs a subject position that rewards voyeuristic narrative absorption. The film industry's assumption of this subject facilitated the efficient production of films with repeatable codes, and the reproduction of standardized cinematic pleasures. VR and the Internet as currently imagined pose a particular threat to the persistence of classical film, however, for they hang their discursive identities on alternative communication forms—for example, the availability of Internet-accessible MUDs (multi-user dimensions) and MOOs (MUD–object-oriented) in which users wander through virtual spaces and converse via text with people they've never physically met— possibilities that contradict the individuated media reception that classical cinema assumes.[18] Interactive media, even more than radio and TV, appear to facilitate (rather than invent) their own version of subjectivity, definable more by its slippage between different registers of representation and communication than by reproducible codes like classical editing and framing.

Allucquere Rosanne Stone has drawn provocative conclusions about this virtual subjectivity in her studies of interactions within "virtual communities." By virtual communities, Stone primarily means live, text-based role-playing games where large groups of people assume fictional identities and move from "room" to "room" casting spells, trading virtual goods, and talking about life and events both in cyberspace and out. Against protests that cyberspace is merely escapist, Stone argues that cyberspace is rapidly becoming an experience of everyday life and a unique form of social confrontation that cannot simply be dismissed as a simulation of "real" relationships. Users exhibit a shared sense of what Oscar Negt and Alexander Kluge term a horizon of experience or, better, a matrix of social experience set apart from face-to-face communication by such elements as the keyboard/monitor interface and flexibility of individual identity but not reducible to any one of these media-specific elements.[19] Cyberspace is finally defined for its users not by keyboards and monitors or slick graphics but by the social interactions that take place there.

Virtuality, then, comes into its own for Stone not as a visualizable "place" but as an organizing principle, a hazy model for some future form of interaction now under construction and contestation: "The meaning of locality and privacy [in virtual communities in general] is not settled. The field is rife with debates about the legal status of communications within the networks."[20] Although its own most exuberant and inventive phase has already passed, in the mid-nineties MOO culture represented two interrelated threats to the continuation of preexisting modes of mass-media reception, threats that persist insofar as MUDs and MOOs still house thriving virtual subcultures: first, this well-developed form of Internet interaction requires that users see nothing but a screen full of paragraphs that jerkily appear on a computer monitor as they're posted in real time by citizens of the MOO (the presence of visible avatars in such MOO-like environments as the Palace does not undermine the primacy of written speech in the interactions occurring there); and second, however banal or self-consciously fantasized their encounters may be, MOO users have the opportunity to experiment with methods of self-expression within a subculture whose finite boundaries and role-playing imperative nearly force this ersatz community to recognize itself as such a unit.

The unifying and individuating principles of cinematic or even video visuality seem anachronistic when compared to this virtual visuality, despite the hysterical claims of cyberphobic films that only the force of the visual can prove to the world the dangers of the digital. Where critics like Stone and novelists like the cyberpunks and postcyberpunks (William Gibson, Melissa Scott, Neal Stephenson) focus on the productive ambiguity of emergent digital cultures, digital media films simply drain all the ambiguity out of new electronic worlds, envisioning VR and the Internet as tempting but poisoned media, dangerous exactly because intersubjectivity is such an unpredictable basis for the formation of a media public.

One reason for this one-sided response might be that the coming-to-consciousness of cyber-subjectivity described by Stone would seem to place the cinema's subject position somewhere between mortal wounding and extinction. The "ideal" digital subject barely exists as a category in the sense of the Subject constructed by bourgeois art, the novel, and classical cinema: absorbed in and engaged with the text but answerable to no one while in the act of viewing and interpreting it. Stone takes issue with Vivian Sobchack's characterization of "electronic space" as "spatially decentered, weakly temporalized and quasi-disembodied" compared to cinematic space, arguing that the very spectator presumed by classical cinema suggests otherwise:

> It is the potential for interaction that . . . distinguishes the computer from the cinematic mode, and that transforms the small, low-resolution, and frequently monochromatic electronic screen from a novelty to a powerfully gripping force. Interaction is the physical concretization of a desire to escape the flatness [of the screen] and merge into the created system. It is the sense in which the "spectator" is more than a participant, but becomes both participant in and creator of the simulation.[21]

The earliest of the willful denizens of cyberspace, typing/chatting from the distracting spaces of offices, libraries, or homes but acutely conscious of their mediated relationship to other users, more closely resembled the unabsorbed audiences of early cinema, whose responses to films had as much or more to do with particular venues and felt affinities among spectators than with the films actually shown, than they did classical spectators.

This "new" media possibility is, in effect, a return of the cinematic repressed, a return that cyberphobic films actually stimulate in the act of attempting to banish it. Hansen argues that early cinema, with its inconsistent exhibition practices and dependence on sensational attractions, offered a unique opportunity for diverse publics to organize their reception of this quintessentially public form. Without narrative codes or prerecorded soundtracks to direct spectatorship, early audiences had relative freedom to interpret films, collectively as well as individually (since silence was not yet golden), with respect to interests based on such factors as neighborhood politics, ethnicity, and gender.[22] As Hansen has noted in her essay "Early Cinema/Late Cinema: Transformations of the Public

Sphere," contemporary commercial cinema has harbored a resurgence of such ambiguities, due in part to the influences of new media on film form. By defining the new media in terms of the social interactions they facilitate, Hollywood's cyberphobia draws attention to the intersubjective limits of Hollywood spectatorship as limits that exclude more self-consciously social kinds of reception.

But media films' obsession with interactivity does not begin and end with cyberphobia. Even a preliminary attempt to characterize the subject position of digital fantasy films reveals how much the discourses of interactive media have already changed the cinema. As I have discussed in previous chapters, the expansion of cinematic experience to include interaction (in the informatic sense of user-technology relations) begins much earlier than the 1980s and '90s, with the synchronized-sound film "performances" of the late 1920s, and picks up steam with widescreen, color, 3-D, and stereo sound experiments of the 1940s and 1950s. The appearance of new media has also affected film production in less apparent ways. The studios eventually gave in to TV by increasing the number of close-ups per film, avoiding framing characters and objects outside the "safe action area" that represents the aspect ratio of the television screen,[23] increasing editing speed (primarily under the influence of MTV), and acquiescing to smaller screens and remote-happy home viewers by packing action films with pyrotechnic effects that even the most liberal user of the fast-forward button can scarcely miss. The cost of pious adherence to classical codes was obvious to the studios: the loss of the enormous revenue to be made from selling or leasing films to network TV, cable, and home video. But as Timothy Corrigan argues, these apparently minor changes in film aesthetics make a decisive impact on how spectators perceive cinematic space and how they interpret films:

> Surrounded by the fragmented images of a domestic space or before the
> spectacular backgrounds of public outings, contemporary audiences . . .
> view movies and their histories on the visual fringes of their public or
> domestic experiences, disengaged from any unilateral bond through
> which those movies and those experiences might once have reflected
> each other. . . . The contemporary viewer . . . activates an image of self
> and subjectivity that is fractured and emptied through the *possibility*
> of multiple other viewing and social positions.[24]

As if in response to the spectator's ambivalent relation to the image, Corrigan says, postmodern films exhibit "nostalgia for [older] relationships with images that they nonetheless never provide."

Cyberphobic films' attacks on interactive media would seem to support Corrigan's claim that spectators remain nostalgic for classicality; nevertheless, the transformation of the subject position pushes on. If anything, the cinema has become more self-consciously interactive in both the informatic and sociological senses in the past three decades than it has been since the first decade of the twentieth century: more visceral (e.g., the ubiquity of slasher and porno films),[25] more concerned with spectacle, more distracting, and—recalling again the heterogeneity of early cinema—more difficult to interpret in any way that could be properly called universal. While these changes don't suggest "interaction" in the same sense as using a keyboard or having an argument or sexual encounter with another PC user, they do imply different forms of involvement in the cinematic experience, and different paradigms for thinking about the relationship of spectators to the film before them and the spectators around them, than were available before the television age.

The new distractions in/from film spectatorship may indeed represent the dissolution of a "unilateral bond" among viewers of the same film, but these situations in which films register only in the "visual fringes of . . . public or domestic experiences" introduce a new unilateral bond: the experience of distracted viewing itself, which spectators have in common whether they watch the same film on video, cable, broadcast television, CD-ROM, DVD, or even at the theater. Siegfried Kracauer argues that in Berlin in the 1920s, the cinema's continuous stream of distractions, from events on the screen to the accompanying orchestra to the opulent theater decor, was the manifest content of all cinematic experience. This fact had potentially explosive consequences, for the foregrounding of distraction could "convey precisely and openly to thousands of eyes and ears the *disorder* of society—this is precisely what would enable [such shows] to evoke and maintain the tension that must precede the inevitable and radical change."[26] Although the naturalization of media white noise over the course of the century may have cooled the volatility of distraction, the new cult of digital media distraction has already revised Hollywood cinema's institutional identity and posited the possibility of a future cinema in which public interaction becomes central and films themselves enter only the corner of the eye.

Cyberphobia's discourse about *vision* directly addresses this shift in the dominant form of mass-media subjectivity. By using the less-developed, hypervisual medium of VR to trope the more familiar—and visually much more mundane—medium of the Internet circa 1994–95, cyberphobic films gave cinema a level playing field on which to compete with digital media. Even nineties digital fantasy films that focus on Internet-based espionage obsessively visualize such unspectacular media experiences as hacking data or conversing in a MOO. Johnny Mnemonic (Keanu Reeves) performs the digital equivalent of blasting a flea with an elephant gun when he dons datagloves and eyephones to dial up his modem and dig a number out of a hotel's fax machine buffer (Figure 32). In *Hackers,* cyberpunks Crash Overdrive (Johnny Lee Miller) and Acid Burn (Angelina Jolie) sit in front of monitors that inexplicably project images back onto their faces (Figure 33), while their hacks, performed without VR gear, appear on our screen as sweeping movements through a virtual cityscape.

Joel Schumacher's *Batman Forever* (1995) presents us even more forcefully with a cinema whose constructions of visuality and publicness oppose digital constructions of the same concepts, even while it predicts the dissolution of these cinematic preserves in the face of their media revisions. *Batman Forever*'s cyberphobia is metonymized by the figure of "the Box," an amalgam of VR, cable/satellite video, and digital TV, that promises to bring "the joy of 3-D entertainment into your living room." The secret purpose of the Box, however, is to siphon off the brainwaves of the global village, which the Riddler (Jim Carrey) then uses to make himself smarter. The Box scenario resonates tellingly with Wasko's critique of the U.S. Federal Communications Commission's (FCC's) policy regarding what counts as "public interest" in media broadcasting: A new "choice" in entertainment disguises itself as a public service but actually serves only

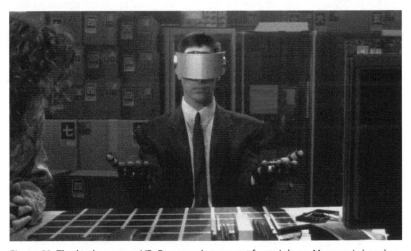

Figure 32. The hacker enters VR. Frame enlargement from *Johnny Mnemonic* (1995).

Figure 33. An ordinary PC monitor manages to project images onto its users' faces. Frame enlargement from *Hackers* (1995).

the producers marketing this choice and fulfills no need expressed by any real "public." As Wasko writes, this situation has become so normalized that even the FCC has come to see media audiences as media consumers and nothing else (74).

But the spectator is not the only one to suffer from this violation. Hollywood film also suffers a blow to its classical identity in *Batman Forever*'s media scenario, articulating a potential for institutional losses that might outweigh the economic gains to be made by exploiting digital media. In the film's opening sequence, a helicopter controlled by the villain Two-Face (Tommy Lee Jones) crashes first through an enormous effigy of an eye—a billboard ad for eye drops that reads "Tired Eyes?" (Figures 34 and 35), then directly into the eyes of Gotham City's version of the Statue of Liberty, where the rotors obliterate everything between nose and crown (Figure 36). *Batman Forever* affirms the potency of scopophilia with these special effects but taints that affirmation by reversing *The King of Jazz*'s own reversal of Méliès's punctured eye. Instead of celebrating the potency of classical narrative and its informatically engaged spectator, as the suspense of the scene might suggest (will Batman manage to avert serious disaster while dangling from a moving helicopter? Of course, but *how*?), this set piece allegorically sacrifices the unified, classical eye in a '90s Hollywood answer to the opening of *Un Chien andalou* (Luis Buñuel, 1929). One of the tasks of Buñuel's own eyeball-slicing prologue was to threaten the destruction of the spectatorial eye produced by a "realist" system of narration that was less than two decades old and yet was as restricted by convention as any bourgeois painter the Surrealists protested.

Figure 34. Batman and Two-Face smash into "tired eyes." Frame enlargement from *Batman Forever* (1995).

Figure 35. Frame enlargement from *Batman Forever*.

Batman Forever answers Buñuel's iconoclastic gesture in the 1990s by promising to blow out the same tired eye of voyeuristic spectatorship—ironically the very eye whose sacrifice to an informatically and sociologically interactive, digital consumption paradigm the film's "Box" scenario fears and laments.

If cinematic potency has to be affirmed here by sacrifice, a spectacular convergence of visual *jouissance* and self-castration, the sacrifice has the

Figure 36. Frame enlargement from *Batman Forever.*

virtue of wiping the slate clean, leaving room for film to reinvent scopo-philia in a way that could compete with the promises of the digital. This move gives away unified narrative vision in favor of a bubbling up of the mode of attractions, one of the conditions that Hansen argues made early cinema such potentially fertile ground for alternative public spheres. If the cinema of attractions went "underground" once the industry's priorities shifted to storytelling and character psychology, cyberphobic films provide strong evidence for Gunning's argument that the "exhibitionist tendency" of early cinema continually returns in the era of classical narrative film and provides pleasures that exceed classical cinema's imperative of absorption in the diegesis.[27]

To be sure, all films show us something, but cyberphobic films overstress the power of the visual in their reliance on digital technology to produce spectacle at the expense of narrative, a consequence that Bukatman has argued is latent in all special effects (Bukatman, 14). Despite the goal-driven classicality of nearly all the films I've discussed, few of them add up to classical films so much as trick films, the early genre pioneered by Méliès. The main thrills of cyberphobic films come from watching figures morph and electronic universes transform themselves, wondering how such effects are accomplished, and imagining what we might do in such a world. *The Lawnmower Man* and *Johnny Mnemonic* are rife with subjective shots of VR, during which the spectator can imagine that her head is the one behind the eyephones; pairs of hands often jut into the frame, ostensibly attached to *our* arms (Figure 37). Although many spectators may never pick up a pair of eyephones or datagloves (just as many travelogue film viewers and Hale's Tours passengers could not afford an actual train ride), the viewer seems to get the next best thing out of such scenes, as she "interacts" with the virtual world along with the characters with whom she becomes informatically intimate. Unlike classical point-of-view shots, the point of these first-person VR shots is to be noticed as technologically produced representations that embody the ephemeral and mobile classical gaze, while at the same time anchoring it to a machine. The classicality of these films is undermined by the generic necessity of peppering them with VR attractions for their own sake, to the point where the narrative line of *Freejack* (Geoff Murphy, 1992), on the B-film end of the media film scale, hardly makes any sense at all.

If the example of early cinema is any indication, unclassical narratives confound the culture industry's economic imperative to provoke consistent interpretations from viewer to viewer and thus threaten the cinematic institution's stability at the textual level. To compete for a piece of the multimediated spectator, however, the studios have no choice but to gesture in multiple directions of address and pleasure, and thus tear an opening in their own products for contemplation and discussion, not only about what a cyberphobic film means but what it implies about the media currently in use. By default, and perhaps only for fleeting moments, these ambivalent media films give us glimpses of the kind of counterpublic cinematic experience that the films themselves would construct as wholly opposed to the nature of film.

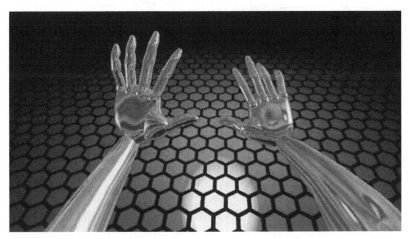

Figure 37. "Look, it's my hand[s]!" Frame enlargement from *The Lawnmower Man*.

Race to the Rescue: Time to Get Real

Back in 1998, I sat through *The Truman Show* transfixed by, in turn, its old-fashioned, *Network*-style critique of the tube—one where liveness and the elision of distance guarantee lies rather than truth—and its digital-era concern with the transformation of the world into its simulacrum.[28] However, in *The Truman Show* the latter problem always refers us to the former in a way I can only call nostalgic, for the simulacrum in question here is explicitly Truman's TV-land of Seahaven, not ours, the space of spectatorship. Not the TV viewers' lives but Truman's life alone is a fabrication, his real feelings and experiences always bound to artifice: friends and lovers who wear earphones to receive their dialogue, endless moments of product placement, and even an artificial sun, a painted-flat sky. The simulacrum, discursively contained by the show-within-the-film just as Seahaven is literally contained by a geodesic bubble, does not leak out into the world of the TV spectators, who know very well that Truman's life has been invented for them. The myth of total media plays out entirely on the stage side of the fourth wall, which never entirely breaks down, even when Truman sees a floodlight fall from the sky or a spotlight of rain follows him across a beach; the fact that Truman, in the eyes of his fans, has merely exited his stage at the end of the film is underscored by their thunderous applause at his escape.

The Truman Show ignores new digital media entirely, casting the contemporary mediascape as straw man, its lies all very obvious, its penetration of the real made palpable by the continuous attention it draws from its audience but its effects on that audience ultimately harmless. Even the fantasized damage done by staged "reality" TV, which *Network* cast as a question of turning the masses into herds, is here distilled into an unfair imprisonment of one individual who simply wants the right to travel physically as his audience has traveled virtually to Seahaven. The viewers within the film may look to Seahaven to find a fantasy version of quotidian life, but aside from taking up a lot of their time, *The Truman Show* has harmed them very little. But the film still marks its mild rebuttal of TV as "serious" critique by refusing to display any actual products in the show's product placement spots (soft drinks and other commodities with parodic names replace the conspicuous Pepsi cans of other Hollywood blockbusters). The distraction and antinarrativity of new media never enter our purview.

And what if they did? Is classicality really on its last legs (again), besieged to the point where commercial films need to defend it from the media that would fragment its form and reception? Although as a critic I feel little nostalgia for classicality, in practice I often morph into a poster child for its continuance; after the sixth ice cube narrowly missed me, I scolded the kids in the front row, who promptly left me, my notebook, and the other spectators to finish the film without further distraction. I will return to the question of classicality's persistence in the concluding section. But as a spectator, particularly one whose attention to films is focused by research as well as narrative pleasure, I find it easy to imagine late classical cinema edging its audiences to recognize the public nature of spectatorship and the materiality of film, but I find it much more difficult actually to let go of the classical subject position *while I'm watching a Hollywood film in a theater*. It seems that my every recognition of the recession of classicality is at the same time an indication of its persistence as an ideal, if not a reality that Hollywood film texts can fully materialize. This purely institutional identity sticks so tenaciously to the medium that it flips on like a projector bulb behind my eyes as the lights go down, structuring my relationship to the lit wall we all stare at, together and alone, in the dark.

But even in proto-postclassical Hollywood, a few digital fantasy films manage to eke out fantasies about cinematic publics that, like the publics linked by technological dispossession that never quite materialize in the media noirs, might trump even the interactive possibilities of the Web. I'd like to isolate an example of a cyberphobic film that modulates its nostalgia for film's dominance into a fantasy of media ambiguity and spectator ambivalence in a very near future: *Strange Days* (1995). Its director, Kathryn Bigelow, has made a career of embracing ambiguity and scattershot spectacle in such genres as horror (*Near Dark*, 1990) and crime drama (*Blue Steel*, 1992), and has in the process made narrative excesses part of her authorial signature. Steven Shaviro describes *Blue Steel*'s peculiar attraction this way: "I am drawn into a condition of excessive undischargeable excitation. I am depositioned and dispossessed by the film's incessant modulations of visibility. . . . Vision . . . is excruciatingly, preternaturally vivid; reality is heightened into feverish hallucination."[29] If Shaviro is right that these characteristics constitute Bigelow's authorial signature, then *Strange Days*, at least at first glance, looks and feels like no other Bigelow film, for its framing, editing, and plot construction are all quite conventional. Rather than Bigelow taking over the cyberphobia cycle, the cycle and its anxieties seem to have taken over Bigelow. Lenny Nero (Ralph Fiennes) makes his living in turn-of-the-millennium Los Angeles by using a recording device nicknamed "the wire" to produce "clips" (digital disks) of people's firsthand sensory experiences that he then sells on the black market, realizing in the most vulgar and dystopian way de Groot's capitalist fantasy of VR as "mass-produced direct experience." In the film, manufacturing, selling, or buying the clips is illegal, presumably because the inevitable market for legally forbidden experiences would require someone to break the law in order to produce the software. Lenny receives a clip from an anonymous source, a recording of the rape of his ex-lover Faith's best friend Iris that ends with her murder as experienced from the point of view of her killer—a monstrously perverse snuff clip.

Out of desperate concern for Faith (Juliette Lewis), Lenny tries to get to the bottom of the situation, only to be drawn into a plot to cover up the existence of a clip that contains evidence of police corruption. Two members of the LAPD have murdered Jeriko One (Glenn Plummer), an African American rap star and activist, while the appropriately named character Iris (Brigitte Bako), whose camera-eyes accidentally recorded the murder, was killed on the orders of Jeriko's producer to keep her from telling his other talent that he spies on them through agents like Iris herself. As this synopsis suggests, the film is plot driven, and the VR conceit functions primarily to keep that plot moving.

What makes *Strange Days* an aberrant digital fantasy film, however, is its conflation of real experience, virtual reality, and cinema. The film contains several long and gratuitous virtual experiences, including the commission of a robbery and a sexual encounter between Lenny and Faith that resonates with the VR sequences in *The Lawnmower Man,* but with a difference: no digital graphics or other traces of the computer enter into these experiences. The only virtual reality the film offers to the spectator looks almost identical to the experience of film, for both the film itself and the postfilmic "clips" within it provide images from someone else's past that situate us as the organizing consciousness of little narratives. As Jay Bolter and Richard Grusin have written, "if the wire itself is cinematic, the whole of *Strange Days* is also conscious of its own cinematic tradition. . . . Although Lenny insists that the wire is 'not TV only better,' the film ends up representing the wire as 'film only better.'"[30] But the clips turn out to have uses beyond multisensory cinematic entertainment. While classical film invents pasts that never happened, the clips, named after snippets of the medium that first made visual experience of distant places and people possible, are marked by *Strange Days* as historical documents—if they're (mis)used properly. For film and photography theorists from Benjamin and Kracauer to Bazin, the photographic image and the cinematic event attest to a past, profilmic event—and finally signify history itself—with an intensity that drives most commercial film production into smoothing over referentiality with narrative pleasure, out of concern that the spectator will recognize the presence of the apparatus. But the focus of this film *is* the apparatus, that of VR and, by analogy, the cinema. The primary goal of both film and VR here is to expose a historical truth that corrupt authority figures—the policemen who murdered Jeriko One—try to keep from seeing daylight. Only by literally sharing the horrible experiences of Iris, witnessing as she witnessed first the rap star's murder and then her own, can Lenny and Macie empathetically understand the past and bring it to bear on the present and the future. "I can't tell you," Lenny says, pleading with Macie to watch this clip. "You gotta see it. It's that important."

Whatever ambiguity the film carries over from Bigelow's earlier work is, appropriately enough, concentrated in the clips, in which widescreen whip-pans, cinema verité reframings, and the frustration of the spectator's desire to make the camera show what she wants to see "ground" the spectator in a bewildering sensorium.[31] *Strange Days* gives away coherence and spectatorial absorption during these scenes in order to stress VR as a remarkable experience in itself, apart from the narrative spectacle of the film—an experience that disembodies the spectator but at the same time powerfully reembodies her in the experiences of another. In turn, since for us as viewers VR and film occupy the same frame—making us the audience for someone else's experience even more obviously than usual—the film recognizes in a new way the old horizon of collective experience that film has always made possible. Under the sign of a new medium the uses of which were still subject to intensive debate in 1995, *Strange Days* reinvents an unpredictable cinema and a diverse public, or rather a proliferation of publics who could contest not only their interpretations of media texts but also the institutionalized uses of those media.

The anchor for the film's radical position in the debate about film's futures is its restaging of amateur videographer George Holliday's own "clip" of Rodney King being beaten by police in Los Angeles on March 3, 1991. That video unexpectedly proved how momentous the commandeering of an "old" medium could be when its airing on news broadcasts prompted riots and renewed the vigor—temporarily, at least—of the U.S. debate on racial discrimination. A shot near the end of the film reproduces the King video's high-angle framing, not in the diegetic presentation of the clip of Jeriko's murder, or even the event of Macie's own assault by policemen, but in the nondiegetic framing of the crowd standing up to the corrupt officers to stop them from continuing to pummel a downed "perp" (Figure 38). As the King tape prompted a public discussion of videotape as evidence and the tactical use of camcorders, Bigelow's film sketches out terms for two key media counterdiscourses: one about digital media as a purveyor of individual experience to others, and a second about film as a medium that might still make private instances of injustice public, even (and perhaps especially) to an audience that conceives of media engagement primarily in digital, interactive terms. Retaining the famous angled shot of the King tape while reversing the roles played by police and civilians may not reverse the power relations of King's actual beating, but it does allow Bigelow to envision her own act of filmmaking as commensurate, in however symbolic fashion, with Macie's act of hijacking the clip technology.

None of this changes the fact that *Strange Days*'s faith in the progressive force of recorded evidence seems pat and naive—and not a little self-interested on Hollywood's part. Bigelow, like Macie, turns the clip into yet another evidentiary medium in a long line of such quasi-filmic devices that affirm the cinema as a sentinel against social disorder. And, as Mark Berrettini argues, simply using the clips "for the right purpose" seems to magically improve "interracial personal and social relations" in the film, with all the force of a determinist fantasy that offers Macie's act of volition merely as a sop to those who doubt the intrinsic goodness of progress. What troubles Berrettini is not so much the happy ending as the film's refusal to fully resolve Jeriko One's murder by exposing it as an act born of systematic, politically driven racism rather than the actions of a few proverbial bad apples. "We are left to assume that the personal can resolve all social conflicts, that individuals can overcome and reform the problems

Figure 38. The Rodney King tape revisited. Frame enlargement from *Strange Days* (1995).

of the political system, and that human contact produces more reliable bonds than technology, even if the technology provides the key evidence for social action and reform."[32]

While I don't entirely disagree with this assessment, which might fairly be leveled at *all* classical films involving guilt and innocence, it seems to deny the possibility that the rather sudden and shocking rehearsal of the amateur King video might push the main force of *Strange Days*'s intermedia imagination right out of the film plot and into the broader political context of the King moment. The film specifically points to the problem of visual culture that Hamid Naficy argues the King beating and the LA riots that followed it were really about: the uses of media images to perpetuate racial stereotypes and maintain the power relations such stereotypes support.[33] As a film not merely "about" Jeriko One's murder or Lenny and Macie's love affair or even about the "wire," but about film and the crowds it gathers in the theater as well as on the screen for its grand finishing spectacle of a righteous counterpublic taking action, *Strange Days* fantasizes an alternate ending to the King controversy. In that conclusion, both allegorically depicted in the film's final images and floating at its periphery in the intertextual electron cloud those images ignite, the utopian value of the photo-video-digital image as an objective snapshot of racial profiling taken to its logical conclusion is affirmed over the use to which the LAPD's defense counsel put the Holliday tape: an abstraction that means whatever its careful captions tell the public it means and a narrow circuit that "regulates the flow of recognition" and predetermines "the assignment of blame."[34]

As a defense against the expanding subgenre of mediaphobic films that suppress the digital present—including *The Truman Show* and *Pleasantville* (Gary Ross, 1998), in which two kids get trapped in the unrealistically bucolic world of a 1950s TV sitcom—*Strange Days* is worth latching onto as an example of the regenerative potential of explicit, presentist cyberphobia in Hollywood cinema. Although it adheres to the same myth of total media as *The Lawnmower Man,* it addresses the dystopianism of that myth as itself a problem, a half-truth at best, for when the total medium of VR is aimed at corruption in the dominant social structure, justice is actually served. Lenny's transformation is a model for our own as film spectators. He lives mainly in the playback world of his happy past with Faith and deals in pieces of others' lives, until Macie finally demands that he face the crisis of Jeriko's murder and use the past moment recorded on Iris's first clip to change not his own state of mind but history: "This is your life, right here, right now. This is real time, real time. It's time to get real." And Lenny does get real, by entering a struggle that concerns someone other than himself. He makes himself part of a public seeking justice by giving the clip to Macie to use as evidence against the corrupt police, instead of using it to bargain with Jeriko's producer to get Faith back for himself. The problems driving the current media crisis aren't with media technologies themselves, the film reports, but rather with the regressive and opportunistic purposes they're made to serve, and with our silence while medium after medium sheds its transformative possibilities to be dressed in the emperor's clothing, the safe and stable identity of an entertainment institution.

Perhaps it was too optimistic of me as an idealistic graduate student to expect anything more from cyberphobic cinema than reminders like this that media could have functions other than those we usually see. But without such speculations based on not simply faith alone (recall that Juliette Lewis's character, Faith, betrays Lenny by using his blind obsession with her against him) but on "amateurish" *uses* of the strange, powerful, and unpredictable medium in question, the transformative energies of all new media will continue to flounder, trapped in the amber of ahistorical, uncritical myths of progress. What concerns me much more than the conservative themes of cyberphobic films is the fact that such hysterical wish images have faded from Hollywood films since 1995. The closing of this intermedia frontier signals, I fear, the end of the most energetic period of digital media speculation and of Hollywood's productively ambivalent engagement with the possibilities of interactivity.

Let me explain this last point by using my very first film example, Jobe and Marnie's VR confrontation from *The Lawnmower Man,* to excavate perhaps the most important theoretical subtext underwriting my thinking about media fantasy films. When Walter Benjamin examined technological fantasy—and it could be argued that his most trenchant writings do exactly that—he argued that Western culture's propensity to develop new technologies by casting them in the mold of older cultural forms, however historically and politically conservative an impulse this may be, also speaks to an unconscious wish for an imagined past free from oppression. "Too-early" technologies and their products mediate the collective fantasy of a utopian past, transforming it into a glimmer of the "not-yet-known," a future utopia in which machines might be used not to dominate humans and nature under the aegis of capital (as much the case today as in the Paris that Benjamin describes) but to reconcile humans with the new technological nature and, finally, with each other. The Paris Arcades of the nineteenth century, for example, bear for Benjamin the "residues of a dream world. The realization of dream elements in waking is the textbook example of dialectical thinking. For this reason dialectical thinking is the organ of historical awakening. Each epoch not only dreams the next, but also, in dreaming, strives toward the moment of waking."[35]

As a dream from the digital epoch, *The Lawnmower Man,* like *Strange Days* with its cinematic "clips," enacts the "too-early" element of technological fantasy by associating VR with existing forms of entertainment such as video games, cinematic special effects, and even phone sex (seeing a TV ad inviting viewers to listen to young women's bizarre "fantasies" gives Jobe the idea to take Marnie to the VR lab). At the same time, the VR scene acknowledges the "not-yet-known" of fantasy to a degree that the glass and iron arcades and the locomotives of Benjamin's writings do not. The film tries actively to disperse whatever utopian fantasies may collect around VR and the Internet by making the digital environment overtly hostile to individual rights of privacy, even the right to live in and protect one's own brain—at least at the level of narrative and denouement. But even as it portrays Jobe invading homes and bodies, the film's fascination with cyberspace as an *image* of an impossible world that need be only scantly based on the physical, material one makes visible the social stakes that "new" media have historically represented: change itself, the possibility of a new social order (even if that new order is not concretely represented) organized around a truly alternative public sphere, one that would recognize difference and its self-expression rather than collapse or efface that expression by foreclosing the radical intersubjectivity that media fantasies insist on. When Jobe and Marnie meld into a two-headed dragonfly during their erotic encounter in cyberspace, the image of this new joint being, floating through a landscape of Mandelbrot patterns and oceans of color, flashes across the screen the spark of some barely imaginable but still possible mode of future social interaction (Figure 39). *The Lawnmower Man* scapegoats VR for Marnie's psychological rape by Jobe at the end of the scene, but not even this brutal fact can completely dissipate the potential for transformation contained in its fleeting images of virtual intimacy.

However phantasmatic cyberphobic films may be, and however regressive their visions of media and intermedia politics, they nevertheless force film back into the institutional and historical contexts from which classicality tended to divorce it. By getting real about the constructedness of media identities, they make visible the mutability of the relationship

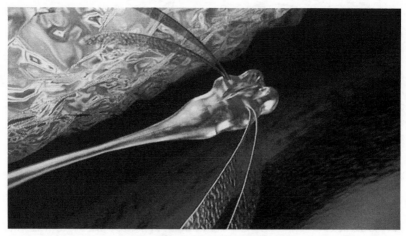

Figure 39. *The Lawnmower Man*'s sole moment of digital bliss.

between Hollywood cinema and its audiences and thus underscore the fact of difference and dissent among the constituencies that continue to collect in and around the cinema, in evanescent rehearsals of politicized public spheres.

Closing Credits: If New Media Are Never New, Old Media Are Never Old

For all intents and purposes, this study ends in 1995, a milestone year in the corporatization of the Internet and a glut year for Internet- and VR-themed Hollywood flops—a mistake Hollywood would not repeat. I did not choose this year arbitrarily; these events seem to be leading indicators that the emergence of digital interactivity had tipped over into a dominant phase. Despite my justifications, however, the break can only seem abrupt. In the years since 1995, film and digital media production have only continued to converge, transforming the technological bases of filmmaking and exhibition in fundamental ways that are already becoming de rigueur properties of films and their exhibition: multichannel digital sound recorded on digitally synchronized CDs and DVDs, and CG (computer-generated) imagery that visualizes everything from the fantastic to the banal but cost effective. Digital crowd scenes mean never having to pay central casting. And the film experience continues to expand into the private sphere in novel ways. Movie Web sites and video games provide spectators intertexts without which the film's stories and worlds appear to be incomplete. Consider, for instance, *The Blair Witch Project*'s cagey, unadvertised Web site, complete with "bootlegged" snatches of the film and the fan sites that popped up to debate whether the film was documentary or fiction even before its theatrical release in 1999; or *The Matrix Reloaded*'s remediation as a multiplatform video game with heavy Web presence, which only added to the film's overexposure and thus may have contributed to its poor word-of-mouth publicity and its underwhelming box office returns.

In fact, the book stops here because this is the point at which digital telecom and audiovisual representation began to structure everyday life rather than surprise and disturb it. The estimated number of computers connected to the Internet jumped from over one million in 1992 to "up to" 30 million by 1995.[36] By the end of 1995, Internet access was available through dial-up providers like AOL and CompuServe that had previously offered domains only on private, nonnetworked mainframes; Ethiopia, Nigeria, Micronesia, and many other nations across the First and Third Worlds had registered country domains; and the browser company of the hour, Netscape, had garnered enough hype and steam to open itself to public trading. The Internet had begun to acquire specific, relatively mundane institutional conventions of both content and user behavior such as e-advertising, e-shopping, spam, instant-access pornography, topic-specific chatrooms, and the rapid retrieval of information previously available through other sources: news, weather, library holdings, and music, for example, and later television programs and, of course, movies.[37] Browser software producers, search engine companies, and marketers from all walks of capitalism staked out territory on a virtual frontier that was practically closed to freeform fantasy even before the dot-com business "revolution" picked up steam. Their investments transformed the Net in near-record time from a quasi-underground medium that alarmed some potential users to a user-friendly digital marketplace.

In 1995, one reviewer argued that *The Net* succeeded where other Internet fantasy films failed because it exploited the audience's anxiety that everyone else knows more about computers and netsurfing than they do: "The hidden fear that drives *The Net* is the creepy thought: 'If *she* can't prevent what's happened to her, what hope is there for the rest of us?'"[38] Now, neither Hollywood nor the everyday network user could perform many quotidian tasks at work or at home without the Internet. When we think movies and the Web these days, the first thing many Americans are likely to think is, Did I order my next Netflix rental yet?

To put all too fine a point on it, when the futures of the Web and digital telecom gained institutional conventions and clearer practical boundaries, mass fantasy about an intersubjective digital future went almost entirely underground. Outside of the media labs, military and scientific communities, multi-user dimensions, and classrooms that once had the Internet to themselves, creative speculation was traded in for economic speculation. When the dot-com bubble began to leak the hot air of autoeconomic fantasy in 1999, nearly the only matters of public debate the Web had left to it were vital and interesting but less than visionary: censorship, sexual predation, hacking, multi-user gaming using PCs and the Internet-ready Xbox game deck, and the workmanlike development of digital media forms that would find ready markets. Radical communicative and aesthetic practices persist on the Web, to be sure, though to discuss them in detail is beyond the scope of this study of mainstream media fantasy. But in 2004, as I wrote the first draft of this conclusion, the press mainly dreamed that the NASDAQ exchange would someday return to its former glory. The Internet as a relatively accessible network for creative, one-to-one (and one-to-one-to-one) communication has become an incidental factor in its own mass discourse, buried beneath the thrill of gambled fortunes.

Of course there is a "real" Internet hidden within speculation about its fiscal futures, a medium through which possibilities are tested and retested constantly in issues ranging from the constitution of human identity to aesthetic forms bound to hyperlinks and temporality in previously unimagined ways. But it would be shortsighted to underestimate the shaping power that the economy exerts on the collective imagination of digital interactivity. Its influence may be tracked with particular clarity in the search for "viable" (that is, marketable) digital media experiences. Game design has begun to outrank social and critical theory even in some academic departments in humanities and social sciences divisions of colleges and universities. Even departments that were founded on the principles of cultural studies of technology bend in that direction, ostensibly because students looking for jobs in an overstuffed market for digital skills have an understandably urgent need for material educational "results."

Yet the narrowing of mainstream digital fantasy has not been reflected by the lion's share of critical appraisals of culture "after" the Web. I wish I could share Mark Poster's certainty that the Internet will transform both subjectivity and the concept of the subject itself, that it will disseminate knowledge evenly and reverse the exclusiveness of the bourgeois public sphere by renegotiating the very definitions of *public* and *difference*.[39] I agree completely that, like the classical public sphere itself and the classical cinema that mirrors its democratic ideals as well as its exclusionary blind spots, the Web produces a structural *possibility* for radical public interaction and political intervention. Such a claim that this or that technological future *must* someday come, however, leans so heavily on technological determinism (something that Poster criticizes but oddly reaffirms by insisting upon the inherent "underdetermination" of digital textuality) that it must table the unpostponable questions of praxis, markets, and the tendency to mistake a time-bound institutional form for the nature of the medium, as if the latter could wriggle free of the former on its own (Poster, 16, 118). The Internet as currently structured requires complex interfacing skills (the point-and-click interface, for example, seems self-explanatory to those who work with it daily and have for ten or even twenty years, but try teaching your parents or grandparents not only how to use it but to *think* with it), a reliable and preferably digital telecom infrastructure, and a stable or relatively stable economy. No such medium, however underdetermined, stands much of a chance against a so-called Third World nation's lack of the material resources that would make it attractive to global technological powers willing to wire its networks, or its crises of quotidian survival—continuous hunger, continuous public health disasters, low literacy rates and strapped education systems, continuous war—that place modem installation far to the rear of the priorities queue.

I would add to this institutional wall the equally bricklike fact that the most structurally radical intersubjective Web game available in the United States in 2004, *The Sims* and its multiple sequels, is structured not only by narrow interactive protocols but also by the fantasy that the healthy market is the ultimate communal goal. There's no denying that one objective of the game is to acquire the most stuff. Media fantasy does matter to the future of a medium. If marketing language, everyday uses, and mass-production formulae like the classical Hollywood cinema manage to lock a medium into a pen in which fantasies are identical to "options" and "choices"—where multiple genres of narrative entertainment, for example, or new combinations of conventional elements (Brad Pitt and Tom Cruise, starring together at last! A first-person shooter game that combines Western frontier themes with sword-and-sorcery action!) stand in where possibilities for user entry, manipulation, appropriation, and poaching used to stand—then what can be said and thought about a medium and its possible futures will have a very difficult time escaping that pen, no matter what futures the technology itself can, or could, support.

In this thinning imaginative atmosphere, the search for even the slenderest fantasies of a countermedium becomes more crucial than ever. If Web users are ever to piece together a truly inclusive, user-controlled medium of expression from the fragments of mainstream technological development, there needs to be a shared language of fantasy—a body of ideas about what is possible that can be spoken with, through, against—that pushes the current mediascape beyond current economic and institutional conditions. Lacking serious media fantasy that enjoys a plethora of channels to which the large proportion of PC-less Americans have access (movies, television, fiction, the press, billboards, and so on), it will be difficult to invent a legitimately *public* syntax of dissatisfaction, or even one of satisfaction, in the United States.

Although mainstream cinema approaches new media under the most conservative rubric of preserving classical spectatorship, its mass availability and the exuberant incoherence of its approaches to new media make the media fantasy film a primary vehicle on which to found media publicness in the emphatic, alternative sense in the early twenty-first century. If this hypothesis has any chance of being true, then no final chapter to this study or any other can drop the other shoe once and for all. Instead, like the best or worst Saturday serial matinee of the 1940s, Hollywood media fantasies will continue to envision impossibly interactive media and imply impossibly public cinemas. It seems fair to speculate that, as long as capitalist enterprise needs to create and supply new markets, "new" audiovisual entertainment media will be developed out of the digital, and fantasies will collect around those media. And as long as interactivity, access, and regulation remain central points of contention in those fantasies, media fantasy films will persist. And Hollywood cinema will have to claim spot after novel spot on the changing landscape of the technological imagination. It will continue to highlight and protect its private-in-public address from alternate paradigms. Although new media tend to lose their sheen of possibility, media fantasy films continue to concentrate on individuated, aberrant media experiences, to interrogate each medium's formal properties and scrutinize its reception, to find anarchy wherever media-based interaction lies, on the one hand, and discover liberation wherever a public witnesses and acts, on the other. This last paradox over the relationship between publics and media is the mark of possible media-social relations that Hollywood never fully imagines, never expresses except under its breath and in flickers of peripheral vision, and never admits except through its hesitancy about bringing them fully to light. But it always discovers their negated traces, by dreaming its rivals with reckless abandon, even when these fantasies reflect back on its own volatile hybrid of public and private media consumption.

But is classical spectatorship really in danger? Theatrical film exhibition appears to have hit a post-postmodern renaissance after half a century of market losses connected to competitors for Hollywood's mindshare as diverse as suburban migration, television, the VCR, and MTV. Although 2003's summer business dipped along with the U.S. economy, 2002 was one of the biggest box-office years in the history of the industry, thanks to conventional classical successes like *Spider-Man* and the indie-in-name-only sleeper hit *My Big Fat Greek Wedding*. The film industry promotes theatrical releases as aggressively as ever, even though public exhibition now functions primarily as advertising for the more profitable forms the film will take later: home video purchase and rental, basic and premium cable runs, and pay-per-view. Although its markets seem to have restabilized, however, the definition of film now faces a novel crisis: the disappearance of photographic film. George Lucas decided to shoot *Star Wars: Episode II—Attack of the Clones* (2002) entirely on digital video and demanded that a certain number of theaters project it in that format. This forced a handful of urban theaters to install digital projectors that would only be useful to them for this film, at least for the moment. Lucas got action from distributors and theaters thanks to his industry clout, but it remains to be seen whether his innovations, which recall the promises of Theater TV (beamed video rather than physically transported cans of celluloid) without the liveness that justified it, will become industry standards like CinemaScope-ratio screens and Lucasfilm's THX digital stereo before it. In the realm of production, however, the ease and low cost of storing and editing "films" on computer hard drives have edged the industry closer to replacing celluloid as the (im)material basis of production and projection.

In media fantasy films since 1995, wired computers and other digital communicators have turned from thematically charged fetish objects to auxiliary plot helpers, informants, or complicators, much as tape recorders, televisions, and camcorders had before it. In *The Ring* (Gore Verbinski, 2002), a horror film about a videotape that kills its viewers seven days after they watch it, Rachel (Naomi Watts), a newspaper reporter, uses the Internet frequently, without comment or negative incident, to research the origins of the tape. This is not to say that digital media no longer bear connotations specific to their histories outside the films; *The Blair Witch Project* (written and directed by film school students Daniel Myrick and Eduardo

Sánchez, 1999) switches back and forth between analog videotape and 16-millimeter film so unnervingly that the difference between the media and the cultural associations that come with that difference (ease of use versus prestige, which relate subtly to the gender biases of the three students sharing the filming duties) become a subtle theme of the film.

Digital media's shift from central plot material to supporting roles parallels the shift in Hollywood's industrial approach to digitality. Where pre-1995 media fantasy films frequently chronicled clashes between digital interactivity and classical address, Hollywood ten years on has adopted digital media identities into the zero degree of classical Hollywood cinema in the form of CG, digital video, and video-game concepts. AOL-Time Warner's premiere of *The Matrix Reloaded* (Andy Wachowski and Larry Wachowski, 2003) was synchronized with the release of Atari's *Enter the Matrix*, a multiplatform game qua film "written" and "directed" by the Wachowski Brothers and "starring" Jada Pinkett Smith, who plays a small supporting role in *Reloaded* but "had to memorize game scripts several times longer than their film [scene] equivalents" and endured six months of intensive motion capturing to become a digital star.[40]

If Hollywood continues to reap profits from tie-in video games, classical action films will probably come to resemble game action even more than they do already, so that games can be more easily modeled after them—and vice versa. (The endlessly protracted final battle to save the besieged community of Zion in *The Matrix Revolutions* [Andy Wachowski and Larry Wachowski, 2003], which includes almost none of the principal characters, would likely never have been approved by the studio if not for its potential as video-game content. If PlayStation and Game Cube games seem more and more like movies, this is in part because action movies have progressively adjusted the proportion of action scenes to characterization and psychologically motivated plot events to resemble that of the most popular games.) And, if Hollywood does indeed adopt high-definition digital video (DV) as its new base standard, films will probably also become less expensive to produce and easier to distribute, at least theoretically. I would hazard a guess that most spectators will agree that the new format is better, perhaps because it looks glossier and newer, perhaps simply because it looks different from film projection, or perhaps even because their DVDs will look more "cinematic" once the cinema becomes more like TV. But let us be clear about this point: the perception of similarities and difference among these two media, film and DV, will depend on standards of media "look and feel," to borrow a term from HTML-VRML Web design, that are constantly being revised in both radical and nearly imperceptible ways. As Rick Altman so aptly puts it, "One reason why linear history is an illusion is that even the most basic objects and categories on which that history would be based have no permanent identity."[41]

But let me revel in a little media fantasy of my own, at least for a moment: Shifts in the identity of "film" that will attend a switch from celluloid to DVD, particularly those changes in image texture and the continual possibility that image artifacts (visible as streaks or distracting blocks of aberrant pixels that accompany figure or camera movement, often caused by common incompatibilities between content and playback equipment), could put producers and consumers on a collision course with each other over the definition of the medium. The reason for this possibility is that DV and Avid or Adobe editing grant broader access to the state of the art than photographic filmmaking—not universal access, of course, but equipment similar to that used by the mainstream film industry can now be afforded by shoestring independents who no longer have to suffer the slings and arrows of getting film developed without the benefit of professional color timers and the like. In the past, the American cinema has made it as difficult as possible for audiences to make of film what they will or to define the cinema according to a public mandate instead of being defined by the cinema. Media like film, to which few have productive access in the traditional sense, can be limited to specific markets and uses with relative ease. But in the case of digital video, where everything from editing and main titles to international distribution can be accomplished with a DV camera, publicly available "professional" editing software, a Firewired iMac, and a 56K modem, the war to define film multiplies its fronts to a tremendous extent. The collective imagination of film is now as close to edging into the truly *public* domain as it has been since Bobby snapped shots of his family and servants behaving badly on nickelodeon screens in 1908, or at least since avant-garde filmmakers of the fifties, sixties, and seventies discovered 16-millimeter technology. How the cinematic institution will spank its twenty-first century amateurs, however, remains to be seen.

At the moment, however, most public thrashings incited by the digital revolution are aimed not at amateur and independent filmmakers but at Hollywood, especially its fairly banal "experiments" with computer-generated images. Most films that employ CG are not films *about* CG or DV in the direct sense, with the exceptions of *Wag the Dog* (Barry Levinson, 1997), the virtual Pygmalion fantasy *S1m0ne* (Andrew Niccol, 2002), about a Hollywood star who exists only in CG form (and thus must be digitally composited into her talk show appearances), and likely a few others. But CG films nevertheless become films *about* CG in extratheatrical discourse, when critics use them to argue about whether and how DV and CG will change the "nature" of Hollywood film. Consider the conflicted opinions expressed about George Lucas's recent films by the best-known film critic in America. Roger Ebert's three-and-a-half-star (out of four) review of *Star Wars: Episode I—The Phantom Menace* (1999) argues that the film's spectacular set pieces make the film great; viewers desiring complex human emotions and relationships should watch *Star Trek* movies instead.

> The stories of the "Star Wars" movies have always been space operas, and . . . the importance of the movies comes from their energy, their sense of fun, their colorful inventions and their state-of-the-art special effects. I do not attend with the hope of gaining insights into human behavior. . . . Dialogue isn't the point, anyway: These movies are about new things to look at. . . . Yet within the rules he has established, Lucas tells a good story.

Ebert even "proves" the quality of the story by comparing it to the Greatest Story Ever Told, when he suggests that Qui-Gon Jinn's realization that Anakin Skywalker will contribute to the salvation of the galaxy alludes to John the Baptist's certainty that Jesus was the savior whose way he was to prepare.[42]

Three years later, however, Ebert's two-star review of *Star Wars: Episode II—Attack of the Clones* criticizes the latter film for collapsing under the weight of its interesting but overwhelming set pieces, largely because its wooden acting and unmemorable lines offer little of human interest to tie the spectacles together. His *Phantom Menace* review, of course, labeled these same flaws mere liabilities that were overcome by Lucas's auteuristic vision. "It's not what's there on the screen that disappoints me [in *Attack of the Clones*] but what's not there. It is easy to hail the imaginative computer images. . . . [But] in the classic movie adventures that inspired 'Star Wars,' dialogue was often colorful, energetic, witty, and memorable. The dialogue in 'Episode II' exists primarily to advance the plot. . . . [The film is] a technological exercise that lacks juice and delight."[43]

I'm not chastising Ebert for inconsistency; the critic has every right to reconsider and even disavow earlier judgments (this is one of many reasons why Robin Wood's forty-year career in film criticism has never failed to astonish and delight his avid readers). Rather, Ebert's turnabout, which he does not overtly acknowledge, strikes me as symptomatic of the difficulty Hollywood spectators experience when they reach for stable evaluative criteria at moments of technological transition. When Ebert finds one movie's asset to be the other's liability, he demonstrates that, for the viewer, the pleasures and satisfactions of classicality depend on the filmmakers' ability to strike a delicate balance between presentation and representation—a balance that, like investment returns that fluctuate according to interest rates, hinges on an ever-changing systemic definition of "classicality." If achieved, that balance makes it possible for thoroughly classical viewers to enjoy explosive, epic, erotic, or fantastic spectacle without finding the attractions superfluous to, or utterly distracting from, the story and characters. But without such a balance, one's mind begins to wander from the story and audiovisuals and could meander into considering critically the technologies behind them both, whether mechanical, electronic, or discursive. When the thrill of attractions for their own sake wears off, Ebert's standards of quality for a space opera, his memories of adventure movies, and perhaps even his experience of *The Phantom Menace,* change. In order to get absorbed—his duty as a die-hard classical spectator—he needs thicker characterization and better speeches, exactly the classical elements also missing from the first film in Ebert's positive review.

Attractions, as early cinema history teaches us, can be distracting, and distraction is exactly what makes Ebert pay attention to how *Episode II* diverges from the "dominant" definition of classical film and presses him to ponder aloud what film is, really, in the first place. For Ebert, this accidental reflexivity is very bad news. He spends much of the 2002 review to complain about the way the film looks at its most basic level, as an image on the screen. He finds the look of the "second-generation" film print (i.e., a photographic copy of a digitally produced image track) muddy and irritating, and he worries that, if Lucas convinces the industry to follow his lead into DV production and projection, celluloid film and the denser photographic information it contains will cease to exist.[44]

Ebert's criticisms also give us another glimpse of the anticlassical spectatorship possibilities that classical cinema never fully contains. Echoing the vague dissatisfaction many viewers have expressed with the film, he finds himself caught here in the perpetual paradox of classical address, its tendency to present and represent by turns, and quite often simultaneously. Excesses of CG only make the paradox more visible. But as unpleasurable as classical displeasure may be, Ebert's dyspepsia suggests that even in the absence of explicit new-media fantasies *in* films, technological adjustments made *to* film can turn spectators away from the screen and toward each other to complain, or express their delight, or simply speculate about film qua film.

The fork that DV installs in Hollywood's path through the twenty-first century has already led aspiring filmmakers to rethink the cinematic institution itself by distributing their works to each other, primarily via streaming video, and encouraging feedback. Such a virtual collective would lack the physical and spatial contiguity that has kept American cinema a classically public institution, but as the experience of millions of hardcore Netizens suggests, one does not have to be in public to behave like a public, and the anonymity of Net discussion, not to mention the very fact of the keyboard, invites opinionated responses that many spectators would never think of expressing to the screen, other spectators, the exhibitor, or the producer of the film (who would have to be contacted outside the theater anyway). Ironically, some of the most circulated independent DV films loose on the Net, at least as of this writing, are poached, loosely authorized films based on *Star Wars, Batman,* and other successful films. Some create alternate story arcs with characters from Lucas's trilogies, while others—the only uncopyrighted amateur works that Lucasfilm refuses out of hand to tolerate—are reedited versions of *The Phantom Menace* that, according to those lucky enough to view them, improve by leaps and bounds the sluglike pacing and bland characterization of what even many diehard fans find a tepid entry in the series.

But the "freedom" from the classical institution that DV and CG offer can be too easily overestimated. Digital artist, game designer, and critic Mary Flanagan argues that "virtual stars"—video game characters who, like "S1m0ne" in her eponymous film, have no incarnation outside 3-D computer graphics—"are here to stay" and claims that this development is liberating without making entirely clear precisely what it liberates anyone *from* that one might perceive as an untenable constraint.[45] Nor does Flanagan offer much besides the virtuality of these stars to mark their difference from "fleshly" Hollywood stars, whom most viewers encounter only in virtual form anyway, as star discourses. Perhaps it is true that "you can own [Lara Croft]. She's yours," but only in the sense that one exerts more control over her image than one does over the image of Colin Farrell or, for that matter, Angelina Jolie. One can no more purchase the "real" Lara Croft as a fleshly body than one can purchase the "real" Jolie by paying for a movie ticket. In any event—not withstanding the fact that Croft has no fleshly body, existing (like the star) at the intersection of textual and metatextual discourses—there's a remarkable, unacknowledged irony to the idea that *owning* another human being, even a virtual one, might free anyone from anything but the right to act even more solipsistically to "fulfil[l] our fantasies" as consumers of both texts and people.[46]

From classical film's side of the media-ontology fence, virtual stardom looks less like an opportunity for the gamer to push the limits of identity—Lara Croft meets Sherry Turkle—than like an opening for game producers to negotiate killer licensing packages with movie studios. To put it cynically, Hollywood films based on games that feature virtual stars like Croft/Jolie (cf. *Lara Croft: Tomb Raider,* 2001; *Final Fantasy: The Spirits Within,* 2000; *Resident Evil,* 2002; *Ballistic: Ecks vs. Sever,* 2002) are presold film properties that wrest the viewer away from her game self, her rule-bound powers to negotiate her game avatar and the world it inhabits, and mold her into the more unidirectional form of interactivity I have referred to as informatic intimacy. Call it the film as game as film: the *Tomb Raider* movies might heighten the illusion of viewer-film interaction for those who have played the game, which itself contains many of the "cinematics," or "lavish . . . noninteractive cinematic sequences" that became a major convention of action games in the 1990s (Manovich, 82). The player's heightened experience of involvement in the game's tie-in film might well draw on the precise definition of "informatic" interactivity I drew from Jens Jensen in the introduction (i.e., giving instructions to a machine) and thus produce a very different kind of spectatorship than the nongamer would experience.

But the film as game as film, by its very nature, permanently fixes some of the same parameters that the game leaves "open." The actors cast to play familiar game characters, changes made to the game's plot to adhere to classical necessities, the ways in which particular game events with multiple exit routes for the player are narrated as a plot with only one outcome, no matter how many times you attend the film: all these elements could limit or change the associations the seasoned player had previously formed with the elements of the actual game. One reviewer of *Final Fantasy: The Spirits Within* at the Internet Movie Database (imdb.com) lists among the film's weaknesses its lack of any familiar plot points from the games. Game tie-in films also invent continuities between film and game as discrete media that threaten to restrict the media identity of the video game to Hollywood's classical specifications, even as the emphasis on building games out of movies changes how action sequences are plotted. To name only one Hollywood-ized "actioner" among hundreds, *Batman: Vengeance*

(2002) dispenses all the rules for game play via movie sequences rather than the written pamphlets of the Atari and early Nintendo eras, and creates continuity between game spaces and events by "narrating" the story with more extended cinematic sequences, complete with master shots and shot–reverse shot editing, dialogue across shots, and orchestral music that swells to heighten dramatic intensity.[47]

In fact, to borrow William Gibson's eloquently masturbatory verb, digital media fantasy has jacked itself into classical Hollywood cinema as eagerly as Hollywood has incorporated digital media into the cinematic institution, and thus into its definition of film. While Hollywood stays Hollywood as far as the game industry sees it, game designers come out fairly regularly as closeted auteurs who use game coding merely as a career stepping stone, a medium in which to hone the media craft to which they actually aspire. In 1999, *Wired* published an interview in its annual "Life after Hollywood" issue with Robyn Miller, the codesigner of *Myst,* one of the most popular and influential computer games ever produced. But beneath a front cover that bears the sassy aphorism "Question Auteurity," Miller reports that he finds interactive game design a disappointing field. Discontented with his limited agency over the gaming audience's imagination, he wants desperately to be the very film auteur that the cover blurb "questions." Why? Because, he says, classical film is more like life than interactive gaming is. "The one interactive story that works is our lives," Miller says. "And the story of our lives is a linear thing."

> "I'm interested in pushing interactive further to accomplish one of two things: to find ways to affect people in an interactive world, or to convince myself that an interactive medium is not suitable for affecting people." . . .
>
> [Miller's] faith in storytelling is part of a larger conviction: that the real world itself is a narrative, in which each detail is saturated with meaning. The stories in films and books, he believes, are one way that we come to read that narrative.
>
> "Finally," he says, "I wanted that power. I wanted the power just to tell a story."[48]

Miller defines the legitimacy of film, digital media, and life itself according to a single standard: classical narrative integration. His invocation of classicality as not merely a genre or a standard but a natural, Platonic Good is a useful reminder that new media change nothing by themselves, least of all our thinking about communication by media or about the political and social limitations of dominant media institutions. New-media fantasies *can* punch multiple windows into classicality that allow specta-tors to look outside it onto other ways of imagining film, but Miller exem-plifies the subject who identifies not with other spectators but with clas-sicality itself—or perhaps the classical Hollywood cinema as a prestigious historical institution to which he, too, wants to belong. He portrays him-self as standing outside the studios' windows looking in, dreaming of the autotelic power of the cinema auteurs he thinks he glimpses inside. In his fantasy future of the new medium he wants to escape, the "better" video games will shed interactivity, while the cinema will accept none of the sur-plus interactivity for itself. Even the informatic interactivity of first-person video games will crumble before the superior power and attractiveness of digital (cinematic) storytelling.

In the creative climate Miller represents, where classicality is the high-est evolutionary form of mass cultural "exchange," making filmmaking accessible to the masses seems identical to spreading the standards of classical filmmaking across the amateur production market. Even a crude but serviceable piece of DV editing software like Apple's "free" program iMovie offers its user an implicit ultimatum: I will give you tools to make your video production less time-consuming and more pleasing to you, but you must make your final copy look like a classical Hollywood film if you wish to "succeed" at the game to which I have supplied the rules, in the form of classical syntactical codes. Fade to black.

Indeed, whether it's due to the CG/DV crisis or the paradox of clas-sicality in general, conservative definitions of film as nothing more nor less than classicality seem extraordinarily popular at the moment. In a recent article in the *Los Angeles Times Magazine,* to which I was alerted by my friend Corinne Scheiner just as I completed a draft of this conclusion, University of Southern California film school grad and Sam Peckinpah biographer David Weddle shakes his head over the "occult and arcane language" that film theorists use to mystify contemporary film students like his own daughter, a student at UC-Santa Barbara. As he interviews film theorists and critics ranging from the academy's Constance Penley to mainstreamer Ebert, he runs into a lot of negative definitions of film ("Film theory has nothing to do with film," Ebert proclaims, after Weddle has gone over his daughter's bewildering exam on semiotics and Russian formalist narrative theory) and exactly one positive definition that Weddle's other interlocutors from the industry all find so obvious that it isn't worth mentioning. "That's what your daughter's being taught?" asks Gary A. Randall, former president of Spelling Television, no bunker of auteurism (but probably an exciting place to get a production job after film school). "That's just elitist psychobabble. . . . That has absolutely no bearing on the real world. It sounds like an awfully myopic perspective of what film is really supposed to be about: touching hearts and minds and providing provocative thoughts."[49]

Now of course, most of the article's ire stems from its complaint that "people" go to film school *to learn about film*—that is, to break into the film or television production business by learning the craft, logistics, and economics of producing film and video texts—and that "psychobabble" doesn't get them any closer to that expensive goal. But Randall, Ebert, and game designer Miller would probably all agree on what film students ought to be taught, that is, classicality and nothing but, because otherwise spectators will begin to notice that film is actually a historical object shaped by a cinematic institution that persists in part because it promises reproducible, familiar pleasures, and in part because it is taught, learned, produced, and consumed as if the media could do nothing else or be consumed in no other way than that which the conventions of private-in-public viewing (or even private-in-private viewing on home video equipment that promises interactive agency but supplies only "choices") decree. If you want to stay on top of the market, it seems, your film actually must *not* attract provocative thoughts, at least not about the medium itself and the chances with style or narration that commercial films rarely if ever take. Rather, it must provide "provocative thoughts" *for* the audience. It must touch them; it must "affect" them. If the spectators do anything to it besides consuming it, including noticing how it goes about affecting and touching them, and talking or even (horrors) theorizing about the process, Randall implies, your film has failed. In fact, it's not even a film.

Even for a president of Spelling Productions, Randall sells his audience remarkably short, imagining them as consumers and nothing but when they watch TV or movies, even if they produce their own amateur DV films upon leaving the couch after a *Beverly Hills 90210* rerun or talk idealistically about how different film could or should be in the digital era (as thousands and thousands of high school and college students do, to name only the demographic I know best as a teacher). The denial of the validity of alternate visions of the American cinema implicit in the statement "Film theory is not about film" should be familiar by now as of a piece with the institutional denials I have been tracking throughout the book, the construction of exteriors for film that deny sociological interaction a constitutive, or even acknowledged, place in cinematic experience. Academic film theory spends at least as much time on the fundamental contexts of making and viewing—spectatorship and subjectivity, race, ideology, cognitive psychology, gender, cultural and historical difference, class—as it does on film aesthetics or semiotics. And of course, film theory speaks the unspoken aspects of making and viewing—the original sin of classical spectatorship. As even Ebert realizes, however, the classical narrative that is "official" film history has melted in the projector yet again thanks to the onset of digital, interactive entertainment media, and we have no choice but to notice that thinkers outside the academy, whether or not they have the official organs and cultural legitimacy to air their views widely, are also wondering what broke and how, or whether, it can be repaired.

Let me conclude, then, by getting into a friendly argument with Ebert about American film's ontological future among its media rivals and accomplices, as we sit together in the American Film History Googolplex among catcalling fellow spectators, waiting to see how the projectionist will try to get things moving again. I sympathize with Ebert's interest in preserving photographic film, but if he is implying that all-DV "films" circa 2002 represent a drastic change from the mainstream cinema of 1999, or 2001, he is mistaken. Remarkably, Ebert loves the way *The Phantom Menace* looks on film, even though it is nearly a purebred digital creature. Could it be that simply knowing that Lucas shot *Attack of the Clones* entirely on DV changed how Ebert perceived the latter film? And if so, what does that do to his and other critics' certainty that film is an irreducible thing that only nutty professors consider an issue of culture or perception? Where, ultimately, does the difference rest between *Final Fantasy*, a fully animated digital film with realistic-looking human protagonists, and *The Phantom Menace,* which contains countless effects shots of spaceships, explosions, desertscapes, and a massive battle between robots and anthropomorphic wallabies—shots that are as nonphotographic as every shot in *Final Fantasy*? Can we say with certainty that even shots of "real" profilmic events are vestiges of a near-lost, photographic cinema, considering that Lucas "cyberdirected" many shots from *The Phantom Menace* by "chang[ing] the actors' performances" in the editing room, moving their images around within finished shots using digital compositing? And to what degree is *The Phantom Menace* "new" in the sense that it is a product of what Manovich calls a "modular" strategy, a strategy based on compositing within single shots, rather than a "linear" one that bases the making of meaning on montage and shot-to-shot continuity, when both preclassical trick films and classical films from *Metropolis, King Kong,* and *Citizen Kane* to the original *Star Wars* trilogy, not to mention every film ever to use a process shot of any sort, fits Manovich's definition of a specifically digital "modularity" quite comfortably?[50] What is "old" and what is "new" about Sam Raimi's *Spider-Man* (2002), which includes among its many effects shots of the digitally created web-swinger "real" images of New York with its main landmarks squeezed closer together than they are in life?

I could take a few stabs at "objective" answers to these questions, all of which would be instantly disputable on countless grounds. But that contestation is really the point. I list such questions to suggest that contemporary film begs us to rethink Hollywood's present place among discourses of film history, and also its place among grander discourses such as history itself and the problems that human subjectivity and mechanical "objectivity" pose to the possibility of writing history, recording it, and accepting it as something shared. Rarely have film and its futures become such overt objects of cinematic discourse before now—except, perhaps, during the emergence of television. This could be film theory's golden moment to suggest that spectatorship theory, and the contingencies of filmic meaning on which contemporary theory focuses, do indeed have something to do with film.

Although the scary Internet of the early nineties has receded behind the clouds of marketeering, phantoms of self-reflexive media fantasy still bounce around in Hollywood film, though now that CG and DV inhabit its very fabric, movies that chastise digital simulacra for overtaking the real world feel anachronistic, even self-defeating. Hollywood cinema could no longer function, economically or stylistically, without CG enhancements as seemingly minor as the digital fog in Ang Lee's *Sense and Sensibility* (1995). If *The Lawnmower Man* were made today, it would surely be a B-film or a straight-to-video exploitation piece rather than a major release with an A-film budget. Yet anachronistic media fantasies may be the best kind of fantasies for keeping the seams in film's identity visible. Compared even to the least imaginative cyberphobic fantasy films of the mid-nineties, *FearDotCom* (William Malone, 2002) is a ludicrous cheapie about a supernatural serial killer (Stephen Rea) who snares victims through the Internet and murders them in front of live Webcams. Its glimpses of the Internet through numerous PC screens look as clunky as the keyed-video composites that appear on the amateurs' screens in *Hackers*. And as a toucher of hearts and minds, *FearDotCom* has scarcely a redeeming facet; the film bristles with misogynist stereotypes and brutal victimizations that just happen to expose a good deal of female skin.

But even *FearDotCom* manages to get across a fantasy of cinema as a critical "space" distinct from digital media—even distinct from Hollywood cinema itself—by refusing the kinds of effects that make *The Lawnmower Man* at best a hypocritical critique of a digital wave that it advertises as thoroughly as it demonizes (Time Warner Interactive timed a *Lawnmower Man* game for the Sega Genesis 16-bit video game to the film's theatrical release). While Rea (somehow) manipulates the Internet to violate the minds of his audience and push them to madness and suicide, effectively raping even accidental witnesses to his murders, *FearDotCom* refuses to let CG penetrate its mise-en-scène. Indeed, its producers apparently re-solved to make the film look and feel as old-fashioned in terms of contem-porary Hollywood technology and technique as possible. Shot in Germany, *FearDotCom* is set in New York, but instead of providing digitized sky-lines and enhanced locales to fudge the differences, *FearDotCom* simply plunges the city into the dark. Dank soundstages are dressed to evoke a generic urban-ness rather than any particular locale, and the actors who mill about its apparently sparsely populated downtown hide their German and British accents the old-fashioned way, badly, with the help of diction coaches rather than overdubbing or digital alteration.

In effect, *FearDotCom* manages to incarnate a sense what film "was" before CG, a sense it underscores by building its Monogram B-film en-vironment around the Internet. The film preaches a shrill sermon about the ethics of live cybervoyeurism and the "virus" with which it infects the lonely or bored PC user, while setting up filmic properties—past-tense narrative viewed from a distanced, informed position—as media saviors once again in the symbolic form of an amateur videotape of two of Rea's murder victims' final days. As it had in countless films before this one, film yields a narrative of evidence that leads to dramatic and social reso-lution. But this praise for cinematic oversight at the expense of Internet prurience cannot escape the hailstorm of voyeuristic thrills that the film itself fires at its audience.

The Net voyeurs the film presumes, eager to experience the serial killer's sadism and the agony of his victims, are structurally identical to the film spectator, as *FearDotCom* hinges our visual pleasure on the torture of female bodies and reduces both diegetic and nondiegetic oglers—the latter being, of course, we spectators—to statistics generated by the film; those Net voyeurs I mentioned are represented only by the rapidly increasing number of hits that registers on the "feardotcom.com" homepage (Figure 40). Although the videotaped evidence helps the heroic police detective Reilly (Stephen

Figure 40. Internet users reduced to raw statistics. Frame enlargement from
FearDotCom (2002).

Dorff) put the killer away, the character whose gaze at the videotape mirrors our own dies in the end. Considering the general ugliness of the film's
production design as well as its gender politics, Reilly's death functions as
a ritualized suicide of the classical gaze akin to the eye-blowing scene in
Batman Forever. Unlike that film, however, *FearDotCom* pieces together a
new spectator out of the fragments of the shattered gaze: Reilly, the avatar
of classical spectatorship, gets reborn in the Web, his resurrection signified
by the telephone call from beyond the grave he makes to Terry (Natascha
McElhone) that closes the film.

It bears mentioning that I interpreted this phone call unequivocally
as a sign of rebirth, even though Reilly's voice is never heard, based on
an intertextual reference that in turn led me to draw a rather unexpected
contrast between this scene and its reference. *The Lawnmower Man* also
ends with a Net-based resurrection signified by a ringing phone, but in the
earlier film, Jobe's signal of his global takeover is just another instantiation of one-way authority calling a two-way medium—and the populace
linked by it—to heel. *FearDotCom*'s concluding phone call, however, gestures toward the rebirth of media consumption in some networked yet
individuated form. Whatever this consumption might look like, it seems
to be stuck, and aware that it is stuck, somewhere between telephone use
and theatrical film spectatorship, between invisibility and visibility, between presence before others and disappearance, thanks to Dorff's uncertain status between (physical) death and (digital) life. To its credit,
FearDotCom has the perspicacity not to envision the media textuality
that would draw such a community together, only to suggest it via loud,
scratchy, telephonic static. It's as if to represent such a spectator would

implicate *FearDotCom*'s own spectator in the informatic voyeurism of classicality and, by extension, in the real-time voyeurism of the Webcam. Seen in this light, the film's refusal of spectacular CG is not merely an act of Luddite resistance to progress but a resistance to hypostatizing a form of spectatorship, and for that matter an institutional form for film, that might yet be founded on a similar resistance to objectifying the Other.

eXistenZ (David Cronenberg, 1999), a film set mainly in the world of a VR video game, does pinpoint a fantasy of postclassical cinema and spectatorship more directly, but it, too, builds that position on a nebulous foundation, an interstitial zone where the predigital and postdigital cinemas meet without quite touching. Like *FearDotCom, eXistenZ* avoids spectacular digital animation despite its digital theme. The proof that "eXistenZ," the multiplayer-game-within-the-movie, simulates real life perfectly is that *everything in it looks real*—in other words, the world of "eXistenZ" refers more directly to film than to video games, the Internet, or VR because this world's realism depends on it looking exactly like a movie, just as the VR "clips" in *Strange Days* guarantee their experiential realism by aping widescreen point-of-view shots (which is, of course, exactly what the clips are to the spectator in the theater).[51] The game, designed by Allegra Geller (Jennifer Jason Leigh), utilizes "slave pods," which resemble PlayStation controllers covered with pink, veiny flesh, to network the players into the game and with each other. The folds of flesh on the pods give them a resemblance to female genitalia that was surely intentional, but they appear more immediately like eyeless zygotes of some half-formed creature, complete with patch-cords that plug into the user's spine—umbilical cords, that is, right down to the barely visible blue vein.

It is difficult not to see Cronenberg's pod, by turns emotionally needy and in physical agony but unable to achieve relief for either pain on its own, as a figure for the contested fetus in an era flush with religious fundamentalism. But while the pro-life movement locates human authenticity and divine authority alike in the uterus it so wishes to control, *eXistenZ* revels in the inhumanity of the pod while insisting on it as an extension of humanity, nearly in the McLuhanist sense of interconnecting its master-players into a community. Even as a VR game with rules, informatic controls, and intersubjective engagements, however, the "eXistenZ" game resonates more immediately with classical cinema than with any digitally networked dream world yet invented, even by 2006. If the players enslave the pods, they become each others' slaves in the Hegelian sense: they only achieve self-realization—winning the game—by reducing the other players to the Other, merely an embodied *relationship* to the Self, an obstacle to each player's successful negotiation through a game with a clear beginning, middle, and end, and an object of her or his gaze. Rather than members of a self-conscious community, the players are individuated spectators in their own first-person "shooter" classical films, using each other for profit or pleasure and discarding each other without remorse when their services are no longer required. When Pikul (Jude Law) screams at Allegra to consider the implications of pulling the trigger on an "enemy" when neither of them is certain any longer whether they're in "eXistenZ" or physical Existence, she is oblivious to any fleshly implications of the question. A few seconds later, they have betrayed each other and Pikul's avatar lies "dead," while Allegra looks to the sky and calls out, "Is it over? Did I win?"

Win she does, but *eXistenZ* makes clear that its confounding of game world and real world is not merely an exercise in Baudrillardian rhetoric about the loss of distinction between the real and the simulacrum. *The Matrix* (Andy Wachowski and Larry Wachowski, 1999) traffics in that rhetoric and nothing but, yet undermines its own hip cynicism by insisting that there is a real reality after all. *eXistenZ,* by contrast, parodies that very point of view via the Realists, a group of radical pod-killers who are as fanatical for authenticity, and as oblivious to the other lives they sacrifice in the name of their belief, as any religious fundamentalist. The perpetual blurring of the two realities is, in fact, a means of criticizing Miller's analogy between classical narrative and one's life story. Cronenberg parodies the unrealism of classical characterization, the dizzying changes that melodramatic characters must suffer in order to bring the plot to its resolution, in the form of the "game urges" the players find themselves submitting to—preprogrammed "scripts" that, like all filmmaking, turn humans into props and special effects. When the "game" needs to make a transition from one place or time to another, it simply makes a straight cut to a new setting just as *eXistenZ* does. But the difference between the cuts in *eXistenZ* and the cuts in "eXistenZ" is, in the latter, the player-characters find the cuts extremely disturbing—and unnatural. Suddenly they are standing in locations they don't recognize, wearing clothes they weren't wearing just a second before, performing tasks in medias res that they weren't even aware they knew how to do. By making a simple, conventional cut into a diegetic event that is also recognized as colossally disorienting, *eXistenZ* manages to make classicality strange with only the *theme* of digital media at its disposal. Allegra, Pikul, and the rest take pleasure in the game/film they "live" in, but they regularly experience their classically structured game-lives as cages rather than routes to the liberation of their identities.

Ultimately, the pod is the key to the door leading away from a confounded sense of reality as narrative, and into a critical position with respect to both classical film and the subjectivity it constructs. Near the end of the film, when the players "wake up" from the game like viewers after an extraordinarily absorbing movie, we find that the pod existed only in the game; the central interface through which the gamers apparently experienced this interactive event—the very anchor by which the film's own spectator makes sense of the game's parameters—is a fiction. This fact suggests to me how much weight the film places on media fantasy itself, symbolized by the pod, as an *escape* pod through which film's publics might imagine if not a definitive ideal of a posthuman or posthumanist cinema then at least the perpetual murder of one definition of film and its perpetual rebirth into unexpected, indeed hybridized forms, at the hands of its spectators and amateur producers rather than those of its institutionally legitimated producers and commentators alone. *eXistenZ* imagines this unimaginable cinema as irreducibly a creature of empathy—an abject blob that is utterly simple, a slave to its creator's wishes, yet unutterably complex at the same time. The image of its electrical-umbilical cord tears this little bundle of media machinery out of the loop of technological determinism and connects it back to its human creators in the bluntest fashion possible—by symbolically citing biology as the tie that binds them. The cord also arrests the idea of the "new medium," as a category of thought and practice as well as technology, in a frozen state of invention or testing that is also, inevitably, a state of hybridity: not human, but not the Other of technology or nature, either—a being processed from mutant frogs and lab-grown tissues that exists symbiotically with its human "masters." Because its cord penetrates the human body at the base of the spine rather than the navel, one can never say unequivocally which is giving birth to which. All that is certain is that some of the fluids and genes pumping through the throbbing pods are, in fact, human.

Why must this avatar for media fantasy die in the end? Because the Realists want it dead, in the name of unadulterated reality. They give the pods diseases and even torch them with flamethrowers, like villagers chasing Boris Karloff, while ejaculating comic-book victory cries like "Die, diseased pod!" in ludicrous amalgams of stock foreign accents. The radical Realists defend something very like the classical cinema that Miller defends as "natural"—a dimension of experience that obscures its own control panel, seemingly free of all manipulation, like Benjamin's "blue flower in the land of technology"; it seems no coincidence that the group shares its name with self-conscious movements in theater and literature that achieved illusionism by carefully cloistering the element of craft. But unlike *The Matrix,* which trades in its Baudrillardian posturing for an ideal of a gritty, unadulterated reality in a heartbeat, *eXistenZ* does not envision any clear reality for the viewer. It only offers films within films. The Realists play tug-of-war against a group of go-for-broke gamers who don't want to kill the pods, but only to forget the pods are necessary to make this realm exist. *eXistenZ* makes both groups look equally self-delusional, not to mention imaginatively impoverished, regarding the alternatives to present social organization and hierarchization with which a digital game-cinema could allow its users to experiment. Like Miller, all these players want is to be the star consciousnesses of their own linear narratives. Gas (Willem Dafoe) sums up this solipsistic wish when he quotes the tagline for Allegra's previous hit game, "ArtGod," "Thou, the Player, Art God."

What a waste it seems, then, that the pod—a new life-form whose chance at achieving its own consciousness has never been tested—is reduced to the role of tug-of-war rope between Cinema Ancients and Cinema Moderns. Cronenberg envisions "eXistenZ," the game, as a form of willing mind control, but he doesn't envision mind control as its only possibility. No one can predict what kind of ultimatum it would strike with its willing participants to co-define new subjectivities, if the players could escape the dueling visions that define it to death. Its edges are as lumpy, and its worlds as interpenetrable, as film's turn out to be even after ninety years of classicality—at least, that is, if one defines film first and foremost by its mutability, its intermedia transformations and the contingencies of individual and group reception, rather than by the continuities that we fetishize in our quest to assemble a classical narrative of film history.

I will not conclude this discussion with some ultimate definition of film, only a transhistorical definition of Hollywood cinema, which is that it looks much like Cronenberg's pod: an institution that mobilizes its medium to shift users in time and space, and that remains frozen in the early stages of its own development as a creature of, by, and for publicness because it must be continually reconstructed out of the parts of other media animals whenever its "old-fashionedness" becomes too visible to the viewers who have learned to want to forget its presence. Ironically, the continual surgeries to which Hollywood subjects film—sync sound, CinemaScope, digital animation—temporarily make the technology even more visible, and in turn make its spectators more aware that the thing they are experiencing not only produces an alternate world but attracts a nebulous mass of beings that collectively, like the pod, appear suspiciously human. The only intrinsic aspect of public film exhibition is a gathered audience—a wondrous, unpredictable, self-contradictory thing—that goes to the movies to be something other than it is for a while, even if it can't imagine exactly what that would look like. All it knows, subconsciously at least, is that it would like a shot at deciding that future for itself.

Acknowledgments

No one will excuse the blind spots of this book if I call it a preliminary study, nor should they, but preliminary it is—an attempt to map a different path through the history of Hollywood's relationships to a particular set of media competitors. Intermedia studies has become an important subfield within cinema and media criticism. The revisionist histories of the beginnings of particular media and technologies undertaken by Robert C. Allen, Rick Altman, Christopher Anderson, Tino Balio, John Belton, William Boddy, Jay Bolter, Lisa Cartwright, Timothy Corrigan, Sean Cubitt, Daniel Czitrom, Susan Douglas, Anne Friedberg, Lisa Gitelman, Richard Grusin, Tom Gunning, Michele Hilmes, James Lastra, Lev Manovich, Carolyn Marvin, Margaret Morse, Lauren Rabinowitz, Lynn Spigel, Cecelia Tichi, Yuri Tsivian, Janet Wasko, Alan Williams, Justin Wyatt, and others during the past two decades have helped push media studies past its understandable tendency to think of the question of media identity primarily as one of technological specificity and ontology. Scholars in the field of film, sound, and music such as Jacques Attali, James Lastra, Claudia Gorbman, Michel Chion, Arthur Knight, Pamela Robertson Wojcik, and Tim Anderson, and established scholars in other film fields who have recently turned to intermedia issues such as Thomas Elsaesser and William Uricchio, lend both inspiration and authority to the continuing project of "thinking" media through the technologies they either resemble in technological capabilities or are made to resemble by the rhetorics used to describe, market, and understand them.

It seems to have taken the arrival of yet another new and malleable mass consumer medium that communicates texts—the PC-Internet dyad, coupled with the mainstreaming and honing of video-game forms throughout the 1990s—to conjure back into being the burst of creative energy that gave rise to television studies more than twenty years ago. But to my knowledge there has been no attempt at a theoretical overview of the American cinema's intermedia history. It seems past time to try to remove the unfortunate wedge that often keeps theoretical and historical conceptions of film's relationships to its media rivals distinct from each other. In recent years "theory" has too often been made to sound like a dirty word in the American academy, particularly in media studies fields and in film studies, even though cultural and textual theories arguably put the discipline on the map. This book is unapologetically theoretical in approach but refuses, I hope, the tendency of many "pure" poetics of media to shield the object of study from the historical conditions that have as much to do with what a medium "is" in a given culture as do its technological properties.

This book wants to be a revisionist history of the American commercial cinema. What it does not want to do is replace or displace other histories written from other points of reference. Rather, it identifies one rhetorical mode among potentially many modes by which certain Hollywood films construct a medium as "other." If I don't spend enough time with the histories of the representational and rhetorical strategies developed for radio, television, or the Web to inform the reader fully on these crucial issues—and I surely do not—this is because I take the point of view of the film industry and its constructions of these media from both within (when Hollywood participates in these other industries at the levels of economic and textual development) and without (in cinematic texts that regularly ignore, and even contradict, Hollywood's material interests in the new medium in question). I hope that my suggestion to approach intermedia history as a history of media fantasy as much as one of technology, capital, or ideology will draw responses that home in on much more specific territories, whether to prove my claims right or wrong.

If the book accomplishes anything like what I've just described, I have many people to thank for that.

My dissertation advisors, Miriam Hansen, Bill Brown, and Jim Lastra, were tremendously patient and trenchant readers of my original research. Their influence on my thinking has been so profound that the book exhibits even more of their influence now than the dissertation did eight years ago. I am responsible for any misprisions or misapplications of their ideas and advice. Tom Campbell, John Wojtowicz, Brooks Landon, Tom Lutz, Cheryl Herr, Kate Hayles, and Dudley Andrew deserve thanks for setting me down the intellectual path that let to this book.

I thank my editors Andrea Kleinhuber and Carrie Mullen, acquiring editor Jennifer Moore, and the staff of the University of Minnesota Press for their help and nearly infinite patience.

At the University of Chicago, I want to thank Loren Kruger, Bruce Redford, Ken Warren, Jim Chandler, Jay Schleusener, and especially Tom Mitchell for invaluable mentorship. Tom Gunning's generosity, painstaking attention to detail, and marvelous suggestions leave him with few peers in the field. Don Crafton's film noir seminar in 1993 taught me essential lessons about film historiography, and his encouragement since then has gone beyond the call of duty. I'll have to thank my graduate school colleagues in no particular order, for it's too difficult to rank the value of things like friendship and general intellectual influence: Pat Chu, Shoshanna Cohen, Alicia Tomasian, Corinne Scheiner, Dave Stewart, Michael Caldwell, Ruth Feingold, Jennifer Peterson, John Paul Ricco, Anthony Miller, Pamela Robertson Wojcik, Arthur Knight, Shari Roberts, Priscilla Barlow, Hank Sartin, Rick Wojcik, Temby Caprio, Neda Ulaby, Jackie Cooper, Elisabeth Ceppi, David Grubbs, Scott Johnson, Colin Johnson, John O'Brien, Vicki Olwell, Jacqueline Stewart, and the members of the Mass Culture Workshop. Andrew Hoberek deserves special mention for looking out for my interests on so many levels for as long as he did.

At Georgia Tech, I want to thank (again in no particular order) Richard Grusin, Lisa Yaszek, Jami Moss, Patrick Sharp, Jay Telotte, Alan Rauch, Robert Kolker, Carol Senf, Sara Putzell, Hugh Crawford, and Blake Leland for their ideas and support. I owe my early-career sanity to Ellen Strain-Seymour, Ian Strain-Seymour, Kavita Philip, Ward Smith, Sha Xin Wei and his family, and Chris Shaw and Diane Gromala. Thank you for being such wonderful coteachers, co-conspirators, film freaks, gourmands, cat lovers, and friends. And thanks to Christian Doolin for believing.

Friends I've made since my stint in Atlanta have helped by providing advice, encouragement, energetic conversation, criticism, and a great deal of friendship: Roger Cook, Carsten Strathausen, Valerie Kaussen, Maurice Lee, Catherine Parke, Tom Quirk, Nancy West, Kristin Schwain, Martin Camargo, Sandy Camargo, Devoney Looser, George Justice, John Evelev, Emma Lipton, Ines Segert, Keith Eggener, Karen Piper, Jeff Williams, Jeff Williams (what are the odds?), and Brad Prager at the University of Missouri–Columbia; and Carolyn Dever, Mark Wollaeger, Jerry Christensen, Jay Clayton, Cecelia Tichi, Jennifer Lena, Shawn Salvant, Tina Chen, Sean Goudie, Teresa Goddu, Yoshi Igarashi, Joy Calico, Mark Schoenfield, Gregg Horowitz, Ellen Levy, Katherine Carroll, Sam Girgus, Beth Bachmann,

Brian Bachmann, Dennis Kezar, and Deak Nabers at Vanderbilt University. Mark Wollaeger in particular has been a great supporter and a great reader who also happens to have a great family and a great back patio. Carolyn Dever has already helped me push various vehicles out of the mud more times than I can count.

While researching chapters 1, 2, and 3, I received generous grants from the Georgia Tech Foundation for archival travel. For making my visit to the Library of Congress's Motion Picture, Broadcasting, and Recorded Sound Division in June 2000 so fruitful, I thank Joe Balian, Zoran Sinobad, Madeleine Matz, and especially Rosemary Hanes. Karen Everson, Becky Simmons, and Todd Gustavson at the George Eastman House discovered unusual items that expanded my research questions in provocative directions, and they were generous hosts as well.

Scott Curtis at the Margaret Herrick Library (now of Northwestern University) guided me through the Paramount Collection when I began my research into film noir. He and Jennifer Barker were also kind enough to house me and watch Wilder and Kazan movies with me during my visit to Los Angeles.

The Society for Cinema Studies (now the Society for Cinema and Media Studies) awarded me second place in its student essay competition in 1995 for an essay that later became the heart of chapter 4.

Without music and other pleasant, often unexpected distractions, work suffers. With that in mind, I thank the fine people at the Vanderbilt area CD Warehouse—Ryan, Mia, Ryan (what are the odds?), and Isaac—for supplying me with eclectic, labor-inspiring tunes, honest opinions, and a lot of much-needed laughter.

I am grateful to the editors of *Convergence: The Journal of Research into New Media Technologies* for permission to reprint previously published sections of chapter 5 here. Thanks also to Andy Hoberek and Jeff Williams for the opportunity to test an alternate direction for my television research in the essay "(Not) The Last Noir Essay: Film Noir and the Crisis of Postwar Interpretation" (*The Minnesota Review* 55–57 [2002]: 203–21). Special gratitude goes to Lisa Gitelman and Geoff Pingree, kind and enthusiastic readers of my somewhat different work on telegraphy and early cinema.

My parents, Joann and David Young, have encouraged me unflaggingly throughout my education and my career. Anything remotely funny in the book is dedicated to my brother, Tim Young, and his family: Chieko, Jenny Fujie, Christy Ayumi, William Shotoro, and Julia Shiori. Many thanks to my sister, Deb Henderson, and her children Deontáe, AJ, and Dacarra, with whom I have spent many wonderful days since I began the book in earnest.

This book is for Caitilin McNeal. Her demand that my writing be as frank as possible without skimping on complexity has kept my research honest. We once spent an entire afternoon and evening on her back porch in New Mexico, eating franks and beans heated in a toaster oven and arguing loudly about the merits of Peter Greenaway's multimedia pastiche. To whom else could I dedicate a book about the intermedial character of cinema?

Notes

Introduction

1. Donna Haraway, "A Manifesto for Cyborgs," in *Simians, Cyborgs, and Women: The Reinvention of Nature* (New York: Routledge, 1991), 149–81.

2. On *The Lawnmower Man*'s "preoccup[ation] with gender roles" and Jobe's VR avatar as a manifestation of "the rage of the patriarchal unconscious," see Claudia Springer, *Electronic Eros: Bodies and Desire in the Postindustrial Age* (Austin: University of Texas Press, 1996), 91–94. For a wide-ranging discussion of the successes and failures of cyborgian experimentation in cyberspace up to the mid-nineties, see Ann Balsamo, *Technologies of the Gendered Body: Reading Cyborg Women* (Durham, NC: Duke University Press, 1996), esp. 116–32.

3. William Uricchio, "Television, Film, and the Struggle for Media Identity," *Film History* 10 (1998): 118–27.

4. John Ellis, *Visible Fictions: Cinema, Television, Video* (1982; rev. ed., London: Routledge, 1992).

5. I am indebted to Rick Altman's rhetorical frankness in studies like *Film/Genre* for this straightforward approach to excavating and describing deep-seated assumptions of a field. See Altman, "What Is Generally Understood by the Notion of Film Genre?" in *Film/Genre* (London: British Film Institute, 1999), 13–29.

6. Philip Rosen succeeds admirably at the formidable task of redeeming Bazin from this view by exposing the provisional nature of Bazin's approach to film's ontology and by exploring the implications of its intermedial, intertextual basis. See Rosen's *Change Mummified: Cinema, Historicity, Theory* (Minneapolis: University of Minnesota Press, 2001), chapter 1.

For the origin of the term "Grand Theory," coined by David Bordwell and Noël Carroll to criticize what they see as the dogmatic, excessive, and anti-empirical uses of psychoanalysis, Marxism, and "the modernity thesis" to analyze film, see Bordwell, "Contemporary Film Studies and the Vicissitudes of Grand Theory," in *Post-Theory: Reconstructing Film Studies*, ed. Bordwell and Carroll (Madison:

University of Wisconsin Press, 1996), 3–36. On the modernity thesis, which postulates that the rapid expansion of urban and technological experience at the end of the nineteenth century greatly influenced the invention of moving pictures and the attractions mode of early cinema, see David Bordwell, *On the History of Film Style* (Cambridge, MA: Harvard University Press, 1997), esp. 141–46. A remarkable response to Bordwell's attempt to disprove the modernity thesis appears in Ben Singer, *Melodrama and Modernity: Early Sensational Cinema and Its Contexts* (New York: Columbia University Press, 2001), chapter 4.

7. André Bazin, "The Ontology of the Photographic Image," in *What Is Cinema?* trans. Hugh Gray (Berkeley and Los Angeles: University of California Press, 1967), 9–16; "The Myth of Total Cinema," in *What Is Cinema?* 17–22; "The Evolution of the Language of Cinema," in *What Is Cinema?* 23–40.

8. Friedrich Kittler, *Discourse Networks 1800/1900,* trans. Michael Metteer with Chris Cullens (Stanford, CA: Stanford University Press, 1985), 265.

9. Kittler, "Die Laterna magica der Literatur: Schillers und Hoffmanns Medienstrategien" (1994), quoted in Geoffrey Winthrop-Young and Michael Wutz, "Translator's Introduction: Friedrich Kittler and Media Discourse Analysis," in Friedrich Kittler, *Gramophone, Film, Typewriter* (Stanford, CA: Stanford University Press, 1999), xiv.

10. Jean Baudrillard, "Requiem for the Media" (1981), quoted in Winthrop-Young and Wutz, "Translator's Introduction," xv.

11. Raymond Williams, *Television: Technology and Cultural Form* (1974; repr., Hanover, NH: Wesleyan University Press, 1992), 120, 121, 124.

12. Vachel Lindsay, *The Art of the Moving Picture* (1915; rev. ed. 1922; repr. New York: Liveright, 1970); Hugo Münsterberg, *The Photoplay* (1916), republished as *The Film: A Psychological Study: The Photoplay in 1916* (New York: Dover, 1970).

13. Studios initially planned to treat synchronized sound as an "attraction" or a special effect, and there was even discussion (though it's difficult to tell how serious it was) of dividing all film production into two categories: sound films and silent narratives with recorded musical accompaniment. See Donald Crafton, *The Talkies: American Cinema's Transition to Sound, 1926–1931* (Berkeley and Los Angeles: University of California Press, 1997), 167, 169, 171.

14. See John Belton, *Widescreen Cinema* (Cambridge, MA: Harvard University Press, 1992), chapter 4 and 183–97.

15. See Janet Wasko, *Hollywood in the Information Age* (Austin: University of Texas Press, 1994), 8 and chapter 2.

16. Michele Hilmes, *Hollywood and Broadcasting: From Radio to Cable* (Urbana: University of Illinois Press, 1990), 55–60.

17. Marshall McLuhan, *Understanding Media: The Extensions of Man* (1964; repr. Cambridge, MA: MIT Press, 1994), 311.

18. Lev Manovich, *The Language of New Media* (Cambridge, MA: MIT Press, 2001), 86.

19. Jay David Bolter and Richard Grusin, *Remediation: Understanding New Media* (Cambridge, MA: MIT Press, 1999), 65.

20. James Lastra, "Standards and Practices: Aesthetic Norm and Technological Innovation in the American Cinema," in *The Studio System,* ed. Janet Staiger (New Brunswick, NJ: Rutgers University Press, 1995), 200–225.

21. See Rick Altman, "Deep-Focus Sound: *Citizen Kane* and the Radio Aesthetic," *Quarterly Review of Film and Video* 15, no. 3 (1994): 21 and passim.

22. Uricchio, 118–21.

23. Carolyn Marvin, *When Old Technologies Were New: Thinking about Electric Communication in the Late Nineteenth Century* (New York: Oxford University Press, 1988), 8.

24. Arjun Appadurai, *Modernity at Large: Cultural Dimensions of Globalization* (Minneapolis: University of Minnesota Press, 1996), 8.

25. Max Horkheimer and Theodor W. Adorno specifically contest this dream in *Dialectic of Enlightenment* (1944): "The ruled accept as unquestionable necessity the course of development that with every decreed rise in the standard of living makes them so much more powerless. . . . The absurdity of a state of affairs in which the enforced power of the system over men grows with every step that takes it out of the power of nature, denounces the rationality of the rational society as obsolete" (trans. John Cumming [New York: Continuum, 1991], 38–39).

26. David Bordwell, Janet Staiger, and Kristin Thompson, *The Classical Hollywood Cinema: Film Style and Mode of Production to 1960* (New York: Columbia University Press, 1985).

27. For two early and definitive descriptions of the filmmaking practices and narrative-spectacle strategies of the "New Hollywood," see Thomas Schatz, "The New Hollywood," in *Film Theory Goes to the Movies,* ed. Jim Collins, Hilary Radner, and Ava Preacher Collins, 8–36 (New York: Routledge/American Film Institute, 1993) and Justin Wyatt, *High Concept: Movies and Marketing in Hollywood* (Austin: University of Texas Press, 1994). More recent collections of descriptions and historical-theoretical placements of American films after *Jaws* (as well as essays on international cinema and the future[s] of cinema in the digital age) include Jon Lewis, ed., *The New American Cinema* (Durham, NC: Duke University Press, 1998); Jon Lewis, ed., *The End of Cinema as We Know It: American Film in the Nineties* (New York: New York University Press, 2001); Thomas Elsaesser and Kay Hoffman, eds., *Cinema Futures: Cain, Abel, or Cable?* (Amsterdam: Amsterdam University Press, 1998); and Steve Neale and Murray Smith, eds., *Contemporary Hollywood Cinema* (London: Routledge, 1998).

28. See the following essays in *Classical Hollywood Narrative: The Paradigm Wars,* ed. Jane Gaines (Durham: Duke University Press, 1992): Rick Altman, "Dickens, Griffith, and Film Theory Today" (9–47) and Bill Nichols, "Form Wars: The Political Unconscious of Formalist Theory" (49–77), and see Miriam Hansen, "Male Star, Female Fans," in *Babel and Babylon: Spectatorship in American*

Silent Film (Cambridge, MA: Harvard University Press, 1991), chapter 11. See also Hansen's most recent entries in this discussion, "The Mass Production of the Senses: Classical Cinema as Vernacular Modernism," *Modernism/Modernity* 6, no. 2 (1999): 57–59; and "Fallen Women, Rising Stars: Shanghai Silent Film as Vernacular Modernism," *Film Quarterly* 54, no. 1 (Fall 2000): 10–22.

29. The period of classical dominance begins roughly in 1917 for Bordwell et al., and ends roughly in 1960, though Thompson has since argued that the same dominant overdetermines contemporary Hollywood narrative. See Kristin Thompson, *Storytelling in the New Hollywood: Understanding Classical Narrative Technique* (Cambridge, MA: Harvard University Press, 1999).

30. Pierre Bourdieu, *Outline of a Theory of Practice*, trans. Richard Nice (Cambridge: Cambridge University Press, 1977), 78, quoted in Lastra, "Standards and Practices," 201, and see especially 205–8 and 215–20. For an expanded version of the argument about the transition to sound, see James Lastra, *Sound Technology and the American Cinema: Perception, Representation, Modernity* (New York: Columbia University Press, 2000), chapters 4–6.

31. See Sigmund Freud, "Fragment of an Analysis of a Case of Hysteria" (1905 [1901]), in *The Standard Edition of the Complete Psychological Works of Sigmund Freud*, trans. and ed. James Strachey (London: Hogarth Press and the Institute of Psychoanalysis, 1953), 7:30–31.

32. Fredric Jameson, "Reification and Utopia in Mass Culture" (1979), in *Signatures of the Visible* (New York: Routledge, 1990), 9–34.

33. See Michel de Certeau, *The Practice of Everyday Life*, trans. Steven Rendall (Berkeley and Los Angeles: University of California Press, 1984).

34. See Philip Auslander, *Liveness: Performance in a Mediated Culture* (New York: Routledge, 1999), 24–25. For the full version of the careful argument I have drastically summarized here, see chapters 1 and 2.

35. Jens F. Jensen, "'Interactivity'—Tracking a New Concept in Media and Communication Studies," in *Computer Media and Communication: A Reader,* ed. Paul Mayer, 160–87 (New York: Clarendon, 1999). Roman Jakobson might refer to what Jensen calls *informatic* interactivity as a postmodern instance of communication performing a *phatic* function, in which, as Lev Manovich aptly phrases it when describing the point-and-click structure of Web surfing, "communication comes to be dominated by contact . . . [and] centered on the physical channel and the very act of connection between addresser"—the user—"and addressee"—in this case, the computer that makes various links available to the user as well as displaying the progress of the loading of a page. Roman Jakobson, "Closing Statement: Linguistics and Poetics," in *Style in Language,* ed. Thomas Sebeok (Cambridge, MA: MIT Press, 1960), 355–56; see Manovich, *The Language of New Media,* 206.

36. For example, Marie-Laure Ryan, following the readership theories of Wolfgang Iser, defines interactivity strictly in terms of informatic or phatic relationships between user and (digital) text: "figural" interactivity means "the

collaboration between the reader and the text in the production of meaning," and "literal" interactivity means that "the text undergoes physical changes during the reading process." Ryan, "Cyberspace, Virtuality, and the Text," in *Cyberspace Textuality: Computer Technology and Literary Theory,* ed. Marie-Laure Ryan (Bloomington: Indiana University Press, 1999), 97–98.

37. See Benedict Anderson, *Imagined Communities: Reflections on the Origin and Spread of Nationalism,* rev. ed. (London: Verso, 1991), esp. chapter 2.

38. See Howard Rheingold, *Virtual Reality* (New York: Summit, 1991), chapters 1–4.

39. Scott Bukatman, *Terminal Identity: The Virtual Subject in Postmodern Science Fiction* (Durham, NC: Duke University Press, 1993), 189–90.

1. Rubes, Camera Fiends, Filmmakers, and Other Amateurs

1. For an account of the distinction between film qua medium and film qua institution, and how the French film industry constructed the latter as a means to manage the former, see André Gaudreault, "Les vues cinématographiques selon Georges Méliès, ou: comment Mitry et Sadoul avaient peut-être raison d'avoir tort (même si c'est surtout Deslandes qu'il faut lire et relire)," *Georges Méliès, l'illusionniste fin de siècle,* ed Jacques Malthête and Michel Marie (Paris: Presses de la Sorbonne Nouvelle/College de Cerisy, 1997), 111–31.

2. Stephen Neale, *Genre* (London: British Film Institute, 1980), 50–51.

3. See Sumiko Higashi, *Cecil B. DeMille and American Culture: The Silent Era* (Berkeley and Los Angeles: University of California Press, 1994), esp. chapters 1 and 4.

4. Barry Salt, *Film Style and Technology: History and Analysis* (London: Starword, 1983).

5. Raymond Williams, "Dominant, Residual, and Emergent," in *Marxism and Literature* (Oxford: Oxford University Press, 1977), 121–27.

6. See Anne Friedberg, *Window Shopping: Cinema and the Postmodern* (Berkeley and Los Angeles: University of California Press, 1993), 109–48 and 181–90, and Timothy Corrigan, *A Cinema without Walls: Movies and Culture after Vietnam* (New Brunswick, NJ: Rutgers University Press, 1991) for what are still the definitive statements about these phenomena.

7. Laura Mulvey, "Visual Pleasure and Narrative Cinema," in *Narrative, Apparatus, Ideology,* ed. Philip Rosen, 198–209 (New York: Columbia University Press, 1986) and Jean-Louis Baudry, "Ideological Effects of the Basic Cinematographic Apparatus," in *Narrative, Apparatus, Ideology,* 286–98.

8. Terry Ramsaye, *A Million and One Nights: A History of the Motion Picture,* 2 vols. (New York: Simon and Schuster, 1926), 1:lxvi; Janet Murray, *Hamlet on the Holodeck: The Future of Narrative in Cyberspace* (New York: The Free Press, 1997).

9. Rick Altman, *Film/Genre* (London: British Film Institute, 1999), 121.

10. This hypothetical example is not taken from a specific film, but scenes resembling it appeared in many films after Griffith's one- and two-reelers for Biograph began to do big business. Griffith's "narrator-function" actually tended not to implement matte shots; he was brave enough at this early juncture to use editing alone to suggest that one character pined after another and hope that the audience would understand his peculiar editing syntax well enough to get the connotation by, for example, following the shot of the woman staring into space with a shot of the man, in the same space and dress as before, suddenly looking up in half-realization, as if he knew that someone was thinking about him.

Tom Gunning defines this narrator-function as an implied narrating agent, "an abstraction [that may be derived] from the films that Griffith directed in his first years at Biograph which describes Griffith's systematic approach to narrative form. . . . It is one particular synthesis of filmic discourse" that focuses on "the task of storytelling" above all other discursive concerns. Elements that point to the existence of the implied narrator would include psychological characterization, emphasis on narrative objects and character reactions, the delineation of tense (flashback, present events, etc.), and systematic indications of the spatial and temporal relations among discrete shots (Gunning, *D. W. Griffith and the Origins of American Narrative Film: The Early Years at Biograph* [Urbana: University of Illinois Press, 1991], 25; see also chapters 1 and 2).

11. Carolyn Marvin, *When Old Technologies Were New: Thinking about Electric Communication in the Late Nineteenth Century* (New York: Oxford University Press, 1988), 6.

12. Donald Crafton, *The Talkies: American Cinema's Transition to Sound, 1926–1931* (Berkeley and Los Angeles: University of California Press, 1997), 28.

13. Gunning, "Weaving a Narrative: Style and Economic Background in Griffith's Biograph Films" (1981), in *Early Cinema: Space, Frame, Narrative,* ed. Thomas Elsaesser with Adam Barker (London: British Film Institute, 1990), 336–40; Bordwell, Staiger, and Thompson, *The Classical Hollywood Cinema.*

14. See, for example, Yuri Tsivian, "Media Fantasies and Penetrating Vision: Some Links between X-Rays, the Microscope, and Film," in *The Laboratory of Dreams: The Russian Avant-Garde and Cultural Experiment,* ed. John E. Bowlt and Olga Matich (Stanford, CA: Stanford University Press, 1996), 81–99.

15. Lynne Kirby, "Male Hysteria and Early Cinema," *Camera Obscura* 17 (1988): 113 and *Parallel Tracks: The Railroad and Silent Cinema* (Durham, NC: Duke University Press, 1997), 42–48; and Daniel Czitrom, *Media and the American Mind* (Chapel Hill: University of North Carolina Press, 1982), 11. On the uncanny effect that splitting moving image from physical object may have had on the first spectators, see Tom Gunning, "An Aesthetic of Astonishment: Early Film and the (In)credulous Spectator" (1989), in *Film Theory and Criticism,* 5th ed., ed. Leo Braudy and Marshall Cohen (New York: Oxford University Press, 1999), esp. 818–24.

16. *Electrical Review,* October 3, 1885, 7; quoted in Marvin, 199.

17. Pecqueur, *Économie sociale,* vol. 1 (Paris, 1839), 335–36; quoted in Wolfgang Schivelbusch, *The Railway Journey: The Industrialization of Time and Space in the Nineteenth Century* (1976; repr. Berkeley and Los Angeles: University of California Press, 1986), 71.

18. The railroad engine's power as a symbol of American technological and economic progress repeatedly tipped over into a fantasy similar to Pecqueur's, which Leo Marx terms a belief in "the overall progress of the race," a narrative that teleologically pursued utopian democracy (Marx, *The Machine in the Garden: Technology and the Pastoral Ideal in America* [New York: Oxford University Press, 1964], 27). Quoting the American orator Daniel Webster's 1847 comments on the railroad, Marx exemplifies this impulse as it continued to operate regarding the train for the remainder of the nineteenth century: "The railroad breaks down regional barriers. Those who came from Boston might have brought along 'fish taken out of the sea at sunrise.' . . . The new inventions hold the promise of national unity and, even more exciting, social equality. Nothing could be as important to the 'great mass of the community' as this innovation 'calculated . . . to equalize the condition of men.' It is a mode of conveyance available to rich and poor alike, and [Webster] is pleased to report that the people regard it as their own" (210). As the "shrinking" of time and space had clear and present effects on social relations, so too it perpetually held out the promise of a more profound democratization of American society, as progress continued to unfold in its current, industrial-mechanical manifestation.

19. "The Future of the Telephone," *Scientific American,* January 10, 1880, 16; quoted in Marvin, 65.

20. "The allusion of train window with the screen's rectangle was frequent within [the railway] sub-genre [of the travelogue film]; it found its ultimate expression with Hale's Tours" (Charles Musser, "The Travel Genre in 1903–04: Moving toward Fictional Narrative," in *Early Cinema: Space, Frame, Narrative,* ed. Thomas Elsaesser with Adam Barker [London: British Film Institute, 1990], 127). For a brief but thorough and descriptive history of Hale's Tours, see Raymond Fielding, "Hale's Tours: Ultrarealism in the Pre-1910 Motion Picture," in *Film before Griffith,* ed. John L. Fell (Berkeley and Los Angeles: University of California Press, 1983), 116–30.

21. Miriam Hansen, "Universal Language and Democratic Culture: Myths of Origin in Early American Cinema," in *Myth and Enlightenment in American Literature,* ed. Dieter Meindl and Friedrich W. Horlacher, with Martin Christadler (Erlangen-Nürnberg: Universitätsbund, 1985), 328.

22. Morse, quoted in Richard Rudisill, *Mirror Image* (Albuquerque: University of New Mexico Press, 1971), 57; see Dan Schiller, "Realism, Photography, and Journalistic Objectivity in 19th Century America," *Studies in the Anthropology of Visual Communication* 4, no. 2 (1977): 89.

23. Ithiel de Sola Pool, *Forecasting the Telephone: A Retrospective Technology Assessment of the Telephone* (Norwood, NJ: Ablex, 1983), 107–8.

24. Indeed, Hansen writes, the "intrinsically egalitarian effect [imputed] to the media of technological reproduction" depended on the capitalist structure driving that reproduction, which in turn depended on masses of poor and working-class consumers (Hansen, "Universal Language," 326). On cinematic self-legitimation and the ideology of uplift, see Gunning, *D. W. Griffith,* esp. 89–91, and William Uricchio and Roberta Pearson, *Reframing Culture: The Case of the Vitagraph Quality Films* (Princeton, NJ: Princeton University Press, 1993).

25. See Hansen, "Universal Language" and *Babel and Babylon: Spectatorship in American Silent Film* (Cambridge, MA: Harvard University Press, 1991), 76–86.

26. Charles Musser, *The Emergence of Cinema: The American Screen to 1907* (Berkeley and Los Angeles: University of California Press, 1990), 241, 244.

27. Marvin, 198; Kirby, *Parallel Tracks,* 34. See also Schivelbusch, 73.

28. William Uricchio, "Television, Film, and the Struggle for Media Identity," *Film History* 10 (1998): 119.

29. *Electrical Review,* May 25, 1889, quoted in Marvin, 197; "The Industrial Development of Electricity," *All The Year Round* (London), October 6, 1894, 330, quoted in Marvin, 260 n. 22.

30. Charles Henry Cochrane, *The Wonders of Modern Mechanism* (Philadelphia: Lippincott, 1896), 73.

31. Paul Young, "Media on Display: A Telegraphic History of Early Cinema," in *New Media 1740–1915,* ed. Lisa Gitelman and Geoffrey B. Pingree (Cambridge, MA: MIT Press, 2003), esp. 232–49.

32. On the (courted) confusion between documentary and staged news films during the Spanish-American War, see Bill Brown, *The Material Unconscious* (Cambridge, MA: Harvard University Press, 1996), 134. On film as a quasi-telegraphic news medium, see Musser, *The Emergence of Cinema,* 315–16; and Young, 237–43.

33. Hansen, *Babel and Babylon,* 8. See Jürgen Habermas, *The Structural Transformation of the Public Sphere* (1962), trans. Thomas Burger with Frederick Lawrence (Cambridge, MA: MIT Press, 1992), esp. 27–31.

34. See also Nancy Fraser, "Rethinking the Public Sphere: A Contribution to the Critique of Actually Existing Democracy," in *The Phantom Public Sphere,* ed. Bruce Robbins (Minneapolis: University of Minnesota Press, 1993), 4–23.

35. Oskar Negt and Alexander Kluge, *Public Sphere and Experience: Toward an Analysis of the Bourgeois and Proletarian Public Sphere,* trans. Peter Labanyi, Jamie Owen Daniel, and Assenka Oksiloff (Minneapolis: University of Minnesota Press, 1993), 44, 173–74. Negt and Kluge differ fundamentally from Habermas in their recognition of the mass media as less an institution hovering over industrial culture than one integrated with—and expressive of—the realities of both capital and labor, or to put it in less classically Marxist terms, both the imperatives of the economy and the quotidian experience of those who serve those imperatives in order to subsist: *"The public sphere of production has its nucleus in the sensual presence of the public sphere that emanates from the objective production process—*

of society, just as it is" (13, n. 23; see also 12–18). On the ambivalence of television broadcasting and the possibility of counterreadings, see chapter 3, esp. 99–109.

36. Hansen, *Babel and Babylon,* 90 (emphasis in original), 60.

37. Musser, *The Emergence of Cinema,* 4. See also Hansen, *Babel and Babylon,* 61–62.

38. On the centrality of the apparatus in early film shows, see Tom Gunning, "The Cinema of Attractions: Early Film, Its Spectator, and the Avant-Garde," in *Early Cinema: Space, Frame, Narrative,* ed. Thomas Elsaesser with Adam Barker (London: British Film Institute, 1990), 58, and "An Aesthetic of Astonishment." On the democratic-symbolic context of technological display in the nineteenth century, see Kirby, *Parallel Tracks,* 34–35; Czitrom, 11; Marx, 209–14; and David E. Nye, *American Technological Sublime* (Cambridge, MA: MIT Press, 1994).

39. For *Elephants Shooting the Chutes at Luna Park* (Edison, 1904), see Charles Musser's documentary film *Before the Nickelodeon* (Kino International, 1982). "Edison's failure to create its own original story films" at this point, based on a business decision to cuts costs by emphasizing documentary subjects and duplicating the films of foreign competitors, "undercut the company's commercial position" (Musser, *The Emergence of Cinema,* 389).

40. Ibid., 241, 261.

41. *Austin Statesman,* January 11, 1900, 3, quoted in Burnes St. Patrick Hollyman, "The First Picture Shows: Austin, Texas, 1894–1913," in *Film before Griffith,* ed. John L. Fell (Berkeley and Los Angeles: University of California Press, 1983), 191. Although each uses his own terminology, Walter Benjamin and Martin Heidegger both describe the urge for a "world picture" as a commodifying, post-auratic urge. See Benjamin, "The Work of Art in the Age of Mechanical Reproduction" (1936), in *Illuminations,* ed. Hannah Arendt, trans. Harry Zohn (New York: Schocken, 1968), 221–23, and Martin Heidegger, "The Age of the World Picture" (1938), in *The Question Concerning Technology and Other Essays,* trans. William Lovitt (New York: Harper Colophon, 1977), 126–36.

42. Charlie Keil, *Early American Cinema in Transition* (Madison: University of Wisconsin Press, 2001), esp. chapters 2 and 3.

43. Friedberg, 20–38 and chapter 2.

44. See Siegfried Kracauer, "Cult of Distraction: On Berlin's Picture Palaces" (1926), in *The Mass Ornament,* trans. and ed. Thomas Y. Levin (Cambridge, MA: Harvard University Press, 1995), 325–27, and Benjamin, "The Work of Art in the Age of Mechanical Reproduction," 239–41. The "modernity thesis" is a semi-pejorative term coined by David Bordwell to challenge the recent theories, influenced primarily by Benjamin and Kracauer, that attribute both the stuttering attractions of early cinema and viewers' peculiar attraction to them to fundamental changes to visual perception effected by urban industrial life. See Bordwell, *On the History of Film Style* (Cambridge, MA: Harvard University Press, 1997), 141–46. For a remarkable counter to Bordwell's critique, see Ben Singer, *Melodrama and*

Modernity: Early Sensational Cinema and Its Contexts (New York: Columbia University Press, 2001), chapter 4.

45. Walter Benjamin, "On Some Motifs in Baudelaire," in *Illuminations,* 175.

46. *New York Times,* April 24, 1896, 5; quoted in *Selected Film Criticism 1896–1911,* ed. Anthony Slide (Metuchen, NJ: Scarecrow, 1982), 34.

47. W. Stephen Bush, "The Human Voice as a Factor in the Moving Picture Show," *Moving Picture World* 4, no. 4 (January 23, 1909): 86; quoted in Hansen, *Babel and Babylon,* 97.

48. See Marvin, chapter 2.

49. See T. J. Jackson Lears, *No Place of Grace: Antimodernism and the Transformation of American Culture, 1880–1920* (1981; repr. Chicago: University of Chicago Press, 1994), 26–32, and Lawrence W. Levine, *Highbrow/Lowbrow: The Emergence of Cultural Hierarchy in America* (Cambridge, MA: Harvard University Press, 1988), esp. 200–242.

50. See Levine, chapter 1 and 171–200.

51. See Uricchio and Pearson, chapter 2, esp. 54.

52. Gunning, *D. W. Griffith,* 22–25, chapter 2, and passim.

53. See Anna McCarthy, *Ambient Television: Visual Culture and Public Space* (Durham, NC: Duke University Press, 2001), 1–20 and passim.

54. Hansen, *Babel and Babylon,* 28.

55. For the invaluable filmographic information as well as facsimiles of the *Bulletins* themselves, see Kemp R. Niver, compiler, *Biograph Bulletins 1896–1908,* ed. Bebe Bergstrom (Los Angeles: Locare Research Group, 1971).

56. Niver, 336. The only print of this film I have seen, a 16-millimeter print at the Library of Congress, omits the shots of the slides. I am guessing, based on the construction of *The Story the Biograph Told* and on the fact that the shots are missing, that the slides did not appear matted into the screen within the frame but as full-screen images that could be detached from the film and shown separately. I have no way of knowing from this print whether these "slides" were stills or moving images, though I don't believe this makes a tremendous difference to my argument. I should note that in *Uncle Josh at the Moving Picture Show,* an earlier precedent for this film, Porter has matted the images into Josh's in-frame screen.

57. On the conventions of the bad-boy genre, one of the earliest and most prolific of film genres, see Musser, *The Emergence of Cinema,* 4–5.

58. See ibid., 109–28.

59. Hansen, *Babel and Babylon,* 91.

60. Nancy Martha West, *Kodak and the Lens of Nostalgia* (Charlottesville: University Press of Virginia, 2000), 43–44.

61. See Keil, chapters 3 and 4.

62. Tom Gunning, "Tracing the Individual Body: Photography, Detectives, and Early Cinema," in *Cinema and the Invention of Modern Life,* ed. Leo Charney

and Vanessa R. Schwartz (Berkeley and Los Angeles: University of California Press, 1995), 37, 36.

63. Carol J. Clover, "Judging Audiences: The Case of the Trial Movie," in *Reinventing Film Studies,* ed. Christine Gledhill and Linda Williams (London: Arnold, 2000), 246.

64. David E. Nye, *Electrifying America: Social Meanings of a New Technology, 1880–1940* (Cambridge, MA: MIT Press, 1990), 105.

65. Judith Mayne, *The Woman at the Keyhole: Feminism and Women's Cinema* (Bloomington: Indiana University Press, 1990), 31, 32.

66. Christian Metz, *The Imaginary Signifier: Psychoanalysis and the Cinema,* trans. Celia Britton, Annwyl Williams, Ben Brewster, and Alfred Guzzetti (Bloomington: Indiana University Press, 1982), esp. 91–119; Baudry, passim.

67. Hansen, *Babel and Babylon,* 36.

68. "Film Realism," *Moving Picture World* 3, no. 22 (November 28, 1908): 427. For an examination of the further intermedia implications of this story, see Young, 252.

2. A Cinema without Wires

1. Michel Chion, *The Voice in Cinema,* ed. and trans. Claudia Gorbman (1982; repr. New York: Columbia University Press, 1999), 24.

2. See Jeffrey Sconce, *Haunted Media: Electronic Presence from Telegraphy to Television* (Durham, NC: Duke University Press, 2000), chapters 2 and 3.

3. Susan J. Douglas, *Inventing American Broadcasting, 1899–1922* (Baltimore: The Johns Hopkins University Press, 1987), 191.

4. Erik Barnouw, *A Tower in Babel,* vol. 1 of *A History of Broadcasting in the United States* (London: Oxford University Press, 1966), 31.

5. See Sidney H. Aronson, "Bell's Electrical Toy: What's the Use? The Sociology of Early Telephone Usage," in *The Social Impact of the Telephone,* ed. Ithiel de Sola Pool (Cambridge, MA: MIT Press, 1988), 20, 32; and Paul Young, "Media on Display: A Telegraphic History of Early Cinema," in *New Media 1740–1915,* ed. Lisa Gitelman and Geoffrey B. Pingree (Cambridge, MA: MIT Press, 2003), 243–44.

6. See Peter J. Hugill, *Global Communications since 1844: Geopolitics and Technology* (Baltimore: The Johns Hopkins University Press, 1999), 87.

7. "*Caught by Wireless*: The Efficacy of the Marconigram Shown in Motion Pictures," *Biograph Bulletin* 129 (March 21, 1908), repr. in *Biograph Bulletins 1896–1908,* compiler Kemp R. Niver, ed. Bebe Bergstrom (Los Angeles: Locare Research Group, 1971), 343.

8. Entrepreneur and science fiction author Hugo Gernsback sold wireless equipment by mail order from New York as early as 1906; the *New York Times Magazine* published a major story on wireless "boy" Walter J. Willenborg in 1907. See

Douglas, 188, 199. On Gernsback's seminal role in constructing an amateur market, see Andrew Ross, "Getting Out of the Gernsback Continuum," in *Strange Weather: Culture, Science, and Technology in the Age of Limits* (London: Verso, 1991), 107–17.

9. Carolyn Marvin, *When Old Technologies Were New: Thinking about Electric Communication in the Late Nineteenth Century* (New York: Oxford University Press, 1988), 52.

10. Marvin, 194; Douglas, 60. See also Sconce, 61.

11. See, for example, Marvin, 194. Susan Smulyan finds vestiges of this sort of "faith" in the advertising industry's arguments for allowing advertisements on the radio at the beginning of the 1930s: "Radio . . . could protect the listener/consumer by automatically exposing lies," though less because the technology itself could not lie than because "'nation-wide audience response is so sensitive that no intelligent advertiser can long misuse this wonderful medium'" (Smulyan, *Selling Radio: The Commercialization of American Broadcasting, 1920–1934* [Washington, DC: Smithsonian Institution Press, 1994], 78).

12. V. C. Jewel, "A Song of Wireless," *The Wireless Age* 4, no. 6 (1917): 426.

13. See Douglas, chapter 6.

14. See Cecelia Tichi, *Shifting Gears: Technology, Literature, Culture in Modernist America* (Chapel Hill: University of North Carolina Press, 1987), chapter 3, esp. 97–104. For accounts of Hoover's "strategic" use of the "small boys" label to contain and stigmatize independent wireless use, see Michele Hilmes, *Radio Voices: American Broadcasting, 1922–1952* (Minneapolis: University of Minnesota Press, 1997), 39.

15. See Douglas, 209–15, and Hilmes, *Radio Voices,* 39–41.

16. For an account of Claude Chappe's optical *télégraphe* and its successors, see Tom Standage, *The Victorian Internet: The Remarkable Story of the Telegraph and the Nineteenth Century's On-line Pioneers* (New York: Berkley, 1999), 6–21.

17. Tom Gunning, "Heard over the Phone: *The Lonely Villa* and the de Lorde Tradition of the Terrors of Technology" *Screen* 32 (1991): 186–87; and Eileen Bowser, *The Transformation of Cinema: 1907–1915* (Berkeley and Los Angeles: University of California Press, 1990), 64–71.

18. See Young, 253–55.

19. For a description of this lost film, see Patricia King Hanson, executive editor, *The American Film Institute Catalog of Motion Pictures Produced in the United States,* vol. F1, *Feature Films, 1911–1920: Film Entries* (Berkeley and Los Angeles: University of California Press, 1988), 936.

20. For a discussion of the gendering of telegraph operators in fiction, film, and media practice at the turn of the twentieth century, see Tom Gunning, "Systematizing the Electric Message: Narrative Form, Gender, and Modernity in *The Lonedale Operator,*" in *American Cinema's Transitional Era: Audiences, Institutions, Practices,* ed. Charlie Keil and Shelley Stamp (Berkeley and Los Angeles: University of California Press, 2004), 15–50.

21. Harle Oren Cummings, "The Space Annihilator," in *Ancestral Voices: An Anthology of Early Science Fiction,* ed. Douglas Menville and R. Reginald (New York: Arno, 1975), 62. Although the text as published here is clearly a photographic reprint of the original publication, I have not been able to determine the source of the story.

22. See Gayatri Chakravorty Spivak, "Can the Subaltern Speak?" in *The Post-Colonial Studies Reader,* ed. Bill Ashcroft, Gareth Griffiths, and Helen Tiffin (London: Routledge, 1995), 27–28.

23. Tom Gunning, "From the Kaleidoscope to the X-Ray: Urban Spectatorship, Poe, Benjamin, and *Traffic in Souls* (1913)," *Wide Angle* 19, no. 4 (1997): 48–49.

24. Kristen Whissel, "Regulating Mobility: Technology, Modernity, and Feature-Length Narrativity in *Traffic in Souls," Camera Obscura* 49 (2002): 15.

25. "Full Cast and Crew for *Traffic in Souls* (1913)," Internet Movie Database, http://www.imdb.com/title/tt0003471/fullcredits. Although I have not been able to corroborate this credit with another source, I have found the Internet Movie Database surprisingly reliable regarding other, similarly obscure credits.

26. Whissel refers to Shelley Stamp, *Movie-Struck Girls: Women and Motion Picture Culture after the Nickelodeon* (Princeton, NJ: Princeton University Press, 2000), and Lee Grieveson, "Policing the Cinema: *Traffic in Souls* at Ellis Island," *Screen* 38, no. 2 (1997): 166.

27. Donald Crafton, *The Talkies: American Cinema's Transition to Sound, 1926–1931* (Berkeley and Los Angeles: University of California Press, 1997), 40, 47.

3. Eating the Other Medium

The title of this chapter was inspired by bell hooks's essay "Eating the Other: Desire and Resistance," in *Black Looks: Race and Representation* (Boston, MA: South End Press, 1992), 21–39.

1. Susan J. Douglas, *Inventing American Broadcasting, 1899–1922* (Baltimore: The Johns Hopkins University Press, 1987), 238.

2. Ralph Milne Farley, *The Radio Beasts* (1925; repr. New York: Ace, n.d.). *The Radio Beasts* was a sequel to Milne Farley's *The Radio Man,* to which this novel refers directly (but which I have not been able to locate).

3. "World-wide Broadcasting at Hand," *Literary Digest* 79 (December 29, 1923): 23.

4. Erik Barnouw, *A Tower in Babel,* vol. 1 of *A History of Broadcasting in the United States* (London: Oxford University Press, 1966), 7; Douglas, 306. See also Michele Hilmes, *Radio Voices: American Broadcasting, 1922–1952* (Minneapolis: University of Minnesota Press, 1997), 13.

5. Richard Butsch, "Crystal Sets and Scarf-Pin Radios: Gender, Technology, and the Construction of American Radio Listening in the 1920s," *Media, Culture, and Society* 20 (1998): 566, 562.

6. The first radio stars were announcers, all of whom were shocked by the adoration heaped on them simply because they enunciated well over the wireless. Nevertheless, they were the foundation for a cult of personality that spread to comedians, singers, newsreaders, and other radio voices. See Barnouw, 163–64 and 167.

7. See Gerhard Schulte, "Walter Benjamin's Lichtenberg," *Performing Arts Journal* 42 [14, no. 3] (1992): 34–35; Bertolt Brecht, "An Example of Paedagogics (Notes to *Der Flug der Lindberghs*)" (1930), in *Brecht on Theatre,* trans. John Willett (New York: Hill and Wang, 1964), 32.

8. Rudolf Arnheim, *Radio: An Art of Sound,* trans. Margaret Ludwig and Herbert Read (London: Faber and Faber, 1936), 158.

9. Arthur Knight, *Disintegrating the Musical: Black Performance and American Musical Film* (Durham: Duke University Press, 2002), 94.

10. Hilmes, *Radio Voices,* 135–36, 142–43; emphasis added.

11. Henry O. Osgood, *So This Is Jazz* (Boston: Little, Brown, 1926); Neil Leonard, *Jazz and the White Americans: The Acceptance of a New Art Form* (Chicago: University of Chicago Press, 1962), 36–37.

12. Nicholas M. Evans, *Writing Jazz: Race, Nationalism, and Modern Culture in the 1920s* (New York: Garland, 2000), 102.

13. Susan Smulyan, *Selling Radio: The Commercialization of American Broadcasting 1920–1934* (Washington, DC: Smithsonian Institution Press, 1994), 87, 55.

14. MacDonald Smith Moore, *Yankee Blues: Musical Culture and American Identity* (Bloomington: Indiana University Press, 1985), 149.

15. Matthew Murray, "'The Tendency to Deprave and Corrupt Morals': Regulations and Irregular Sexuality in Golden Age Radio Comedy," in *Radio Reader: Essays in the Cultural History of Radio,* ed. Michele Hilmes and Jason Loviglio (New York: Routledge, 2002), 141.

16. Quoted in Moore, 90; Hilmes, 49.

17. "The Jazz Cannibal," *Literary Digest* 84 (January 10, 1925): 36. The poem, originally published in *Punch* on an unspecified date, is headed thus: "Punch proposes a conundrum on the change of manners: THE JAZZ CANNIBAL[.] ('The noisy beats of jazz-bands are merely a disguised and modern form of the tom-toms of old, which incited savages to fury and fired the fierce energy of cannibals.'—*From a letter in 'The Daily Graphic*')."

18. American composer Virgil Thompson, quoted in Hilmes, 78.

19. Alison McCracken, "Real Men Don't Sing Ballads: The Radio Crooner in Hollywood, 1929–1933," in *Soundtrack Available: Essays on Film and Popular Music,* ed. Pamela Robertson Wojcik and Arthur Knight (Durham, NC: Duke University Press, 2001), 114, 130 n. 15, and 109–10.

20. See Barnouw, 82–83 and 130; Hilmes, 49–50, 54.

21. *The Jazz Singer* was not the first "talking picture," only the first full-length feature film to include synchronized speech and singing, and then only in short and isolated sequences; Warner Bros., the studio that brought Al Jolson to the screen,

had been producing Vitaphone short-subject programs featuring vaudeville-like performances since 1926, to accompany screenings of all-music synchronized features like *Don Juan* (which introduced the Vitaphone sound-on-disk system to the world, also directed by *The Jazz Singer* director Alan Crosland) and *The First Auto* (Roy Del Ruth, 1926).

22. "The most obvious fact about *The Jazz Singer*, unmentioned in all the critical commentary, is that it contains no jazz" (Michael Rogin, "Blackface, White Noise: The Jewish Jazz Singer Finds His Voice," *Critical Inquiry* 18 [1992]: 447). Rogin later attenuated this claim but did not give it up entirely: "Jazz may have been the Jazz Age's name for any up-tempo music . . . but the indiscriminate use of the term no more excuses *The Jazz Singer*'s missing sound than blackface compensates for the absence of blacks. Signifying the omitted referent claims possession of it. . . . In the silenced, racial, black story, Jolson's white noise obliterates jazz" (Michael Rogin, *Blackface, White Noise: Jewish Immigrants in the Hollywood Melting Pot* [Berkeley and Los Angeles: University of California Press, 1996], 115).

On the plasticity of "jazz" as a musical label in the 1910s, '20s, and '30s in particular, see Krin Gabbard, *Jammin' at the Margins: Jazz and the American Cinema* (Chicago: University of Chicago Press, 1996), 15–17; Richard M. Sudhalter, "Hot Music in the 1920s: The 'Jazz Age,' Appearances and Realities," in *The Oxford Companion to Jazz*, ed. Bill Kirchner (New York: Oxford University Press, 2000), 149; and Evans, 105.

23. See Rogin, *Blackface, White Noise*, 112. For the classic discussion of minstrelsy's history of white curiosity about blacks and white exploitation of black musical forms and black bodies, see Eric Lott, *Love & Theft: Blackface Minstrelsy and the American Working Class* (New York: Oxford University Press, 1993); see also Lisa Gitelman's extension of Lott's argument into the emergence of recorded music in *Scripts, Grooves, and Writing Machines* (Stanford, CA: Stanford University Press, 1999), chapter 3.

24. Donald Crafton, *The Talkies: American Cinema's Transition to Sound, 1926–1931* (Berkeley and Los Angeles: University of California Press, 1997), 160.

25. Crafton, 40. For the debate among sound engineers on which medium's standards of representation should guide the continuing development of film sound aesthetics, see James Lastra, *Sound Technology and the American Cinema: Perception, Representation, Modernity* (New York: Columbia University Press, 2000), esp. chapters 4, 5, and 6.

26. Rick Altman, "Sound/History," in *Sound Theory/Sound Practice*, ed. Rick Altman (New York: Routledge, 1992), 118–19; Crafton, 41; and "'Talking Movies,' by Radiophone," *Wireless Age* (June 1922): 112.

27. It is crucial to recall that Hollywood did not develop synchronized sound film in order to "catch up" with any other medium. Rather, two small studios, Warner Bros. and William Fox, introduced rival sound systems in separate gambits to rise in the industry; they also hoped to save their theaters the overhead cost of

hiring musicians to play along with the films. The rest of the industry followed suit, though cautiously at first. See Michele Hilmes, *Hollywood and Broadcasting: From Radio to Cable* (Urbana: University of Illinois Press, 1990), 33; and Crafton, 217–21. But as the broadcasting market boomed after 1922, the film industry sought ways to ride the wave of radiomania. Hilmes reports that even the much-touted 1932 Hollywood "ban" on film stars crossing over into radio lasted less than a year, and that it was brought about by exhibitors' complaints that radio gave away star appearances for "free" rather than the studios' aggravation over competition. In fact, Warner Bros. and Paramount began purchasing radio stations by 1925, hoping to use the new medium to promote their theatrical releases (Hilmes, *Hollywood and Broadcasting,* 55, 34).

28. Charles Wolfe, "Vitaphone Shorts and *The Jazz Singer,*" *Wide Angle* 12, no. 3 (1990): 62.

29. Crafton, 21. For a discussion of "film as phonography," "film as radio," and other contemporary intermedial fantasies about sync sound, see Altman, "Introduction: Sound/History," in *Sound Theory/Sound Practice,* ed. Rick Altman (New York: Routledge, 1992), 113–25.

30. Crafton, 109. Robert E. Sherwood's review in the October 27, 1927 issue of *The Silent Drama* recognized these scenes as revelations of the star: "Al Jolson as an actor is only fair. But when Al Jolson starts to sing . . . well, bring on your super-spectacles, your million-dollar thrills. . . . I'll trade them all for any ham song that Al cares to put on" (quoted in Alexander Walker, *The Shattered Silents: How the Talkies Came to Stay* [1978; repr., London: Harrap, 1986], 38).

31. It is not known whether Costello really lisped so terribly—"Merthy, merthy, have you no thithter of your own?"—or whether crude miking and poor playback were to blame, but whatever the case, "the spectators were moved to loud mirth during the spoken episodes of this lurid film" (Mordaunt Hall, *New York Times,* March 15, 1928; quoted in Walker, 49).

32. Paramount mogul Jesse Lasky predicted in 1928 that the "all-dialogue picture" would remain primarily a theatrical enterprise and be "radically different from anything we know at present," while silent films would continue with sound accompaniment, eschewing dialogue but exploiting sound "thoughtful[ly]" to heighten dramatic effect (Crafton, 169–70).

33. For Porter's comments on Méliès's rudiments of narration through editing and a discussion of Porter's *Jack and the Beanstalk* (1902) in relation to films like *Le Voyage dans la lune,* see Charles Musser's documentary *Before the Nickelodeon* (Kino, 1982).

34. See Lastra, esp. chap. 6.

35. Brecht, "The Radio as an Apparatus of Communication" (1932), in *Brecht on Theatre,* 52.

36. Alice Maurice, "'Cinema at Its Source': Synchronizing Race and Sound in the Early Talkies," *Camera Obscura* 49 (2002): 42.

37. See Krin Gabbard, *Jammin' at the Margins: Jazz and the American Cinema* (Chicago: University of Chicago Press, 1996), 205.

38. Strain also cites Johannes Fabian's further development of the world picture concept. Ellen Strain, *Public Places, Private Journeys: Ethnography, Entertainment, and the Tourist Gaze* (New Brunswick, NJ: Rutgers University Press, 2003), 25.

39. Cynthia Erb, *Tracking King Kong: A Hollywood Icon in World Culture* (Detroit, MI: Wayne State University Press, 1998), 68. For Erb's sources, see Susan Sontag, *On Photography* (New York: Anchor-Doubleday, 1973), 8–16, and Donna Haraway, *Primate Visions: Gender, Race, and Nature in the World of Modern Science* (New York: Routledge, 1989), esp. 26–58.

40. Whiteman here echoes a more explicitly imperialist, and more ethically vulnerable, origin story he tells in his autobiography, in which jazz "came to America 300 years ago in chains." See Arthur Knight, "*Jammin' the Blues,* or the Sight of Jazz, 1944," in *Representing Jazz,* ed. Krin Gabbard (Durham, NC: Duke University Press, 1995), 19.

41. On minstrelsy's expropriation of black culture for cultural and economic capital, see Lott, 39. White jazz musicians replicated the logic of minstrelsy that Lott theorizes in ways that have yet to be explored. Like antebellum minstrels and their working-class male audiences, white jazz musicians identified themselves with the musical and social rebellions perpetrated by black ragtime and hot musicians but exploited jazz as a free space for experimenting with subversive identities, a luxury that black musicians did not have. Whiteman once described jazz in terms that mimic minstrelsy's attraction to black suffering as a channeling device for white working-class dissatisfaction: jazz's optimism, Whiteman said, is the "optimism of the pessimist" who looks for something better; it oscillates between expressions of dissatisfaction and an inarticulate but productive desire for change. See Leonard, 87–88.

42. Fatimah Tobing Rony, *The Third Eye: Race, Cinema, and Ethnographic Spectacle* (Durham, NC: Duke University Press, 1996), 157, 155.

43. Ella Shohat and Robert Stam, *Unthinking Eurocentrism: Multiculturalism and the Media* (London: Routledge, 1994), 107.

44. Pascal James Imperato and Eleanor M. Imperato, *They Married Adventure: The Wandering Lives of Martin and Osa Johnson* (New Brunswick, NJ: Rutgers University Press, 1992), 168.

45. Like the photo captions that Roland Barthes deconstructs in "The Photographic Message," the intertitles of *Grass* and *Congorilla* exploit the indexical connotation of cinematography to disguise themselves as mere annotations to obvious realities. See Barthes, "The Photographic Message" (1961), in *Image-Music-Text,* ed. and trans. Stephen Heath (New York: Noonday, 1977), 25–27.

46. For the cover of the *Congorilla* sheet music, see the unpaginated section of Imperato and Imperato, *They Married Adventure.*

47. Jeff Taylor, "The Early Origins of Jazz," in Kirchner, *The Oxford Companion to Jazz,* 47.

48. Walter Kingsley (1917), quoted in Osgood, 12.

49. Claudia Gorbman, *Unheard Melodies: Narrative Film Music* (Bloomington: Indiana University Press, 1987), 74, 88.

50. Andrew R. Boone, "Prehistoric Monsters Roar and Hiss for Sound Film," *Popular Science Monthly,* April 1933, 20–21, 106.

51. See E. Ann Kaplan, *Looking for the Other: Feminism, Film, and the Imperial Gaze* (New York: Routledge, 1997), and Jane M. Gaines, *Fire and Desire: Mixed-Race Movies in the Silent Era* (Chicago: University of Chicago Press, 2001), 90.

52. Gaylyn Studlar, *In the Realm of Pleasure: Von Sternberg, Dietrich, and the Masochistic Aesthetic* (Urbana: University of Illinois Press, 1988), 114.

53. The classic studies of female identity as masquerade are Mary Ann Doane, "Film and the Masquerade: Theorizing the Female Spectator" and "Masquerade Reconsidered: Further Thoughts on the Female Spectator," in *Femmes Fatales: Feminism, Film Theory, Psychoanalysis* (New York: Routledge, 1991), 17–32 and 33–43, and Judith Butler, "Bodily Inscriptions, Performative Subversions," in *Gender Trouble: Feminism and the Subversion of Identity* (New York: Routledge, 1990), 163–80.

54. Fredric Jameson, "Reification and Utopia in Mass Culture" (1979), in *Signatures of the Visible* (New York: Routledge, 1990), 9–34.

55. Mark McGurl, "Making It Big: Picturing the Radio Age in *King Kong,*" *Critical Inquiry* 22 (1996): 431.

56. Noël Carroll, "*King Kong*: Ape and Essence" (1984), in *Interpreting the Moving Image* (Cambridge: Cambridge University Press, 1998), 129.

57. James Snead, *White Screens/Black Images: Hollywood from the Dark Side,* ed. Colin MacCabe and Cornel West (New York: Routledge, 1994), 21.

58. On "protection" as justification for colonialism in *Kong* and in the pulp jungle tales of the previous two decades, see Carroll, 122.

59. For a discussion of Spencerian pseudo-Darwinism as it was applied to spirituals and ragtime by racialist music critics in the late nineteenth and early twentieth centuries, see Evans, chapter 1, and Moore, 131–57.

60. Jenny Sharpe, "Figures of Colonial Resistance," in *The Post-Colonial Studies Reader,* ed. Bill Ashcroft, Gareth Griffiths, and Helen Tiffin (London: Routledge, 1995), 102.

61. After World War I, many white Americans took jazz seriously as an expression of "social and moral problems which could not be ignored" and took to listening to, dancing to, and playing jazz as a means to express those dissatisfactions themselves as well as gain release from Victorian social norms that the Great War rendered superfluous (Leonard, 30, 47–61). See also Burton W. Peretti, *Jazz in American Culture* (Chicago: Ivan R. Dee, 1997), 14, 29, and 44.

62. Homi Bhabha, "Signs Taken for Wonders: Questions of Ambivalence and

Authority under a Tree outside Dehli, May 1817," in *The Location of Culture*, 2d ed. (London: Routledge, 2004), 145–74.

63. Brown uses Charlie McCarthy, whom he tracks through the puppet's appearance as a figure for Bergen's unconscious and as a "character" in a number of more recent novels by American writers of immigrant descent, as a primary exemplar of how "the hybrid object . . . may be figured as a participant in the intersubjective constitution of reality." Shawn Wong's *Homebase* (1979), he writes, finally "tells the story of a Chinese American boy making use of an Irish American instantiation of what was taken to be an ancient Chinese practice of enabling some other self (or the body itself) to attain audibility." See Bill Brown, "How to Do Things with Things (A Toy Story)," *Critical Inquiry* 24 (1998): 942, 959. See also 940–47 and 958.

64. Rick Altman, "Moving Lips: Cinema as Ventriloquism," *Yale French Studies* 60 (1980): 69, 76–77.

65. "As a form of splitting and multiple belief, the stereotype requires, for its successful signification, a continual and repetitive chain of other stereotypes. The process by which the metaphoric 'masking' is inscribed on a lack which must then be concealed gives the stereotype both its fixity and its phantasmatic quality—the *same old* stories of the Negro's animality, the Coolie's inscrutability or the stupidity of the Irish *must* be told (compulsively) again and afresh, and are differently gratifying and terrifying each time." Bhabha, "The Other Question: Stereotype, Discrimination and the Discourse of Colonialism," in *The Location of Culture*, 77.

66. See Erb, chapter 2, for a detailed discussion of the parallels between the plot of *King Kong* and Cooper and Schoedsack's own career as adventurers.

67. Smith, writing nearly sixty years after the fact, recounts his partner J. Stuart Blackton's introductory "lecture" to Edison's *The Black Diamond Express* thus: "In just a moment, a cataclysmic moment, my friends, a moment without equal in the history of our times, you will see this train take life in a [marvelous] and most astounding manner. It will rush towards you, belching smoke and fire from its monstrous iron throat" (Albert E. Smith with Phil A. Koury, *Two Reels and a Crank* [Garden City, NY: Doubleday, 1952] 39–40; quoted in Tom Gunning, "An Aesthetic of Astonishment: Early Film and the (In)credulous Spectator" [1989], in *Film Theory and Criticism*, ed. Leo Braudy and Marshall Cohen, 5th ed. [New York: Oxford University Press, 1999], 824).

68. Kaja Silverman, *The Acoustic Mirror: The Female Voice in Psychoanalysis and Cinema* (Bloomington: Indiana University Press, 1988), 77–78.

69. Snead, 17–18, 24; Carroll, 137–39. Cynthia Erb reveals that Willis O'Brien was a boxing enthusiast and a sports cartoonist before he turned to stop-motion film animation, and suggests that his modeling of Kong's fighting blows and "choke holds" on prominent boxers, both black and white, implies less omnidirectional rage on Kong's part than a concerted, tactical approach to "dismantl[ing]" both Denham's spectacle, which represents the explorer-showman's "power base," and

"the base of modern culture itself" as signified by New York City and the ultra-modern Empire State Building (Erb, 117).

70. Bhabha, "The Other Question," 82.

71. Gareth Griffiths provides a useful paraphrase of Bhabha's central argument in "Signs Taken for Wonders": "The possibility of subaltern speech exists principally and crucially when its mediation through mimicry and parody of the dominant discourse subverts and menaces the authority within which it necessarily comes into being" ("The Myth of Authenticity," in *The Postcolonial Studies Reader,* ed. Ashcroft et al., 240).

72. *Variety,* March 7, 1933, 21.

73. The appearance of Cooper and Schoedsack in the fighter plane that brings Kong down from the Empire State Building may be the most famous directorial cameo this side of Hitchcock's self-portrait with string bass in 1951's *Strangers on a Train* (see Erb, 118).

74. Mary Carbine, "The Finest outside the Loop: Motion Picture Exhibition in Chicago's Black Metropolis, 1905–1928," *Camera Obscura* 23 (1990): 9–41. For a discussion of such practices from the perspective of the concerned film studios, see Lastra, 111–21.

75. Noël Carroll, *The Philosophy of Horror* (New York: Routledge, 1990), 31–34, quoted in Rony, 161.

76. Alison Griffiths, *Wondrous Difference: Cinema, Anthropology, and Turn-of-the-Century Visual Culture* (New York: Columbia University Press, 2002), 213–18.

4. The Glass Web

1. Christopher Anderson, *Hollywood TV: The Studio System in the Fifties* (Austin: University of Texas Press, 1994), 2.

2. Lisa Gitelman, *Scripts, Grooves, and Writing Machines: Representing Technology in the Edison Era* (Stanford, CA: Stanford University Press, 1999), chapter 4, esp. 148–65.

3. William Boddy, *Fifties Television: The Industry and Its Critics* (Urbana: University of Illinois Press, 1990), 17.

4. Anderson, chapter 7; Michele Hilmes, *Hollywood and Broadcasting: From Radio to Cable* (Urbana: University of Illinois Press, 1990), 150–67.

5. Anderson, 17–18.

6. Frank Krutnik, *In a Lonely Street: Film Noir, Genre, Masculinity* (London: Routledge, 1991), 147.

7. J. P. Telotte's work on communications technologies in film noir lifts up the media literally presented by noir to discover a sensibility less Oedipal than Foucauldian in its obsession with "discourse" in all its social forms. Protagonists like Leona (Barbara Stanwyck) in *Sorry, Wrong Number* exploit telephones and other media to extend their limited powers but are ultimately thwarted by those very

technologies. See Telotte, "The Call of Desire and the Film Noir," *Film/Literature Quarterly* 17, no. 1 (1989): 52–54. For the full version of the Foucauldian argument touched on by this essay, see Telotte, *Voices in the Dark: The Narrative Patterns of Film Noir* (Urbana: University of Illinois Press, 1989).

8. Edward Dimendberg, "From Berlin to Bunker Hill: Urban Space, Late Modernity, and Film Noir in Fritz Lang's and Joseph Losey's *M*," *Wide Angle* 19 no. 4 (1997): 87.

9. Anna McCarthy, *Ambient Television: Visual Culture and Public Space* (Durham, NC: Duke University Press, 2001), esp. chapter 1.

10. Raymond Williams, *Television: Technology and Cultural Form* (1974; Hanover, NH: Wesleyan University Press, 1992), chapter 4, esp. 83–89.

11. On the various studio gambles on theater TV between 1947 and 1953, see Timothy R. White, "Hollywood's Attempt at Appropriating Television: The Case of Paramount Pictures," in *Hollywood in the Age of Television*, ed. Tino Balio (Boston, MA: Unwin Hyman, 1990), 149–55.

12. Richard Koszarski, "Coming Next Week: Images of Television in Pre-war Motion Pictures," *Film History* 10 (1998): 133.

13. Garrett Stewart, *Between Film and Screen: Modernism's Photo Synthesis* (Chicago: University of Chicago Press, 1999), 196. Stewart also argues that an "improbable lap dissolve" marks Frederson's closed-circuit TV system as a transmitter of "quasi-cinematic rather than . . . fully televised space" (194).

14. It should be stressed that baseball is a time-specific entertainment; thus the video feed is more a form of reporting than a cinematic form of entertainment.

15. Stewart, 198–99.

16. Lynn Spigel, *Make Room for TV: Television and the Family Ideal in Postwar America* (Chicago: University of Chicago Press, 1992), 102–6. Although Spigel shows how the picture window was both a kind of shield for the private sphere and a trace of a legitimate expansion of the concept of "home" to incorporate and integrate social space, I would suggest—as Spigel does, and as the films I will discuss below also imply, notably *In a Lonely Place*—that the discourse on *the social* articulated by the trend toward panoramic windows in suburban homes left the imaginary line between public and private experience in postwar culture relatively undisturbed and may even have fortified that boundary.

17. "With the exception of theater television . . . nonbroadcast uses of television did not receive general public recognition or debate after the 1920s" (Boddy, *Fifties Television*, 17). See also Spigel, 30, and Boddy, "Spread Like a Monster Blanket over the Country: CBS and Television, 1929–33," *Screen* 32, no. 2 (1991): 172–74 and passim.

18. Cecelia Tichi, *Electronic Hearth: Creating an American Television Culture* (New York: Oxford University Press, 1991), 16.

19. Ibid., 15.

20. DuMont advertisement, *Atlantic Monthly*, November 1944, 23.

21. Boddy, *Fifties Television,* 80; emphasis added.

22. Philip Auslander, *Liveness: Performance in a Mediatized Culture* (London: Routledge, 1999), chapter 2.

23. Telotte, *Voices in the Dark,* 48, 14.

24. For more thorough discussions of the automobile as mediator of modern experience, see Mary Morley Cohen, "Forgotten Audiences in the Passion Pits: Drive-in Theatres and Changing Spectator Practices in Postwar America," *Film History* 6 (1994): 474–75; and Edward Dimendberg, "The Will to Motorization: Cinema, Highways, and Modernity," *October* 73 (1995): 91–137.

25. Elaine Tyler May, *Homeward Bound: American Families in the Cold War Era* (New York: Basic, 1988), 166.

26. For example, see Erik Barnouw, *The Golden Web* (New York: Oxford University Press, 1968) on the eventual silencing of the FCC's scathing 1946 report on radio commercialism known as the "blue book" (227–36). Without sensing (or at least acknowledging) conflict of interest, the government quickly granted NBC and CBS carte blanche to program whatever could be reasonably (or unreasonably) defined as "public service" as required by the Radio Act of 1927, in which the Federal Radio Commission (after 1933 the Federal Communications Commission) states its purpose as to "generally encourage the large and more effective use of radio in the public interest." To explain Hollywood's continual failures to control broadcasting, Michele Hilmes refers to the work of Vincent Mosco, who "trace[s] the evolution of [the FRC-FCC's] simple and vaguely defined purpose over the years to a strong perceived mandate to protect existing broadcasting interests and structures from outside interference." See Hilmes, 134. Boddy nails the cynicism and tautology underlying the definition of "service" and "public interest" in broadcasting when he quotes CBS president Frank Stanton's testimony to the FCC in 1960: "I suggest that a [television] program in which a large part of the audience is interested is by that very fact a program in the public interest" (Boddy, *Fifties Television,* 237). Stanton, of course, neglected to mention that this abstracted audience had no input into this hypothetical program and precious few viewing alternatives.

27. *Variety,* March 29, 1944, 2.

28. "Studios Take New Slaps at Radio: Showdown Sought," *Variety,* March 8, 1944, 3 (the article does not attribute the quote to a specific "agency man"). Like the Hollywood "radio ban" of 1932, which (contrary to myth) was as brief as it was toothless, the 1944 "edicts" reflected Hollywood's interest in gaining future control over broadcasting rather than its fear of broadcasting's current competition. Nevertheless, in each case, issuing the edicts was a powerfully symbolic move that collected Hollywood's various anxieties about the postwar future around the imposing figure of broadcasting. For a discussion of the politics and implications of the 1932 ban, see Hilmes, 55.

29. Robert Gessner, "Film Industry to Mature—or Else," *Variety,* January 5, 1944, 30.

30. Howard P. Segal, "The Technological Utopians," in *Imagining Tomorrow: History, Technology, and the American Future,* ed. Joseph J. Corn (Cambridge, MA: MIT Press, 1986), 132.

31. Warren I. Susman, *Culture as History: The Transformation of American Society in the Twentieth Century* (1973; repr. New York: Pantheon, 1984), 268; quoted in Spigel, 47.

32. Amy Sue Bix, *Inventing Ourselves out of Jobs? America's Debate over Technological Unemployment* (Baltimore: The Johns Hopkins University Press, 2000), esp. chapters 4, 5, and 6.

33. Martin Glaberman, *Wartime Strikes: The Struggle against the No-Strike Pledge in the UAW during World War II* (Detroit, MI: Bewick, 1980), i, 4–7, 90.

34. George Lipsitz, *Rainbow at Midnight: Labor and Culture in the 1940s* (Urbana: University of Illinois Press, 1994), 58, 59.

35. Stephanie Coontz also challenges the myth of universal financial security by citing high unemployment and divorce rates immediately after the war and the continuation of high rates of poverty (25 percent, by Coontz's count) into the 1950s (*The Way We Never Were: American Families and the Nostalgia Trap* [New York: Basic, 1992], 29).

36. "Food spending rose by only 33 percent in the five years following the Second World War, and clothing expenditures rose by 20 percent, but purchases of household furnishings and appliances climbed 240 percent" during the same period (Coontz, 25).

37. Zanuck, *Hollywood Reporter,* October 26, 1953; quoted in John Belton, *Widescreen Cinema* (Cambridge, MA: Harvard University Press, 1992), 78.

38. Robert E. Lee, *Television: The Revolution* (New York: Essential Books, 1944), 137, 138.

39. See Miriam Hansen, "Benjamin, Cinema, and Experience: 'The Blue Flower in the Land of Technology,'" *New German Critique* 40 (1987): 196; Walter Benjamin, "On the Mimetic Faculty," in *Reflections,* ed. Peter Demetz, trans. Edmund Jephcott (New York: Harcourt Brace Jovanovich, 1978), 333–36.

40. Dimendberg, "The Will to Motorization," 134.

41. Nancy Fraser, "Rethinking the Public Sphere: A Contribution to the Critique of Actually Existing Democracy," in *The Phantom Public Sphere,* ed. Bruce Robbins (Minneapolis: University of Minnesota Press, 1993), 22; Coontz, 29.

42. Sylvia Harvey, "Woman's Place: The Absent Family of Film Noir," in *Women in Film Noir,* ed. E. Ann Kaplan, rev. ed. (London: British Film Institute, 1980), 22.

43. Oskar Negt and Alexander Kluge, *Public Sphere and Experience,* trans. Peter Labanyi, Jamie Owen Daniel, and Assenka Oksiloff (Minneapolis: University of Minnesota Press, 1993), 17.

44. Christine Gledhill, "*Klute* I: A Contemporary Film Noir and Feminist Criticism," in *Women in Film Noir,* ed. E. Ann Kaplan, 15.

45. Belton, 70.

46. See Andreas Huyssen, "Mass Culture as Woman: Modernism's Other," in *After the Great Divide: Modernism, Mass Culture, Postmodernism* (Bloomington: Indiana University Press, 1986), 44–53.

47. The referent for Laurel and Dix's stormy affair was probably Ray's own marriage to Gloria Grahame, which collapsed during shooting of *In a Lonely Place*. Dix's alternately tender and violent relationship with Laurel was by no means an idiosyncratic projection of postwar domesticity: "Beneath the polished facades of many 'ideal' families, suburban as well as urban, was violence, terror, or simply grinding misery that only occasionally came to light. Although Colorado researchers found 302 battered-child cases, including 33 deaths, in their state during one year alone, the major journal of American family sociology did not carry a single article on family violence between 1939 and 1969. Psychiatrists in the 1950s, following Helen Deutsch, 'regarded the battered woman as a masochist who provoked her husband into beating her'" (Coontz, 35).

48. Raymond Williams, *The Country and the City* (New York: Oxford University Press, 1973), 155. The Dickens quotation is from *Dombey and Son*.

49. Jane Feuer argues that the backstage musical "manages to incorporate the immediate performer-audience relationship [of popular theater] into films, thus gaining all the advantages of both media" ("The Self-Reflective Musical and the Myth of Entertainment," in *Genre: The Musical,* ed. Rick Altman [London: Routledge, 1981], 169).

50. James Naremore, *More Than Night: Film Noir in Its Contexts* (Berkeley and Los Angeles: University of California Press, 1998), 30.

51. See Richard Schickel, *Double Indemnity* (London: British Film Institute, 1992), 43.

52. On the establishment of mutual advertising relations between Hollywood producers and department stores, see Charles Eckert, "The Carole Lombard in Macy's Window" (1978), in *Stardom: Industry of Desire,* ed. Christine Gledhill (London: Routledge, 1991), 33–39.

53. Cohen, 475, 481.

54. This loss did more long-term damage than immediate devastation—Belton reports that "many of the majors successfully delayed divestment proceedings for years," with Loew's, Warners, and Twentieth Century Fox keeping some of their theaters for nearly a decade after the 1948 decision—but it remains part of an avalanche of woes facing the industry at the time, a threat of future lost revenue that salted the wounds caused by real losses in the present. See Belton, 70–71.

55. Balio, 15; Anderson, 40. Anderson also writes, following Boddy and Hilmes, that, coupled with "the FCC's reluctance to support alternative technologies," the freeze virtually ruined the studios' chances of success not only with broadcasting but also in-theater video technologies. The freeze could not have come at a worse time, for film attendance declined sharply after the previous year's record num-

bers, and studios like Paramount and Warners looked increasingly to television as a possible means to bolster sagging profits. See Anderson, chapter 2, 37–41, and passim; see also Boddy, *Fifties Television,* 50–52, and Hilmes, 130.

56. Anderson, 221. Anderson characterizes selling all television rights to films as a "conservative" approach to raising studio capital, for such a move sacrificed the long-term rental rights, which brought huge long-term gains to shrewder studios like Columbia. The outright sales of pre-1948 catalogues by RKO, Warners, and Paramount "demonstrated the studio[s'] failure to imagine the future of television in Hollywood" (221–22).

57. Hilmes, 153.

58. Charles A. Siepmann, *Radio, Television, and Society* (New York: Oxford University Press, 1950), 347 (emphasis added).

59. William Paul ("The Aesthetics of Emergence," *Film History* 5 [1993]: 323) writes that a 3-D process had been used as early as 1936 by MGM to produce short subjects; John Belton (51) shows that a 70-millimeter widescreen format had been briefly toyed with by Fox in 1929; and Charles Musser reports the use of a similar format by the American Mutoscope (Biograph) Company in 1895–96 to differentiate its films from Edison's (*The Emergence of Cinema: The American Screen to 1907* [New York: Scribners, 1990], 145–46).

60. Paul, 325.

61. Feuer, 172.

62. Belton, 187.

63. Belton, "Glorious Color, Breathtaking CinemaScope, and Stereophonic Sound," in *Hollywood in the Age of Television,* ed. Tino Balio, 187.

64. The algorithmic quality of "live" performances has only become more palpable since the 1950s, as "big" Broadway musicals such as *Cats, Les Misérables, Miss Saigon,* and *The Lion King* are sold to touring groups as packaged shows, complete with production and direction details that must be followed no matter who "directs" an individual performance. See Auslander, 49–51.

65. For an account of 3-D as an excessively antinarrative and distracting process, one that continually foregrounded both itself and its status as a technology, see Paul, 329–34 and passim.

66. "It is impossible to prophesy what will become of television; its current state has nothing to do with the invention itself, not even the particular forms of its commercial exploitation, but with the social totality in and by which the miracle is harnessed. . . . For television *[Fernsehen]* to realize the promise that still resides in its name, it would have to emancipate itself from everything that revokes its innermost principle, the most daring sense of wish fulfillment, by betraying the Great Happiness to the department store of the small comforts" (Theodor Adorno, *Eingriffe* [Frankfurt: Suhrkamp, 1963], 80; quoted in and trans. Hansen, "Benjamin, Cinema, and Experience," 223–24).

67. See Spigel's influential discussion of this scene (123).

68. "How can a mother of grown children overcome the taboo against her continued sexual activity in 'civilised society,' when the object of her desire is reduced to child-like dependence on her ministrations?" (Laura Mulvey, "Notes on Sirk and Melodrama" [1977], in *Home Is Where the Heart Is: Studies in Melodrama and the Woman's Film,* ed. Christine Gledhill [London: British Film Institute, 1987], 79).

5. The Negative Reinvention of Cinema

1. Lauren Rabinovitz, "From Hale's Tours to *Star Tours*: Virtual Voyages and the Delirium of the Hyper-Real," *Iris* 25 (1998): 134–35.

2. William Gibson, *Neuromancer* (New York: Ace, 1984).

3. New York: Touchstone/Simon and Schuster, 1991.

4. Bruce Sterling, *The Hacker Crackdown: Law and Disorder on the Electronic Frontier* (New York: Bantam, 1992), 52.

5. I'm grateful to Ann Eaton for this insight about cyberspace "consensus" in *The Lawnmower Man.*

6. Constance Penley has made a similar link between everyday experience of faulty domestic and business machines and full-scale technological disaster in *The Terminator*: "The film seems to suggest that if technology can go wrong or be abused, it will be" (*The Future of an Illusion: Film, Feminism, and Psychoanalysis* [London: Routledge, 1989], 124); on the feminization of this sense of unknowable electronic chaos, see Claudia Springer, *Electronic Eros: Bodies and Desire in the Postindustrial Age* (Austin: University of Texas Press, 1996), 106.

7. See André Bazin, *What Is Cinema?* vol. 1, trans. Hugh Gray (Berkeley and Los Angeles: University of California Press, 1967), 21, and Jean Baudrillard, "The Procession of Simulacra," in *Art after Modernism,* ed. Brian Wallis, 253–81 (New York: Godine, 1984). Scott Bukatman discusses the resonances of VR and its attendant discourse with Bazin's myth of total cinema; see Bukatman, *Terminal Identity: The Virtual Subject in Postmodern Science Fiction* (Durham, NC: Duke University Press, 1993), 191.

8. See Doug Stewart, "Through the Looking Glass into an Artificial World— Via Computer," *Smithsonian* 21, no. 10 (January 1991): 38, 39. Bricken worked at the Human Interface Technology Lab (HITL); Walser was head of the Cyberspace Project at Autodesk.

9. The most literal Hollywood vision of digital media harboring an invasion of the material world is Brett Leonard's latest entry in the cycle, *Virtuosity* (1995), where the equipment itself becomes the saboteur, literally hacking human bodies rather than hardware. SID 6.7 (Russell Crowe) is a software composite of various serial killers' personalities who is released from his mainframe to roam the earth and perform spectacular murders. Here the myth of total media reaches its logical conclusion: the world of the Net now so thoroughly permeates RL (the serious Internet chat room user's abbreviation for "real life")

that one need not be jacked into a computer or even own a telephone to fall prey to its deadly force.

10. Janet Wasko, *Hollywood in the Information Age: Beyond the Silver Screen* (Austin: University of Texas Press, 1994), 210.

11. Harold Bloom, *Kabbalah and Criticism* (New York: Seabury Press, 1975), 97.

12. Media films engage these others more frontally than do Bloom's anxious poems but equivocate no less about the true stakes of that engagement, pretending autonomy while actually speaking their debt to the new with every denial that the cinema could foster interaction or intersubjectivity. The films I examine place the cinema in as contradictory a situation as that in which Bloom finds the poet, but here the anxiety centers on newer competitors rather than on powerful precursors and is born of institutional conservatism rather than the egoism of the youthful upstart.

13. Fredric Jameson, "Reification and Utopia in Mass Culture" (1979), in *Signatures of the Visible* (New York: Routledge, 1990), 29.

14. Douglas Rushkoff, *Cyberia: Life in the Trenches of Hyperspace* (San Francisco, CA: HarperSanFrancisco, 1994), 42.

15. On such fantasies as they appeared in the writings of Vachel Lindsay, D. W. Griffith, and a host of newspaper critics, trade press writers, and social reformers, see Miriam Hansen, "Universal Language and Democratic Culture: Myths of Origin in Early American Cinema," in *Myth and Enlightenment in American Culture,* ed. Dieter Meindl and Friedrich W. Horlacher with Martin Christadler (Erlangen-Nürnberg: Univeritätsbund, 1985), 321–51.

16. Rushkoff, 57. Comments like de Groot's and McKenna's attest to the validity of Benjamin's observation that new technologies alter our perception of previous phenomena, natural or manufactured; see "A Short History of Photography," in which Benjamin argues that early nature photography, especially at the microscopic level, was widely understood to prove that natural forms presciently rehearsed designs in wrought iron and other human-made materials: "Photography uncovers . . . material physiognomic aspects of pictorial worlds which live in the smallest things, perceptible yet covert enough to find shelter in daydreams, but which, once enlarged and capable of formulation, show the difference between technology and magic to be entirely a matter of historical variables" ("A Short History of Photography" [1931], trans. Stanley Mitchell, *Screen* 13 [1972]: 7–8). In de Groot and McKenna's remarks, the history of language becomes a teleological search for a materialized visible world, a search that ends with the linkage of metaphor and real object through VR.

17. Anne Friedberg, *Window Shopping: Cinema and the Postmodern* (Berkeley and Los Angeles: University of California Press, 1993), 2, 125.

18. *Wired* magazine has already published a number of pieces on the impending death of cinema, which it envisions as self-euthanised by lame plots and lack of any user-friendliness commensurate with the expectations of Internet users.

See in particular Scott Rosenberg, "The Net Net on Net Films: Crapola," *Wired* 3, no. 7 (July 1995): 117–18.

19. Miriam Hansen has used the appropriately digital term "matrix" to update Negt and Kluge's "horizon" of experience to reflect the increasing complexity of both global media and the experience of media publics. See Hansen, "Early Cinema/Late Cinema: Transformations of the Public Sphere," in *Viewing Positions: Ways of Seeing Film,* ed. Linda Williams (New Brunswick, NJ: Rutgers University Press, 1995), 134–52.

20. Allucquere Rosanne Stone, "Will the Real Body Please Stand Up? Boundary Stories about Virtual Cultures," in *Cyberspace: First Steps,* ed. Michael Benedikt (Cambridge, MA: MIT Press, 1991), 105.

21. Stone, 106, 107. Stone quotes from Vivian Sobchack, *Screening Space: The American Science Fiction Film* (New York: Ungar, 1987) without a page citation.

22. Miriam Hansen, *Babel and Babylon: Spectatorship in American Silent Film* (Cambridge, MA: Harvard University Press, 1991), chapter 3, and "Early Cinema/Late Cinema."

23. The American Society of Cinematographers established this practice in 1962. See Belton, 225.

24. Timothy Corrigan, *A Cinema without Walls: Movies and Culture after Vietnam* (New Brunswick, NJ: Rutgers University Press, 1991), 32. Friedberg also discusses the effects of such video-age developments as "time shifting" (videotaping a program to be watched after its broadcast time), rewinding and fast-forwarding video, and channel changing on the paradigms of temporality and viewer attention that stem from cinematic spectatorship (Friedberg, 136–42).

25. On the viscerality of "body genres," see Linda Williams, "Film Bodies: Gender, Genre, and Excess," in *Film Genre Reader II,* ed. Barry Keith Grant (Austin: University of Texas Press, 1995), 40–58.

26. Siegfried Kracauer, "Cult of Distraction: On Berlin's Picture Palaces" (1926), in *The Mass Ornament,* trans. and ed. Thomas Y. Levin (Cambridge, MA: Harvard University Press, 1995), 327.

27. Tom Gunning, "The Cinema of Attractions: Early Film, Its Spectator, and the Avant-Garde" (1986), in *Early Cinema: Space, Frame, Narrative,* ed. Thomas Elsaesser with Adam Barker (London: British Film Institute, 1990), 57, 60–61.

28. This concern reaches back to earlier decades of TV, as the 1960s and '70s writings of Baudrillard and Guy Debord attest, but by the late 1990s, worry over the waning of "actual" experience in the face of all-encompassing spectacle has become irrevocably intertwined with a myth of total media specific to the digital age.

29. Steven Shaviro, *The Cinematic Body* (Minneapolis: University of Minnesota Press, 1993), 9.

30. Jay David Bolter and Richard Grusin, "Remediation," *Configurations* 3 (1996): 313.

31. Thanks to Colin Johnson for pointing out that the VR sequences in *Strange Days* represent the primary traces of Bigelow's directorial "presence."

32. Mark Berrettini, "Can 'We All' Get Along? Social Difference, the Future, and *Strange Days*," *Camera Obscura* 50 (2002): 183–84.

33. See Hamid Naficy, "King Rodney: The Rodney King Video and Textual Analysis," in *The End of Cinema as We Know It: American Film in the Nineties*, ed. Jon Lewis (New York: New York University Press, 2001), 302–3.

34. See Tom Gunning's remark on the King tape and trial, "Tracing the Individual Body: Photography, Detectives, and Early Cinema," in *Cinema and the Invention of Modern Life*, ed. Leo Charney and Vanessa R. Schwartz (Berkeley and Los Angeles: University of California Press, 1995), 41.

35. Walter Benjamin, "Paris, Capital of the Nineteenth Century," in *Reflections*, ed. Peter Demetz, trans. Edmund Jephcott (New York: Harcourt Brace Jovanovich, 1979), 162.

36. James Coates, "Exploring Planet Internet," *Chicago Tribune*, March 26, 1995, 7.1.

37. Robert "Hobbes" Zakon, "Hobbes' Internet Timeline, v6.1," http://www.zakon.org/robert/Internet/timeline/.

38. Caryn James, "Got Killer Chips on Our Minds," *New York Times*, October 8, 1995, H24.

39. Mark Poster, *What's the Matter with the Internet?* (Minneapolis: University of Minnesota Press, 2001), esp. chapters 4 and 6.

40. Evan Ratliff, "How to Be a Real Hollywood Player: And the Oscar for Best Actress in a Supporting Game goes to . . . Jada Pinkett Smith!" *Wired* 11, no. 5 (May 2003): 119.

41. Rick Altman, "Deep Focus Sound: *Citizen Kane* and the Radio Aesthetic," *Quarterly Review of Film and Video* 15, no. 3 (1994): 21.

42. Roger Ebert, review of *Star Wars: Episode I—The Phantom Menace*, *Chicago Sun-Times*, May 5, 1999, http://www.suntimes.com/ebert/ebert_reviews/1999/05/051701.html.

43. Roger Ebert, review of *Star Wars: Episode II—Attack of the Clones*, *Chicago Sun-Times*, May 5, 2002, http://www.suntimes.com/ebert/ebert_reviews/2002/05/051001.html.

44. I use the term "density" here expressly to challenge Lev Manovich's claim that some digital composite images "achieve an information density unprecedented in film. . . . Some shots of [Christian Boustani's digital film *A Viagem*, 1998] use as many as one thousand six hundred layers." This is a typical example of Manovich's understandable but often-problematic tendency to identify with media producers to the exclusion of textual experience when defining the "language" of new media. Surely the digital artist experiences her own labor to create a thickly imagined image as much more intensive and painstaking than that of a cinematographer, but does labor intensity automatically make a layered digital

image "denser" *to the viewer's eye* than that of a celluloid frame covered with tens of millions of grains of nitrate that, as Poe wrote of the Daguerreotype in 1840, render more detail rather than less the closer one's view? See Manovich, *The Language of New Media* (Cambridge, MA: MIT Press, 2001), 328; Edgar Allan Poe, "The Daguerreotype," in *Classic Essays on Photography*, ed. Alan Trachtenberg (New Haven, CT: Leete's Island Books, 1980), 37–38.

45. Mary Flanagan, "Digital Stars Are Here to Stay," *Convergence* 5, no. 2 (1999): 20.

46. Richard Dyer's groundbreaking works on stardom articulate how fans "know" stars through discourses—the fan press, film appearances, personal appearances and autobiographies, and biographical criticism—and *only* through these discourses. See Dyer, *Stars* (1979; new ed., London: British Film Institute, 1998).

47. "Frequently [in the 1990s], [a] whole game would be structured as an oscillation between interactive fragments requiring the user's input and noninteractive cinematic sequences" (Manovich, 83).

48. Steve Silberman, "Mystery Man: He Invented a New Gaming Genre. Now Robyn Miller Is Exploring a New Medium: Movies," *Wired* 7, no. 10 (October 1999): 233, 234, 235.

49. David Weddle, "Lights, Camera, Action. Marxism, Semiotics, Narratology. Film School Isn't What It Used to Be, One Father Discovers," *Los Angeles Times Magazine,* July 13, 2003, http://www.latimes.com/features/printedition/magazine/la-tm-filmschool28jul13.story.

50. For a look at Lucas "cyberdirecting" a shot of people standing in the cockpit of a starship, see the documentary on disk 2 of the *Star Wars: Episode I—The Phantom Menace* special edition DVD (Fox Home Video, 2000).

51. Thanks to Tom Mitchell for conversing with me so long ago about this remarkable aspect of *eXistenZ.*

Filmography

Africa Speaks! (Walter Futter, 1930)
Africa Speaks . . . English (Roy Mack, 1932)
All That Heaven Allows (Douglas Sirk, 1955)
The Apartment (Billy Wilder, 1960)
L'arrivée d'un train à la Ciotat (Lumière Brothers, 1895)
L'arroseur arrosé (Louis Lumière, 1895)
Ballistic: Ecks vs. Sever (Wych Kaosayananda, 2002)
Batman Forever (Joel Schumacher, 1995)
Before the Nickelodeon (Charles Musser, 1982)
The Big Broadcast (Frank Tuttle, 1932)
The Birth of a Nation (D. W. Griffith, 1915)
Black and Tan Fantasy (Dudley Murphy, 1929)
The Black Diamond Express (Edison, 1896)
The Blair Witch Project (Daniel Myrick and Eduardo Sánchez, 1999)
Blonde Venus (Josef von Sternberg, 1932)
Blue Steel (Kathryn Bigelow, 1992)
Bobby's Kodak (Biograph, 1908)
Brigadoon (Vincente Minnelli, 1954)
Broadcast News (James L. Brooks, 1987)
The Camera Fiend (AMB, 1903)
Capturing the Friedmans (Andrew Jarecki, 2003)
Caught by Wireless (Wallace McCutcheon, 1908)
Chang: A Drama of the Wilderness (Merian C. Cooper and Ernest B. Schoedsack, 1927)
The Charge at Feather River (Gordon Douglas, 1953)
The Cheat (Cecil B. DeMille, 1915)
Check and Double Check (Melville W. Brown, 1930)
Un Chien andalou (Luis Buñuel, 1929)

Citizen Kane (Orson Welles, 1941)

The Cohens and Kellys in Africa (Vin Moore, 1930)

Congorilla (Martin Johnson and Osa Johnson, 1932)

CQD, or Saved by Wireless: A True Story of the "Wreck of the Republic" (Vitagraph, 1909)

The Critic (Biograph 1906)

The Crowd (King Vidor, 1928)

Don Juan (Alan Crosland, 1926)

Double Indemnity (Billy Wilder, 1944)

The Dude Operator (Saul Harrison, 1917)

EdTV (Ron Howard, 1999)

Electrocuting an Elephant (Edison, 1903)

Elephants Shooting the Chutes at Luna Park (Edison, 1904)

Execution of Czolgosz with Panorama of Auburn Prison (Edwin S. Porter and George S. Fleming, 1901)

eXistenZ (David Cronenberg, 1999)

Explosion of a Motor Car (Cecil M. Hepworth, 1900)

A Face in the Crowd (Elia Kazan, 1957)

Fahrenheit 9/11 (Michael Moore, 2004)

Falsely Accused! (Biograph, 1908)

FearDotCom (William Malone, 2002)

Final Fantasy: The Spirits Within (Hironobu Sakaguchi and Moto Sakakibara, 2000)

The First Auto (Roy Del Ruth, 1926)

Flash Gordon (Frederick Stephani, 1936; serial)

Forrest Gump (Robert Zemeckis, 1994)

Freejack (Geoff Murphy, 1992)

The Glass Web (Jack Arnold, 1953)

Golddiggers of 1933 (Mervyn LeRoy, 1933)

Grandpa's Reading Glass (Biograph, 1902)

Grass: A Nation's Battle for Life (Merian C. Cooper and Ernest B. Schoedsack, 1925)

The Great Train Robbery (Edwin S. Porter, 1903)

Gun Crazy (Joseph H. Lewis, 1949)

Hackers (Iain Softley, 1995)

Hallelujah! (King Vidor, 1929)

How It Feels to Be Run Over (Cecil M. Hepworth, 1900)

How to Marry a Millionaire (Jean Negulesco, 1953)

I Am a Fugitive from a Chain Gang (Mervyn LeRoy, 1932)

I'll Be Glad When You're Dead (Max Fleischer, 1932)

In a Lonely Place (Nicholas Ray, 1950)

Intolerance (D. W. Griffith, 1916)

It Happened One Night (Frank Capra, 1934)

It's Always Fair Weather (Gene Kelly and Stanley Donen, 1955)

It's Got Me Again (Roy Mack, 1932)

Jaws (Steven Spielberg, 1975)

The Jazz Singer (Alan Crosland, 1927)

Johnny Mnemonic (Robert Longo, 1995)

Jurassic Park (Steven Spielberg, 1993)

Just Imagination (Kleine, 1916)

Kansas Saloon Smashers (Edwin S. Porter and George S. Fleming, 1901)

King Kong (Merian C. Cooper and Ernest B. Schoedsack, 1933)

The King of Jazz (John Murray Anderson, 1929)

King of Kings (Cecil B. DeMille, 1927)

Lara Croft: Tomb Raider (Simon West, 2001)

The Lawnmower Man (Brett Leonard, 1992)

The Lights of New York (Bryan Foy, 1928)

The Man with the Movie Camera (Dziga Vertov, 1929)

The Matrix (Andy Wachowski and Larry Wachowski, 1999)

The Matrix Reloaded (Andy Wachowski and Larry Wachowski, 2003)

The Matrix Revolutions (Andy Wachowski and Larry Wachowski, 2003)

Metropolis (Fritz Lang, 1927)

Modern Times (Charles Chaplin, 1936)

Murder by Television (Clifford Sanforth, 1935)

Murder by Television (Del Lord, 1936)

The Musical Doctor (Ray Cozine, 1932)

My Big Fat Greek Wedding (Joel Zwick, 2002)

The Mystery of the Double Cross (William Parke, 1917; serial)

Near Dark (Kathryn Bigelow, 1990)

The Net (Irwin Winkler, 1995)

Network (Sidney Lumet, 1976)

On a Good Old 5 Cent Trolley Ride (Edison, 1905)

One Kind of Wireless (Saul Harrison, 1917)

Panoramic View of the White Pass Railroad (Edison, 1901)

Photographer's Mishap (Edison, 1901)

Pleasantville (Gary Ross, 1998)

Poltergeist (Tobe Hooper, 1982)

Resident Evil (Paul W. S. Anderson, 2002)

A Rhapsody in Black and Blue (Aubrey Scotto, 1932)

The Ring (Gore Verbinski, 2002)

The Robe (Henry Koster, 1953)

SIm0ne (Andrew Niccol, 2002)

Samson and Delilah (Cecil B. DeMille, 1949)

A Search for Evidence (Biograph, 1903)

Sense and Sensibility (Ang Lee, 1995)

The Seven Year Itch (Billy Wilder, 1955)

The Show of Shows (John G. Adolfi, 1929)

Simba, The King of Beasts (Martin Johnson and Osa Johnson, 1928)

Sing, Bing, Sing (Babe Stafford, 1933)

Singin' in the Rain (Gene Kelly and Stanley Donen, 1952)

Sorry, Wrong Number (Anatole Litvak, 1948)

Spider-Man (Sam Raimi, 2002)

Star Wars: Episode I—The Phantom Menace (George Lucas, 1999)

Star Wars: Episode II—Attack of the Clones (George Lucas, 2002)

The Story the Biograph Told (Biograph, 1904; aka *Caught by Moving Pictures*)

Strange Days (Kathryn Bigelow, 1995)

Streetcar Chivalry (Edison, 1903)

Sunset Boulevard (Billy Wilder, 1950)

The Telegraph Operators (Éclair, undated)

Tenderloin (Michael Curtiz, 1928)

Terminator 2: Judgment Day (James Cameron, 1991)

The Testament of Dr. Mabuse (Fritz Lang, 1933)

Things to Come (William Cameron Menzies, 1936)

Titanic (James Cameron, 1997)

To Hell with the Kaiser (George Irving, 1918)

Traffic in Souls (George Loane Tucker, 1913)

Trapped by Television (Del Lord, 1936)

Tron (Steven Lisberger, 1982)

The Truman Show (Peter Weir, 1998)

Uncle Josh at the Moving Picture Show (Edwin S. Porter, 1902)

A Viagem (Christian Boustani, 1998)

Videodrome (David Cronenberg, 1983)

Virtuosity (Brett Leonard, 1995)

Le Voyage dans la lune (Georges Méliès, 1902)

Wag the Dog (Barry Levinson, 1997)

WarGames (John Badham, 1983)

White Heat (Raoul Walsh, 1949)

Will Success Spoil Rock Hunter? (Frank Tashlin, 1957)

Index

munal interaction and, 96–97; communicative realism and, 58; cultural production and, 43–47; digital media, 207–8; distracted, 207–8, 210; drive-in theaters, 178; early cinema, xxxiii, 24, 208–9; exhibition practices and, 28, 34; informatic intimacy and, xxxi, 44–45, 55; interactivity, xxxi, 44–45; liveness of, 148–51; narrative absorption, 26, 57–58, 206, 207–8; postmodern subjectivity of, 206; postwar cinema, 178; private-in-public, 91–92, 145–46; private sphere and, 148–51; "process of systematization" of, 46; public sphere and, 46, 62; race and, 59; realism and, 44–45; spectator-auditors, 91–92, 98–99; storytelling and, 26; television and, 139–40; television fantasy films and, 144; theatrical, 2; time/temporality and, 98, 282n.24; virtual reality and, 214–15; voyeurism and, 150–51, 212–13; wireless, 53–54

Spider-Man (2002), 240

Spielberg, Steven: *Jaws* (1975), xvi, xxv, 257n.27; *Jurassic Park* (1993), 202

Spigel, Lynn, 147, 151, 275n.16

Spivack, Murray, 111–12, 128

Spivak, Gayatri Chakravorty, 63–64

Staiger, Janet, xxv–xxvii

Stanton, Frank, 276n.26

Stanwyck, Barbara, 141, 153–54, 274n.7

Star Wars: Episode I—The Phantom Menace (1999), 232, 233, 239–40

Star Wars: Episode II—Attack of the Clones (2002), 229, 232–33

Stephenson, Neal, 207–8

stereotypes. *See* race

Sterling, Bruce, 198–99

Stewart, Doug, 200

Stewart, Garrett, 145, 275n.13

Stone, Allucquere Rosanne, 206–7

story films, 28–29, 44–45, 214

storytelling: classical cinema, 2, 4, 7, 26, 145–46, 214; digital films, 236–37; early cinema, 2–3, 4, 26, 62, 214, 260n.10; Hollywood cinema and, 6; narrative practices, 7; narrator-function, 260n.10, 269n.10; postwar cinema, 157–58

Story the Biograph Told, The (Biograph, 1904; aka *Caught by Moving Pictures*), 28, 56, 133, 188, 264n.56

Strain, Ellen, 102

Strange Days (1995), xxxiv, 217–22, 243, 283n.31

Streetcar Chivalry (1903), 39

Studlar, Gaylyn, 113

Sudhalter, Richard M., 87

Sunset Boulevard (1950), 170–71, 172–73

surveillance: audio/wireless, 65; classical cinema, 133–34; early cinema, 36–39; film vs. television, 145; movie cameras and, 146, 180, 185–86. *See also* voyeurism

Swanson, Gloria, 171

tableaux films, xvi–xvii

talkies. *See* sound cinema

technological fantasies, 222–23

technological progress: access to, 52; amateurs and, 165–66, 168–69; computer graphics, xxi; domestic space, 151, 168–70; economic development and, xvi–xvii; electricity and, 23; film noir, 153–56; historical conditions and, 163–64; individuals and, 153; intimacy and, 85; jazz music and, 85; postwar economy and, 158–62; private-in-public,

Paul Young is director of film studies and assistant professor of English at Vanderbilt University.